Global *Woman*

Global *Woman*

Nannies, Maids, and Sex Workers
in the New Economy

Barbara Ehrenreich and Arlie Russell Hochschild

EDITORS

METROPOLITAN BOOKS
Henry Holt and Company | New York

Metropolitan Books
Henry Holt and Company, LLC
Publishers since 1866
115 West 18th Street
New York, New York 10011

Metropolitan Books™ is a registered
trademark of Henry Holt and Company, LLC.

Library of Congress Cataloging-in-Publication Data
Global woman : nannies, maids, and sex workers in the new economy / Barbara Ehrenreich and Arlie Russell Hochschild, editors.
    p. cm.
  Includes bibliographical references.
  ISBN 0-8050-6995-X (hc.)
  1. Women domestics. 2. Women alien labor. 3. Women—Employment 4. Minority women—Employment. 5. Immigrant women—Employment. 6. Nannies 7. Prostitution. I. Ehrenreich, Barbara. II. Hochschild, Arlie Russell, 1940–
HD6072 .G55 2003
331.4'8164046'08691—dc21   2002071912

First Edition 2003

Designed by Paula Russell Szafranski

Maps designed by James Sinclair

Printed in the United States of America
1 3 5 7 9 10 8 6 4 2

Contents

Contents

Global *Woman*

Introduction

BARBARA EHRENREICH AND
ARLIE RUSSELL HOCHSCHILD

"Whose baby are you?" Josephine Perera, a nanny from Sri Lanka, asks Isadora, her pudgy two-year-old charge in Athens, Greece.

Thoughtful for a moment, the child glances toward the closed door of the next room, in which her mother is working, as if to say, "That's my mother in there."

"No, you're *my* baby," Josephine teases, tickling Isadora lightly. Then, to settle the issue, Isadora answers, "Together!" She has two mommies—her mother and Josephine. And surely a child loved by many adults is richly blessed.

In some ways, Josephine's story—which unfolds in an extraordinary documentary film, *When Mother Comes Home for Christmas,* directed by Nilita Vachani—describes an unparalleled success. Josephine has ventured around the world, achieving a degree of independence her mother could not have imagined, and amply supporting her three children with no help from her ex-husband, their father. Each month she mails a remittance check from Athens to Hatton, Sri Lanka, to pay the children's living expenses and school fees. On her Christmas visit home, she bears gifts of pots, pans, and dishes. While she makes payments on a new bus that Suresh, her oldest son, now drives for a living, she is also saving for a modest dowry for her daughter, Norma. She dreams of buying a new house in which the whole family can live. In the meantime, her work as a nanny enables Isadora's parents to devote themselves to their careers and avocations.

But Josephine's story is also one of wrenching global inequality. While Isadora enjoys the attention of three adults, Josephine's three children in Sri Lanka have been far less lucky. According to Vachani, Josephine's youngest child, Suminda, was two—Isadora's age—when his mother first left home to work in Saudi Arabia. Her middle child, Norma, was nine; her oldest son, Suresh, thirteen. From Saudi Arabia, Josephine found her way first to Kuwait, then to Greece. Except for one two-month trip home, she has lived apart from her children for ten years. She writes them weekly letters, seeking news of relatives, asking about school, and complaining that Norma doesn't write back.

Although Josephine left the children under her sister's supervision, the two youngest have shown signs of real distress. Norma has attempted suicide three times. Suminda, who was twelve when the film was made, boards in a grim, Dickensian orphanage that forbids talk during meals and showers. He visits his aunt on holidays. Although the oldest, Suresh, seems to be on good terms with his mother, Norma is tearful and sullen, and Suminda does poorly in school, picks quarrels, and otherwise seems withdrawn from the world. Still, at the end of the film, we see Josephine once again leave her three children in Sri Lanka to return to Isadora in Athens. For Josephine can either live with her children in desperate poverty or make money by living apart from them. Unlike her affluent First World employers, she cannot both live with her family and support it.

Thanks to the process we loosely call "globalization," women are on the move as never before in history. In images familiar to the West from television commercials for credit cards, cell phones, and airlines, female executives jet about the world, phoning home from luxury hotels and reuniting with eager children in airports. But we hear much less about a far more prodigious flow of female labor and energy: the increasing migration of millions of women from poor countries to rich ones, where they serve as nannies, maids, and sometimes sex workers. In the absence of help from male partners, many women have succeeded in tough "male world" careers only by turning over the care of their children, elderly parents, and homes to women from the

Third World. This is the female underside of globalization, whereby millions of Josephines from poor countries in the south migrate to do the "women's work" of the north—work that affluent women are no longer able or willing to do. These migrant workers often leave their own children in the care of grandmothers, sisters, and sisters-in-law. Sometimes a young daughter is drawn out of school to care for her younger siblings.

This pattern of female migration reflects what could be called a worldwide gender revolution. In both rich and poor countries, fewer families can rely solely on a male breadwinner. In the United States, the earning power of most men has declined since 1970, and many women have gone out to "make up the difference." By one recent estimate, women were the sole, primary, or coequal earners in more than half of American families.[1] So the question arises: Who will take care of the children, the sick, the elderly? Who will make dinner and clean house?

While the European or American woman commutes to work an average twenty-eight minutes a day, many nannies from the Philippines, Sri Lanka, and India cross the globe to get to their jobs. Some female migrants from the Third World do find something like "liberation," or at least the chance to become independent breadwinners and to improve their children's material lives. Other, less fortunate migrant women end up in the control of criminal employers—their passports stolen, their mobility blocked, forced to work without pay in brothels or to provide sex along with cleaning and child-care services in affluent homes. But even in more typical cases, where benign employers pay wages on time, Third World migrant women achieve their success only by assuming the cast-off domestic roles of middle- and high-income women in the First World—roles that have been previously rejected, of course, by men. And their "commute" entails a cost we have yet to fully comprehend.

The migration of women from the Third World to do "women's work" in affluent countries has so far received little scholarly or media attention—for reasons that are easy enough to guess. First, many, though by no means all, of the new female migrant workers are women of color, and therefore subject to the racial "discounting" routinely experienced by, say, Algerians in France, Mexicans in the United States, and Asians in the United Kingdom. Add to racism the private "indoor" nature of so much of the new migrants' work. Unlike factory workers, who congregate in large numbers, or taxi drivers, who are visible on the street, nannies and maids are often hidden away, one or two at a time, behind closed doors in private homes. Because of the illegal nature of their work, most sex workers are even further concealed from public view.

At least in the case of nannies and maids, another factor contributes to the invisibility of migrant women and their work—one that, for their affluent employers, touches closer to home. The Western culture of individualism, which finds extreme expression in the United States, militates against acknowledging help or human interdependency of nearly any kind. Thus, in the time-pressed upper middle class, servants are no longer displayed as status symbols, decked out in white caps and aprons, but often remain in the background, or disappear when company comes. Furthermore, affluent careerwomen increasingly earn their status not through leisure, as they might have a century ago, but by apparently "doing it all"—producing a full-time career, thriving children, a contented spouse, and a well-managed home. In order to preserve this illusion, domestic workers and nannies make the house hotel-room perfect, feed and bathe the children, cook and clean up—and then magically fade from sight.

The lifestyles of the First World are made possible by a global transfer of the services associated with a wife's traditional role—child care, home-making, and sex—from poor countries to rich ones. To generalize and perhaps oversimplify: in an earlier phase of imperialism, northern countries extracted natural resources and agricultural products—rubber, metals, and sugar, for example—from lands they conquered and colonized. Today, while still relying on Third World countries for agricultural and industrial labor, the wealthy countries also seek to extract something harder to measure and quantify, something that can look very much like love. Nannies like Josephine bring the distant families that employ them real maternal affection, no doubt enhanced by the heartbreaking absence of their own children in the poor countries they leave behind. Similarly, women who migrate from country to country to work as maids bring not only their muscle power but an attentiveness to detail and to the human relationships in the household that might otherwise have been invested in their own families. Sex workers offer the simulation of sexual and romantic love, or at least transient sexual companionship. It is as if the wealthy parts of the world are running short on precious emotional and sexual resources and have had to turn to poorer regions for fresh supplies.

There are plenty of historical precedents for this globalization of traditional female services. In the ancient Middle East, the women of populations defeated in war were routinely enslaved and hauled off to serve as household workers and concubines for the victors. Among the Africans brought to North America as slaves in the sixteenth through nineteenth centuries, about a third were women and children, and many of those women were pressed to be concubines, domestic servants, or both. Nineteenth-century Irishwomen—along with many rural Englishwomen—migrated to English towns and cities to work as domestics in the homes of the growing upper middle class. Services thought to be innately feminine—child care, housework, and sex—often win little recognition or pay. But they have always been sufficiently in demand to transport over long distances if necessary. What is new today is the sheer number of female migrants and the very long distances they travel. Immigration statistics show huge numbers of women in motion, typically from poor countries to rich. Although the gross statistics give little clue as to the jobs women eventually take, there are reasons to infer that much of their work is "caring work," performed either in private homes or in institutional settings such as hospitals, hospices, child-care centers, and nursing homes.

The statistics are, in many ways, frustrating. We have information on legal migrants but not on illegal migrants, who, experts tell us, travel in equal if not greater numbers. Furthermore, many Third World countries lack data for past years, which makes it hard to trace trends over time; or they use varying methods of gathering information, which makes it hard to compare one country with another. Nevertheless, the trend is clear enough for some scholars, including Stephen Castles, Mark Miller, and Janet Momsen, to speak of a "feminization of migration."[2] From 1950 to 1970, for example, men predominated in labor migration to northern Europe from Turkey, Greece, and North Africa. Since then, women have been replacing men. In 1946, women were fewer than 3 percent of the Algerians and Moroccans living in France; by 1990, they were more than 40 percent.[3] Overall, half of the world's 120 million legal and illegal migrants are now believed to be women.

Patterns of international migration vary from region to region, but women migrants from a surprising number of sending countries actually outnumber men, sometimes by a wide margin. For example, in the 1990s, women make up over half of Filipino migrants to all countries and 84 percent of Sri Lankan migrants to the Middle East.[4] Indeed, by 1993 statistics, Sri Lankan women such as Josephine vastly outnumbered Sri Lankan men as migrant workers who'd left for Saudi Arabia, Kuwait, Lebanon, Oman, Bahrain, Jordan, and Qatar, as well as to all countries of the Far East, Africa, and Asia.[5] About half of the migrants leaving Mexico, India, Korea, Malaysia, Cyprus, and Swaziland to work elsewhere are also women. Throughout the 1990s women outnumbered men among migrants to the United States, Canada, Sweden, the United Kingdom, Argentina, and Israel.[6]

Most women, like men, migrate from the south to the north and from poor countries to rich ones. Typically, migrants go to the nearest comparatively rich country, preferably one whose language they speak or whose religion and culture they share. There are also local migratory flows: from northern to southern Thailand, for instance, or from East Germany to West. But of the regional or cross-regional flows, four stand out. One goes from Southeast Asia to the oil-rich Middle and Far East—from Bangladesh, Indonesia, the Philippines, and Sri Lanka to Bahrain, Oman, Kuwait, Saudi Arabia, Hong Kong, Malaysia, and Singapore. Another stream of migration goes from the former Soviet bloc to western Europe—from Russia, Romania, Bulgaria, and Albania to Scandinavia, Germany, France, Spain, Portugal, and England. A third goes from south to north in the Americas, including the stream from Mexico to the United States, which scholars say is the longest-running labor migration in the world. A fourth stream moves from Africa to various parts of Europe. France receives many female migrants from Morocco, Tunisia, and Algeria. Italy receives female workers from Ethiopia, Eritrea, and Cape Verde.

Female migrants overwhelmingly take up work as maids or domestics. As women have become an ever greater proportion of migrant workers, receiving countries reflect a dramatic influx of foreign-born domestics. In the United States, African-American women, who accounted for 60 percent of domestics in the 1940s, have been largely replaced by Latinas, many of them recent migrants from Mexico and Central America. In England, Asian migrant women have displaced the Irish and Portuguese domestics of the past. In French cities, North African women have replaced rural French girls. In western Germany, Turks and women from the former East Germany have replaced rural native-born women. Foreign females from countries outside the European Union made up only 6 percent of all domestic workers in 1984. By 1987, the percentage had jumped to 52, with most coming from the Philippines, Sri Lanka, Thailand, Argentina, Colombia, Brazil, El Salvador, and Peru.[7]

The governments of some sending countries actively encourage women to migrate in search of domestic jobs, reasoning that migrant women are more likely than their male counterparts to send their hard-earned wages to their families rather than spending the money on themselves. In general, women send home anywhere from half to nearly all of what they earn. These remittances have a significant impact on the lives of children, parents, siblings, and wider networks of kin—as well as on cash-strapped Third World governments. Thus, before Josephine left for Athens, a program sponsored by the Sri Lankan government taught her how to use a microwave oven, a vacuum cleaner, and an electric mixer. As she awaited her flight, a song piped into the airport departure lounge extolled the opportunity to earn money abroad. The songwriter was in the pay of the Sri Lanka Bureau of Foreign Employment, an office devised to encourage women to migrate. The lyrics say:

> *After much hardship, such difficult times*
> *How lucky I am to work in a foreign land.*
> *As the gold gathers so do many greedy flies.*
> *But our good government protects us from them.*
> *After much hardship, such difficult times,*
> *How lucky I am to work in a foreign land.*
> *I promise to return home with treasures for everyone.*

Why this transfer of women's traditional services from poor to rich parts of the world? The reasons are, in a crude way, easy to guess. Women in Western countries have increasingly taken on paid work, and hence need other— paid domestics and caretakers for children and elderly people—to replace them.[8] For their part, women in poor countries have an obvious incentive to migrate: relative and absolute poverty. The "care deficit" that has emerged in the wealthier countries as women enter the workforce *pulls* migrants from the Third World and postcommunist nations; poverty *pushes* them.

In broad outline, this explanation holds true. Throughout western Europe, Taiwan, and Japan, but above all in the United States, England, and Sweden, women's employment has increased dramatically since the 1970s. In the United States, for example, the proportion of women in paid work rose from 15 percent of mothers of children six and under in 1950 to 65 percent today. Women now make up 46 percent of the U.S. labor force. Three-quarters of mothers of children eighteen and under and nearly two-thirds of mothers of children age one and younger now work for pay. Furthermore, according to a recent International Labor Organization study, working Americans averaged longer hours at work in the late 1990s than they did in the 1970s. By some measures, the number of hours spent at work have increased more for women than for men, and especially for women in managerial and professional jobs.

Meanwhile, over the last thirty years, as the rich countries have grown much richer, the poor countries have become—in both absolute and relative terms—poorer. Global inequalities in wages are particularly striking. In Hong Kong, for instance, the wages of a Filipina domestic are about fifteen times the amount she could make as a schoolteacher back in the Philippines. In addition, poor countries turning to the IMF or World Bank for loans are often forced to undertake measures of so-called structural adjustment, with disastrous results for the poor and especially for poor women and children. To qualify for loans, governments are usually required to devalue their currencies, which turns the hard currencies of rich countries into gold and the soft currencies of poor countries into straw. Structural adjustment programs also call for cuts in support for "noncompetitive industries," and for the reduction of public services such as health care and food subsidies for the poor. Citizens of poor countries, women as well as men, thus have a strong incentive to seek work in more fortunate parts of the world.

But it would be a mistake to attribute the globalization of women's work to a simple synergy of needs among women—one group, in the affluent countries, needing help and the other, in poor countries, needing jobs. For one thing, this formulation fails to account for the marked failure of First World governments to meet the needs created by its women's entry into the workforce. The downsized American—and to a lesser degree, western European—welfare state has become a "deadbeat dad." Unlike the rest of the industrialized world, the United States does not offer public child care for working mothers, nor does it ensure paid family and medical leave. Moreover, a series of state tax revolts in the 1980s reduced the number of hours public libraries were open and slashed school-enrichment and after-school programs. Europe did not experience anything comparable. Still, tens of millions of western European women are in the workforce who were not before—and there has been no proportionate expansion in public services.

Secondly, any view of the globalization of domestic work as simply an arrangement among women completely omits the role of men. Numerous studies, including some of our own, have shown that as American women took on paid employment, the men in their families did little to increase their contribution to the work of the home. For example, only one out of every five men among the working couples whom Hochschild interviewed for *The Second Shift* in the 1980s shared the work at home, and later studies suggest that while working mothers are doing somewhat less housework than their counterparts twenty years ago, most men are doing only a little more.[9] With divorce, men frequently abdicate their child-care responsibilities to their ex-wives. In most cultures of the First World outside the United States, powerful traditions even more firmly discourage husbands from doing "women's work." So, strictly speaking, the presence of immigrant nannies does not enable affluent women to enter the workforce; it enables affluent *men* to continue avoiding the second shift.

The men in wealthier countries are also, of course, directly responsible for the demand for immigrant sex workers—as well as for the sexual abuse of many migrant women who work as domestics. Why, we wondered, is there a particular demand for "imported" sexual partners? Part of the answer may lie in the fact that new immigrants often take up the least desirable work, and, thanks to the AIDS epidemic, prostitution has become a job that ever fewer women deliberately choose. But perhaps some of this demand, as we see in Denise Brennan's chapter on sex tourism, grows out of the erotic lure of the "exotic." Immigrant women may seem desirable sexual partners for the same reason that First World employers believe them to be especially gifted as caregivers: they are thought to embody the traditional feminine qualities of nurturance, docility, and eagerness to please. Some men feel nostalgic for these qualities, which they associate with a bygone way of life. Even as many wage-earning Western women assimilate to the competitive culture of "male" work and ask respect for making it in a man's world, some men seek in the "exotic Orient" or "hot-blooded tropics" a woman from the imagined past.

Of course, not all sex workers migrate voluntarily. An alarming number of women and girls are trafficked by smugglers and sold into bondage. Because trafficking is illegal and secret, the numbers are hard to know with any certainty. Kevin Bales estimates that in Thailand alone, a country of 60 million, half a million to a million women are prostitutes, and one out of every twenty of these is enslaved.[10] As Bales's chapter in this book shows, many of these women are daughters whom northern hill-tribe families have sold to brothels in the cities of the south. Believing the promises of jobs and money, some begin the voyage willingly, only to discover days later that the "arrangers" are traffickers who steal their passports, define them as debtors, and enslave them as prostitutes. Other women and girls are kidnapped, or sold by their impoverished families, and then trafficked to brothels. Even worse fates befall women from neighboring Laos and Burma, who flee crushing poverty and repression at home only to fall into the hands of Thai slave traders.

If the factors that pull migrant women workers to affluent countries are not as simple as they at first appear, neither are the factors that push them. Certainly relative poverty plays a major role, but, interestingly, migrant women often do not come from the poorest classes of their societies.[11] In fact, they are typically more affluent and better educated than male migrants. Many female migrants from the Philippines and Mexico, for example, have high school or college diplomas and have held middle-class—albeit low-paid—jobs back home. One study of Mexican migrants suggests that the trend is toward increasingly better-educated female migrants. Thirty years ago, most Mexican-born maids in the United States had been poorly educated maids in Mexico. Now a majority have high school degrees and have held clerical, retail, or professional jobs before leaving for the United States.[12] Such women are likely to be enterprising and adventurous enough to resist the social pressures to stay home and accept their lot in life.

Noneconomic factors—or at least factors that are not immediately and directly economic—also influence a woman's decision to emigrate. By migrating, a woman may escape the expectation that she care for elderly family members, relinquish her paycheck to a husband or father, or defer to an abusive husband. Migration may also be a practical response to a failed marriage and the need to provide for children without male help. In the Philippines, contributor Rhacel Salazar Parreñas tells us, migration is sometimes called a "Philippine divorce." And there are forces at work that may be making the men of poor countries less desirable as husbands. Male unemployment runs high in the countries that supply female domestics to the First World. Unable to make a living, these men often grow demoralized and cease contributing to their families in other ways. Many female migrants, including those in Michele Gamburd's chapter in this volume, tell of unemployed husbands who drink or gamble their remittances away. Notes one study of Sri Lankan women working as maids in the Persian Gulf: "It is not unusual . . . for the women to find upon their return that their Gulf wages by and large have been squandered on alcohol, gambling and other dubious undertakings while they were away."[13]

To an extent then, the globalization of child care and housework brings the ambitious and independent women of the world together: the career-oriented upper-middle-class woman of an affluent nation and the striving woman from a crumbling Third World or postcommunist economy. Only it does not bring them together in the way that second-wave feminists in affluent countries once liked to imagine—as sisters and allies struggling to achieve common goals. Instead, they come together as mistress and maid, employer and employee, across a great divide of privilege and opportunity.

This trend toward global redivision of women's traditional work throws new light on the entire process of globalization. Conventionally, it is the poorer countries that are thought to be dependent on the richer ones—a dependency symbolized by the huge debt they owe to global financial institutions. What we explore in this book, however, is a dependency that works in the other direction, and it is a dependency of a particularly intimate kind. Increasingly often, as affluent and middle-class families in the First World come to depend on migrants from poorer regions to provide child care, homemaking, and sexual services, a global relationship arises that in some ways mirrors the traditional relationship between the sexes. The First World takes on a role like that of the old-fashioned male in the family—pampered, entitled, unable to cook, clean, or find his socks. Poor countries take on a role like that of the traditional woman within the family—patient, nurturing, and self-denying. A division of labor feminists critiqued when it was "local" has now, metaphorically speaking, gone global.

To press this metaphor a bit further, the resulting relationship is by no means a "marriage," in the sense of being openly acknowledged. In fact, it is striking how invisible the globalization of women's work remains, how little it is noted or discussed in the First World. Trend spotters have had almost nothing to say about the fact that increasing numbers of affluent First World children and elderly persons are tended by immigrant care workers or live in homes cleaned by immigrant maids. Even the political groups we might expect to be concerned about this trend—antiglobalization and feminist activists—often seem to have noticed only the most extravagant abuses, such as trafficking and female enslavement. So if a metaphorically gendered relationship has developed between rich and poor countries, it is less like a marriage and more like a secret affair.

But it is a "secret affair" conducted in plain view of the children. Little Isadora and the other children of the First World raised by "two mommies" may be learning more than their ABC's from a loving surrogate parent. In their own living rooms, they are learning a vast and tragic global politics.[14] Children see. But they also learn how to disregard what they see. They learn how adults make the visible invisible. That is their "early childhood education."

In this volume, we hope to make the invisible visible again. The essays we bring together range from personal recollection to economic analysis, and they span the globe from Taiwan to Mexico, from Thailand to the Dominican Republic. Some essays describe a global transfer of emotional resources (Hochschild, Parreñas), while others consider the pressures global capitalism puts on women and their families (Sassen). Some point to the dilemmas migrant domestic workers raise for First World feminism (Ehrenreich, Anderson) and inquire into the similarities and differences between the situations of employed and employer (Cheever, Hondagneu-Sotelo, Constable, Rivas, Zarembka). Several essays focus on how immigrant nannies and maids have assumed the tasks associated with traditional family relationships, like the obligations of daughters-in-law in Hong Kong (Lan). Still others investigate the ways that women's migration has modified relationships between men and women—both in marriage and through the global sex trade (Brennan, Gamburd, Bales, Thai).

The globalization of women's traditional role poses important challenges to anyone concerned about gender and economic inequity. How can we improve the lives and opportunities of migrant women engaged in legal occupations such as nannies and maids? How can we prevent trafficking and enslavement? More basically, can we find a way to counterbalance the systematic transfer of caring work from poor countries to rich, and the inevitable trauma of the children left behind? Our contributors do not have easy answers, but their essays, many based on recent and extensive fieldwork, do help us take that essential first step—to bring the world's most invisible women into the light. Before we can hope to find activist solutions, we need to see these women as full human beings. They are strivers as well as victims, wives and mothers as well as workers—sisters, in other words, with whom we in the First World may someday define a common agenda.

Love and Gold

ARLIE RUSSELL HOCHSCHILD

Whether they know it or not, Clinton and Princela Bautista, two children growing up in a small town in the Philippines apart from their two migrant parents, are the recipients of an international pledge. It says that a child "should grow up in a family environment, in an atmosphere of happiness, love, and understanding," and "not be separated from his or her parents against their will . . ." Part of Article 9 of the United Nations Declaration on the Rights of the Child (1959), these words stand now as a fairy-tale ideal, the promise of a shield between children and the costs of globalization.

At the moment this shield is not protecting the Bautista family from those human costs. In the basement bedroom of her employer's home in Washington, D.C., Rowena Bautista keeps four pictures on her dresser: two of her own children, back in Camiling, a Philippine farming village, and two of children she has cared for as a nanny in the United States. The pictures of her own children, Clinton and Princela, are from five years ago. As she recently told *Wall Street Journal* reporter Robert Frank, the recent photos "remind me how much I've missed."[1] She has missed the last two Christmases, and on her last visit home, her son Clinton, now eight, refused to touch his mother. "Why," he asked, "did you come back?"

The daughter of a teacher and an engineer, Rowena Bautista worked three years toward an engineering degree before she quit and went abroad for work and adventure. A few years later, during her travels, she fell in love with a Ghanaian construction worker, had two children with him, and returned to the Philippines with them. Unable to find a job in the Philippines, the father of her children went to Korea in search of work and, over time, he faded from his children's lives.

Rowena again traveled north, joining the growing ranks of Third World mothers who work abroad for long periods of time because they cannot make ends meet at home. She left her children with her mother, hired a nanny to help out at home, and flew to Washington, D.C., where she took a job as a nanny for the same pay that a small-town doctor would make in the Philippines. Of the 792,000 legal household workers in the United States, 40 percent were born abroad, like Rowena. Of Filipino migrants, 70 percent, like Rowena, are women.

Rowena calls Noa, the American child she tends, "my baby." One of Noa's first words was "Ena," short for Rowena. And Noa has started babbling in Tagalog, the language Rowena spoke in the Philippines. Rowena lifts Noa from her crib mornings at 7:00 A.M., takes her to the library, pushes her on the swing at the playground, and curls up with her for naps. As Rowena explained to Frank, "I give Noa what I can't give to my children." In turn, the American child gives Rowena what she doesn't get at home. As Rowena puts it, "She makes me feel like a mother."

Rowena's own children live in a four-bedroom house with her parents and twelve other family members—eight of them children, some of whom also have mothers who work abroad. The central figure in the children's lives—the person they call "Mama"—is Grandma, Rowena's mother. But Grandma works surprisingly long hours as a teacher—from 7:00 A.M. to 9:00 P.M. As Rowena tells her story to Frank, she says little about her father, the children's grandfather (men are discouraged from participating actively in child rearing in the Philippines). And Rowena's father is not much involved with his grandchildren. So, she has hired Anna de la Cruz, who arrives daily at 8:00 A.M. to cook, clean, and care for the children. Meanwhile,

Anna de la Cruz leaves her teenage son in the care of her eighty-year-old mother-in-law.

Rowena's life reflects an important and growing global trend: the importation of care and love from poor countries to rich ones. For some time now, promising and highly trained professionals have been moving from ill-equipped hospitals, impoverished schools, antiquated banks, and other beleaguered workplaces of the Third World to better opportunities and higher pay in the First World. As rich nations become richer and poor nations become poorer, this one-way flow of talent and training continuously widens the gap between the two. But in addition to this brain drain, there is now a parallel but more hidden and wrenching trend, as women who normally care for the young, the old, and the sick in their own poor countries move to care for the young, the old, and the sick in rich countries, whether as maids and nannies or as day-care and nursing-home aides. It's a care drain.

The movement of care workers from south to north is not altogether new. What is unprecedented, however, is the scope and speed of women's migration to these jobs. Many factors contribute to the growing feminization of migration. One is the growing split between the global rich and poor. In 1949 Harry S. Truman declared in his inaugural speech that the Southern Hemisphere—encompassing the postcolonial nations of Africa, Asia, and Latin America—was underdeveloped, and that it was the role of the north to help the south "catch up." But in the years since then, the gap between north and south has only widened. In 1960, for example, the nations of the north were twenty times richer than those of the south. By 1980, that gap had more than doubled, and the north was forty-six times richer than the south. In fact, according to a United Nations Development Program study, sixty countries are *worse off* in 1999 than they were in 1980.[2] Multinational corporations are the "muscle and brains" behind the new global system with its growing inequality, as William Greider points out, and the 500 largest such corporations (168 in Europe, 157 in the United States, and 119 in Japan) have in the last twenty years increased their sales sevenfold.[3]

As a result of this polarization, the middle class of the Third World now earns less than the poor of the First World. Before the domestic workers Rhacel Parreñas interviewed in the 1990s migrated from the

Philippines to the United States and Italy, they had averaged $176 a month, often as teachers, nurses, and administrative and clerical workers. But by doing less skilled—though no less difficult—work as nannies, maids, and care-service workers, they can earn $200 a month in Singapore, $410 a month in Hong Kong, $700 a month in Italy, or $1,400 a month in Los Angeles. To take one example, as a fifth-grade dropout in Colombo, Sri Lanka, a woman could earn $30 a month plus room and board as a house-maid, or she could earn $30 a month as a salesgirl in a shop, without food or lodging. But as a nanny in Athens she could earn $500 a month, plus room and board.

The remittances these women send home provide food and shelter for their families and often a nest egg with which to start a small business. Of the $750 Rowena Bautista earns each month in the United States, she mails $400 home for her children's food, clothes, and schooling, and $50 to Anna de la Cruz, who shares some of that with her mother-in-law and her children. As Rowena's story demonstrates, one way to respond to the gap between rich and poor countries is to close it privately—by moving to a better paying job.

Even as the gap between the globe's rich and poor grows wider, the globe itself—its capital, cultural images, consumer tastes, and peoples—becomes more integrated. Thanks to the spread of Western, and especially American, movies and television programs, the people of the poor south now know a great deal about the rich north. But what they learn about the north is what people *have*, in what often seems like a material striptease.

Certainly, rising inequality and the lure of northern prosperity have contributed to what Stephen Castles and Mark Miller call a "globalization of migration."[4] For men and women alike, migration has become a private solution to a public problem. Since 1945 and especially since the mid-1980s, a small but growing proportion of the world's population is migrating. They come from and go to more different countries. Migration is by no means an inexorable process, but as Castles and Miller observe, "migrations are growing in volume in all major regions at the present time."[5] The International Organization for Migration estimates that 120 million people moved from one country to another, legally or illegally, in 1994. Of this group, about 2 percent of the world's population, 15 to 23 million are refugees and asylum seekers. Of the rest, some move to join family members who have previously migrated. But most move to find work.

As a number of studies show, most migration takes place through personal contact with networks of migrants composed of relatives and friends and relatives and friends of relatives and friends. One migrant inducts another. Whole networks and neighborhoods leave to work abroad, bringing back stories, money, know-how, and contacts. Just as men form networks along which information about jobs are passed, so one domestic worker in New York, Dubai, or Paris passes on information to female relatives or friends about how to arrange papers, travel, find a job, and settle.

Today, half of all the world's migrants are women. In Sri Lanka, one out of every ten citizens—a majority of them women—works abroad. That figure excludes returnees who have worked abroad in the past. As Castles and Miller explain:

> Women play an increasing role in all regions and all types of migration. In the past, most labor migrations and many refugee movements were male dominated, and women were often dealt with under the category of family reunion. Since the 1960s, women have played a major role in labor migration. Today women workers form the majority in movements as diverse as those of Cape Verdians to Italy, Filipinos to the Middle East and Thais to Japan.[6]

Of these female workers, a great many migrate to fill domestic jobs. Demand for domestic servants has risen both in developed countries, where it had nearly vanished, and in fast-growing economies such as Hong Kong and Singapore, where, write Miller and Castles, "immigrant servants—from the Philippines, Indonesia, Thailand, Korea and Sri Lanka—allow women in the richer economies to take up new employment opportunities."[7]

Vastly more middle-class women in the First World do paid work now than in the past. They work longer hours for more months a year and more years. So they need help caring for the family.[8] In the United States in 1950, 15 percent of mothers of children aged six and under did paid work while 65 percent of such women do today. Seventy-two percent of all American women now work. Among them are the grandmothers and sisters who thirty years ago might have stayed home to care for the children of relatives. Just as Third World grandmothers may be doing paid care work abroad in the Third World, so more grandmothers are working in the First World too—another reason First World families are looking outside the family for good care.

Women who want to succeed in a professional or managerial job in the First World thus face strong pressures at work. Most careers are still based on a well-known (male) pattern: doing professional work, competing with fellow professionals, getting credit for work, building a reputation, doing it while you are young, hoarding scarce time, and minimizing family work by finding someone else to do it. In the past, the professional was a man; the "someone else" was his wife. The wife oversaw the family, itself a flexible, preindustrial institution concerned with human experiences the workplace excluded: birth, child rearing, sickness, death. Today, a growing "care industry" has stepped into the traditional wife's role, creating a very real demand for migrant women.

But if First World middle-class women are building careers that are molded according to the old male model, by putting in long hours at demanding jobs, their nannies and other domestic workers suffer a greatly exaggerated version of the same thing. Two women working for pay is not a bad idea. But two working mothers giving their all to work is a good idea gone haywire. In the end, both First and Third World women are small players in a larger economic game whose rules they have not written.

The trends outlined above—global polarization, increasing contact, and the establishment of transcontinental female networks—have caused more women to migrate. They have also changed women's motives for migrating. Fewer women move for "family reunification" and more move in search of work. And when they find work, it is often within the growing "care sector," which, according to the economist Nancy Folbre, currently encompasses 20 percent of all American jobs.[9]

A good number of the women who migrate to fill these positions seem to be single mothers. After all, about a fifth of the world's households are headed by women: 24 percent in the industrial world, 19 percent in Africa, 18 percent in Latin America and the Caribbean, and 13 percent in Asia and the Pacific. Some such women are on their own because their husbands have left them or because they have escaped abusive marriages. In addition to these single mothers, there is also a shadow group of "almost" single mothers, only nominally married to men who are alcoholics, gamblers, or just too worn down by the hardships of life to make a go of it. For example, one Filipina nanny now working in California was married to a man whose small business collapsed as a result of overseas competition. He could find no well-paid job abroad that he found acceptable, so he urged his wife to "go and earn good money" as a lap dancer in a café in Japan. With that money, he hoped to restart his business. Appalled by his proposal, she separated from him to become a nanny in the United States.

Many if not most women migrants have children. The average age of women migrants into the United States is twenty-nine, and most come from countries, such as the Philippines and Sri Lanka, where female identity centers on motherhood, and where the birth rate is high. Often migrants, especially the undocumented ones, cannot bring their children with them. Most mothers try to leave their children in the care of grandmothers, aunts, and fathers, in roughly that order. An orphanage is a last resort. A number of nannies working in rich countries hire nannies to care for their own children back home either as solo caretakers or as aides to the female relatives left in charge back home. Carmen Ronquillo, for example, migrated from the Philippines to Rome to work as a maid for an architect and single mother of two. She left behind her husband, two teenagers—and a maid.[10]

Whatever arrangements these mothers make for their children, however, most feel the separation acutely, expressing guilt and remorse to the researchers who interview them. Says one migrant mother who left her two-month-old baby in the care of a relative, "The first two years I felt like I was going crazy. You have to believe me when I say that it was like I was having intense psychological problems. I would catch myself gazing at nothing, thinking about my child."[11] Recounted another migrant nanny through tears, "When I saw my children again, I thought, 'Oh children do grow up even without their mother.' I left my youngest when she was only five years old. She was already nine when I saw her again, but she still wanted me to carry her."[12]

Many more migrant female workers than migrant male workers stay in their adopted countries—in fact, most do. In staying, these mothers remain separated from their children, a choice freighted, for many, with a terrible sadness. Some migrant nannies, isolated in their employers' homes and faced with what is often depressing work, find solace in lavishing their affluent charges with the love and care they wish they could provide their own children. In an interview with Rhacel Parreñas, Vicky Diaz, a college-educated schoolteacher who left behind five children in the Philippines, said, "the only thing you can do is to give all your love to the child [in your care]. In my absence from my children, the most I could do with my situation was to give all my love to that child."[13] Without intending it, she has taken part in a global heart transplant.

As much as these mothers suffer, their children suffer more. And there are a lot of them. An estimated 30 percent of Filipino children—some eight million—live in households where at least one parent has gone overseas. These children have counterparts in Africa, India, Sri Lanka, Latin America, and the former Soviet Union. How are these children doing? Not very well, according to a survey Manila's Scalabrini Migration Center conducted with more than seven hundred children in 1996. Compared to their classmates, the children of migrant workers more frequently fell ill; they were more likely to express anger, confusion, and apathy; and they performed particularly poorly in school. Other studies of this population show a rise in delinquency and child suicide.[14] When such children were asked whether they would also migrate when they grew up, leaving their own children in the care of others, they all said no.

Faced with these facts, one senses some sort of injustice at work, linking the emotional deprivation of these children with the surfeit of affection their First World counterparts enjoy. In her study of native-born women of color who do domestic work, Sau-Ling Wong argues that the time and energy these workers devote to the children of their employers is diverted from their own children.[15] But time and energy are not all that's involved; so, too, is love. In this sense, we can speak about love as an unfairly distributed resource—extracted from one place and enjoyed somewhere else.

Is love really a "resource" to which a child has a right? Certainly the United Nations Declaration on the Rights of the Child asserts all children's right to an "atmosphere of happiness, love, and understanding." Yet in some ways, this claim is hard to make. The more we love and are loved, the more deeply we can love. Love is not fixed in the same way that most material resources are fixed. Put another way, if love is a resource, it's a *renewable* resource; it creates more of itself. And yet Rowena Bautista can't be in two places at once. Her day has only so many hours. It may also be true that the more love she gives to Noa, the less she gives to her own three children back in the Philippines. Noa in the First World gets more love, and Clinton and Princela in the Third World get less. In this sense, love does appear scarce and limited, like a mineral extracted from the earth.

Perhaps, then, feelings *are* distributable resources, but they behave somewhat differently from either scarce or renewable material resources. According to Freud, we don't "withdraw" and "invest" feeling but rather *displace* or redirect it. The process is an unconscious one, whereby we don't actually give up a feeling of, say, love or hate, so much as we find a new object for it—in the case of sexual feeling, a more appropriate object than the original one, whom Freud presumed to be our opposite-sex parent. While Freud applied the idea of displacement mainly to relationships within the nuclear family, it seems only a small stretch to apply it to relationships like Rowena's to Noa. As Rowena told Frank, the *Wall Street Journal* reporter, "I give Noa what I can't give my children."

Understandably, First World parents welcome and even invite nannies to redirect their love in this manner. The way some employers describe it, a nanny's love of her employer's child is a natural product of her more loving Third World culture, with its warm family ties, strong community life, and long tradition of patient maternal love of children. In hiring a nanny, many such employers implicitly hope to import a poor country's "native culture," thereby replenishing their own rich country's depleted culture of care. They import the benefits of Third World "family values." Says the director of a co-op nursery in the San Francisco Bay Area, "This may be odd to say, but the teacher's aides we hire from Mexico and Guatemala know how to love a child better than the middle-class white parents. They are more relaxed, patient, and joyful. They enjoy the kids more. These professional parents are pressured for time and anxious to develop their kids' talents. I tell the parents that they can really learn how to love from the Latinas and the Filipinas."

When asked why Anglo mothers should relate to children so differently than do Filipina teacher's aides, the nursery director speculated, "The Filipinas are brought up in a more relaxed, loving environment. They aren't as rich as we are, but they aren't so pressured for time, so materialistic, so anxious. They have a more loving, family-oriented culture." One mother, an American lawyer, expressed a similar view:

> Carmen just enjoys my son. She doesn't worry whether . . . he's learning his letters, or whether he'll get into a good preschool. She just enjoys him. And actually, with anxious busy parents like us, that's really what Thomas needs. I love my son more than anyone in this world. But at this stage Carmen is better for him.

Filipina nannies I have interviewed in California paint a very different picture of the love they share with their First World charges. Theirs is not an import of happy peasant mothering but a love that partly develops on American shores, informed by an American ideology of mother-child bonding and fostered by intense loneliness and longing for their own children. If love is a precious resource, it is not one simply extracted from the Third World and implanted in the First; rather, it owes its very existence to a peculiar cultural alchemy that occurs in the land to which it is imported.

For María Gutierrez, who cares for the eight-month-old baby of two hard-working professionals (a lawyer and a doctor, born in the Philippines but now living in San Jose, California), loneliness and long work hours feed a love for her employers' child. "I love Ana more than my own two children. Yes, more! It's strange, I know. But I have time to be with her. I'm paid. I am lonely here. I work ten hours a day, with one day off. I don't know any neighbors on the block. And so this child gives me what I need."

Not only that, but she is able to provide her employer's child with a different sort of attention and nurturance than she could deliver to her own children. "I'm more patient," she explains, "more relaxed. I put the child first. My kids, I treated them the way my mother treated me."

I asked her how her mother had treated her and she replied:

> "My mother grew up in a farming family. It was a hard life. My mother wasn't warm to me. She didn't touch me or say 'I love you.' She didn't think she should do that. Before I was born she had lost

four babies—two in miscarriage and two died as babies. I think she was afraid to love me as a baby because she thought I might die too. Then she put me to work as a 'little mother' caring for my four younger brothers and sisters. I didn't have time to play."

Fortunately, an older woman who lived next door took an affectionate interest in María, often feeding her and even taking her in overnight when she was sick. María felt closer to this woman's relatives than she did to her biological aunts and cousins. She had been, in some measure, informally adopted—a practice she describes as common in the Philippine countryside and even in some towns during the 1960s and 1970s.

In a sense, María experienced a premodern childhood, marked by high infant mortality, child labor, and an absence of sentimentality, set within a culture of strong family commitment and community support. Reminiscent of fifteenth-century France, as Philippe Ariès describes it in *Centuries of Childhood,* this was a childhood before the romanticization of the child and before the modern middle-class ideology of intensive mothering.[16] Sentiment wasn't the point; commitment was.

María's commitment to her own children, aged twelve and thirteen when she left to work abroad, bears the mark of that upbringing. Through all of their anger and tears, María sends remittances and calls, come hell or high water. The commitment is there. The sentiment, she has to work at. When she calls home now, María says, "I tell my daughter 'I love you.' At first it sounded fake. But after a while it became natural. And now she says it back. It's strange, but I think I learned that it was okay to say that from being in the United States."

María's story points to a paradox. On the one hand, the First World extracts love from the Third World. But what is being extracted is partly produced or "assembled" here: the leisure, the money, the ideology of the child, the intense loneliness and yearning for one's own children. In María's case, a premodern childhood in the Philippines, a postmodern ideology of mothering and childhood in the United States, and the loneliness of migration blend to produce the love she gives to her employers' child. That love is also a product of the nanny's freedom from the time pressure and school anxiety parents feel in a culture that lacks a social safety net—one where both parent and child have to "make it" at work because no state policy, community, or marital tie is reliable enough to sustain them. In that sense, the love María gives as a nanny does not suffer from the disabling effects of the American version of late capitalism.

If all this is true—if, in fact, the nanny's love is something at least partially produced by the conditions under which it is given—is María's love of a First World child really being extracted from her own Third World children? Yes, because her daily presence has been removed, and with it the daily expression of her love. It is, of course, the nanny herself who is doing the extracting. Still, if her children suffer the loss of her affection, she suffers with them. This, indeed, is globalization's pound of flesh.

Curiously, the suffering of migrant women and their children is rarely visible to the First World beneficiaries of nanny love. Noa's mother focuses on her daughter's relationship with Rowena. Ana's mother focuses on her daughter's relationship with María. Rowena loves Noa, María loves Ana. That's all there is to it. The nanny's love is a thing in itself. It is unique, private—fetishized. Marx talked about the fetishization of things, not feelings. When we make a fetish of an object—an SUV, for example—we see that object as independent of its context. We disregard, he would argue, the men who harvested the rubber latex, the assembly-line workers who bolted on the tires, and so on. Just as we mentally isolate our idea of an object from the human scene within which it was made, so, too, we unwittingly separate the love between nanny and child from the global capitalist order of love to which it very much belongs.

The notion of extracting resources from the Third World in order to enrich the First World is hardly new. It harks back to imperialism in its most literal form: the nineteenth-century extraction of gold, ivory, and rubber from the Third World. That openly coercive, male-centered imperialism, which persists today, was always paralleled by a quieter imperialism in which women were more central. Today, as love and care become the "new gold," the female part of the story has grown in prominence. In both cases, through the death or displacement of their parents, Third World children pay the price.

Imperialism in its classic form involved the north's plunder of physical resources from the south. Its main protagonists were virtually all men: explorers, kings, missionaries, soldiers, and the local men who were forced at gunpoint to harvest wild rubber latex and the like. European states lent their legitimacy to these endeavors, and an ideology emerged to support them: "the white man's burden" in Britain and *la mission civilisatrice* in France, both of which emphasized the benefits of colonization for the colonized.

The brutality of that era's imperialism is not to be minimized, even as we compare the extraction of material resources from the Third World of that time to the extraction of emotional resources today. Today's north does not extract love from the south by force: there are no colonial officers in tan helmets, no invading armies, no ships bearing arms sailing off to the colonies. Instead, we see a benign scene of Third World women pushing baby carriages, elder care workers patiently walking, arms linked, with elderly clients on streets or sitting beside them in First World parks.

Today, coercion operates differently. While the sex trade and some domestic service is brutally enforced, in the main the new emotional imperialism does not issue from the barrel of a gun. Women choose to migrate for domestic work. But they choose it because economic pressures all but coerce them to. That yawning gap between rich and poor countries is itself a form of coercion, pushing Third World mothers to seek work in the First for lack of options closer to home. But given the prevailing free market ideology, migration is viewed as a "personal choice." Its consequences are seen as "personal problems." In this sense, migration creates not a white man's burden but, through a series of invisible links, a dark child's burden.

Some children of migrant mothers in the Philippines, Sri Lanka, Mexico, and elsewhere may be well cared for by loving kin in their communities. We need more data if we are to find out how such children are really doing. But if we discover that they aren't doing very well, how are we to respond? I can think of three possible approaches. First, we might say that all women everywhere should stay home and take care of their own families. The problem with Rowena is not migration but neglect of her traditional role. A second approach might be to deny that a problem exists: the care drain is an inevitable outcome of globalization, which is itself good for the world. A supply of labor has met a demand—what's the problem? If the first approach condemns global migration, the second celebrates it. Neither acknowledges its human costs.

According to a third approach—the one I take—loving, paid child care with reasonable hours is a very good thing. And globalization brings with it new opportunities, such as a nanny's access to good pay. But it also introduces painful new emotional realities for Third World children. We need to embrace the needs of Third World societies, including their children. We need to develop a global sense of ethics to match emerging global economic realities. If we go out to buy a pair of Nike shoes, we want to know how low the wage and how long the hours were for the Third World worker who made them. Likewise, if Rowena is taking care of a two-year-old six thousand miles from her home, we should want to know what is happening to her own children.

If we take this third approach, what should we or others in the Third World do? One obvious course would be to develop the Philippine and other Third World economies to such a degree that their citizens can earn as much money inside their countries as outside them. Then the Rowenas of the world could support their children in jobs they'd find at home. While such an obvious solution would seem ideal—if not easily achieved—Douglas Massey, a specialist in migration, points to some unexpected problems, at least in the short run. In Massey's view, it is not underdevelopment that sends migrants like Rowena off to the First World but development itself. The higher the percentage of women working in local manufacturing, he finds, the greater the chance that any one woman will leave on a first, undocumented trip abroad. Perhaps these women's horizons broaden. Perhaps they meet others who have gone abroad. Perhaps they come to want better jobs and more goods. Whatever the original motive, the more people in one's community migrate, the more likely one is to migrate too.

If development creates migration, and if we favor some form of development, we need to find more humane responses to the migration such development is likely to cause. For those women who migrate in order to flee abusive husbands, one part of the answer would be to create solutions to that problem closer to home—domestic-violence shelters in these women's home countries, for instance. Another might be to find ways to make it easier for migrating nannies to bring their children with them. Or as a last resort, employers could be required to finance a nanny's regular visits home.

A more basic solution, of course, is to raise the value of caring work itself, so that whoever does it gets more rewards for it. Care, in this case, would no longer be such a "pass-on" job. And now here's the rub: the value of the labor of raising a child—always low relative to the value of other kinds of labor—has, under the impact of globalization, sunk lower still. Children matter to their parents immeasurably, of course, but the labor of raising them does not earn much credit in the eyes of the world. When middle-class housewives raised children as an unpaid, full-time role, the work was dignified by its aura of middle-classness. That was the one upside to the otherwise confining cult of middle-class, nineteenth- and early-twentieth-century American womanhood. But when the unpaid work of raising a child became the paid work of child-care workers, its low market value revealed the abidingly low value of caring work generally—and further lowered it.

The low value placed on caring work results neither from an absence of a need for it nor from the simplicity or ease of doing it. Rather, the declining value of child care results from a cultural politics of inequality. It can be compared with the declining value of basic food crops relative to manufactured goods on the international market. Though clearly more necessary to life, crops such as wheat and rice fetch low and declining prices, while manufactured goods are more highly valued. Just as the market price of primary produce keeps the Third World low in the community of nations, so the low market value of care keeps the status of the women who do it—and, ultimately, all women—low.

One excellent way to raise the value of care is to involve fathers in it. If men shared the care of family members worldwide, care would spread laterally instead of being passed down a social class ladder. In Norway, for example, all employed men are eligible for a year's paternity leave at 90 percent pay. Some 80 percent of Norwegian men now take over a month of parental leave. In this way, Norway is a model to the world. For indeed it is men who have for the most part stepped aside from caring work, and it is with them that the "care drain" truly begins.

In all developed societies, women work at paid jobs. According to the International Labor Organization, half of the world's women between ages fifteen and sixty-four do paid work. Between 1960 and 1980, sixty-nine out of eighty-eight countries surveyed showed a growing proportion of women in paid work. Since 1950, the rate of increase has skyrocketed in the United States, while remaining high in Scandinavia and the United Kingdom and moderate in France and Germany. If we want developed societies with women doctors, political leaders, teachers, bus drivers, and computer programmers, we will need qualified people to give loving care to their children. And there is no reason why every society should not enjoy such loving paid child care. It may even be true that Rowena Bautista or María Guttierez are the people to provide it, so long as their own children either come with them or otherwise receive all the care they need. In the end, Article 9 of the United Nations Declaration on the Rights of the Child—which the United States has not yet signed—states an important goal for both Clinton and Princela Bautista and for feminism. It says we need to value care as our most precious resource, and to notice where it comes from and ends up. For, these days, the personal is global.

The Nanny Dilemma

SUSAN CHEEVER

Dominique came to New York eight years ago, but she says it would take a lifetime to figure out New Yorkers. We teach our kids that money can't buy love, and then we go right ahead and buy it for them—hiring strangers to love them, because we have more important things to do. "You are workaholics, that's for sure," she tells me, in the lilting island accent she uses for unpleasant truths. "It's work, work, work with you, and money, money, money. You analyze every little stupid thing, and then you run off to some therapist to get the answers." She shakes her head and laughs, fiddling with a red plastic Thunderzord my five-year-old son has left on the table. Strangest of all, she says, we supersmart New Yorkers are afraid of our children—afraid to say no, afraid to deny them anything that other kids have. "It's hard for the nannies to adjust to our New York way," says Eileen Stein of Town & Country, an agency that has placed Dominique in several jobs. "Here children are the boss. The children run the home. The parents let the children do whatever they want."

If there's a good woman behind every great man, behind every great woman there's a good nanny. The restructuring of the American family has created a huge demand for child care. According to a 1992 Department of

Consumer Affairs report that calls the nanny-placement industry a "free-for-all," there are almost 400,000 children under thirteen in New York City whose parents both work, and fewer than 100,000 places for them in after-school and day-care programs. The demand for child care at home has been met by an unregulated patchwork of agencies, a few experienced nannies, and thousands of immigrant women looking for jobs that require no training, no degrees, and, often, no papers. "It's hard to make a living back home," says Dominique, who came from Trinidad on a tourist visa when she was twenty, leaving behind a job that paid the equivalent of $130 a week. "Working here and sending money home is the only way I can take care of my family."

This collision of necessity and need is a disaster for working mothers, who have to find reliable child care in an unreliable market, and for the nannies who work for them with no protection or guarantees. Many New York nannies are from the Caribbean—Trinidad, Jamaica, other islands of the West Indies—but there are thousands of Philippine, Irish, and South and Central American nannies, too. (A nanny is a full-time worker who lives in or out and is paid between $250 and $600 a week. A baby nurse lives in for twenty-four hours a day during the first weeks of an infant's life and gets $100 a day or more.) Usually, nannies arrive with visas that are valid for a few months. But finding a good legal nanny is so difficult that many families are willing to break the law. And agencies sometimes lie about the legal status of the nannies they place.

Dominique is lucky; she got her green card through one of the first families she worked for. But in eight years she has had eight jobs—some good, some bad, some ugly. These days, she lives in Brooklyn—like most nannies, she can't afford Manhattan rents—and works for a professional couple who live with their two children in a big postwar building on East Eighty-sixth Street. She has worked in Greenwich Village (she loves it), on the Upper West Side (she hates it), and in the suburbs (trapped!). From 1992 to 1994, she worked for me, taking care of my two children. I had always thought of myself as the perfect employer; when I interviewed Dominique for this article—in which I have changed some names and identifying details—she gently set me straight.

Dominique's morning begins in the dark, in the heart of Brooklyn. She switches on CD 101.9 radio and Channel 5 TV (*Good Day New York*), and slides a worn Bible out from under her pillow. "Consider the lilies of the field, how they grow," she reads. "They toil not, neither do they spin." It's 6:08 A.M., and the temperature is thirty-six degrees. There are tie-ups on the George Washington Bridge and ten-minute delays on the Lexington Avenue line. "Take therefore no thought for the morrow," she reads. "Sufficient unto the day is the evil thereof." Her apartment, a studio that costs $504 a month, is sparsely furnished, with a glass-topped dining room table and chairs from Workbench, and a bed; Dominique would rather have no furniture than the tacky stuff some of her friends crowd into their apartments. Next to the stereo system are neat piles of Toni Braxton and Luther Vandross tapes and the eight-pound dumbbells that Dominique uses three or four times a week—she does half an hour of lifting and twenty minutes of aerobics. Out the window, beyond the fire escape, she can see the Sears sign over near Flatbush Avenue and the outline of Canarsie out toward Jamaica Bay.

Out on Eighty-sixth Street, an icy wind is blowing off the East River. Dominique thinks of New York as home, but she'll never get used to how cold it is here and the way night falls at four o'clock in the winter. She stops to buy an orange and a Snapple. The people she works for eat out, and their children live on sweet cereal, bread, boxed fruit juice, and peanut butter and jelly that are premixed in the jar. Dominique nurses her Snapple (guava or pink-grapefruit flavored) all day, eats the orange when she's hungry, and tries to make herself a proper dinner when she gets home. On a good night, she makes some curried chicken and steams some broccoli. On a bad night, she stops at Burger King for a shake. Now, shouldering her way through the crowds, she passes the health-food store where kids eat vegetarian pizza. She avoids looking in the windows of a new, expensive shoe store: she loves to buy shoes.

At York Avenue, she turns away from her destination and goes around the corner of Eighty-seventh Street to St. Joseph's Church. Inside, she crosses herself with holy water, lights a candle, and kneels near the back, where stained-glass windows throw splashes of color on the whitewashed walls. It's almost eight o'clock. The people she works for are just getting out of bed. But as she kneels Dominique daydreams for a minute, remembering home: the big white-and-blue house in Valencia where she lived after her mother married the small town's unofficial mayor, Big Daddy Will Diamond. The candle is for her mother. She also prays for her own eight-year-old daughter,

Crystal, who lives in Valencia with Dominique's sister. Dominique hasn't seen her daughter in three years. As she prays, she feels a familiar, sharp sadness about Crystal. Then she reminds herself that the money she is making will buy her daughter an education, so that she can get a stable job with good wages—*she* won't end up in New York taking care of other people's children.

When Dominique was growing up, she always knew she wasn't going to be a typical Trini girl—hanging out in Valencia, with its dead-end jobs and girls who had children when *they* were still children. She was going a lot farther than Sangre Grande, the nearest big town, which everyone called Sandy Grandy. Dominique had an aunt who lived in London, but she favored New York. She saw *Saturday Night Fever* four times. Every Sunday she watched *Fame,* the TV show starring the lucky kids at the New York School of Performing Arts, who stopped traffic with their dancing. Dominique loved to dance. She still does, turning up the volume and pulling down the shades and prancing alone around her little room. But now she knows that nothing stops New York traffic. "Take therefore no thought for the morrow," she remembers as she crosses Eighty-sixth Street to work. "Sufficient unto the day is the evil thereof."

Dominique smiles at the doorman and lets herself into the apartment. Suzanne is desperately jiggling the crying baby on one hip while she tries to make a peanut-butter-and-jelly sandwich. The dog is yapping. Emily, the five-year-old, is giggling and eating Froot Loops at the kitchen table. There's a puddle of milk on the floor. Suzanne's nightgown is stained with applesauce and instant coffee. Dominique says good morning; in response, Suzanne groans and hands her the baby. Dominique can hear the shower: Henry is getting ready for work.

It's a modern apartment, with lots of light, but it's crowded with furniture, and unopened mover's boxes are piled in one corner. The kitchen counters are overflowing with dishes, and the cabinets are filled with paper plates and appliances that are still in bubble wrap. When Dominique took this job, six months ago, Suzanne explained that they had just moved in. Later, Dominique found out that they had "just moved in" in 1992; she has often heard Henry boast that they got the apartment for a great price in a buyer's market.

The baby screeches with delight and then grunts with satisfaction, wiggling his whole body in Dominique's arms. Dominique kisses him on the top of his downy head and silently tells him to chill. She doesn't want Suzanne to be jealous. She doesn't like dealing with parents' jealousy of the bonds that she forms with their children. "They want us to be mother and father to these children," she says. "They're the ones who brought the kids into the world, but then they don't have time to raise them. So the kids get attached to you, because you're the one who's always there. Then the parents get angry."

This is part of what Dominique and her friends call the attachment factor—one of the most intransigent problems of being a New York nanny. "The kids see you all the time, and they assume you are going to be part of their life," says Sally, an Irish nanny, who is Dominique's closest friend in the building. Sally has had three jobs in five years. Two years ago, she applied for a position with a rich, prominent New York family. When she was interviewed, she was told she would wear a uniform, would have to be available for traveling, and would never under any circumstances speak directly with the parents of the children she was caring for—the family had hired a liaison person for that. She took the job on East Eighty-sixth Street instead.

"When you leave, the children can be devastated—and it can break your heart too," Sally says. Nannies rarely get notice. Then there's the problem of the hours, which seem to get more flexible (i.e., longer) the longer you work for a family. There's also the problem of being asked to do work—dog walking, ironing, serving at dinner parties—that was not part of the job description and was not included in the original salary. And if the job can sometimes be too flexible, the salary is often inflexible: many employers count minutes and deduct dollars when a nanny is late. Sometimes nannies get farmed out to clean or baby-sit for their employers' friends, too. "When they act as if my services are their property—property they can lend out whenever they want—that really makes me feel bought," Sally says.

There is the problem of summers. Many families offer nannies a Hobson's choice: either go away with them and be trapped in some all-white resort (in nanny circles, the Hamptons are a synonym for Hell) or take token wages while they're gone. There is the problem of a family's dependence on their nanny. "Some weekends, they call me five or six times," Dominique says. "Basically, I'm on call around the clock. I feel like my life isn't mine even when I'm at home."

Many nannies wonder why their employers bothered to have children at all. "I see these women struggling between being the careerperson who gets self-esteem from her job and being the parent who really loves her children," Sally says. "But you shouldn't have kids if you're not ready to make adjustments. Sometimes it blows me away when I'll come in to work and there will be no milk and no cereal and no money for groceries. Two people without kids who eat out don't have to have groceries, but with kids you need to have something for them to eat."

Worst of all, being a nanny is a job with negative stability. When children go to school—and in New York they sometimes go to school at age two—the job begins to evaporate. Many New York children are in school from 9:00 A.M. to 3:00 P.M. by the time they are five. Nannies have to get along with their employers in a relationship that is in certain respects more intimate than a marriage. Sometimes they are treated like servants; sometimes they are treated like best friends. They are required to be completely reliable and completely discreet. They are asked to ignore drug problems. They must see no evil, hear no evil, speak no evil—like the nanny in Jamaica Kincaid's novel *Lucy*, who walks in on her employer licking the neck of his wife's best friend. (The intensity of the connection between nannies, mothers, and children has attracted storytellers from Homer, who made Odysseus's nurse the only woman who could identify him, to Charlotte Brontë, who made her most sympathetic heroine, Jane Eyre, a governess. The nanny canon also includes the evil Miss Jessel from Henry James's *The Turn of the Screw*, the precursor to dozens of malign child-care professionals, all acting out a mother's worst fears, right up to *The Hand That Rocks the Cradle*.)

Nannies want to be treated as professionals. Dominique's friend Maria took a nanny-awareness class in Brooklyn last year. "The main thing they told us was to be businesslike," she says. "Businesslike, businesslike! But it's hard to be businesslike when you're going into someone's house and taking care of their children." I heard one or two horror stories from the nannies I spoke to: an employer who would give a reference only in exchange for sex; a man who left pornographic pictures around and watched the nanny's reaction; a woman who checked the garbage to see what her children had eaten; another woman who came home at 2:00 A.M. and broke all the windows in her apartment with a heavy copper saucepan. But the real horrors are more subtle: employers who tell their nannies what to wear, employers who depend on them so much that the nannies go to work even when they're sick. Sally says, "I lie there in bed when I'm sick and I think, Did anyone get Laurie's lunch? Do they know that it's library day? Do they know that she has a play date with Joan after school? I might as well go to work." And when a nanny leaves, it can be as devastating for the parents as it is for the children.

"We would close down the city," says Myrtle Johnson, a child-care veteran who works as a short-term baby nurse because she believes that nannies always end up getting treated badly. "If we didn't go to work, the mothers would go crazy, and they'd drive their husbands crazy, and no one could work. If there's a garbage strike, the trash just lies there. If there's a postal strike, the mail doesn't get delivered. But if the nannies were to strike it would be different. You can't just leave a baby around until there's someone ready to take care of it."

In twenty-five years as a baby nurse, Myrtle has traveled with families to Calgary (for the Olympics) and London (where she stayed at Claridge's) and has saved enough to buy a big brick house on Grant Avenue in the Bronx. In her kitchen there's a double Garland stove—the best. Upstairs, she has installed a pink-and-gold bathroom with a wicker basket of fluffy towels; it could fit right in on Park Avenue. But success hasn't changed her attitude. "The nannies are there for the duration," she says. "The employers get to think they own them, and it's just like anything else. You have a boyfriend, you do anything to keep him, you give him cocktails and lobsters. Then, when he marries you, it's no more cocktails and no more lobsters."

In the thirteen years I have been raising children in New York, I've employed three full-time nannies, supplemented by about a dozen baby-sitters. Our generation has made a religion of parenting. Our mothers had Dr. Spock; we have books to fill a ten-foot shelf. They had a family doctor; we have pediatric endocrinologists who specialize in glandular disorders. We love our children passionately, and for me, at least, leaving them—for a week, or even for a day—is the hardest thing I've ever had to do. This makes the person who takes care of them in my absence both indispensable and somehow an agent of separation and doom—much more than a simple employee. In many families, where women take on most of the job of raising the children, along with doing their outside jobs, the nanny becomes the true significant other. It's the nanny who works with the mother to create a place where the children can thrive; the husband is at best an assistant to the team and at worst an obstacle to their aims. "It's a fragile situation," Sally says. "I have to come in every morning and assess the mood in the house and take up the slack. In these marriages, the mothers depend on us so that they can work, and the fathers sometimes get off scot-free—a lot of the time it's as if they didn't even have children." Dominique and Sally have decided that the perfect employer would be a single mother with one child.

Honesty and professionalism go a long way toward helping nannies and families get along, but the circumstances of their employment will always be colored by our worst fears. The nannies know everything about us, and we know little about them. They come from alien cultures to fill our culture's most important job: raising our kids. We've decided to let other women take care of our children so that we can give those children a better life. It's an excruciating decision, as the nannies know better than anyone. The truth is, we are more like our nannies than we realize—strung out between the old ways and the new, between the demands of money and the demands of love. They have chosen to give their children less mothering so that they can make more money, and so have we. There are bad nannies and good nannies, just as there are bad mothers and good mothers, but it's our similarities rather than our differences that make the situation so painful.

The Care Crisis in the Philippines: Children and Transnational Families in the New Global Economy

RHACEL SALAZAR PARREÑAS

A growing crisis of care troubles the world's most developed nations.[1] Even as demand for care has increased, its supply has dwindled. The result is a care deficit,[2] to which women from the Philippines have responded in force. Roughly two-thirds[3] of Filipino migrant workers are women, and their exodus, usually to fill domestic jobs,[4] has generated tremendous social change in the Philippines. When female migrants are mothers, they leave behind their own children, usually in the care of other women.[5] Many Filipino children now grow up in divided households, where geographic separation places children under serious emotional strain. And yet it is impossible to overlook the significance of migrant labor to the Philippine economy. Some 34 to 54 percent of the Filipino population is sustained by remittances from migrant workers.[6]

Women in the Philippines, just like their counterparts in postindustrial nations, suffer from a "stalled revolution." Local gender ideology remains a few steps behind the economic reality, which has produced numerous female-headed, transnational households.[7] Consequently, a far greater degree of anxiety attends the quality of family life for the dependents of migrant mothers than for those of migrant fathers. The dominant gender ideology, after all, holds that a woman's rightful place is in the home, and the households of migrant mothers present a challenge to this view. In response, government officials and journalists denounce migrating mothers, claiming that they have caused the Filipino family to deteriorate, children to be abandoned, and a crisis of care to take root in the Philippines. To end this crisis, critics admonish, these mothers must return. Indeed, in May 1995, Philippine president Fidel Ramos called for initiatives to keep migrant mothers at home. He declared, "We are not against overseas employment of Filipino women. We are against overseas employment at the cost of family solidarity."[8] Migration, Ramos strongly implied, is morally acceptable only when it is undertaken by single, childless women.

The Philippine media reinforce this position by consistently publishing sensationalist reports on the suffering of children in transnational families.[9] These reports tend to vilify migrant mothers, suggesting that their children face more profound problems than do those of migrant fathers; and despite the fact that most of the children in question are left with relatives, journalists tend to refer to them as having been "abandoned." One article reports, "A child's sense of loss appears to be greater when it is the mother who leaves to work abroad."[10] Others link the emigration of mothers to the inadequate child care and unstable family life that eventually lead such children to "drugs, gambling, and drinking."[11] Writes one columnist, "Incest and rapes within blood relatives are alarmingly on the rise not only within Metro Manila but also in the provinces. There are some indications that the absence of mothers who have become OCWs [overseas contract workers] has something to do with the situation."[12] The same columnist elsewhere expresses the popular view that the children of migrants become a burden on the larger society: "Guidance counselors and social welfare agencies can show grim statistics on how many children have turned into liabilities to our society because of absentee parents."[13]

From January to July 2000, I conducted sixty-nine in-depth interviews with young adults who grew up in transnational households in the Philippines. Almost none of these children have yet reunited with their migrant parents. I interviewed thirty children with migrant mothers, twenty-six with migrant fathers, and thirteen with two migrant parents. The children I spoke to certainly had endured emotional hardships; but contrary to the media's dark presentation, they did not all experience their mothers' migration as abandonment. The hardships in their lives were frequently diminished when they received support from extended families and communities, when they enjoyed open communication with their migrant parents, and when they clearly understood the limited financial options that led their parents to migrate in the first place.

To call for the return of migrant mothers is to ignore the fact that the Philippines has grown increasingly dependent on their remittances. To acknowledge this reality could lead the Philippines toward a more egalitarian gender ideology. Casting blame on migrant mothers, however, serves only to divert the society's attention away from these children's needs, finally aggravating their difficulties by stigmatizing their family's choices.

The Philippine media has certainly sensationalized the issue of child welfare in migrating families, but that should not obscure the fact that the Philippines faces a genuine care crisis. Care is now the country's primary export. Remittances—mostly from migrant domestic workers—constitute the economy's largest source of foreign currency, totaling almost $7 billion in 1999.[14] With limited choices in the Philippines, women migrate to help sustain their families financially, but the price is very high. Both mothers and children suffer from family separation, even under the best of circumstances.

Migrant mothers who work as nannies often face the painful prospect of caring for other people's children while being unable to tend to their own. One such mother in Rome, Rosemarie Samaniego,[15] describes this predicament:

> When the girl that I take care of calls her mother "Mama," my heart jumps all the time because my children also call me "Mama." I feel the gap caused by our physical separation especially in the morning, when I pack [her] lunch, because that's what I used to do for my children. . . . I used to do that very same thing for them. I begin thinking that at this hour I should be taking care of my very own children and not someone else's, someone who is not related to me in any way, shape, or form. . . . The work that I do here is done for my family, but the problem is they are not close to me but are far away in the Philippines. Sometimes, you feel the separation and you

start to cry. Some days, I just start crying while I am sweeping the floor because I am thinking about my children in the Philippines. Sometimes, when I receive a letter from my children telling me that they are sick, I look up out the window and ask the Lord to look after them and make sure they get better even without me around to care after them. [*Starts crying.*] If I had wings, I would fly home to my children. Just for a moment, to see my children and take care of their needs, help them, then fly back over here to continue my work.

The children of migrant workers also suffer an incalculable loss when a parent disappears overseas. As Ellen Seneriches,[16] a twenty-one-year-old daughter of a domestic worker in New York, says:

There are times when you want to talk to her, but she is not there. That is really hard, very difficult. . . . There are times when I want to call her, speak to her, cry to her, and I cannot. It is difficult. The only thing that I can do is write to her. And I cannot cry through the e-mails and sometimes I just want to cry on her shoulder.

Children like Ellen, who was only ten years old when her mother left for New York, often repress their longings to reunite with their mothers. Knowing that their families have few financial options, they are left with no choice but to put their emotional needs aside. Often, they do so knowing that their mothers' care and attention have been diverted to other children. When I asked her how she felt about her mother's wards in New York, Ellen responded:

Very jealous. I am very, very jealous. There was even a time when she told the children she was caring for that they are very lucky that she was taking care of them, while her children back in the Philippines don't even have a mom to take care of them. It's pathetic, but it's true. We were left alone by ourselves and we had to be responsible at a very young age without a mother. Can you imagine?

Children like Ellen do experience emotional stress when they grow up in transnational households. But it is worth emphasizing that many migrant mothers attempt to sustain ties with their children, and their children often recognize and appreciate these efforts. Although her mother, undocumented in the United States, has not returned once to the Philippines in twelve years, Ellen does not doubt that she has struggled to remain close to her children despite the distance. In fact, although Ellen lives only three hours away from her father, she feels closer to and communicates more frequently with her mother. Says Ellen:

> I realize that my mother loves us very much. Even if she is far away, she would send us her love. She would make us feel like she really loved us. She would do this by always being there. She would just assure us that whenever we have problems to just call her and tell her. [*Pauses.*] And so I know that it has been more difficult for her than other mothers. She has had to do extra work because she is so far away from us.

Like Ellen's mother, who managed to "be there" despite a vast distance, other migrant mothers do not necessarily "abandon" their traditional duty of nurturing their families. Rather, they provide emotional care and guidance from afar.[17] Ellen even credits her mother for her success in school. Now a second-year medical school student, Ellen graduated at the top of her class in both high school and college. She says that the constant, open communication she shares with her mother provided the key to her success. She reflects:

> We communicate as often as we can, like twice or thrice a week through e-mails. Then she would call us every week. And it is very expensive, I know. . . . My mother and I have a very open relationship. We are like best friends. She would give me advice whenever I had problems. . . . She understands everything I do. She understands why I would act this or that way. She knows me really well. And she is also transparent to me. She always knows when I have problems, and likewise I know when she does. I am closer to her than to my father.

Ellen is clearly not the abandoned child or social liability the Philippine media describe. She not only benefits from sufficient parental support—from both her geographically distant mother and her nearby father—but also exceeds the bar of excellence in schooling. Her story indicates that children of migrant parents can overcome the emotional strains of transnational family life, and that they can enjoy sufficient family support, even from their geographically distant parent.

Of course, her good fortune is not universal. But it does raise questions about how children withstand such geographical strains; whether and how they maintain solid ties with their distant parents; and what circumstances lead some children to feel that those ties have weakened or given out. The Philippine media tend to equate the absence of a child's biological mother with abandonment, which leads to the assumption that all such children, lacking familial support, will become social liabilities.[18] But I found that positive surrogate parental figures and open communication with the migrant parent, along with acknowledgment of the migrant parent's contribution to the collective mobility of the family, allay many of the emotional insecurities that arise from transnational household arrangements. Children who lack these resources have greater difficulty adjusting.

Extensive research bears out this observation. The Scalabrini Migration Center, a nongovernmental organization for migration research in the Philippines, surveyed 709 elementary-school-age Filipino children in 2000, comparing the experiences of those with a father absent, a mother absent, both parents absent, and both parents present. While the researchers observed that parental absence does prompt feelings of abandonment and loneliness among children, they concluded that "it does not necessarily become an occasion for laziness and unruliness." Rather, if the extended family supports the child and makes him or her aware of the material benefits migration brings, the child may actually be spurred toward greater self-reliance and ambition, despite continued longings for family unity.

Jeek Pereno's life has been defined by those longings. At twenty-five, he is a merchandiser for a large department store in the Philippines. His mother more than adequately provided for her children, managing with her meager wages first as a domestic worker and then as a nurse's aide, to send them $200 a month and even to purchase a house in a fairly exclusive neighborhood in the city center. But Jeek still feels abandoned and insecure in his mother's affection, he believes that growing up without his parents robbed him of the discipline he needed. Like other children of migrant workers, Jeek does not feel that his faraway mother's financial support has been enough. Instead, he wishes she had offered him more guidance, concern, and emotional care.

Jeek was eight years old when his parents relocated to New York and left him, along with his three brothers, in the care of their aunt. Eight years later, Jeek's father passed away, and two of his brothers (the oldest and youngest) joined their mother in New York. Visa complications have prevented Jeek and his other brother from following—but their mother has not once returned to visit them in the Philippines. When I expressed surprise at this, Jeek solemnly replied: "Never. It will cost too much, she said."

Years of separation breed unfamiliarity among family members, and Jeek does not have the emotional security of knowing that his mother has genuinely tried to lessen that estrangement. For Jeek, only a visit could shore up this security after seventeen years of separation. His mother's weekly phone calls do not suffice. And because he experiences his mother's absence as indifference, he does not feel comfortable communicating with her openly about his unmet needs. The result is repression, which in turn aggravates the resentment he feels. Jeek told me:

> I talk to my mother once in a while. But what happens, whenever she asks how I am doing, I just say okay. It's not like I am really going to tell her that I have problems here. . . . It's not like she can do anything about my problems if I told her about them. Financial problems, yes she can help. But not the other problems, like emotional problems. . . . She will try to give advice, but I am not very interested to talk to her about things like that. . . . Of course, you are still young, you don't really know what is going to happen in the future. Before you realize that your parents left you, you can't do anything about it anymore. You are not in a position to tell them not to leave you. They should have not left us. (*Sobs.*)

I asked Jeek if his mother knew he felt this way. "No," he said, "she doesn't know." Asked if he received emotional support from anyone, Jeek replied, "As much as possible, if I can handle it, I try not to get emotional support from anyone. I just keep everything inside me."

Jeek feels that his mother not only abandoned him but failed to leave him with an adequate surrogate. His aunt had a family and children of her own. Jeek recalled, "While I do know that my aunt loves me and she took care of us to the best of her ability, I am not convinced that it was enough. . . . Because we were not disciplined enough. She let us do whatever we wanted to do." Jeek feels that his education suffered from this lack of discipline, and he greatly regrets not having concentrated on his studies. Having completed only a two-year vocational program in electronics, he doubts his competency to pursue a college degree. At twenty-five, he feels stuck, with only the limited option of turning from one low-paying job to another.

Children who, unlike Jeek, received good surrogate parenting managed to concentrate on their studies and in the end to fare much better. Rudy Montoya, a nineteen-year-old whose mother has done domestic work in Hong Kong for more than twelve years, credits his mother's brother for helping him succeed in high school:

> My uncle is the most influential person in my life. Well, he is in Saudi Arabia now. . . . He would tell me that my mother loves me and not to resent her, and that whatever happens, I should write her. He would encourage me and he would tell me to trust the Lord. And then, I remember in high school, he would push me to study. I learned a lot from him in high school. Showing his love for me, he would help me with my schoolwork. . . . The time that I spent with my uncle was short, but he is the person who helped me grow up to be a better person.

Unlike Jeek's aunt, Rudy's uncle did not have a family of his own. He was able to devote more time to Rudy, instilling discipline in his young charge as well as reassuring him that his mother, who is the sole income provider for her family, did not abandon him. Although his mother has returned to visit him only twice—once when he was in the fourth grade and again two years later—Rudy, who is now a college student, sees his mother as a "good provider" who has made tremendous sacrifices for his sake. This knowledge offers him emotional security, as well as a strong feeling of gratitude. When I asked him about the importance of education, he replied, "I haven't given anything back to my mother for the sacrifices that she has made for me. The least I could do for her is graduate, so that I can find a good job, so that eventually I will be able to help her out, too."

Many children resolve the emotional insecurity of being left by their parents the way that Rudy has: by viewing migration as a sacrifice to be repaid by adult children. Children who believe that their migrant mothers are struggling for the sake of the family's collective mobility, rather than leaving to live the "good life," are less likely to feel abandoned and more likely to accept their mothers' efforts to sustain close relationships from a distance. One such child is Theresa Bascara, an eighteen-year-old college student whose mother has worked as a domestic in Hong Kong since 1984. As she puts it, "[My inspiration is] my mother, because she is the one suffering over there. So the least I can give back to her is doing well in school."

For Ellen Seneriches, the image of her suffering mother compels her to reciprocate. She explained:

Especially after my mother left, I became more motivated to study harder. I did because my mother was sacrificing a lot and I had to compensate for how hard it is to be away from your children and then crying a lot at night, not knowing what we are doing. She would tell us in voice tapes. She would send us voice tapes every month, twice a month, and we would hear her cry in these tapes.

Having witnessed her mother's suffering even from a distance, Ellen can acknowledge the sacrifices her mother has made and the hardships she has endured in order to be a "good provider" for her family. This knowledge assuaged the resentment Ellen frequently felt when her mother first migrated.

Many of the children I interviewed harbored images of their mothers as martyrs, and they often found comfort in their mothers' grief over not being able to nurture them directly. The expectation among such children that they will continue to receive a significant part of their nurturing from their mothers, despite the distance, points to the conservative gender ideology most of them maintain.[19] But whether or not they see their mothers as martyrs, children of migrant women feel best cared for when their mothers make consistent efforts to show parental concern from a distance. As Jeek's and Ellen's stories indicate, open communication with the migrant parent soothes feelings of abandonment; those who enjoy such open channels fare much better than those who lack them. Not only does communication ease children's emotional difficulties; it also fosters a sense of family unity, and it promotes the view that migration is a survival strategy that requires sacrifices from both children and parents for the good of the family.

For daughters of migrant mothers, such sacrifices commonly take the form of assuming some of their absent mothers' responsibilities, including the care of younger siblings. As Ellen told me:

> It was a strategy, and all of us had to sacrifice for it. . . . We all had to adjust, every day of our lives. . . . Imagine waking up without a mother calling you for breakfast. Then there would be no one to prepare the clothes for my brothers. We are all going to school. . . . I had to wake up earlier. I had to prepare their clothes. I had to wake them up and help them prepare for school. Then I also had to help them with their homework at night. I had to tutor them.

Asked if she resented this extra work, Ellen replied, "No. I saw it as training, a training that helped me become a leader. It makes you more of a leader doing that every day. I guess that is an advantage to me, and to my siblings as well."

Ellen's effort to assist in the household's daily maintenance was another way she reciprocated for her mother's emotional and financial support. Viewing her added work as a positive life lesson, Ellen believes that these responsibilities enabled her to develop leadership skills. Notably, her high school selected her as its first ever female commander for its government-mandated military training corps.

Unlike Jeek, Ellen is secure in her mother's love. She feels that her mother has struggled to "be there"; Jeek feels that his has not. Hence, Ellen has managed to successfully adjust to her household arrangement, while Jeek has not. The continual open communication between Ellen and her mother has had ramifications for their entire family: in return for her mother's sacrifices, Ellen assumed the role of second mother to her younger siblings, visiting them every weekend during her college years in order to spend quality time with them.

In general, eldest daughters of migrant mothers assume substantial familial responsibilities, often becoming substitute mothers for their siblings. Similarly, eldest sons stand in for migrant fathers. Armando Martinez, a twenty-nine-year-old entrepreneur whose father worked in Dubai for six months while he was in high school, related his experiences:

> I became a father during those six months. It was like, ugghhh, I made the rules. . . . I was able to see that it was hard if your family is not complete, you feel that there is something missing. . . . It's because the major decisions, sometimes, I was not old enough for them. I was only a teenager, and I was not that strong in my convictions when it came to making decisions. It was like work that I should not have been responsible for. I still wanted to play. So it was an added burden on my side.

Even when there is a parent left behind, children of migrant workers tend to assume added familial responsibilities, and these responsibilities vary along gender lines. Nonetheless, the weight tends to fall most heavily on children of migrant mothers, who are often left to struggle with the lack of male responsibility for care work in the Philippines. While a great number of children with migrant fathers receive full-time care from stay-at-home mothers, those with migrant mothers do not receive the same amount of care. Their fathers are likely to hold full-time jobs, and they rarely have the time to assume the role of primary caregiver. Of thirty children of migrant mothers I interviewed, only four had stay-at-home fathers. Most fathers passed the caregiving responsibilities on to other relatives, many of whom, like Jeek's aunt, already had families of their own to care for and regarded the children of migrant relatives as an extra burden. Families of migrant fathers are less likely to rely on the care work of extended kin.[20] Among my interviewees, thirteen of twenty-six children with migrant fathers lived with and were cared for primarily by their stay-at-home mothers.

Children of migrant mothers, unlike those of migrant fathers, have the added burden of accepting nontraditional gender roles in their families. The Scalabrini Migration Center reports that these children "tend to be more angry, confused, apathetic, and more afraid than other children."[21] They are caught within an "ideological stall" in the societal acceptance of female-headed transnational households. Because her family does not fit the traditional nuclear household model, Theresa Bascara sees her family as "broken," even though she describes her relationship to her mother as "very close." She says, "A family, I can say, is only whole if your father is the one working and your mother is only staying at home. It's okay if your mother works too, but somewhere close to you."

Some children in transnational families adjust to their household arrangements with greater success than others do. Those who feel that their mothers strive to nurture them as well as to be good providers are more likely to be accepting. The support of extended kin, or perhaps a sense of public accountability for their welfare, also helps children combat feelings of abandonment. Likewise, a more gender-egalitarian value system enables children to appreciate their mothers as good providers, which in turn allows them to see their mothers' migrations as demonstrations of love.

Even if they are well-adjusted, however, children in transnational families still suffer the loss of family intimacy. They are often forced to compensate by accepting commodities, rather than affection, as the most tangible reassurance of their parents' love. By putting family intimacy on hold, children can only wait for the opportunity to spend quality time with their migrant parents. Even when that time comes, it can be painful. As Theresa related:

> When my mother is home, I just sit next to her. I stare at her face, to see the changes in her face, to see how she aged during the years that she was away from us. But when she is about to go back to Hong Kong, it's like my heart is going to burst. I would just cry and cry. I really can't explain the feeling. Sometimes, when my mother is home, preparing to leave for Hong Kong, I would just start crying, because I already start missing her. I ask myself, how many more years will it be until we see each other again?
>
> . . . Telephone calls. That's not enough. You can't hug her, kiss her, feel her, everything. You can't feel her presence. It's just words that you have. What I want is to have my mother close to me, to see her grow older, and when she is sick, you are the one taking care of her and when you are sick, she is the one taking care of you.

Not surprisingly, when asked if they would leave their own children to take jobs as migrant workers, almost all of my respondents answered, "Never." When I asked why not, most said that they would never want their children to go through what they had gone through, or to be denied what they were denied, in their childhoods. Armando Martinez best summed up what children in transnational families lose when he said:

> You just cannot buy the times when your family is together. Isn't that right? Time together is something that money can neither buy nor replace. . . . The first time your baby speaks, you are not there. Other people would experience that joy. And when your child graduates with honors, you are also not there. . . . Is that right? When your child wins a basketball game, no one will be there to ask him how his game went, how many points he made. Is that right? Your family loses, don't you think?

Children of transnational families repeatedly stress that they lack the pleasure and comfort of daily interaction with their parents. Nonetheless, these children do not necessarily become "delinquent," nor are their families necessarily broken, in the manner the Philippine media depicts. Armando mirrored the opinion of most of the children in my study when he defended transnational families: "Even if [parents] are far away, they are still there. I get that from basketball, specifically zone defense." [He laughed.] "If someone is not there, you just have to adjust. It's like a slight hindrance that you just have to adjust to. Then when they come back, you get a chance to recover. It's like that."

Recognizing that the family is an adaptive unit that responds to external forces, many children make do, even if doing so requires tremendous sacrifices. They give up intimacy and familiarity with their parents. Often, they attempt to make up for their migrant parents' hardships by maintaining close bonds across great distances, even though most of them feel that such bonds could never possibly draw their distant parent close enough. But their efforts are frequently sustained by the belief that such emotional sacrifices are not without meaning—that they are ultimately for the greater good of their families and their future. Jason Halili's mother provided care for elderly persons in Los Angeles for fifteen years. Jason, now twenty-one, reasons, "If she did not leave, I would not be here right now. So it was the hardest route to take, but at the same time, the best route to take."

Transnational families were not always equated with "broken homes" in the Philippine public discourse. Nor did labor migration emerge as a perceived threat to family life before the late 1980s, when the number of migrant women significantly increased. This suggests that changes to the gendered division of family labor may have as much as anything else to do with the Philippine care crisis.

The Philippine public simply assumes that the proliferation of female-headed transnational households will wreak havoc on the lives of children. The Scalabrini Migration Center explains that children of migrant mothers suffer more than those of migrant fathers because child rearing is "a role women are more adept at, are better prepared for, and pay more attention to."[22] The center's study, like the Philippine media, recommends that mothers be kept from migrating. The researchers suggest that "economic programs should be targeted particularly toward the absorption of the female labor force, to facilitate the possibility for mothers to remain in the family."[23] Yet the return migration of mothers is neither a plausible nor a desirable solution. Rather, it implicitly accepts gender inequities in the family, even as it ignores the economic pressures generated by globalization.

As national discourse on the care crisis in the Philippines vilifies migrant women, it also downplays the contributions these women make to the country's economy. Such hand-wringing merely offers the public an opportunity to discipline women morally and to resist reconstituting family life in a manner that reflects the country's increasing dependence on women's foreign remittances. This pattern is not exclusive to the Philippines. As Arjun Appadurai observes, globalization has commonly led to "ideas about gender and modernity that create large female work forces at the same time that cross-national ideologies of 'culture,' 'authenticity,' and national honor put increasing pressure on various communities to morally discipline working women."[24]

The moral disciplining of women, however, hurts those who most need protection. It pathologizes the children of migrants, and it downplays the emotional difficulties that mothers like Rosemarie Samaniego face. Moreover, it ignores the struggles of migrant mothers who attempt to nurture their children from a distance. Vilifying migrant women as bad mothers promotes the view that the return to the nuclear family is the only viable solution to the emotional difficulties of children in transnational families. In so doing, it directs attention away from the special needs of children in transnational families—for instance, the need for community projects that would improve communication among far-flung family members, or for special school programs, the like of which did not exist at my field research site. It's also a strategy that sidelines the agency and adaptability of the children themselves.

To say that children are perfectly capable of adjusting to nontraditional households is not to say that they don't suffer hardships. But the overwhelming public support for keeping migrant mothers at home does have a negative impact on these children's adjustment. Implicit in such views is a rejection of the division of labor in families with migrant mothers, and the message such children receive is that their household arrangements are simply wrong. Moreover, calling for the return migration of women does not necessarily solve the problems plaguing families in the Philippines. Domestic violence and male infidelity, for instance—two social problems the government has never adequately addressed—would still threaten the well-being of children.[25]

Without a doubt, the children of migrant Filipina domestic workers suffer from the extraction of care from the global south to the global north. The plight of these children is a timely and necessary concern for nongovernmental, governmental, and academic groups in the Philippines. Blaming migrant mothers, however, has not helped, and has even hurt, those whose relationships suffer most from the movement of care in the global economy. Advocates for children in transnational families should focus their attention not on calling for a return to the nuclear family but on trying to meet the special needs transnational families possess. One of those needs is for a reconstituted gender ideology in the Philippines; another is for the elimination of legislation that penalizes migrant families in the nations where they work.

If we want to secure quality care for the children of transnational families, gender egalitarian views of child rearing are essential. Such views can be fostered by recognizing the economic contributions women make to their families and by redefining motherhood to include providing for one's family. Gender should be recognized as a fluid social category, and masculinity should be redefined, as the larger society questions the biologically based assumption that only women have an aptitude to provide care. Government officials and the media could then stop vilifying migrant women, redirecting their attention, instead, to men. They could question the lack of male accountability for care work, and they could demand that men, including migrant fathers, take more responsibility for the emotional welfare of their children.

The host societies of migrant Filipina domestic workers should also be held more accountable for their welfare and for that of their families. These women's work allows First World women to enter the paid labor force. As one Dutch employer states, "There are people who would look after children, but other things are more fun. Carers from other countries, if we can use their surplus carers, that's a solution."[26]

Yet, as we've seen, one cannot simply assume that the care leaving disadvantaged nations is surplus care. What is a solution for rich nations creates a problem in poor nations. Mothers like Rosemarie Samaniego and children like Ellen Seneriches and Jeek Pereno bear the brunt of this problem, while the receiving countries and the employing families benefit.

Most receiving countries have yet to recognize the contributions of their migrant care workers. They have consistently ignored these workers' rights and limited their full incorporation into society. The wages of migrant workers are so low that they cannot afford to bring their own families to join them, or to regularly visit their children in the Philippines; relegated to the status of guest workers, they are restricted to the low-wage employment sector, and with very few exceptions, the migration of their spouses and children is also restricted.[27] These arrangements work to the benefit of employers, since migrant care workers can give the best possible care for their employers' families when they are free of care-giving responsibilities to their own families. But there is a dire need to lobby for more inclusive policies, and for employers to develop a sense of accountability for their workers' children. After all, migrant workers significantly help their employers to reduce *their* families' care deficit.

Blowups and Other Unhappy Endings

PIERRETTE HONDAGNEU-SOTELO

A conflict begins over a mundane issue: a seemingly misspent hour, a seemingly sharp word. Quickly, the confrontation flares, exploding into a screaming match. Both women say harsh, regrettable things—things that reveal deep antipathies, which perhaps always lurked unspoken between them. It is as though the previously invisible fissures in their relationship were suddenly magnified and projected into plain view. The domestic worker is fired, or she walks out in disgust.

It's a dramatic way to end a job, but not an uncommon one for domestic workers, who often spend months or years in daily contact with the most intimate aspects of their employers' lives. Most commonly, blowups result from a lack of trust or respect between mistress and maid—surveillance on the part of the employer, perceived insubordination on the part of the worker, or a feeling of betrayal on either side.

Of course, not all domestic jobs end in blowups. But even less combustible arrangements often end more the way relationships do than the way jobs do: with white lies or alibis, designed to spare feelings or avoid conflict. Often, both parties know that the real reason an employee leaves is not a sick relative or a return to her home country. Like estranged partners, they tacitly agree not to discuss the tensions that rendered their relationship unworkable; but far from being partners, the two women occupy vastly unequal social roles. The worker keeps her silence out of fear; the employer, out of guilt, diffidence, or indifference.

What follow are stories culled from interviews I conducted with nearly seventy Latina immigrant domestic workers and their employers in Los Angeles County during the mid- to late 1990s. Nearly every live-in maid or nanny recounted at least one blowup in her career; employers were less forthcoming with tales of such confrontations. Nonetheless, a close look at how domestic jobs end, from the perspective of the workers if not the employers, tells us a great deal about how they begin and about how the profession is organized; it also exposes the degree to which domestic labor is viewed as something other than "real work."[1]

Blowups

By the time Soraya Sanchez had lived and worked at the Brooks family's three-story home for two months, caring for three young children, she was already dissatisfied. Her hours were too long; she was required to sleep with the children when the parents stayed out late; and her relationships were rocky with both Mrs. Brooks and the family's seven-year-old child, whom Soraya found manipulative and disobedient. Her previous jobs, which were relatively upscale nanny and housekeeper positions, had never demanded that she work major holidays; but the Brooks family coaxed Soraya into accompanying them to a relative's home in Seattle for Thanksgiving. There, things went from bad to worse.

After the catered Thanksgiving dinner, the Brooks's seven-year-old told her mother that Soraya had screamed at her to keep quiet while she put the baby to bed. "The *señora* had been drinking a bit too much at the Thanksgiving dinner," Soraya recalls. "I can't find another explanation, because she came into the baby's room, opened the door, and started yelling at me, saying, 'How dare you speak that way to my child!' She was yelling so exaggeratedly loud that I had to be quiet. . . . She was yelling 'I don't know who you think you are, I've been going out of my way for you.' And I said, 'Justine, you don't go out of the way for nobody, not even your mother!' 'Cause she didn't. 'You don't go out of the way for nobody but yourself!' "

When Mrs. Brooks told Soraya she was fired, Soraya replied, "You know what? You don't have to fire me, I won't work for you! Not for a million dollars! I'm quitting! You know what? Now I'm no longer your maid, and you're no longer my boss, and you and I are equals! Now you are going to hear what I am going to say to you!"

What Soraya had to say was this: "You're the mother and not even you want to take care of your own children. Why I should have to worry? I hope that you find a person who really understands your children, because not even you know how to understand them. I quit, I'm quitting, I'm quitting!"

With that, Soraya packed her things and stormed out of the house. Finding herself alone in a strange city, she took a taxi to the airport and waited there for a morning flight home to Los Angeles.

The work week began as usual for Elvira Areola. Early Monday morning, she arrived at the Johnston family's white-picket-fenced suburban home. She had worked there for eleven years, initially cleaning the Johnstons' house once or twice a week while also working in a plant nursery. When Dr. Johnston and his wife adopted their first child four years ago, they persuaded Elvira to work for them full-time. As a live-out nanny and housekeeper, she worked four ten-hour days a week.

Elvira cared for a newly adopted baby as well as the four-year-old boy, who now attended nursery school two mornings a week. She was also in charge of the upkeep of the Johnstons' sprawling house, which included five bathrooms and many delicate antiques. That Monday morning, Elvira took the baby for a walk, as she had been instructed to do, and visited, as she often did, with a nanny who worked in another home in the neighborhood. As Elvira tells it, Mrs. Johnston tracked her down and told her, in a raised voice, that she had been frantically telephoning in search of her and the baby. Accusing Elvira of not having brought enough food for the baby, Mrs. Johnston immediately took the baby home herself.

Silence descended between them for the remainder of the day, but that wasn't all that unusual. According to Elvira, although they were almost always the only two adults in the house, they rarely spoke. Often, Mrs. Johnston stayed in her bedroom, alone, until two o'clock in the afternoon. But that Monday's silence was pregnant with the resentment both women felt after the incident on the street.

Elvira bristled most at Mrs. Johnston's distrust. It didn't help, however, that she was already quietly smoldering over the increase in her workload that had accompanied the second adoption. Monday mornings, when the boy was in preschool, had previously been Elvira's housecleaning time; she now spent that day caring for the new baby. She knew from friends who worked in neighboring homes that in some households, a weekly or biweekly house cleaner helped pick up the slack for overloaded nannies. Mrs. Johnston, however, no doubt saw an idle employee, neglecting her housecleaning duties and perhaps even the baby's diet in order to socialize. Elvira was being paid to take care of the Johnston house and children, Mrs. Johnston admonished her—not to visit with nearby nannies.

When Elvira returned to the job on Wednesday, Mrs. Johnston took her aside, accused her of having left the house for five hours, and told her to be more responsible. "You're just like one of our family," she said.

No, she wasn't, Elvira replied: she had her own family, and in any case, one didn't treat one's family in this manner.

"Remember, you're just a maid," retorted Mrs. Johnston.

When Mr. Johnston drove Elvira home that evening, he asked her to apologize to his wife. Elvira passed a restless night, wondering if she should quit. She decided to stay and to act civilly but not to apologize, because she felt she'd done nothing wrong.

On Friday, Mrs. Johnston told Elvira to take the boy to the library for story time, and then to meet her at McDonald's, where she would hand over the baby so that Elvira might walk home with both children. Elvira waited at McDonald's for several hours. Her employer never arrived.

Later that afternoon, Elvira told Mrs. Johnston she was quitting.

"Rethink this. You can't quit," said Mrs. Johnston.

Elvira held fast. Mrs. Johnston asked her to put her resignation in writing—but Elvira could not write in English, and Mrs. Johnston knew it. The women traded insults. Mrs. Johnston, a large woman by Elvira's account, attempted to block the doorway, but eventually Elvira slipped past. Downstairs, Mr. Johnston, oblivious to the blowup between the two women, asked, "Elvira, can you please take out the garbage before you leave?" She complied, gathered her purse and sweater, and then walked out of the house for the last time, leaving her employers of eleven years and the four-year-old boy whom she had helped raise since infancy.

Elvira expected she would soon feel sad and remorseful. To her surprise, however, she felt only joyful and relieved. "I thought maybe I wouldn't even feel like searching for a new job, that I'd be depressed. But no! I felt really great!" She had only one regret: she longed to see the little boy she had cared for, but she knew that if she called or visited him, his parents might construe her presence as malicious, or as an attempt to kidnap their son.

A single mother of four, Elvira had her hands full with her job search in any event. "I haven't rested one day," she says. "There's not been one day when I haven't gone out searching for work." Without references, Elvira's job hunt was certainly challenging. She spent her days walking the streets of Pasadena and other cities in the San Gabriel Valley, looking into jobs at plant nurseries, motels, hospitals, shops, and convalescent homes. She left crudely drawn, hand-printed cards advertising her housecleaning services on doorsteps in a middle-class neighborhood, but no one called to inquire.

Finally, after weeks of searching, Elvira was hired for the night shift on a hospital cleaning crew. She still hoped to pick up a few houses to clean during the week. Her pay at the Johnstons had come to approximately $8 an hour, which placed her at the upper end of her occupation's wage scale; at her new job, she would earn only the minimum wage, then $4.25. She was ashamed of the low pay and the odd hours but was optimistic that she would soon do better. What's more, she felt strongly that her dignity was worth the pay cut. "What matters to me most is feeling good, seeing that they like my work," she maintains. "Money is important for material things. I know that without money you've got nothing, but I can't expect to earn the same as I was before."

Candace Ross is the cheerful, thirty-six-year-old wife of a CEO. The mother of three young children, she recently quit her job as a midlevel manager in order to spend more time with her family. That changed things for Carmen, her Salvadoran live-in nanny and housekeeper. As Mrs. Ross recalls, "Carmen's life got a lot easier. I'm very neat and tidy and I do a lot."

As far as Mrs. Ross could see, Carmen's job was now reduced to watching the baby when she went out. She was therefore stunned when Carmen chose that time to ask for a raise. After consulting with her husband, Mrs. Ross decided to consent to a raise, but on the condition that Carmen's duties expand to include regular Friday- and Saturday-night baby-sitting. Carmen initially consented but later objected, since the new schedule would interfere with her Saturday-morning ESL classes.

"We kind of had a blowup, and then she started acting really inconsiderate about her position, in my opinion," recalls Mrs. Ross. "She said, 'Well, you've never given me a bonus.' And I thought, A bonus! I worked all my work years and I never got a bonus from any employer at all. I don't know where she even got that idea! I just felt really bad, and I said, 'Gosh, it's apparent that you don't appreciate what you have here. I try to have a nice house for you to live in, and I never ask you to do something that I wouldn't do myself.' I said, 'You know, you say that I didn't give you a bonus—well, why don't you take back all those Christmas presents I gave you and cash them in? There's your bonus!' You know, that kind of thing. I said, 'Is money just really all that's important to you?'"

Indeed, it was the suggestion that Carmen was motivated as much by her wages as by love for the Ross children that stung her employer most. "I was really hurt," Candace Ross concedes, "and I probably said some things to her that I wish I could take back."

The worst of the things the employer said was that she no longer needed a nanny five days a week, and that she was only keeping Carmen out of pity. "I said, 'So if you want to, go ahead and just leave. Go ahead, and I'll just try to find somebody to come in two or three days a week.'"

Later, Carmen came to her boss, and the women were able to mend their relationship. They came up with a new arrangement, whereby Carmen would work for the Ross family three days a week and work the other two days elsewhere, cleaning houses in the same exclusive residential neighborhood. Carmen remains Candace Ross's live-in, which allows her to save on rent and to send money to her own children in El Salvador; but she now has several employers, which means she is no longer solely dependent on what she earns in the Ross household.

Margarita Gutierrez, a young woman from Mexico City, worked as a live-in nanny and housekeeper. When she decided to leave her job, she gave her employer two weeks' notice—a rare courtesy in this realm of employment. The weeks passed. But the night before what was to have been her last day, the couple came knocking on Margarita's bedroom door. "Here's your money," they told her. "You can go now."

Unexpectedly cast out of her home and job a day early, Margarita called her sister, who also worked as a live-in maid and nanny. Margarita waited outside, in the canyon home's dark driveway, for a ride to her sister's employer's home. Although several years have passed since this incident, she still cries as she tells the story.

Celestina Vitriola lived a middle-class life in El Salvador. But when she came to the United States, she took a job with a family as a Monday-through-Friday live-out nanny and housekeeper. Two years later, the family asked her to move in. Celestina said no; she was taking evening classes at an adult school, and she was living with her boyfriend. The family fired her on the spot, with one week's severance pay. "They didn't even give me time to say, 'Well, let me think about it,' or to find another job! They let me go that same day," she recalls.

For Celestina, the shock was compounded by the fact that she was abruptly forced to part with the two-year-old she had tended since birth, and whom she had grown to love. "I said to myself, 'I'll never work in a house again, and I'll never take care of a child again,'" Celestina recounts. "You get to feeling a lot of attachment for these children. It really hurt me that they took me out like that, so suddenly. So I said, 'No, I'll never take care of a house or children again.'"

Like many vows made in the heat of the moment, Celestina's was a hard one to keep, especially given the scarcity of job options for recent immigrants. She took a job on a catering truck, preparing and selling lunches to Latino factory workers; but before long she was laid off. That was when she returned to domestic work, accepting another position as a live-out nanny and housekeeper.

In order to make her peace with this decision, she drew some protective boundaries with her new employer. "From the beginning, I told her, 'You know what? If you decide to get rid of me someday, tell me three months ahead of time. Don't tell me one day to the next. And I'll do the same, I'll give you plenty of time to find a replacement person.' But to this day [six years later], I still work for her."

Ronalda Saavedras, a young Salvadoran nanny and housekeeper, has seen several jobs end explosively. Once, an employer accused her of torturing and killing the family's cat. She was fired on this basis, despite her claim that the cat had wandered into a nearby canyon, where a coyote probably ate it. A previous employer in Beverly Hills, in a fit of rage, fired Ronalda and three other domestic employees en masse.

That didn't stop Ronalda from taking another job in a multiple-employee household, however. She worked for several months as one of two daily live-out nannies and housekeepers in an upscale home on Los Angeles's West Side. It took no longer than that for a conflict to brew: one Saturday, Ronalda's employer confronted her with a litany of complaints and abruptly fired her. According to the employer, Ronalda was a bad driver, an indulgent nanny, an insubordinate employee, and inattentive to her job. Ronalda says she had heard about none of these failings until the moment she was fired.

After that, the young woman resolved not to seek another job as a nanny and housekeeper but to work instead as a weekly house cleaner. She was well situated to make the switch: she was relatively young, with good physical stamina; her English was rapidly improving; she had a car; and she had an aunt in the housecleaning business who could help her gain a foothold. Within a year, she'd established a viable route of houses to clean. The work was physically demanding and exhausting, but to Ronalda, it was infinitely preferable to the emotional vulnerability she felt as a nanny and housekeeper.

Sarah Cohen is a labor lawyer who specializes in domestic work. The most common complaint she gets from workers is that they have been unjustly terminated, usually following a blowup. The employers, she explains, tend to explode at perceived affronts or suggestions of personal disloyalty. "I think it comes from this idea that the domestic worker is the employer's chattel," Cohen speculates. "She paid for the worker, the employer is getting a life. When the domestic worker shows that she has her own life, her own problems, her own health, and her own kids to attend to, it's threatening. Suddenly it's clear that the worker has concerns that are more important than taking care of some employer's house or kids."

One of Cohen's recent cases involved a Guatemalan live-in who worked for a stay-at-home mother with school-aged children. When the live-in fell ill one weekend, she called in sick from her weekend residence. According to Cohen, "The employer became incensed and commanded her to come immediately. She refused, and she was fired." The employers immediately stopped payment on her last paycheck.

Many live-in nannies and housekeepers erroneously believe that they are entitled to national holidays such as Memorial Day and Labor Day. They are often summarily fired when they return to their jobs. For this reason, the domestic-employment agencies brim with new job seekers after holiday weekends. Conflicts over pay and requests for raises also spark abrupt firings. Cohen recently represented a woman who worked as a live-in at one place for seven years, earning $130 a week, which was well below minimum wage. When the employer added the care of a sick stray dog to her regular list of duties, which already included tending to several animals, the employee asked for a raise. She was fired.

"They lose their job and they think there's something wrong when that happens," says Cohen. "A lot of domestic workers come in complaining about having been wrongfully terminated. I haven't studied other countries' legal systems, but it appears to me that in other countries, the laws around being terminated from a job and your right to a vacation are a lot more progressive than here."

Sociologist Alejandro Portes confirms Cohen's impression. "Many Third World nations have implemented labor regulations that, on paper at least, have little to envy those of the most advanced countries," says Portes. "In Colombia, Peru, and Mexico, it is more difficult to fire a worker with some minimum tenure on the job than in the United States."[2]

In the United States, employers can fire or hire whomever they wish "at will," so long as they do not employ discriminatory criteria. Employment at will means both that an employer can legally fire a worker for no reason and with no notice and that an employee can legally quit without notice. The notion of an equal playing field between employers and employees, however, overlooks the imbalance of power between the two parties. In recent decades, a body of U.S. law called "wrongful termination" has developed, but it generally applies to rich executives with written contracts that they can prove were breached.[3]

Most of Cohen's clients who allege wrongful termination wind up pursuing wage claims. After all, there is not much a lawyer can do to redress a legal, though unpleasant, job termination; but very often, Cohen finds that employers have made illegal deductions from their workers' wages.

Nonetheless, whether they come to Cohen seeking a wrongful-termination claim or a wage claim, many domestic workers emerge from blowups with grievances no lawyer can rectify. The eruption of hostilities, often with longtime employers, whose lives the workers know intimately well, can be emotionally wounding. The loss of contact with children domestic workers helped raise can be nothing short of heartbreaking. And the fact of being fired on the spot, which may also mean being cast out of one's home, bruises the pride of many workers, especially when, like Elvira, they find themselves casting about for lodging and work without references and without roots in the communities where they have landed.

Quitting Through Alibis and Other Fictions

Weekly house cleaners and their employers rarely experience blowups, in part because they only see each other once a week, twice a month, or perhaps not at all. When they do meet, it is typically for fleeting moments, during which it is relatively easy to remain cordial. Since the house cleaners' duties do not include child care, employer-employee relations are less complex and less volatile. Problems do arise, and when that happens, house cleaners and their employers prefer to exit the arrangement with discretion.

Some house cleaners leave jobs by calling in sick a few times, or by relying on a time-tested alibi: "My mother is sick and I must immediately return to Guatemala." The alibi is so well used that some Latina domestic workers joke about it, recalling with laughter their dramaturgical efforts.

Lies and alibis are popular exit strategies for nannies and housekeepers as well as for house cleaners. One domestic worker, Gladys Vargas, recalls, "About a year ago a friend of mine who was working as a housekeeper for a bachelor says to me, 'Look, I'm going to Miami. But I have to tell the *señor* that I'm going back to Honduras . . . because what if something is missing?

And then another thing, and then he calls the police?' That would make her life impossible, so it's just easier to say that she's going to Honduras to be with her sick children even though she's going to Miami for a better job."

As subordinates in relationships marked by asymmetries of race, nationality, citizenship, language, and class, many domestic workers are not accustomed to expressing face-to-face criticism to their superiors. In fact, they fear retribution for doing so. A domestic employee who tells her employer that she is leaving because she has a better job prospect or because she was dissatisfied with her job may be accused of betrayal and disloyalty. She may be accused of theft, justly or unjustly. She may fear that the former employer will call the immigration authorities in retaliation. Or she may fear that by quitting verbally, she will ignite the flame of an unpleasant verbal encounter.

Employers often know that quitting alibis are lies. Several of the employers I spoke with laughingly recalled seeing their former housekeepers, women who supposedly had to leave abruptly to visit sick or dying relatives in their countries of origin, waiting at bus stops in the neighborhood just days or weeks later. When a house cleaner calls in sick for a few days and then just disappears, the employer may interpret her behavior as typical of a lazy, unmotivated, Latina immigrant, not a disgruntled employee who is unhappy with her working conditions. As Julia Wrigley, the author of *Other People's Children,* notes, "AWOL workers are sending their employers a message, but it is not a message employers always choose to understand."[4]

Employers, meanwhile, are not much better at firing domestic workers than the workers are at quitting. Typical employer alibis include extended trips, home remodeling, or the return of a former employee. Many employers find it very difficult either to directly fire a worker or to constructively communicate job deficiencies in ways that might allow the employee to improve.

Teresa Portillo, a weekly house cleaner, made the mistake of offering to do the laundry one week. Thereafter, the employer anticipated that she would do the laundry every time. Teresa explained that their original agreement did not entail her staying until the dryer cycles were completed, but the employer left her a note saying that she would dock Teresa's pay by $5 each time she left clothes in the dryer. Teresa solved the problem: she simply stopped going to that job.

Lupe Velez had a full route of houses to clean. One employer accused her of scratching an old, used stove. "I finished cleaning that house, but my eyes were swollen from crying over that stove that I hadn't scratched. I went home and I didn't return."

Elizabeth Mapplethorpe fired her last maid, a young Latina woman, because she couldn't properly cook and serve a formal dinner for six. Yet she never communicated this grievance to the employee. In spite of Mrs. Mapplethorpe's years of experience with domestic employees, her ample social graces, and her seemingly unflappable confidence in hierarchy and in communicating directives, she wasn't quite sure how to handle this situation. She sought advice from the domestic-employment agency that had initially made the placement, and the agency counseled her to tell the woman that a former housekeeper was returning. That's what Mrs. Mapplethorpe did.

Bonnie Feinstein, who employs a rotating group of cleaners, housekeepers, and nannies, is extremely dissatisfied with two women in her crew—particularly her weekly house cleaner, Sarita. "She started to come to iron, and she didn't have any other work, and so then I let her start cleaning," Mrs. Feinstein explains. "She's not a very good cleaner, and she's not a very good ironer, but I just haven't been able to fire her." She chuckles. "So I just haven't fired her. . . . I'd just rather stick with someone like Sarita who is not perfect, rather than make a change."

But Mrs. Feinstein does not intend to stick with Sarita indefinitely. "We're going to go away next month, and I've told her that I'm thinking about changing things around, and that we're waiting to hear about this thing my husband is doing in France," she says. "I'll use that as an excuse." Asked if she had ever told Sarita that her cleaning was not up to par, Mrs. Feinstein laughed and replied, "No. I know I should, but I just haven't."

In fact, Sarita's cleaning was so substandard that even the other household employees had complained about it to Mrs. Feinstein. She told them to handle it among themselves.

Mrs. Feinstein's across-the-street neighbor, Julia Thomas-Ahib, also employed Sarita, and she acted with less ambivalence. One day, Ms. Thomas-Ahib came home to find Sarita in her house, cleaning, when she was not scheduled to do so. Ms. Thomas-Ahib expressed her anger, but Sarita remained unflustered.

"At that point," recalls Ms. Thomas-Ahib, "I said, 'You know, I really have to think about this, and I'll let you know when I want you to come back.' "

She did her own housecleaning for eight months, and then, just before hosting a party at her home, she called Sarita. Sarita, she reported, returned to clean and acted as though nothing had ever happened between them.

While not all employers are as diffident about communicating displeasure as Mrs. Feinstein, and while few would resume employing someone after a transgression, there is a strong preference among employers for staying with an imperfect house cleaner who is a "known quantity." Most employers prefer this to a confrontation or to the hassle of seeking a replacement. When they do decide to fire someone, they rarely do so straightforwardly.

What Blowups, Excuses, and Other Exits Say About Domestic Work

Domestic work, especially when it involves child care, produces relationships that fall somewhere between family and employment yet are often regarded as neither. Caught betwixt and between, the domestic worker also finds herself on the losing end of a highly asymmetrical balance of power and privilege between employer and employee. Taken together, these conditions comprise a recipe for abuse and abrupt job endings.

Many Latina immigrant employees and their U.S. employers fall easily into a familial rhetoric, referring to the worker as "just like one of the family." Indeed, this attitude has a long history in paid domestic work, and, as many analysts have noted, it helps blur the boundaries between paid work and unpaid favors, which in turn often leads to exploitation. Contemporary employers in Los Angeles, however, sound markedly different from their predecessors. In fact, many of them regard their domestic workers with a new distance and sterility. It's the employees, meanwhile, who *want* personal recognition from their employers. But they do not want to be taken for granted like members of the employer's own family, or to be expected to perform their duties solely out of love for their employer's children. Rather, they want *consideracíon* (understanding) and acknowledgment that they have lives and families of their own.

The complexity of domestic-employment arrangements begins with the very nature of the work involved. Providing daily care for children or the elderly is a personal and idiosyncratic affair. Not only that, but as policy analyst Deborah Stone has noted, care work is inherently relational, whether it consists in routine bodily care, such as bathing and feeding, or in emotional attachment, affiliation, and intimate knowledge.[5] Parents who hire nannies and housekeepers want employees who will really "care about" and show preference for their children; yet such personal engagement remains antithetical to how we normally think about employment. In fact, it can be hard for employers to acknowledge that the domestic employee has her own family life and is in fact tenderly caring for and cooing over the employer's children because she needs the cash.

Nannies *do* form genuine bonds of affection with some of the children in their care, but this does not obviate their need for a living wage and decent working conditions. Moreover, the nannies who open their hearts to the children they care for often express bewilderment, hurt, and rage when the children's parents then treat them with little regard. Many employers go out of their way to minimize interactions with their domestic employees, but Latina immigrant women, especially those who look after children, crave personal contact. The distant employer-employee relations that prevail today exacerbate inequality by denying domestic workers even the modest forms of social recognition that help shore up a worker's dignity and provide emotional sustenance.

The job exits detailed above are not just tales of personal distress or relational conflict. They are also missed opportunities for occupational reform. Many years ago, the development economist Albert O. Hirschman observed that consumers express dissatisfaction with company products by either exiting the relationship (and buying their goods elsewhere) or by voicing complaints.[6] The former is a good deal easier than the latter. Exiting an economic relationship requires neither verbal skill nor negotiating savvy, and it practically ensures that everyone concerned will be spared messy, complex, and unpleasant interactions.

The asymmetries endemic to paid domestic work encourage the painless exit. For both employers and employees, quiet dismissals and alibis are neater, more manageable, less offensive, and thus preferable to heated, honest exchanges. Over time, the accumulation of these quiet exits can lead to explosive blowups. One thing clearly lost amid both the repression and the explosions is the opportunity to exchange constructive criticism; another is the chance to substantively reform the occupation.

As the global marketplace for paid domestic work expands, it cries out for new models of employment. Like all workers, domestic employees have families, concerns, and aspirations of their own. But unlike other workers, nannies and housekeepers tend to face employers who feel threatened by their outside emotional commitments. While we cannot legislate that employers care about their workers' personal lives, we can strive to make domestic work an occupation that allows employees to maintain their dignity, as well as their family and social ties. We could begin with a living wage, benefits, and the simple recognition that domestic work can be both a job and an avocation— one deserving of respect, consideration, and constructive engagement, whether critical or otherwise.

Invisible Labors:
Caring for the Independent Person

LYNN MAY RIVAS

Twenty minutes into the interview,[1] Bill coughs. I notice that his voice is beginning to deteriorate. Earlier, he told me he had a problem with "dehydrating when he talks a lot." We are in his bedroom. On a table next to him is a glass of water with a plastic top and a straw. Since he is unable to use his hands, I offer, "Um, do you want, would you like some water?"

Bill raises his voice and calls, "Joe!" Then he explains, "I have an attendant."

"Okay," I reply. I'm disappointed, because I'm asking questions about his relationship with his attendants, and I was hoping to have privacy during the interview.

Bill again calls, "Joe!" Then, addressing me, he says, "I'm okay." He makes still another cry of "Joe!" and again tells me, "I'll be okay."

Joe does not come. Bill's voice is loud enough to be heard in the rest of the apartment, but just barely. I think I should volunteer to look for Joe, or to call for him with my louder voice. But Bill's insistence that he'll be okay, coupled with his earlier refusal of my offer to hold the water glass, leaves me uncertain what to do. I do nothing.

We continue the interview for another fifteen minutes until Bill again calls out, "Joe! Joe! Hey, Joe—hey, Joe—hey, Joe, Joe."

Bill's roommate pokes his head into the room and says, "I think Joe's out-side." Bill says, "Oh, okay." Then he continues answering my questions. Thirty seconds later, his roommate reappears and says, "Actually, I don't think he's in the house—I don't know where he's at." His roommate leaves and Bill says, "Joe is really wonderful, he probably just cut out for a few minutes."

We continue the interview, but I am uncomfortably aware of the fact that talking without water is causing Bill to dehydrate. Furthermore, his voice is deteriorating and he is getting harder to understand—so much so that when I review the tape for transcription, many of his responses are lost. Neverthe-less, I say nothing. Ten more minutes pass before he again calls, "Joe—hey, Joe—Joe, are you around?"

By this point, I feel frantic. I can't imagine why he won't let me give him water. "Do you want me to go outside and see if I can find him?" I ask in des-peration, not sure what I should do. Bill responds, "Would you?"

I find Joe sitting in the sun directly outside the apartment. I tell him that Bill wants him, and he explains that he was waiting for me to leave. I wonder what Joe will think when he gets to Bill's room. Will he think that I was unwilling to hold the glass of water? I want to tell Joe that I offered to give Bill the water, that I appreciate his giving us privacy, and that I am sorry to interrupt his break. I resist the impulse, however, saying nothing. I follow Joe back to Bill's room, and during the last twenty minutes of our inter-view he stands next to Bill, offering him a sip of water every few minutes, seamlessly.

In 1999 my mother, who is a personal attendant, had to choose between car-ing for her seriously ill client and taking care of her own dying mother. She did not want to abandon her client. She worried that the client's family would not be able to replace her quickly enough, and she feared losing her job. I offered to step in with the client, allowing my mother to care for my grandmother. This strange experience of expressing my love for my mother and grandmother by caring for a stranger marked the beginning of my inter-est in personal-attendant work. Though it was my first experience working as a personal attendant, it was not my last.

My mother, now in her sixties, is an immigrant from Mexico with less than a high school education. Her background is typical among personal attendants.[2] Many, if not most, personal attendants are immigrant women or women of color over the age of forty; but, given that, there are many differences.[3] Some personal attendants are native born, while others are immigrants. Some are African-Americans or other people of color; some are white. Of the immigrants, some are sponsored by family members, some are illegal, and still others are refugees. Some have lived here for forty years, others for forty weeks. They come from China, Indonesia, Afghanistan, Russia, various Latin American countries, and elsewhere. For some, this job is a one-generation stopover: their mothers were not personal attendants, nor will their daughters be. For others, it was the work of their mothers and grandmothers, and it will be the work of their daughters as well. Some have professional degrees but poor English, having fled countries wracked by civil wars. Others grew up in poverty and have only high school degrees. What they share is that they are mostly women and they are overwhelmingly poor.[4]

Bill was one of twenty-one subjects I interviewed between 1999 and 2001, among them eleven personal attendants, two former personal attendants, and eight people with disabilities who used personal attendants. The attendants in my sample fell into two categories. One, made up of immigrant women and women of color, is not too different from the larger population of such workers. The other group is more anomalous, encompassing workers who are mostly white, have had some college, and include some men, such as Joe. The consumers in my sample have also had some college. They are all white, severely disabled, and of working age.[5]

Personal attendants care for people with a range of disabilities who need assistance with daily living. Attendants may be required to prepare meals, shop, assist with baths, or provide bowel and bladder care. Without attendant care, many people with disabilities would be confined to institutions.[6] Most of them do not need care from nine to five, Monday through Friday. Rather, particularly for people considered severely disabled, care must be spaced throughout the day. The consumer who needs help getting out of bed, as well as getting bathed and dressed, may need his or her personal attendant to work a brief morning shift that can range from one to four hours. Someone who needs help eating will require another one or two shifts during the day; another shift will be required to help the consumer get into bed at night.

These shifts may be filled by one personal attendant or, more commonly, by several. The number of attendants involved in the care of one individual can become so large, and the turnover rates so high, that over a lifetime a single consumer will employ literally hundreds of people. One of my interviewees, who had needed attendant services for twenty years and at the time of the interview employed seven people, exclaimed, "I'm like a company. It's exhausting but, you know, every crip on the block is a company."

Although many consumers may feel like small corporations, most do not have the resources of small corporations. In fact, most consumers of personal-attendant services meet the low-income qualifications required for those services to be paid by the government.[7] The state, however, is willing to pay little more than minimum wage; and so consumers with limited financial means are left to hire people, usually immigrant women and women of color, who will work for very little.[8]

Nevertheless, due to extraordinary growth projections, employment trend analysts celebrate the opportunities available in personal attendant work. Some even call it one of the "hot jobs" of the new millennium.[9] Advocates of personal attendant services also insist that those jobs are good first steps for immigrants, in that they can lead to other opportunities, though it is not clear of what kind.[10]

It's true that many immigrant women work as personal attendants as their first jobs. But the women who take these jobs then work in private households, where they are socially isolated, with little potential for collective voice and few prospects for job mobility.[11] There is no formal training, no career ladder, and no hope for advancement.[12] Speaking through an interpreter, one immigrant woman who lived with the elderly disabled couple she cared for bemoaned her lack of opportunities: "The worst part is that even though I have completed my studies in my country, I have not even been able to complete a one-year language course in this country. I want to improve my language skills, but because these people need someone to be with them twenty-four hours a day, and because they speak my own language, I can't improve my English with them."

Personal attendants rarely receive health benefits, vacation time, or sick leave.[13] They can be fired at will, without notice. Their work hours make it difficult for them to get forty hours of work a week with any one client, but traveling among various different employers consumes a significant amount of unpaid time. Taking travel time and expense into account, many of these jobs actually net less than the minimum wage.

Given the striking *lack* of opportunity this job provides, it is not surprising that the demand for personal attendant services is met largely by one of the most vulnerable populations of workers: immigrant women. The low status and social invisibility of immigrant women allows them more easily to achieve the invisibility required for the job. This social invisibility is necessary because personal attendants are essential to the home care consumers' identities as "independent" individuals. Said one consumer of personal-attendant services:

> When I was a kid, my parents . . . they were doing all the stuff that I do now . . . when I turned twelve or thirteen they hired someone . . . to be there with me, help me with my homework and that kind of stuff, so I was slowly getting a taste of independence. But I was still living with my parents.

No longer living with his parents, this consumer considers himself independent. But being independent not only means living apart from his parents; more important, it means not having them care for him. The fact that he believed he got "a taste of independence" as a thirteen-year-old, when his parents paid to have an attendant care for him, demonstrates that his sense of independence does not rest on his ability to pay for his own care. Rather, it rests simply on the fact that his care is *somebody's* paid work. Indeed, although their work may appear identical, paid caregivers deliver a different cultural good than family members or friends can provide: personal attendants deliver the illusion of independence.

American individualism stresses personal independence and autonomy in all its aspects.[14] The archetypal account of self-reliance is Henry David Thoreau's *Walden*. But although Thoreau appeared to have a completely independent day-to-day existence, he came to Walden with a history and with resources. He neither built his home without a hammer nor learned to fish by himself. The nurturing he received as a child allowed him to achieve the robust physical condition he called upon in his time of isolation. Indeed, when we think of all the objects, beliefs, and interactions that make our lives possible, it is difficult to sustain the notion that anyone is self-made. Nevertheless, the idea of the self-reliant, independent man occupies the center of the American imagination.[15] Its persistence as one of our dominant cultural ideals lends it the power to obscure the actual, interdependent state of our lives.[16] Maria, a personal attendant from Mexico, observed:

> I think that American society values independence. . . . If an elderly person [lives alone] . . . I think that's when they say, "She's independent, she's strong." If she's living with somebody . . . I think that's when they say, "Gosh, she's not able to take care of herself." And I think there is a big stigma if you can't stand up on your own feet. I think people lose status, because they only respect the strong.

In American society, rights, respect, and status depend on one's ability to present oneself as independent. Joan Tronto points out that we "prefer to ignore routine forms of care" because they threaten our autonomy.[17] For disabled individuals this often means minimizing the visibility of the paid care that facilitates a disabled person's daily life. The best care workers, according to some consumers and attendants, are those whose presence is barely felt. One immigrant care worker described what he considers quality care:

> It's being able to put yourself in a situation where you are almost not seen . . . where the recipient of care is so able to do what he wants . . . it almost feels like, "I'm doing this," and you're not even in the picture in his mind . . . when he's so in tune with what he's doing, what he wants to do and feels really good, and you're almost nonexistent and yet you're there . . . [It's] like you're there, but you're not there . . . [when they can do something] without even realizing that they're doing it because you're there, that's quality work right there.

For all that, however, personal attendant work consists of literal, physical acts—things one can see and touch. How can that labor be transformed into something unseen? In fact, what is made invisible is not the labor itself, but the worker. When the workers are invisible, consumers can feel that they have accomplished their daily activities by themselves.

Independence, after all, is not simply a passive status: it is something people "do."[18] Personal attendants, beyond performing caregiving tasks, participate in creating an illusion of independence for the disabled individuals they serve. Together with the consumers of their services, personal attendants accomplish this by transferring the authorship of many caregiving tasks from the worker to the consumer. This is a collaborative process, through which not one but two identities are constructed: care receivers are constructed as independent, and caregivers are constructed as invisible.

Women and members of certain ethnic groups are often thought to be "natural" caregivers.[19] Not surprisingly, the consumers I interviewed claimed that workers who were mothers or who came from foreign countries (bearing, as Ron asserted, "old-world values") made the best caregivers. One consumer, Janet, offered that "foreign people stick around longer, and unfortunately, they take better care." Another, Sue, averred that immigrants "just care a lot more and have much more of a helping attitude than, let's say, an American." George, a self-described consumer advocate, agreed, noting that "some feel the best workers are illegal immigrants."

Immigrant women are easily cast into roles that require invisibility, because they already belong to a category that is socially invisible. Furthermore, when care activities are naturalized and essentialized, the *work* they entail is effectively erased. Immigrant women are the caregivers par excellence because both they and their work are often rendered invisible. What's more, caregivers often actively participate in this erasure. D'avian, a woman of color who works as an attendant, says it is important for personal attendants "to do it [the work] like they really want to." When the effort of care turns into something the worker "wants" to do, the labor vanishes.[20]

Nonetheless, care workers and their work are made invisible by a range of factors, including the work itself, the workers' social characteristics and roles, and the degree to which the work does or does not conflict with these roles or characteristics.

Care work is considered women's work, and as a general rule it is undervalued. As one personal attendant observed, "You can make more washing a dog than you can washing a human being." Associated with bodily functions, care work can also be considered humiliating or degrading. Part of the worker's job is to exhibit an absence of disgust.[21] Receivers of care, too, may find the arrangement humiliating. Needing help with bodily functions can be particularly shame-provoking for adults.[22] One consumer told me, "If they're moms it's easy, because they are used to diapers. That's the worst part for people, is dealing with the bowel movement. Because I need help with that too. What I usually say is, Pretend you're changing a diaper, and um, yeah, they usually cope pretty well." I asked this consumer how it felt to know that the workers had to cope. The consumer replied, "In the beginning, it was one of the hardest things in the world. But now it's part of living."

The attendant's job, therefore, is to reduce the amount of shame the consumer feels, first of all by not showing disgust. In a study that compared the care provided by paid caregivers to the care provided by family members, Lise Isaksen found that care related to stressful emotions, such as tasks involving bodily functions, requires "distance." Paid strangers are able to deliver care in a way that is less shaming for the receiver. Women workers are futher enabled to do this kind of work invisibly because it is similar to work like changing diapers, which is considered a part of the female gender role. And what makes the uncomfortable intimacy of the attendant's job comfortable is the attendant's invisibility. After all, a disabled receiver of care cannot retreat to another room for privacy, as an employer of a domestic worker might. Rather, his or her body is central to the attendant's work. "I'm like an extension of his body," said Julie, an attendant. For the consumer, this results in a loss of privacy; for the home-care worker, it produces another kind of burden, as he or she must constantly manage his or her emotions. One consumer responding to my question about the lack of privacy said, "Sometimes you just have to say, I really need to take a nap. Don't talk to me for a half hour or something." When I spoke with attendants, the obligation to manage their emotions emerged as the most oppressive aspect of the job.[23] Ironically, this emotional labor is not recognized as work. Rather, it is invisible.[24]

Invisibility, and the transfer of the authorship of one's efforts to another person, requires the desire, or at the very least the consent, of the caregiver not to be seen.[25] Caregivers hand over authorship of their caring work. This is not to say that care receivers share no responsibility for this situation. Rebecca, for example, expressed a desire for the care she receives to be done without effort or, in other words, to be done invisibly: "Quality care is when that attendant has left, I feel good. I feel refreshed, clean, sitting in my chair correctly. I have everything I need for the day and I have an attendant who has come in and done it effortlessly." Another consumer, who has an attendant assist him at work, uses language to take authorship of his attendant's activities. "I'm running around the office, sending out faxes, photocopying, lazerbeaming, you know that kind of stuff," he recounts, although he is not physically able to carry out any of these activities.[26]

The degree to which care workers participate in their own invisibility varies. Only one attendant in my sample explicitly envisioned quality care as requiring invisibility. Others tended to define quality care as involving a kind of intense focus on the care receiver. Elisa, an immigrant worker, is proud of the fact that she knows what her employer's needs are even before those needs are articulated. "When they were looking toward something or even moving their lips, I knew what they needed. Immediately I provided them with water, tea, food."

There is, however, no reciprocal gaze on the caregiver. It can be argued that the disabled employer's bodily needs are so great that this focus is justified. But one must not underestimate the needs of the caregiver, which are not as obviously embodied, but may nevertheless be great. Personal attendants are often new immigrants, unfamiliar with the customs, norms, laws, and language of their adopted country. Some face additional struggles because they are undocumented. Working in a largely unregulated occupation, personal attendants are especially vulnerable to racism, sexism, sexual harassment, and taxing working conditions. Poor to begin with, these workers tend to be badly compensated. And when they're women, their care workload generally extends beyond their clients, to their families. Often they have no one to take over their care responsibilities or to help them when they need care themselves.

These workers are also vulnerable in that they must constantly struggle for respect. Every time a worker was present in the course of my interviews, sometimes coming within a few feet of me for a brief interaction with the consumer, the consumer failed to introduce us.[27] This was particularly striking given that the subject of the interview was the relationship between caregivers and care receivers. None of the caregivers I observed at consumers' homes introduced themselves, and it was difficult to make eye contact with them in order to introduce myself. By failing to make eye contact, the attendants reinforced and helped produce the invisibility that caused the consumers not to introduce them in the first place.

If we accept the view that the invisibility of personal attendants is particularly demeaning and oppressive, how do we make sense of the idea that personal attendants consent to their invisibility? First of all, not all workers who consent to being invisible desire it. When someone implied that one of my interviewees didn't need to be introduced at a meeting because he was "just the caregiver," the caregiver commented, "It does hurt, you know."

Some attendants do desire invisibility. Since their job is to confer independence, it makes sense that workers who want to do a good job will participate in making themselves invisible. They will be further motivated if they care about their employers.[28] Ironically, handing over the authorship of caring labor may itself be the most caring part of care.

Are workers who articulate a desire to be invisible oppressed by being made so? Must one feel oppressed to be oppressed? I believe that the transfer of authorship is a negative phenomenon even for those who consciously work to make it happen. To be made invisible is the first step toward being considered nonhuman, which is why making another person invisible often precedes treating them inhumanely. To use Marxist terms, invisibility is the most extreme form of alienation—the ultimate manifestation of self-estrangement.

In the traditional capitalist-worker transaction, what is appropriated is surplus value. Here, however, what is produced is the activity of care work, and so it is the authorship of this activity that may be appropriated.

The personal attendants I interviewed recognized and resented the fact that they were unseen and undervalued. One attendant observed: "We should be respected as hardworking people, as doing a hard job. [But] how much respect have we gotten in history books?" These personal attendants want it both ways. They want to be valued and recognized as important people, yet they also want to help the consumer feel independent, which means that they must transfer the authorship of their actions and make themselves invisible. Interestingly, the attendants do not connect their invisibility in relation to the consumer to their invisibility in relation to the larger society.

That many personal attendants fail to see their participation in the transfer of authorship as problematic is not surprising. In a culture like ours, few individuals embrace dependence or interdependence. The attendant may want to do care work in a visible, self-affirming way that neither negates his or her own contribution nor conceals the dependence of the person being cared for. But he or she is often faced with a recipient who experiences being cared for as a painful reminder of dependence. Under these circumstances, workers may feel compelled to hide the true nature of care. Once the worker makes this choice, the necessary result is that he or she will be undervalued for the work. How could something unseen be completely valued? Some will argue that individuals whose job it is to be invisible are valued for their very invisibility. But the jobs of invisible people are the lowest paid, and this low pay reflects the value such workers possess in the eyes not only of society but of the people for whom they are caring.

One consumer, George, questioned my use of the term "caregiver." He said, "Caregiver? That's a controversial term . . . say 'personal attendant' instead." George was referring to a controversy within the disabled community regarding the role of personal attendants and their relationships with consumers of care.[29] Informing this debate is the disability community's history with "care" that imprisoned them in institutions, made them the victims of "care giving" professionals, or left them at the mercy of abusive or controlling familial relationships. Consumers who reject the word *care* see it as implying too much passivity on the part of the care receiver.[30] Others embrace an idea of caregiving in which receivers recognize their dependence on their personal attendants and understand that personal attendants can also fulfill emotional needs.[31]

Most of the consumers I interviewed considered businesslike relationships with their personal attendants to be ideal. Interestingly, however, this expectation directly conflicts with what the attendants felt was the most essential quality for their jobs. Maria explained:

> Of course they need to have their basics. The house needs to be cleaned, they need to eat, they need to shower, that kind of thing. But I think that it goes beyond that, you have to show that you care . . . because they're not objects and it's not just a job, you know; you get attached. . . . You're working with human beings, and that's where the difference lies—between working with people and work-

ing with things. . . . They also need to feel like they're still humans who deserve respect, love, and care.

Jacob, another attendant, agreed:

I enjoy the atmosphere and conversation I create with whoever it is that I'm with, and there really isn't much that happens besides that. [All the physical tasks] are incidental. . . . I think the most important thing in the relationship is that the attendant like the consumer. . . . The absence of a businesslike relationship creates an opportunity for the attendant to like the employer more.

The attendants I interviewed described their work almost as a religious calling. Mohamed, who acted as a translator in my interview with his wife, told me, "She is doing these things for the satisfaction of our conscience, of our spirituality." Working as a personal attendant is a labor of love. Money changes hands, but this is not commodified care. The immigrant women and women of color in my sample unanimously said that good care required that they love the receiver. Patting her chest, D'avian told me, "It has to come from here. . . . You just got to have that love." Nothing brought attendants more satisfaction than when care receivers loved them back. In other words, the ideal employment situation was not one where they were thinking only about the consumer but one in which the consumer also thought about them. These were relationships that seemed more familial than businesslike. Cecilia asserted, "I like to work as a home health-care worker better [than in a nursing home] because when you go to their house it is as if you are going to care for a relative, a family member." Maria, reflecting on the elderly woman, now deceased, for whom she used to care, said, "We became really good friends. . . . I loved her like a grandmother."

The consumers I interviewed, however, including those who were close to their attendants, expressed a desire for a different kind of relationship. Rebecca echoed many of their sentiments when she said, "I tend to like to put up a wall with my attendants." That care receivers are not particularly open to more personal relationships with their care givers is not surprising, since these jobs pay so poorly that few caregivers tend to stay in them for long.[32] Given the expectation of high turnover, consumers I interviewed expected their attendants to do little more than accomplish discrete tasks.[33]

In the past, family members supplied the intimate bodily care that is now performed by personal attendants. The care provided by personal attendants is public care; it is paid and performed by non-kin, albeit in the domestic spheres. Deborah Stone cautions, "When we stop doing care and instead hire someone else to do it, the care becomes commodified and . . . we look at other people as means not ends."[34] When care is commodified, the care receiver becomes an independent purchaser of services to which he or she feels entitled. The care receiver does not experience the caregiver as generously expressing affection and concern through his or her work; rather, the worker is simply doing a paid job. When I asked him what his caregiver had done that was above and beyond the call of duty, Ron replied, "I can't think of a good answer to that. I don't know of anything that I ask of them that isn't what I consider to be part of that attendant's job." Several of the consumers I interviewed responded similarly. At first I thought these answers reflected on the care workers in question. But upon further questioning, I realized that this was not a personal assessment of their attendant so much as a structural assessment. The consumers felt that they had fully purchased the time of their personal attendant; therefore, there was nothing the attendant did within his or her work time that the consumer did not consider part of the job.[35] When the job expands to include everything the attendant does, it becomes impossible for the caregiver to express real caring, because nothing he or she does is understood as a gift.

On the other hand, it's no wonder that disabled consumers want to distance their bodily needs from their personal relationships. Some of the disabled individuals I interviewed involve their friends in their personal care, but most are very careful to draw a line. One consumer explained, "I really try to keep that to a minimum, because that really does cut into the friendships." Those who do rely on friends to provide care often see their friendships suffer as a result. One interviewee told of a friendship that ruptured under the strain of her care needs. She lost not only a friend, but also the person who was meeting her important needs.

What would it be like to live in a society where the need for care and the work of care were supported materially and symbolically? Maybe in such a society, we wouldn't mind when our friends cared for us, and our friends wouldn't find caring for us a burden. The state would enfranchise disabled consumers to choose the "best person for the job." Dependence would not be stigmatized. Under these conditions, consumers and personal attendants could meet each other as equals, forging a mutually respectful relationship that would transcend commodification.

Conclusion

As a Latina woman, I would under many circumstances have no difficulty being invisible enough to provide good care. However, as the anecdote at the beginning of this paper illustrates, in my role as a researcher from the University of California I was not a preferred provider of a certain type of care. Bill could not tolerate my assistance with the glass of water because I was not sufficiently invisible to perform such intimate care. Had I helped Bill drink, he would not have been able to maintain an image of himself as independent. But when his paid caregiver raised the cup to his lips, the act was invisible. In other words, the very same work is either visible or invisible, depending upon who does it.

Furthermore, not all care work requires the same level of invisibility. Physically intimate types of care work, for example, require the most invisibility on the part of the caregiver. Bill allowed me to get his attendant, because this fell within the range of activities not likely to stigmatize the beneficiary as dependent. On the other hand, the fact that he was not comfortable asking me to get his attendant, and that I had to offer, could mean that even this gesture threatened his sense of autonomy.

We are all dependent on others to varying degrees. A language that denies this fact fuels a system that obscures the ways in which other people care for us. Words such as *independence, self-reliance,* and *self-made* help create, and are created by, a dynamic within which people are ignored and devalued. Joan Tronto reminds us that by "not noticing how pervasive and central care is to human life, those who are in positions of power and privilege can continue to ignore and degrade the activities of care and those who give care."

Independence is perhaps the most fundamental of our cultural myths; it supports the organization of our society and justifies the distribution of goods, real and ideal. The labels *independent* and *dependent,* rather than reflecting empirical reality, are myths used to justify inequality.

The transfer of authorship of tasks is ubiquitous in American society. It occurs between executives and secretaries, between children and mothers, between disabled individuals and their caregivers. Nevertheless, two things are true: no one is invisible, and no one is independent. If we recognize our dependence on others, we must acknowledge that we fall short of the cultural ideal of independence. We must further acknowledge our debt to those upon whom we depend.

When individuals with care needs have to worry about whether or not their caregiver will come the next morning, perhaps it is simply too frightening for them to face the extent of their dependency. Rejecting "care" because of its connection to dependence, and embracing a businesslike, commodified relationship (in which the receiver becomes a "consumer"), disabled people can nurture the illusion of choice and control.[36] However, without the resources to pay competitive wages, most of these care receivers have few options regarding who will care for them, or how much care they will receive. Furthermore, in a strictly commodified relationship, care givers and care receivers become means instead of ends, a dynamic that denies the full subjectivity of both.[37]

Consumers of personal-attendant services deserve good care, delivered by people they can rely on. Personal attendants deserve reasonable wages, decent working conditions, and to have their efforts recognized. Both parties deserve arrangements that hold out the possibility for mutual respect and love, for relationship and community.

The fact that some people need more assistance than others should affect the larger polity more than it does. Rather, the workers and their efforts are not the only invisible parties; the disabled population and its needs are invisible as well. All of us need to take responsibility for the caring needs of our society. We need to reject claims of independence when they legitimate the unequal distribution of rights and resources. We need to recognize that independence is a fantasy not just for disabled individuals but for everyone.

Maid to Order

BARBARA EHRENREICH

As class polarization grows, the classic posture of submission makes a stealthy comeback. "We scrub your floors the old-fashioned way," boasts the brochure from Merry Maids, the largest of the residential cleaning services that have sprung up in the last two decades, "on our hands and knees." This is not a posture that independent "cleaning ladies" willingly assume—preferring, like most people who clean their own homes, the sponge mop wielded from a standing position. In her comprehensive guide to homemaking, Cheryl Mendelson warns, "Never ask hired housecleaners to clean your floors on their hands and knees; the request is likely to be regarded as degrading."[1]

But in a society where 40 percent of the wealth is owned by 1 percent of households, while the bottom 20 percent reports negative assets, the degradation of others is readily purchased. Kneepads entered American political discourse as a tool of the sexually subservient, but employees of Merry Maids, The Maids International, and other new corporate-run cleaning services spend hours every day on these kinky devices, wiping up the drippings of the affluent.

I spent three weeks in September 1999 as an employee of The Maids

International in a New England city, cleaning, along with my fellow team members, approximately sixty houses containing a total of about 250 scrubbable floors—bathrooms, kitchens, and entryways requiring the hands-and-knees treatment. It's a different world down there below knee level, one that few adults voluntarily enter. Here you find elaborate dust structures held together by a scaffolding of dog hairs; dried bits of pasta glued to the floor by their sauce; the congealed remains of gravies, jellies, contraceptive creams, vomit, and urine. Sometimes too you encounter some fragment of a human being: a child's legs, stamping by in disgust because the maids are still present when he gets home from school, or, more commonly, the Joan and David–clad feet and electrolyzed calves of the female homeowner. Look up and you may find this person staring at you, arms folded, in anticipation of an overlooked stain. In rare instances, she may try to help in some vague, symbolic way, by moving the cockatoo's cage, for example, or apologizing for the leaves shed by a miniature indoor tree. Mostly though, she will not see you at all, and may even sit down with her mail at a table in the very room you are cleaning, where she will remain completely unaware of your existence—unless you were to crawl under that table and start gnawing away at her ankles.

Housework, as you may recall from the feminist theories of the 1960s and 1970s, was supposed to be the great equalizer of women. Whatever else women did—jobs, school, child care—we also did housework, and if there were some women who hired others to do it for them, they seemed too privileged and rare to include in the theoretical calculus. All women were workers, and the home was their workplace—unpaid and unsupervised to be sure, but a workplace no less than the offices and factories men repaired to every morning. If men thought of the home as a site of leisure and recreation— a "haven in a heartless world"—this was to ignore the invisible female proletariat that kept it cozy and humming. We were on the march then, or so we imagined, united against a society that devalued our labor even as it waxed mawkish over "the family" and "the home." Shoulder to shoulder and arm in arm, women were finally getting up off the floor.

In the most eye-catching elaboration of the home-as-workplace theme, in 1972 Marxist feminists Maria Rosa Dallacosta and Selma James proposed that the home was in fact an economically productive and significant workplace, an extension of the actual factory, since housework served to "reproduce the labor power" of others, particularly men. The male worker would hardly be in shape to punch in for his shift, after all, if some woman had not fed him, laundered his clothes, and cared for the children who were his contribution to the next generation of workers. If the home was a quasi-industrial workplace staffed by women for the ultimate benefit of the capitalists, then "wages for housework" was the obvious demand.

But when most American feminists, Marxist or otherwise, asked the Marxist question *Cui bono?* they tended to come up with a far simpler answer: men. If women were the domestic proletariat, then men made up the class of domestic exploiters, free to lounge while their mates scrubbed. In consciousness-raising groups, we railed over husbands and boyfriends who refused to pick up after themselves, who were unaware of housework at all, unless of course it hadn't been done. The "dropped socks," left by a man for a woman to gather up and launder, joined lipstick and spike heels as emblems of gender oppression. When, somewhere, a man dropped a sock with the calm expectation that his wife would retrieve it, it was a sock heard round the world. Wherever second-wave feminism took root, battles broke out between lovers or spouses over sticky countertops, piled-up laundry, and whose turn it was to do the dishes.

The radical new idea was that housework was not only a relationship between a woman and a dust bunny or an unmade bed; it also defined a relationship between human beings, typically husbands and wives. This marked a departure from the more conservative views of Betty Friedan, who, in *The Feminine Mystique,* never thought to enter men into the equation, either as part of the housework problem or part of an eventual solution. She raged against a society that consigned its educated women to what she saw as essentially janitorial chores, beneath "the abilities of a woman of average or normal intelligence" and, according to unidentified studies she cited, "peculiarly suited to the capacities of feeble-minded girls." But men are virtually exempt from housework in *The Feminine Mystique*—why drag them down too? At one point she even disparaged a "Mrs. G.," who "somehow couldn't get her housework done before her husband came home at night and was so tired then that he had to do it." Educated women would just have to become more efficient so that housework could no longer "expand to fill the time available."

Or they could hire other women to do it—an option Friedan approved in

The Feminine Mystique. So did the National Organization for Women, which Friedan helped launch: at the 1973 congressional hearings on whether to extend the Fair Labor Standards Act to household workers, NOW testified to the affirmative, arguing that improved wages and working conditions would attract more women to the field, and that "the demand for household help inside the home will continue to increase as more women seek occupations outside the home." One young NOW member added, on a personal note, "Like many young women today, I am in school in order to develop a rewarding career for myself. I also have a home to run and can fully conceive of the need for household help as my free time at home becomes more and more restricted. Women know [that] housework is dirty, tedious work, and they are willing to pay to have it done."[2] On the aspirations of the women paid to do it, assuming at least some of them were bright enough to entertain a few, neither Friedan nor these members of NOW had, at the time, a word to say.

So the insight that distinguished the more radical, post-Friedan cohort of feminists was that when we talked about housework, we were really talking, yet again, about power. Housework was not degrading because it was manual labor, as Friedan thought, but because it was embedded in degrading relationships and inevitably served to reinforce them. To make a mess that another person will have to deal with—the dropped socks, the toothpaste sprayed on the bathroom mirror, the dirty dishes left from a late-night snack—is to exert domination in one of its more silent and intimate forms. One person's arrogance—or indifference, or hurry—becomes another person's occasion for toil. And when the person who is cleaned up after is consistently male, while the person who cleans up is consistently female, you have a formula for reproducing male domination from one generation to the next.

Hence the feminist perception of housework as one more way by which men exploit women or, more neutrally stated, as "a symbolic enactment of gender relations." An early German women's-liberation cartoon depicted a woman scrubbing on her hands and knees while her husband, apparently excited by this pose, approaches from behind, unzipping his fly. Hence, too, the second-wave feminists' revulsion at the hiring of maids, especially when they were women of color. At a feminist conference I attended in 1980, the poet Audre Lorde chose to insult the all-too-white audience by accusing them of being present only because they had black housekeepers to look after their children at home. She had the wrong crowd; most of the assembled radical feminists would no sooner have employed a black maid than they would have attached Confederate flag stickers to the rear windows of their cars. But accusations like hers, repeated in countless conferences and meetings, reinforced our rejection of the servant option. There already were at least two able-bodied adults in the average home—a man and a woman—and the hope was that, after a few initial skirmishes, they would learn to share the housework graciously.

A couple of decades later, however, the average household still falls far short of that goal. True, women do less housework than they did before the feminist revolution and the rise of the two-income family: down from an average of 30 hours per week in 1965 to 17.5 hours in 1995, according to a July 1999 study from the University of Maryland. Some of that decline reflects a relaxation of standards rather than a redistribution of chores; women still do two-thirds of whatever housework—including bill paying, pet care, tidying, and lawn maintenance—gets done. The inequity is sharpest for the most despised of household chores: cleaning. Between 1965 and 1995, men increased the time they spent scrubbing, vacuuming, and sweeping by 240 percent—all the way up to 1.7 hours per week—while women decreased their cleaning time by only 7 percent, to 6.7 hours per week.[3] The averages conceal a variety of arrangements, of course, from minutely negotiated sharing to the most clichéd division of labor, as described by one woman to the *Washington Post:* "I take care of the inside, he takes care of the outside."[4] But perhaps the most disturbing finding is that almost all the increase in male participation took place between the 1970s and the mid-1980s. Fifteen years after the apparent cessation of hostilities, it is probably not too soon to call the question: in the "chore wars" of the 1970s and 1980s, women gained a little ground, but overall, and after a few strategic concessions, men won.

Enter then, the cleaning lady as dea ex machina, restoring tranquillity as well as order to the home. Marriage counselors recommend hiring them as an alternative to squabbling, as do many within the residential cleaning industry itself. A Chicago cleaning woman quotes one of her clients as saying that if she were to give up the service, "My husband and I will be divorced in six months." Managers of the new corporate cleaning services, such as the one I worked for, attribute their success not only to the influx of women into the workforce but to the tensions over housework that arose in its wake. When the trend toward hiring out was just beginning to take off, in 1988, the owner of a Merry Maids franchise in Arlington, Massachusetts, told the *Christian Science Monitor,* "I kid some women. I say, 'We even save marriages.' In this new eighties period, you expect more from the male partner, but very often you don't get the cooperation you would like to have. The alternative is to pay somebody to come in." Another Merry Maids franchise owner has learned to capitalize more directly on housework-related spats: he closes 30 to 35 percent of his sales by making follow-up calls on Saturday mornings, the "prime time for arguing over the fact that the house is a mess." The microdefeat of feminism in the household opened a new door for women, only this time it was the servants' entrance.

In 1999, somewhere between 14 and 18 percent of households employed outsiders to do their cleaning, and the numbers have been rising dramatically since. Mediamark Research reports a 53 percent increase, between 1995 and 1999, in the number of households using a hired cleaner or service once a month or more, and Maritz finds that 30 percent of the people who hired help in 1999 did so for the first time that year. Among my middle-class, professional women friends and acquaintances, including some who made important contributions to the early feminist analysis of housework two and a half decades ago, the employment of a cleaning person is now nearly universal. The home, or at least the affluent home, is finally becoming what radical feminists in the 1970s only imagined it was—a "workplace" for women and a tiny, though increasingly visible, part of the capitalist economy. The question is this: As your home becomes a workplace for someone else, is it still a place where you want to live?

Strangely, or perhaps not so strangely at all, no one talks about the "politics of housework" anymore. The demand for "wages for housework" no longer has the power to polarize feminist conferences; it has sunk to the status of a curio, along with the consciousness-raising groups in which women once rallied support in their struggles with messy men. In the academy, according to the feminist sociologists I interviewed, housework has lost much of its former cachet—in part, I suspect, because fewer sociologists actually do it.

Most Americans, more than 80 percent, still clean their homes, but the minority who do not include a sizeable fraction of the nation's opinion makers and culture producers: professors, writers, editors, media decision makers, political figures, talking heads and celebrities of all sorts. In their homes, the politics of housework is becoming a politics not only of gender but also of race and class, and these are subjects that the opinion-making elite, if not most Americans, generally prefer to avoid.

Even the number of paid household workers is hard to pin down. The Census Bureau reports that there were 549,000 domestic workers in 1998, up 9 percent since 1996, but this may be a considerable underestimate, since so much of the servant economy is still underground. In 1993, for example, the year when Zoë Baird lost her chance to be attorney general for paying her undocumented immigrant nanny off the books, the *Los Angeles Times* reported that fewer than 10 percent of those Americans who paid a house-cleaner reported these payments to the IRS. Sociologist Mary Romero, one of the few academics who retains an active interest in housework and the women who do it for pay, offers an example of how severe the undercounting can be. The 1980 census found only 1,063 "private household workers" in El Paso, Texas, although at the same time, that city's Department of Planning, Research and Development estimated these workers' numbers at 13,400, and local bus drivers estimated that half of the 28,300 daily bus trips were taken by maids going to and returning from work.[5] The honesty of employers has increased since the Baird scandal, but most experts believe that household workers remain, in large part, uncounted and invisible to the larger economy.

One thing you can say with certainty about the population of household workers is that they are disproportionately women of color: "lower" kinds of people for a "lower" kind of work. Of the "private household cleaners and servants" it managed to locate in 1998, the Bureau of Labor Statistics reports that 36.8 percent were Hispanic, 15.8 percent black, and 2.7 percent "other." Certainly the association between housecleaning and minority status is well established in the psyches of the white employing class. When my daughter, Rosa, was introduced to the wealthy father of a Harvard classmate, he ventured that she must have been named for a favorite maid. And Audre Lorde can perhaps be forgiven for her intemperate accusation at the feminist conference mentioned above when we consider an experience she had in 1967:

"I wheel my two-year-old daughter in a shopping cart through a supermar-ket . . . and a little white girl riding past in her mother's cart calls out excit-edly, 'Oh look, Mommy, a baby maid.' "[6]

The composition of the household workforce is hardly fixed, and it has changed with the life chances of the different ethnic groups. In the late nine-teenth century, Irish and German immigrants served the urban upper and middle classes, then left for the factories as soon as they could. Black women replaced them, accounting for 60 percent of all domestics in the 1940s and dominating the field until other occupations opened to them. Similarly, West Coast maids were disproportionately Japanese-American until that group found more congenial options.[7] Today, the color of the hand that pushes the sponge varies from region to region: Chicanas in the Southwest, Caribbeans in New York, native Hawaiians in Hawaii, native whites, many of recent rural extraction, in the New England city where I briefly worked.

The great majority—although again, no one knows the exact numbers—of paid housekeepers are freelancers, or "independents," who find their clients through agencies or networks of already employed friends and rela-tives. To my acquaintances in the employing class, the freelance housekeeper seems to be a fairly privileged and prosperous type of worker, sometimes paid $15 an hour or more and usually said to be viewed as a friend or even as "one of the family." But the shifting ethnic composition of the workforce tells another story: many women have been trapped in this kind of work, whether by racism, imperfect English skills, immigration status, or lack of education. Few happily choose it. Interviews with independent maids collected by Romero and by sociologist Judith Rollins, who herself worked as a maid in the Boston area in the early eighties, confirm the undesirability of the work to those who perform it.[8] Even when the pay is deemed acceptable, the hours may be long and unpredictable; there is no job security; there are usually no health benefits; and if the employer has failed to pay Social Security taxes (in some cases because the maid herself prefers to be paid off the books), there are no retirement benefits. And the pay is often far from acceptable. The BLS found full-time "private household workers and servants" earning a median income of $223 a week in 1998, which is $23 a week below the poverty level for a family of three. Recall that in 1993 Zoë Baird paid her undocumented household workers $5 an hour out of her earnings of $507,000 a year.

At the most lurid extreme there is slavery. A few cases of captivity and forced labor pop up in the press every year, most recently involving undocumented women held in servitude by high-ranking staff members of the United Nations, the World Bank, and the International Monetary Fund. Consider the charges brought by Elizabeth Senghor, a Senegalese woman who told the court that her Manhattan employers forced her to work fourteen-hour days without any regular pay and with no accommodations beyond a pull-out bed in her employers' living room. Hers is not a particularly startling instance of domestic slavery; no beatings or sexual assaults were charged, and Ms. Senghor was apparently fed. What gives this case a certain rueful poignancy is that her employer, former U.N. employee Marie Angelique Savane, is one of Senegal's leading women's-rights advocates, and had told the *Christian Science Monitor* in 1986 about her efforts to get the Senegalese to "realize that being a woman can mean other things than simply having children, taking care of the house."

Mostly though, independent maids and their employers complain about the peculiar intimacy of the employer-employee relationship. Domestic service is an occupation that predates the refreshing impersonality of capitalism by several thousand years, conditions of work being still largely defined by the idiosyncrasies of the employers. Some of them seek friendship and even what their maids describe as "therapy," though they are usually quick to redraw the lines once the maid is perceived as overstepping. Others demand deference bordering on servility, while an increasing portion of the nouveau riche is simply out of control. In August 1999, the *New York Times* reported on the growing problem of dinner parties in upscale homes being disrupted by hostesses screaming at their help. To the verbal abuse, add published reports of sexual and physical assaults—the teenage son of an employer, for example, kicking a live-in nanny for refusing to make sandwiches for him and his friends after school.

For better or worse, capitalist rationality is finally making some headway into this preindustrial backwater. Nationwide and even international cleaning services like Merry Maids, Molly Maids, and The Maids International, all of which have arisen since the 1970s, now control 20 to 25 percent of the $1.4

billion housecleaning business, and perhaps their greatest innovation has been to abolish the mistress-maid relationship, with all its quirks and dependencies.

The customer hires the service, not the maid, who has been replaced anyway by a team of two to four uniformed people, only one of whom, the team leader, is usually authorized to speak to the customer about the work at hand. The maids' wages, their Social Security taxes, their green cards, backaches, and child-care problems are the sole concern of the company, meaning the local franchise owner. If there are complaints on either side, they are addressed to the franchise owner; the customer and the actual workers need never interact. Since the franchise owner is usually a middle-class white person, cleaning services are the ideal solution for anyone still sensitive enough to find the traditional employer-maid relationship morally vexing. In a 1997 article about Merry Maids, *Franchise Times* reported tersely that the "category is booming,[and the] niche is hot too, as Americans look to outsource work even at home."

Not all cleaning services do well. There is a high rate of failure among the informal, mom-and-pop services, like one I applied to by phone that did not even require a cursory interview; all I would have had to do was show up at seven the next morning. The "boom" is concentrated among the national and international chains—outfits like Merry Maids, Molly Maids, Mini Maids, Maid Brigade, and The Maids International—all named, curiously enough, to highlight the more antique aspects of the industry, although the "maid" may occasionally be male. In 1996, Merry Maids claimed to be growing at 15 to 20 percent a year, while spokespersons for Molly Maids and The Maids International each told me that their firms' sales are growing by 25 percent a year. Local franchisers are equally bullish. My boss at The Maids confided to me that he could double his business overnight, if only he could find enough reliable employees.

To this end, The Maids offers a week of paid vacation, health insurance after ninety days, and a free breakfast every morning, consisting, at least where I worked, of coffee, doughnuts, bagels, and bananas. Some franchises have dealt with the tight labor market by participating in welfare-to-work projects that not only funnel them employees but often subsidize their paychecks with public money, at least for the first few months of work (which doesn't mean that the newly minted maid earns more, only that the company has to pay her less). The Merry Maids franchise in the city where I worked is conveniently located a block away from the city's welfare office.

Among the women I worked with at The Maids, only one said she had previously worked as an independent, and she professed to be pleased with her new status as a cleaning-service employee. She no longer needed a car to get her from house to house, and she could take a day off—unpaid, of course—to stay home with a sick child without risking the loss of a customer. Cleaning services are an especially appealing option for recent immigrants, who are unlikely to have cars or the contacts they would need to work as independents; large services, like The Maids, have videotapes used for training new hires in Spanish and well as English. I myself could see the advantage of not having to deal directly with the customers, who were sometimes at home while we worked and eager to make use of their supervisory skills. Criticisms of our methods, as well as demands that we perform unscheduled tasks, could simply be referred to the team leader or, beyond her, to the franchise owner.

But workers inevitably face losses when an industry moves from the entrepreneurial to the industrial phase—most strikingly, in this case, in the matter of pay. At Merry Maids, I was promised $200 for a forty-hour week, with the manager hastening to add that "you can't calculate it in dollars per hour," since the forty hours includes all the time spent traveling from house to house—up to five houses a day—which is unpaid. The Maids International, with its straightforward starting rate of $6.63 an hour, seemed preferable, although this rate was conditional on perfect attendance. Miss one day and your wage dropped to $6 an hour for two weeks, a rule that weighed particularly heavily on those who had young children. In addition, I soon learned that management had ways of shaving off nearly an hour's worth of wages a day. We were told to arrive at 7:30 in the morning, but our billable hours began only after we had been teamed up, given our list of houses for the day, and packed off in the company car at around 8:00. At the end of the day, we were no longer paid from the moment we left the car, although as much as fifteen minutes of work—sorting through the rags dirtied in the course of the day, refilling cleaning-fluid bottles, and the like—remained to be done in the office. So for a standard nine-hour day, the actual pay amounted to about $6.06 an hour, unless you were still being punished for an absence, in which case it came out to $5.48 an hour.

Nor are cleaning-service employees likely to receive any of the perks or tips familiar to independents—free lunches and coffee, cast-off clothing, or a Christmas gift of cash. When I asked, only one of my coworkers could recall ever receiving a tip, and that was a voucher for a free meal at a downtown restaurant owned by a customer. More than a year later, she had still hadn't used it, probably because she would have to eat alone, the $20 or so for a companion's meal being out of the question. The customers of cleaning services are probably no stingier than the employers of independents; they just don't know their cleaning people and probably wouldn't recognize them on the street. They may even get a different crew each visit. Besides, customers probably assume that the fee they pay the service—$25 per person-hour in the case of my franchise of The Maids—goes largely to the workers who do the actual cleaning.

The most interesting feature of the cleaning-service chains, at least from an abstract, historical perspective, is that they are finally transforming the home into a fully capitalist-style workplace, and in ways that the old wages-for-housework advocates could never have imagined. A house is an innately difficult workplace to control, especially a house with ten or more rooms, like so many of those we cleaned; workers may remain out of one another's sight for many minutes, as much as an hour at a time. For independents, the ungovernable nature of the home workplace means a certain amount of autonomy. They can take breaks (though this is probably ill-advised if the home owner is on the premises); they can ease the monotony by listening to the radio or television while they work. But cleaning services lay down rules meant to enforce a factorylike—or even conventlike—discipline on their far-flung employees. At The Maids, there were no breaks except for a daily ten-minute stop at a convenience store for coffee or "lunch," meaning something like a slice of pizza. Otherwise, the time spent driving between houses was considered our "break" and was the only chance to eat, drink, or (although this was also officially forbidden) smoke a cigarette. When the houses were spaced well apart, I could eat the sandwich I packed each day in one sitting; otherwise it would have to be divided into as many as three separate, hasty snacks.

Within a customer's house, nothing was to touch our lips at all—not even water. On hot days, I sometimes broke that rule by drinking from a bathroom faucet. Televisions and radios were off-limits, and we were never, ever to curse out loud, even in an ostensibly deserted house. There might be a home owner secreted in some locked room, we were told, ear pressed to the door, or, more likely, a tape recorder or video camera running. At the time, I dismissed this as a scare story, but I have since come across ads for concealable video cameras, like the Tech 7 "incredible coin-sized camera," designed to "get a visual record of your babysitter's actions" and "watch employees to prevent theft." It was the threat or rumor of hidden recording devices, set up by customers to catch one of us stealing, that provided the final capitalist-industrial touch: supervision.

But what makes the work most factory-like is the intense Taylorization imposed by the companies. An independent, or a person cleaning his or her own home, chooses where she will start and, within each room, probably tackles the most egregious dirt first. Or she may plan her work more or less ergonomically, first doing whatever can be done from a standing position and then squatting or crouching to reach the lower levels. But with the special "systems" devised by the cleaning services and imparted to employees through training videos, there are no such decisions to make. In The Maids' "healthy-touch" system, which is similar to what I saw of the Merry Maids' system on the training tape I was shown during my interview, all cleaning is divided into four task areas—dusting, vacuuming, kitchens, and bathrooms—which are in turn divided among the team members. For each task area other than vacuuming, there is a bucket containing rags and the appropriate cleaning fluids, so the biggest decision an employee has to make is which fluid and scrubbing instrument (rag, brush, or Dobie-brand plastic scouring pad) to deploy on which kind of surface; almost everything else has been choreographed in advance. When vacuuming, you begin with the master bedroom; when dusting, with the first room off the kitchen, then you move through the rooms going left to right. When entering each room, you proceed from left to right and top to bottom, and the same with each surface—left to right, top to bottom. Deviations are subject to rebuke, as I discovered when a team leader caught me moving my arm from right to left, then left to right, while wiping Windex over a French door.

It's not easy for anyone with extensive cleaning experience—and I include myself in this category—to accept this loss of autonomy over her movements from minute to minute. But I came to love the system: first, because if you hadn't always been traveling rigorously from left to right, it would have been easy to lose your way in some of the larger houses and to omit or redo a room. Second, many of our houses were already clean when we started, at least by any normal standards, thanks probably to a house-keeper who kept things up between our visits; but the absence of visible dirt did not mean there was less work to do, for no surface could ever be neglected, so it was important to have "the system" to remind you of where you had been and what you had already "cleaned." No doubt the biggest advantage of the system, though, is that it helps you achieve the speed demanded by the company, which allots only so many minutes per domicile (from about forty-five for a smallish apartment up to several hours per house). After a week or two on the job, I found myself moving robotlike from surface to surface, grateful to have been relieved of the thinking-process.

Even ritual work, however, takes its toll on those assigned to perform it. Turnover is dizzyingly high in the cleaning-service industry, and not only because of the usual challenges that confront the working poor, including child-care problems, unreliable transportation, evictions, and prior health conditions. As my longwinded interviewer at Merry Maids warned me, and as my coworkers at The Maids confirmed, this is a physically punishing occupation, something to tide you over for a few months, not year after year. The hands-and-knees posture damages knees, with or without pads; vacu-uming strains the back; constant wiping and scrubbing invite repetitive-stress injuries even in the very young. In my three weeks as a maid, I suffered nothing more than a persistent muscle spasm in the right forearm—from scrubbing, I suppose—but the damage would have been far worse if I'd had to go home every day to my own housework and children, as most of my coworkers did, instead of returning to my motel and indulging in a daily after-work regimen of ice packs and stretches. Chores that seem effortless at home, even almost recreational when undertaken at will for twenty minutes or so at a time, quickly turn nasty when performed hour after hour, with few or no breaks and under relentless time pressure.

So far, the independent, entrepreneurial house cleaner is holding her own, but there are reasons to think that corporate cleaning services will eventually dominate the industry. New users often prefer the impersonal, standardized service offered by the chains, and in a fast-growing industry, new users make up a sizable chunk of the total clientele. Government regulation also favors the corporate chains, whose spokesmen speak gratefully of the "Zoë Baird effect," referring to customers' worries about being caught employing an undocumented immigrant. But the future of housecleaning may depend on the entry of even bigger players into the industry. Merry Maids, the largest of the chains, has the advantage of being a unit within the $6.4 billion ServiceMaster conglomerate, which includes such related businesses as TruGreen ChemLawn, Terminix, Rescue Rooter, and Furniture Medic. A few other large firms are testing, or have tested, the water: Johnson Wax acquired Molly Maid in 1987–88, then abandoned it, according to a Molly Maid spokesperson, because the wax people were too "product oriented" for the "relational" culture of a service-providing company. Swisher International, best known as an industrial toilet-cleaning service, is operating Swisher Maids in Georgia and North Carolina; and Sears may be feeling its way into the business too. If large multinational firms establish a foothold in the industry, the mobile customers sociologist Saskia Sassen calls the "new transnational professionals" will be able to find the same branded and standardized product wherever they relocate. For the actual workers, the change will, in all likelihood, mean a more standardized and speeded-up approach to the work, with less freedom of motion and fewer chances to pause.

The trend toward outsourcing the work of the home seems, at the moment, unstoppable. Two hundred years ago, women manufactured soap, candles, cloth, and clothing in their own homes, and the complaints of some women at the turn of the twentieth century that they had been "robbed . . . by the removal of *creative* work" from the home sound pointlessly reactionary today. Not only have the skilled crafts, like sewing and cooking from scratch, left the home, but many of the "white-collar" tasks are on their way out too. For a fee, new firms like San Francisco–based Les Concierges and Cross It Off Your List in Manhattan will pick up dry cleaning, baby-sit pets, buy groceries, deliver dinner, even do the Christmas shopping. With other firms and individuals offering to buy your clothes, organize your financial files, straighten out your closets and drawers, and wait around in your home for the plumber to show up, why would anyone want to hold on to the toilet cleaning?

Absent a long-term souring of the economy, there is every reason to think that Americans will become increasingly reliant on paid housekeepers and that this reliance will extend ever further into the middle class. For one thing, there is no reason to expect that men will voluntarily take on a greater share of the burden, and much of the need for paid help arises from their abdication. As for children, once a handy source of household help: they are now off at soccer practice or SAT-prep classes, and Grandmother has relocated to warmer weather or taken up a second career. Furthermore, despite the fact that people spend less time at home than ever, the square footage of new homes swelled by 39 percent between 1971 and 1996, to include family rooms, home-entertainment rooms, home offices, bedrooms, and often a bathroom for each family member.[9] By the second quarter of 1999, 17 percent of new homes were larger than three thousand square feet, which is usually considered the size threshold for household help, or the point at which a house becomes unmanageable to the people who live in it.[10]

One more trend impels people to hire outside help, according to cleaning expert Cheryl Mendelson: fewer Americans know how to clean or even to "straighten up." I hear this from professional women defending their decision to hire a maid: "I'm just not very good at it myself" or "I wouldn't really know where to begin." Since most of us learn to clean from our parents (usually our mothers), any diminution of cleaning skills is transmitted from one generation to the next, like a gene that can, in the appropriate environment, turn out to be lethal or disabling. Upper-middle-class children raised in the servant economy of the early twenty-first century are bound to grow up as domestically incompetent as their parents, and no less dependent on others to clean up after them. Mendelson sees this as a metaphysical loss, a "matter of no longer being physically centered in your environment." Having cleaned the rooms of many overprivileged teenagers during my stint with The Maids, I think the problem is a little more urgent than that. The American overclass is raising a generation of young people who will, without constant assistance, suffocate in their own detritus.

___

If there are moral losses, too, as Americans increase their reliance on paid household help, no one has been tactless enough to raise them. Almost everything we buy, after all, is the product of some other person's suffering and miserably underpaid labor. I clean my own house, but I can hardly claim purity in any other area of consumption. I buy my jeans at the Gap, which is reputed to subcontract to sweatshops. I tend to favor decorative objects no doubt ripped off, by their purveyors, from scantily paid Third World craftspersons. Like everyone else, I eat salad greens picked by migrant farmworkers, some of them possibly children. And so on. We can try to minimize the pain that goes into feeding, clothing, and otherwise provisioning ourselves—by observing boycotts, checking for a union label, and so on—but there is no way to avoid it altogether without living in the wilderness on berries. Why should housework, among all the goods and services we consume, arouse any special angst?

Yet it does, as I have found in conversations with liberal-minded employers of maids, perhaps because we all sense that there are ways in which housework is different from other products and services. First is its inevitable proximity to the activities that constitute "private" life. The home that becomes a workplace for other people remains a home, even when that workplace is minutely regulated by the corporate cleaning chains. Someone who has no qualms about purchasing rugs woven by child-slaves in India, or coffee picked by ruined peasants in Guatemala, might still hesitate to tell dinner guests that, surprisingly enough, his or her lovely home doubles as a sweatshop during the day. You can eschew the chain cleaning services of course, hire an independent cleaner at a generous hourly wage, and even encourage, at least in spirit, the unionization of the housecleaning industry—and of course you should do all these things if you are an employer of household help. But none of this will change the fact that someone is working in your home at a job she would almost certainly never have chosen for herself—if she'd had a college education, for example, or was a native-born American with good English skills—or that the place where she works, however enthusiastically or resentfully, is the same as the place where you sleep.

It is also the place where your children are raised, and what they learn pretty quickly is that some people are less worthy than others. Even better wages and working conditions won't erase the hierarchy between an employer and his or her domestic help, since the help is usually there only because the employer has "something better" to do with her time, as one report on the growth of cleaning services puts it, not noticing the obvious implication that the cleaning person herself has *nothing* better to do with her time. In a merely middle-class home, the message may be reinforced by a warning to the children that that's what they'll end up doing if they don't try harder in school. Housework, as radical feminists once proposed, defines a human relationship and, when unequally divided among the social groups, reinforces preexisting inequalities. Dirt, in other words, tends to attach to the people who remove it—"garbagemen" and "cleaning ladies." Or, as cleaning entrepreneur Don Aslett told me with some bitterness—and this is a successful man, the chairman of the board of an industrial cleaning service and a frequent television guest—"The whole mentality out there is that if you clean, you're a scumball."

Increasingly often, the house cleaner is a woman of color and a recent arrival from the Third World, so that the implicit lesson for the household's children is that anyone female with dark skin and broken English is a person of inferior status—someone who has "nothing better" to do. What we risk as domestic work is taken over by immigrant workers is reproducing, within our own homes, the global inequalities that so painfully divide the world.

There is another lesson the servant economy teaches its beneficiaries and, most troublingly, the children among them. To be cleaned up after is to achieve a certain magical weightlessness and immateriality. Almost everyone complains about violent video games, but paid housecleaning has the same consequence-abolishing effect: you blast the villain into a mist of blood droplets and move right along; you drop the socks knowing they will eventually levitate, laundered and folded, back to their normal dwelling place. The result is a kind of virtual existence, in which the trail of litter that follows you seems to evaporate all by itself. Spill syrup on the floor and the cleaning person will scrub it off when she comes on Wednesday. Leave the *Wall Street Journal* scattered around your airplane seat and the flight attendants will deal with it after you've deplaned. Spray toxins into the atmosphere from your factory's smokestacks and they will be filtered out eventually by the lungs of the breathing public. A servant economy may provide opportunities, however limited, for poor and immigrant women. But it also breeds callousness and solipsism in the served, and it does so all the more effectively when the service is performed close up and routinely in the place where they live and reproduce.

Individual situations vary, of course, in ways that elude blanket judgment. Some people—the elderly and disabled, parents of new babies, asthmatics who require an allergen-free environment—may well need help performing what nursing-home staffers call the ADLs, or activities of daily living, and no shame should be attached to their dependency. In a more generous social order, housekeeping services would be subsidized for those who have health-related reasons to need them—a measure that would generate a surfeit of jobs for the entry-level workers who now clean the homes of the affluent. And in a less gender-divided social order, husbands and boyfriends would more readily do their share of the chores. The growing servant economy, with all the quandaries it generates, is largely a result of men's continuing abdication from their domestic responsibilities.

However we resolve the issue in our individual homes, the moral challenge is, put simply, to make work visible again: not only the scrubbing and vacuuming, but all the hoeing, stacking, hammering, drilling, bending, and lifting that goes into creating and maintaining a livable habitat. In an ever more economically unequal world, where so many of the affluent devote their lives to ghostly pursuits like stock trading, image making, and opinion polling, real work, in the old-fashioned sense of labor that engages hand as well as eye, that tires the body and directly alters the physical world tends to vanish from sight. The feminists of my generation tried to bring some of it into the light of day, but, like busy professional women fleeing the house in the morning, they left the project unfinished, the debate broken off in midsentence, the noble intentions unfulfilled. Sooner or later, someone else will have to finish the job.

Just Another Job?
The Commodification of Domestic Labor

Bridget Anderson

Paid domestic work looks in many ways like just another undesirable job. The hours are long, the pay is low, and the tasks are often regarded as demeaning. The same could be said of hamburger flipping or garbage collection. But there is much to distinguish the culture of domestic labor from other kinds of low-wage work. Significantly, domestic work is deeply embedded in status relationships, some of them overt, but others less so. And these relationships are all the more complex because they fall along multiple axes. They are relationships among women, but often women of different races or nationalities—certainly of different classes. They take place in a space that can be intimate, loving, and private but that can also be a form of social plumage, demonstrating to visitors the home owner's comfort and leisure. And the worker, often a migrant without legal protection or proper papers, may depend on the employer for more than her paycheck, just as the employer depends on the worker for more than her elbow grease.

The demand for domestic workers has been steadily rising in Europe, and although one can point to many economic and demographic forces that may have contributed to this trend—the retrenchment of the welfare state, the rise in the ratio of older to younger people, the feminization of the work-force, the rise in divorce, and the decline of the extended family—they leave a good deal unexplained. For instance, many domestic workers are employed by women who do not work outside their homes. Moreover, many paid domestic workers are cleaners rather than carers. While a working couple might need someone to look after their children or elderly relatives, no one *has* to employ a cleaner in the same way. Ironed clothes, dust-gathering ornaments, polished floors, and clean windows are not necessities; but such markers affirm a household's status by displaying its access to financial and human resources.

The migrant domestic workers I interviewed, many of them through a British support organization called Kalayaan, seemed to spend much of their time servicing lifestyles that their employers would have found difficult and even undesirable to sustain had they undertaken their upkeep themselves. Said Aida, a Filipina live-in in Paris:

> Every day I clean for my madam one pair of riding shoes, two pairs of walking shoes, house shoes. That is every day, just for one person. . . . Plus the children: that's one pair of rubbers and one pair of everyday school shoes. . . . Fourteen pairs of shoes every day. My time is already finished. . . . You will be wondering why she has so many bathrobes, one silk and two cotton. I say, Why does madam have so many bathrobes? Every day you have to hang them up. Every day you have to press the back because it is crumpled.

Siryani, a Sri Lankan live-in in Athens, recounted, "They have a very big house, and white carpet everywhere. They have three dogs. I hate those dogs with long, long hair. Even one hair will show on the white carpet."

When a cleaner is not enabling her employers to enjoy an extravagant lifestyle or an impractically appointed home (would Siryani's employers have had both white carpet and dogs if they'd had to clean their own home?), she allows her middle-class, female employer to devote "quality" time to her children and husband. In effect, employing a cleaner enables middle-class women to take on the feminine role of moral and spiritual support to the family, while freeing her of the feminine role of servicer, doer of dirty work. The employment of a paid domestic worker thereby facilitates status reproduction, not only by maintaining status objects but also by allowing the worker to serve as a foil to the lady of the house. Simply by hiring a domestic worker, the employer lowers the status of the work that employee does. After all, the employer has better or more lucrative things to do with her time.

Many middle-class, heterosexual couples in the United Kingdom employ a cleaner once they have children, thereby averting gender and generational conflict over domestic work.[1] But there is no total amount of domestic work that can be divided fairly between equal partners or delegated to someone who is paid to do it. When one does not have to do the work oneself, standards change. Eliska, a Czech au pair in the United Kingdom recounted, "Her teenage daughter changes her clothes five, six times a day and leaves them on the floor. I have to pick them up, wash them, iron them, put them away. I cannot tell her, Tasha, you cannot change your clothes so many times. And my employer does not notice."

Economic explanations, then, fail to fully account for the popularity of domestic workers in middle- to upper-class European households, because they fail to consider the status implications of hiring such workers. Similarly, the prevalence of migrant labor in this sector cannot be attributed only to avoidance of tax and national insurance, for there is a supply of cheap, nonmigrant female laborers willing to work off the books. Despite the relatively high wages of Polish workers in Berlin, they still account for a significant proportion of domestic workers. Filipina workers are the most popular in Athens, and they are also the most expensive.

Significantly, migrant workers are more willing than local ones to live with their employers. Live-in workers may be considerably less expensive than live-out workers, in some cases because their board and lodging are set against their wages, but especially because employers get more labor and greater flexibility for their money. Whatever hours a live-in nanny and housekeeper is supposed to work, there is virtually no time when she can comfortably refuse to "help" her employer with a household task. Domestic workers and au pairs commonly complain of having to be available at both ends of the day, early in the morning for children and late at night for entertaining guests. It is a question not simply of long hours but of permanent availability. Said Teresa, a Filipina domestic in Athens:

> You're working the minute you open your eyes until the minute you close your eyes. You keep your strength and your body going so that you will finish your work. . . . You keep waiting on your employers until they go to sleep because, although you finish your work, for example you finish ironing everything, putting the children or the elder person to bed, even if you put them to bed at ten o'clock, there are still other members of the family. So you keep on observing, "Oh, can I sleep or maybe they will call me to give them food or to give them a yogurt." . . . And even if you are sleeping you sometimes feel that you are still on duty.

A 1998 survey of thirty-nine Kalayaan members found that although the workers were well organized and belonged to a trade union, only 18 percent worked eight hours or less a day. Nearly 30 percent averaged more than twelve hours a day.

Although the long hours, low pay, and lack of privacy render live-in domestic work extremely unpopular among the population in general, migrants, particularly new arrivals, can find it advantageous: problems of accommodations and employment are solved in one, and the worker can both minimize expenses and acclimatize herself to a new language and culture. Moreover, housing is more than a place to live: it is shelter from the police, and many new arrivals are undocumented and terrified of deportation. Employers appreciate live-in migrants because, unlike local domestic workers, migrants cannot leave their employers to go tend to their own sick children or other family obligations. Undocumented workers in particular have extremely limited access to their own families or really, to any life outside the employing home.

Such women, however, isolated in private households, without papers or legal protection, are strikingly vulnerable to abuse. Their work can be singularly degrading: cleaning cats' anuses, flushing employers' toilets, scrubbing the floor with a toothbrush three times a day, or standing by the door in the same position for hours at a time. One worker told a researcher of a par-ticularly degrading experience: "We were three Filipinas, she brought us into the room where her guests were, she made us kneel down and slapped each one of us across the face."[2] Sadly, these are not isolated instances. Kalayaan keeps annual figures detailing the kinds of difficulties faced by the workers they register. In 1996–1997, 84 percent reported psychological abuse, 34 per-cent physical abuse, and 10 percent sexual abuse. Additionally, 54 percent were locked in, 55 percent did not have their own beds, and 38 percent were not fed regularly.

Racial stereotypes play a role both in the abuse of domestic workers and in the selection of migrant workers over local citizens in the first place. Certainly, such stereotypes help manufacture a sense of difference between the female employer and her domestic worker: "other" women are presumed suited to such service work, and these others are so alien that some employers actually fear that the migrants' bodies will contaminate their homes. Workers are typically required to wash their clothes sepa-rately from those of the family, and they are given their own cutlery and plates. Said Rose, a Ghanaian domestic worker in Athens, of her employer's family, "The daughter wouldn't even accept water from my hand, simply because I am black." Irene, a Filipina I interviewed in Athens, recounted the following story: "I heard children playing house. One child said, 'I am a Daddy.' The other child said, 'I am a Mummy,' and then, 'She is a Filipina.' So what does the child mean? Even the child knows or is already learning that if you are a Filipina, you are a servant inside the house."

Agencies and employers tend to express preferences for specific national-ities of domestic workers, and these preferences often reflect racial hierar-chies that rank women by precise shades of skin color. One volunteer from Caritas, the international Catholic social service and relief agency, in Athens told me, "The Ethiopians are very sweet. They are not like the African Africans, who are ugly." Said a worker at an agency in Barcelona, "Moroccans are difficult to place. . . . Their religion is very different, they observe Ramadan. . . . They are very different, though like Peruvians they are brought up to be servile. . . . Filipinas are easiest to place." And according to a community volunteer in Paris, "You know the black people are used to being under the sun, and the people in France think they are very lazy, they are not going very quick, and you know, another breed, but they are very good with children, very maternal."

Some hierarchies are based on particular national or personal prejudices. Greek employers and agencies tend to frown upon Albanians and Ukrainians. In Paris, many employers evince a preference for Haitians, who are generally darker-skinned than the expressly shunned Moroccans and Algerians. Stereotypes differ across European states, but also across households: one household might display an "eccentric" liking for Congolese, for example, on the basis of household myths of an almost folkloric character. A "bad" experience with a domestic worker might lead a family to generalize about her entire nationality. Consider the comments of this Athens employer:

> I have a problem with women from Ethiopia: they are lazy, and they have no sense of duty, though they are good-hearted. . . . I have a lot of experience. I have had ten girls from Ethiopia. They like to be well-dressed—hair, nails; for that they are good. . . . Then the Albanians—that was terrible. They are liars, always telling lies. And telephone maniacs because they have never had telephones. And they had no knowledge of electrical appliances. For seven months I had that girl. . . . Then I had one from Bulgaria. The Bulgarians are more civilized, more sincere, more concerned about work. But they are very unhappy.

Of course, not all employers are racist or abusive. Some women hire migrants in the hope of helping them. Certainly, migrant workers need the money. Why not match the needs of hard-pressed working mothers, on the one hand, with those of desperate migrants on the other?

Many of the domestic workers I met said that traveling abroad had enabled them to make important contributions to their families back home. But most of the more than four thousand workers at Kalayaan had never intended to come to Britain. Some had migrated first to the Middle East, from where they accompanied their employers to London on business trips or holidays; others had taken jobs in their countries of origin and traveled with their employers to the United Kingdom. While domestic workers who had papers felt that their work brought benefits to their families, others, especially those still undocumented, found the price too high. Said Nora, a Filipina working in London, "My life is worse than before. I'm on this dark road with no way out, that's how I feel. . . . All I want to do is go back home, even though we're very poor. But then, what kind of life will my daughter have?"

Hidden costs become apparent to many workers when they return home. They often feel ill at ease in their home countries, where things have changed in their absence, and where they may feel that they no longer belong. When their families meet them at the airport, these women commonly do not recognize their own kin. They talk of the embarrassment of having sex with husbands who have become virtual strangers, and of reuniting with children who doubt their mothers' love. Often a woman's relatives will have died or moved away. It is thus scarcely surprising that such women are very ambivalent when asked whether they would recommend migration to their daughters. Most migrants would prefer that their daughters did not have to make the choice between hunger and moving abroad.

So is employing a migrant domestic worker an act of sisterhood toward a woman in need or of complicity with abusive power structures? Employers often make contact with Kalayaan after they have seen a television program or read an article exposing the situation of migrant domestic workers in London. They want to help, they explain, and to offer board and lodging in return for "help around the house." A place in a British home is proffered as a kind of charity, and the woman's labor power is a little extra on the side. But even under the best of circumstances, the employer has power over the worker, and this power is greatly increased when the worker is an undocumented migrant. How the employer chooses to exercise that power is up to her.

As Judith Rollins has noted, a kind of "maternalism" sometimes marks these relationships, wherein friendliness between the women works to confirm the employer's sense of her own kindness and of the worker's childlike inferiority.[3] Through kindness, pity, and charity, the employer asserts her power. Nina, an employer in Athens, had hired dozens of migrant domestic workers to care for her very disabled mother over the years, because, she said,

"This is the Greek way to help foreigners." She claimed to offer exceptional working conditions (though the wages she told me were extremely low) and a loving household. But her employees, she lamented, have turned out to be gold diggers:

> There is no feeling for what I offer. I'll give you an example of the last woman from Bulgaria. . . . I had a bright idea: 'She needs to see her friends.' Because I was tired of all the turnover, I gave her Sunday off. . . . Now, every morning, including Sundays, the girl wakes, helps grandmother to the toilet and changes her Pamper. . . . Then she goes, but she must be back before seven P.M. . . . Then after all I do for her, the girl says every Sunday she would like to be back at midnight, and not to do any work—that is, not to change the Pamper in the morning.

This worker was being denied twelve consecutive hours off in a week—an arrangement that would still have placed her hours well above the European legal maximum.

Some employers express their maternalism through gifts, giving their domestic workers mostly unwanted, cast-off household goods. Said Maggie, a Zairean working in Athens, "You need the money to feed your children, and in place of pay they give you old clothes. 'I give you this, I give you this.' They give you things, but me, I need the money. Why? I am a human being."

All of these exercises of power, whether through direct abuse, through the insistence that a worker perform degrading tasks, or through acts of maternalism, expose the relationship between worker and employer as something other than a straightforward contractual one. But that is not the only relationship in the domestic workplace that is fraught with ambiguity and complexity. When we hire someone to care for children or the elderly, we cannot pay simply for the physical labor of care, leaving the emotional labor to those who are genetically linked to those cared for. Magnolia, a Dominican nanny in Barcelona, noted, "Sometimes when they say to me that I should give her lots of love, I feel like saying, well, for my family I give love free, and I'm not discriminating, but if it's a job you'll have to pay me."

Indeed, many parents hire nannies rather than sending their children to day care precisely because they want their children to develop personal, emotional relationships with the people who care for them. But can the emotional labor of care really be bought? The worker may carry out the physical work of care, entering into a sort of intimacy with the children, but her caring engenders no mutual obligations, no entry into a community, and no real human relationship—just money. A worker may care for a child over many years, spending many more hours with that child than the child's natural mother does, but should the employer decide to terminate the relationship, the worker will have no further right to see the child. As far as the employer is concerned, money expresses the full extent of her obligation to the worker. To the worker, this view is deeply problematic; indeed, it denies the worker's humanity and the very depth of her feelings. Juliette, a nanny from Côte d'Ivoire working in Parma, recalled, "I cared for a baby for his first year. . . . The child loves you as a mother, but the mother was jealous and I was sent away. I was so depressed then, seriously depressed. All I wanted was to go back and see him. . . . I will never care for a baby again. It hurts too much."

The idea that the worker can be considered "part of the family" allows some employers to negotiate these difficulties. Interestingly, this language even appears in U.K. immigration legislation with reference to au pairs. But the analogy does not withstand scrutiny. A relative who contracts a long-term illness is not expelled from the family; domestic workers usually are, even if they are given a nice severance package. And although being a part of the family does not entitle the worker to unconditional love or support, it does entitle the employer to encroach on the worker's off-duty hours for "favors." In fact, many employers will invoke either a contractual or a family relationship under different circumstances, depending on what is most convenient. Writes Miranda Miles:

> The disadvantages of being "one of the family" far outweighed the advantages. Wages tended to be lower and erratically paid on the premise that the maid would "understand" their financial situation. Incorporating a domestic worker into the family circle is usually, although not always, a sure way of depressing wages and possibly hiding even the most discreet forms of exploitation involved in the employer-employee relationship.[4]

These are vexed questions, for while informality clearly leaves workers open to exploitation—excessive hours, for instance, or low pay—workers also value having personal relationships with their employers, particularly because domestic work can be highly isolating. In some cases, a woman will decide to work for low wages precisely because she feels that a particular family is "nice" or an employer "treats me as part of the family." Professionalizing employment relations and rendering them more anonymous may therefore introduce new difficulties. Labor is a social, not simply an economic process.

This is not to say that labor contracts for domestic work are not important. We should welcome the emergence of domestic labor into the realm of recognized and productive work. Professionalization is a means of giving respect to domestic workers as workers, as well as of managing the personal relationships that develop from care work.

Certainly, it is possible to argue for the social significance of care work. Changing an elderly person's incontinence pads is surely as important and as deserving of social respect and status as the work of a stockbroker. But the work of cleaners and housekeepers sometimes occupies a more problematic space. Cleaning can be part and parcel of caring, and tidying up for a disabled person, for instance, can be construed as socially valuable. But many cleaners, like those described at the start of this essay, do work that simply expresses the employer's status, leisure, and power. Can such race-, class-, and gender-based divisions be resolved through contracts? Undocumented migrants, for example, cannot draw boundaries or refuse work they find demeaning. They simply do not have the power. The most effective way to protect them is to make sure that they have basic employment rights, as well as access to the means to implement those rights. For migrants, these rights begin with work permits.

Because both the workers and the employers in this sector tend to be women, it is tempting to draw on notions of sisterhood in order to reform the relationships between employers and employees. But the power relations among these women are very complex, to the point where even acts of kindness work to reproduce an employer's status and self-image, and they do not always, in the end, benefit the worker. This does not mean that employers should not respect their domestic workers but, rather, that they should also be aware that the very act of employing a domestic worker weaves them into a status relationship. Real sisterhood, then, should take concerned women beyond their own homes: it means campaigning and organizing around issues of migration and domestic labor, having as an important first demand that domestic work be treated, in the best sense, like just another job.

Filipina Workers in Hong Kong Homes: Household Rules and Relations

NICOLE CONSTABLE

When I first met her, in Hong Kong in 1994, Cathy was nineteen years old. As she told me her story in the shade next to St. John's Cathedral, her naive and cheerful demeanor belied the difficulties she had experienced since leaving her home in the Philippines. Cathy is the youngest of six children, and her mother is a widow. She completed secondary school at age seventeen. A promising student, she hoped to study management in college, and eventually to start a small business. But her mother could not afford the tuition, so Cathy decided to go to work as a "helper" in Hong Kong instead. She had to overcome her mother's resistance. "I explained to her that I wanted to go to college," Cathy told me. "If I can earn some money, I will finish one [two-year] contract and then I'll go back home and continue my studies."

To avoid employment-agency expenses, Cathy asked her sister, who had already worked in Hong Kong for six years, to help her find an employer. A friend of her sister's recommended Ms. Leung, a Cantonese woman in her late thirties who ran a small textile business. Cathy was assured that Ms. Leung would be a good employer. She was single and lived alone in a small, middle-class flat. The workload, it seemed, would be reasonable.

Cathy's sister met her at Kai Tak airport the evening of her arrival in

October 1992 and took her to her employer's house. Cathy was surprised to find that the "single" woman lived with her husband and daughter, but Ms. Leung kindly reassured Cathy that she would be treated as a "younger sister."

As it happened, however, Cathy was required to work sixteen hours a day, and to do "illegal work" outside of her employer's home. She was not paid the legal wage stipulated in her contract. As Cathy explained:

> It's written in the contract 3-2 [HK$3,200]. But when I got to Hong Kong ... [Ms. Leung] said to me, "Your salary is 2-3, but don't worry, I will just add [to it] if your performance is good until it reaches minimum [wage]." She promised me, so I expected her to respect that promise. But for six months, no. She didn't add to my salary. So she only gave me 2-3. But in fact I only received 2-1, because she opened a bank account for me but she did not give HK$200 every month. The account was in her name and my name—a joint account. [Now] my bankbook is with her so I cannot get my money. My bankbook—my documents—she took them all. So I still cannot get my money from the bank.

When Cathy ate with the family, she was served last. Other times, she complained, she was given leftovers and rarely received enough to eat. The family slept in air-conditioned quarters, but the room where Cathy slept, which also served as a storeroom, was sweltering hot in the summer and leaked when it rained.

Cathy's work followed a rigid daily schedule, beginning before seven o'clock in the morning and ending around nine o'clock at night. Her duties included washing, shopping, cooking, cleaning, and looking after two dogs. In addition to such "official" duties, she was also required to serve as a messenger and to clean Ms. Leung's mother's flat, Ms. Leung's friend's flat and office, and Ms. Leung's office. Even on her rest day—which was rotated each week, thus curtailing her ability to meet her sister and her friends—she was required to make breakfast, take the dogs out, and do many other household chores.

Ms. Leung gave Cathy a detailed list of rules to follow. She was forbidden to wear makeup, fingernail polish, or perfume; she could not wear dresses or skirts, only pants; and her curfew on her day off was strictly enforced. She was not permitted to use the phone, and Ms. Leung threatened to deduct

HK$10 from her pay even for free local calls. Ms. Leung specified the days when Cathy could wash her hair, and she monitored the length of her showers. She was required to pay replacement costs for broken dishes, and her use of hot water was strictly limited. Ms. Leung claimed the right to change Cathy's day off without notice and to dictate that Cathy be home by nine in the evening. All her work was to be finished before bed. After work, she "must turn off the light and sleep within one hour, at ten o'clock."

Such lists of rules appear to be common among employers of domestic workers in Hong Kong. Staff at employment agencies encourage employers to write them. Although it is difficult to say how widespread they are, I was shown many examples in the course of my research. Significantly, such lists serve to establish the worker's inferior position. Unlike other members of the household, a domestic worker must ask permission to use the phone, the television, or the air conditioner, or to attend to "personal matters" when she has completed her work. Like immature members of the household, she is told when to go to bed and what time to come home. The final rule on Cathy's list takes the form of a threat:

> The employee must not be misconduct himself [sic]. The term misconduct includes insolence, persistent laziness, immorality, dishonesty and drunkenness. Misconduct will justify summary dismissal if it directly interferes with the interest and business of the employer or the employee's ability to perform his services. And all the expenses, including the air ticket, doctor fees, application fee, every thing paid for you in advance for coming to H.K. the employer shall have the right to claim back all the charges and deduct in your salary while you break the contract or found dishonesty at anytime.

In fact, under Hong Kong policies an employer does not have the right to reclaim expenses. But another domestic worker's employer's list ends with a similar warning: "If you are not satisfied with working in this house, you have to give a one month's notice before you can quit. If we are not happy with your work, we can send you back to the Philippines right away according to the contract."[1] This "rule"—like many others—contradicts government policy.

Although many employers create rules and regulations that they present as "law," the official Employment Contract for a Domestic Worker Recruited Outside of Hong Kong is the only contract that is legally recognized in Hong Kong. The contract outlines the rights and obligations of the employer and the worker. It covers a two-year period and can be legally terminated with one month's notice or one month's pay in lieu of notice by either the worker or the employer. A domestic worker whose contract ends or is terminated is usually required to return to the Philippines within two weeks. The contract stipulates the worker's minimum monthly pay (approximately US$460 since the mid 1990s), his or her holidays, and benefits. It also stipulates that he or she work for only one employer, doing only "household work." The employer is required to provide "suitable and furnished accommodation and food free of charge."[2] Although such laws exist to protect foreign domestic workers, they are in fact very difficult to enforce. As we have seen, employers like Ms. Leung try to impose their own idiosyncratic rules and regulations on domestic workers.

Most factory workers, too, are expected to abide by rules of conduct and dress, to follow timetables, and even to fulfill work quotas dictated by their employers. But the situation of foreign domestic workers is far more vulnerable. Large groups of factory workers labor together for the same employer, working a set number of hours per day, usually under similar conditions to one another. Domestic workers, with few exceptions, are dispersed among different employers, where they experience different work conditions. They normally live in the place where they work, which can make work time indistinguishable from time off. They are isolated both by virtue of being foreign and because they work in private homes. Usually outnumbered by the members of the employer's household, the domestic worker can easily be exposed to abuse or exploitation.

The relationship between a household worker and her employer is potentially intense and complicated. Working in her employer's private domain, she often observes behaviors to which only the closest family members are otherwise privy. The Hong Kong Institute of Household Management in Manila, an organization that trains domestic workers for the Hong Kong markets instructs women to "maintain a SAFE-DISTANCE" from their employers. "If you become too familiar with your employer, you may answer back or abuse [sic] without knowing or intentionally doing it."[3] The domestic worker, unlike her employer, is expected to behave "professionally" at all times. She should take the emotional outbursts of the employer and the employer's family in stride, while concealing and repressing her own anger, frustration, and other emotions.

One Philippine employment agency advises workers to "be patient and tolerant to your employer when you are being scolded for your mistakes. Be willing to adjust to your employer's way of cooking, working, and way of living. . . . Be polite and always SMILE. Greet your employer 'GOOD MORNING' 'GOOD NIGHT.' Say 'PLEASE' 'THANK YOU' 'I AM SORRY.' . . . Avoid crying. It is bad luck to your employer." Such agencies routinely warn domestic workers against crying, displaying "long faces," touching employers with any part of a broom, sweeping the house on the first day of the Chinese lunar New Year, or wearing all white or all black (colors associated with death), because some Hong Kong employers believe that these behaviors will bring them bad fortune. The Hong Kong Institute instructs domestic workers to begin the day by "saying 'good morning' to everybody. Even if they don't answer you, continue doing this." After all, "even a difficult employer can be won over by a hardworking and pleasant maid." In addition, "a maid should never shout [at] an employer. Always speak in a normal, pleasant voice. Also, when called . . . respond immediately."[4]

Live-in domestic workers are in some ways less like factory workers than like military recruits, who work and live in the same space and to whom the same rules apply twenty-four hours a day. But military officers are expected to lead by example, and they are bound by many of the same regulations that apply to their recruits. Not so for employers of household workers. As in a factory, the employer creates rules specifically for the worker, and these rules thus highlight the status differences between the two groups. In the case of domestic workers, rules do not usually apply to anyone else, except occasionally to immature members of the household. Rules for children change as a child becomes older, however, whereas rules for the domestic worker remain the same, whether she is eighteen or fifty-five.

Most employers view their domestic workers—and expect those workers to view themselves—as "maids" at all times, but especially in their employers' homes. A worker must obey her employer's rules, even at night, and in her own room. She may be told when and where to bathe, what time to go to bed, and what she can and cannot wear. Only on her day off is she at all free to express herself outside of the role of domestic worker. But even then, she does so under the watchful eye of the public.

Jane, a Filipina in her mid-forties who has several children, has been a domestic worker in Hong Kong for fifteen years. I met her when I volunteered at the Mission for Filipino Migrant Workers, a nongovernmental organization that provides legal and personal support to Filipino workers. She had just received a month's notice because her employers were moving to Canada. Since her employers were willing to document their situation with Hong Kong's Labor and Immigration Departments, Jane was allowed to process a new contract in Hong Kong rather than return to the Philippines within the two weeks stipulated by the employment contract. Thanks to her good "release papers," she was interviewed by several prospective employers. After one interview she rushed excitedly to the mission, not because the interview had gone well but because she had another list to add to my collection. "Where's Nicole?" she shouted. "I have a good one for her!" A volunteer read the list aloud, interrupted by jeers and a chorus of dissent. The list included many "rules" that contradicted the official contract, such as requiring chores on the "rest day" and imposing curfews. Other rules included:

- You are not allowed to rest and lean on sofa of parlour and your employer's bed.
- A maid must always be polite and greet the employer, his family members, relatives, visitors as soon as meeting them by saying: GOOD MORNING, GOOD DAY, GOOD AFTERNOON, GOOD EVENING or GOOD NIGHT (before going to bed), SIR MADAM etc. Don't forget to say THANK YOU at appropriate times.
- DO NOT use any nail polish on fingers and toes. DO NOT put on make up, even when you are going out to do the family shopping. Your hair must be short and tidy. DO NOT wear tight jeans and pants and low-cut T-shirts while you are working. DO NOT go to the parlour in pyjamas.
- Must take bath daily before going to bed. Hand wash your own clothes separately from those of your employers and the children (especially the under-wear), unless your employer allows you to wash your own clothes by the washing-machine together with theirs.

- You will be required to sleep and attend the baby and elderly, even during night time.
- Use separate towels for different purposes, such as a) sweeping floor, b) cleaning furniture, c) cleaning dining table, d) washing oily dishes, e) washing cups, f) washing basin, g) washing toilet; you should use separate towel for each purpose.
- Washing of car and caring for pets (e.g. dogs & cats) are part of your duties with <u>NO EXTRA ALLOWANCE</u>.
- You give [a] very bad impression to your employer if they see you chatting or laughing with your Filipino friends outside their house or down the street. Therefore, <u>NEVER</u> gather with other Filipino maids near your living place, especially when you are bringing their kids down to the street to catch the school bus or going to the market.
- <u>DO NOT</u> write any letters during your working days, do it on your holidays.

Jane accepted a job offer from another employer who seemed to be far less controlling.

Employers' rules not only govern a domestic worker's behavior and attitude but also control her use of time and the pace of her work. The Hong Kong Institute teaches that "there is not [sic] place for LAZINESS in the job you have accepted. There is a difference between a lazy and a slow person. We tend to do things here [in the Philippines] at a slower pace due to the hot weather but in Hong Kong where the weather is cold, people move fast and this is what they expect to see in other people."[5] Women are told to "Learn to CLOCK WATCH. Schedule [your] time and work. . . . During your FREE-TIME, rest if you must, but be ready to answer the door or telephone. Sew clothes or other special chores like re-potting some plants and cleaning kitchen cupboards."[6] The idea that domestic workers need to be taught the "value of time" and how to "budget time" recalls the capitalist discipline imposed on English workers in the eighteenth and nineteenth centuries.[7]

The confluence of home and workplace renders it difficult for household workers to separate their work time from their personal time, either spatially or temporally. Many employers instruct domestic workers that after completing assigned tasks, they should "find" more work to do. One worker I spoke to prided herself on her efficiency and speed. Her employer agreed that she did good work but told her that when she finished a task, she should either find more work or redo what she had done. "I didn't hire you to sit around and do nothing," her employer told her.

Domestic workers are usually expected to follow timetables and schedules.[8] The timetable allows the employer to control the domestic worker's use of time. It also prevents the worker from using her time more efficiently to create "free time." Regardless of whether the floors or windows appear clean, they must be cleaned at the scheduled time. In most cases, workers are not allowed to judge for themselves whether a job needs to be done; they are merely required to follow the schedule. Many domestic workers are not permitted to write letters or take care of their own business on workdays or during work hours regardless of whether they have completed their duties. It is as though the employer has bought the domestic worker's labor power and time, not simply hired her to carry out specific tasks.

Most employers impose restrictive curfews and dictate that a domestic worker return home by eight, nine, or ten in the evening on her day off. Such curfews are common, although the official contract states that employers must "notify the Helper before the beginning of each month" as to the dates of the weekly rest days, and that "a rest day is a continuous period of not less than 24 hours." Employers often rationalize curfews as being for the domestic worker's own good or safety. Domestic workers—often mature and responsible women—more accurately view such restrictions as unfair, overly restrictive, patronizing, or "maternalistic."[9]

Recalling the wealthy owners of *muijai* (bond servants) of the past, many employers claim that they are different from other types of employers since they serve as the domestic worker's "guarantor." As one explained,

> A guarantor . . . has to pay all her lodging and food, and [guarantee her] safety. Safety is the most important. Now that is one misunderstanding with the girls. . . . Some girls want to stay outside. . . . They want to come home late. The employer will ask them, "Oh, next time please come home earlier." She will be very unhappy. "This is my holiday, why will you not allow me to?" But one thing they do not understand [is that it is] because they live in the same house. If

she did not come home, the employers would have to wait for her. They could not go to bed. Another thing is that they worry about her because the guarantor is responsible in case she had an accident outside. The employer would be responsible for her, so she looks after her like her own son and daughter. But the maids don't understand.

For domestic workers whose duties include care of infants, small children, or sick or elderly family members, work hours may extend through the night. Jane's prospective employer specified that she would be required to attend to the babies and the elderly, even at night. Foreign domestic workers often share rooms with children, providing bottles, diaper changes, and comfort when a child wakes up in the night. Domestic workers are commonly expected to serve refreshments at mah-jongg parties, which may take place several nights a week. Although the employer who has been up until the early hours of the morning is free to sleep late, the domestic worker is still expected to prepare breakfast for the children, walk the dog, or resume her normal duties at six or seven in the morning. A domestic worker may theoretically be "allowed" to go to bed whenever she pleases, but if her "bedroom" is in the living room where the family watches television until late, or on the floor of the kitchen, she cannot go to sleep until the rest of the family does, because of the noise, interruptions, or lack of privacy.

Domestic workers sometimes find their use of time monitored by a household member who remains at home. This is often an older member of the household, such as the employer's mother or mother-in-law, or the female employer herself if she does not work outside the home. Occasionally, a Chinese domestic worker, usually referred to as an "amah," supervises the foreign worker. Some employers phone or "check in" on the domestic worker periodically. Workers who have a choice greatly prefer to work in households where no one is at home during the day. Detailed timetables provide the best example of the extreme controls placed on workers' time. Some timetables include daily, weekly, biweekly, and monthly duties. Some employers make up their own schedules; others adapt them from books such as *The Maid's Manual*[10] or from schedules used by friends or proposed by agencies. Along with her rules, Ms. Leung gave Cathy one of the most detailed lists of duties I have ever seen. Monday's schedule was as follows:

6:30 A.M. Wake up, prepare breakfast for Pucci [Ms. Leung's son]

6:50 A.M. Feed Bobo [the dog] (two cups of dry food and one glass of milk). After that bring him to the toilet. But make sure [it's] in the right place. Don't let him [go to the] toilet in the house and the building.

7:30 A.M Prepare breakfast for Mr. and Mrs. [Leung]

8:00 A.M to 12:00 A.M Wash all the cups and dishes. Wash clothes, use washing machine. Clean the living room (including all the windows, furniture, mirror, television, hi-fi, fans, table, chairs and books . . .). Clean the floor (especially the corner and the gap).

At office: Arrive office at 12:30 P.M. After lunch wash bowls and dishes. Rest one hour (1:00–2:00 P.M.). Clean all the tables, chairs, machine, showroom (all the surfaces). Clean the floor.

5–5:30 P.M Go back to home and buy meat for dinner.

Evening Wash all the meat and vegetables. Prepare dinner for Bobo, bring him to the toilet and take the rubbish to the street. Prepare dinner. After dinner clean up all the bowls and dishes. Clean the floor. Iron clothes.

This same schedule was repeated each day of the week, with additional daily variations between 8:30 A.M. and noon. Saturday's schedule included the usual chores, but at 9:30 A.M. Cathy was required to go to Ms. Leung's mother's house and cook, clean, iron, mop, and the like.

Most studies suggest that domestic workers work much more than ten hours a day, and they receive no overtime pay. According to Carolyn French's in-depth random study of one hundred Filipina domestic workers, 15 percent worked fewer than ten hours a day; 40 percent worked eleven to thirteen hours a day; 30 percent worked fourteen to sixteen hours a day; and 10 percent worked more than sixteen hours a day.[11] According to the Asian Migrant Centre study, over 75 percent of all domestic workers surveyed worked more than fourteen hours a day; only about 3 percent of Filipinas worked fewer than eleven hours a day. More than half worked twelve to fifteen hours a day; almost 30 percent worked sixteen to seventeen hours a day, and 4 percent more than eighteen hours a day.[12] The disparity between the two studies may reflect different sampling techniques or difficulties in defining what qualifies as household work. Nonetheless, both surveys point to very long work days.

Domestic workers and representatives of their organizations often express concern over these unlimited working hours. Employers, however, tend to oppose strongly any limit on workers' hours. One reason employers say they hire foreign workers, as opposed to local ones, is that foreign workers live in and can be called on to work at any time. Mrs. Yang, a working mother of three young children, expressed the view of many employers when she said that she would not hire a worker who was restricted to ten hours a day. "Families—working wives—they really need someone who will sleep in and stay. Why do they have to give them the house to live in? Why do they have to allow them to have the bed? Only because they need to have someone to stay in."

Some employers accuse domestic workers of exaggerating the number of hours they work. They say it is impossible to count work hours since domestic workers "work intermittently" and spend part of the day "resting." According to Mrs. Yang,

> You cannot keep account of family work. . . . For family work, as you
> know, [there are] some things you have to do in the morning and
> some things you have to do in the evening, like the meals: breakfast,
> lunch, and dinner. How do you count the time? And actually if you
> count their rest, when the babies go to sleep, they should rest too. I
> mean, family work is not work in the factory! I mean, we have many
> part-time servants in Hong Kong. When they do the part-time they
> really work! Not like the domestic workers in the house now.

In a letter to the editor published in the *South China Morning Post*, A. Lam expressed a similar view:

> It is unfair to say that they [domestic workers] have to work an aver-
> age of fifteen hours a day. It all depends on their own efficiency. . . .
> For those helpers whose employers are working and will not stay at
> home, have they thought of the free time they have during the day?
>
> If, for example, a domestic helper's employers leave home at

8 A.M. and return home at 8 P.M. for dinner, the helper has twelve hours on her own. If she can organize her work better, I'm sure that she could have about three or four hours free time within those twelve hours. One of the reasons for their long working hours, and I think most employers would agree with me, is because most of them do not organize their work.[13]

These statements suggest that "housework" is not "real work." Even employers who were themselves once full-time "housewives" feel justified in demanding extremely long working hours from paid workers. What Lam and Mrs. Yang do not seem to realize is that many domestic workers are not given the option to budget their time more efficiently. Housework, moreover, is never finished. The more a domestic worker does, the more she must do.

The domestic workers who seemed most satisfied with their work were those who felt they were allowed more independence and responsibility. They could budget their time how they liked so long as they did their required work well, and they could use their "spare time" as they pleased. Many of the volunteers at the Mission for Filipino Migrant Workers were workers who completed their tasks quickly, efficiently, and to the satisfaction of their employers. When they finished work, they were allowed to decide how to spend their time.

Other workers, however, are far less fortunate. Their employers attempt to control not only their time but even their personal appearance. Some are required to wear uniforms when their employers expect guests; relatively few have to wear uniforms all the time. It is not uncommon, however, to see women at the market, on the train, at the post office, or at school bus stops wearing "maid's uniforms." Other domestic workers often express pity for women who must wear uniforms in public. Many workers dislike uniforms and consider them demeaning or embarrassing, but as Jane's prospective employer's list specified, "If your employer requests you to wear uniforms you must obey and you have no right to refuse."

Maria, whom I met in the mission's Kowloon shelter, explained that some women oppose their employers' uniform requirement. "We have one woman like that here," she explained. "Her employer requested that she wear a uniform and she said, 'You just want us to look smart so that when you have visitors, they will see us in uniform and think this is a rich family.' We don't like to wear uniforms. . . . Because they can identify you, you are a maid!"

Studies suggest that domestic workers are usually well aware that they serve as status symbols.[14] Workers of different class and racial backgrounds can be especially effective in that capacity,[15] and uniforms and other visible markers further distinguish workers from employers, heightening their usefulness as status markers.[16] Hong Kong employers are also concerned that Chinese amahs be identified as such. Mrs. Chin, a professional who preferred Filipina domestic workers over Chinese ones, was extremely annoyed that Ah Ching, the Chinese domestic worker she had once employed, could successfully pass herself off as Mrs. Chin's children's grandmother.

Even when they are not required to wear uniforms, Filipina workers are usually told what to wear. Often they are told to wear pants that are not too tight and shirts with high necks and at least short sleeves. Skirts and dresses must usually cover the knees. Some employers specify that proper shoes—as opposed to slippers or thongs—must be worn. One worker was told that it would reflect poorly on her employer if she were seen going to the market in slippers. Another worker, Acosta, had a part-time employer complain that she dressed less like a maid than like someone going to a disco.

Some employers take this regime so far as to attempt to control their workers' hygiene and bodily appearance. Almost every part of a worker's body, literally down to her toes, may be subject to the employer's control. Employers sometimes monitor their workers' use of makeup and perfume, as well as the length and style of their hair. The length of fingernails and toenails and even the frequency of nail-cutting may be prescribed by an employer. Few of the women I spoke with were permitted to dress as they pleased; most had some restrictions imposed on them.

Christina, a domestic worker in her late twenties, was subject to particularly harsh restrictions. She had been a domestic worker in Malaysia for three years when she came to work in Hong Kong in January 1993. One steamy afternoon, we met in the crowded two-bedroom shelter where she was staying with fifteen other Filipinas whose contracts had been terminated and who had nowhere else to go. We sat in the corner of one dark room, on top of a tall pile of thin mattresses that would be spread out from wall to wall when it was time for the women to sleep. As we talked, a three-week-old baby cried softly and was passed from one woman to the next. His mother had given birth alone, and since the birth had not been officially recorded, she was having difficulty obtaining a passport to allow him to go back with her to the Philippines. Christina began her story. Her roommates already knew it well; they interjected parts of it for her.

She had arrived at Kai Tak airport a bit tired but excited at the prospect of her new job. Her employer, Mrs. Wong, a woman in her mid-thirties, was there to meet her. In the car, as they headed away from the airport, Mrs. Wong began to recite a long list of duties and regulations. "On your day off you must be home by eight P.M. You cannot wear dresses or skirts, only pants. You must keep your shoulders and upper arms covered at all times, and you cannot wear makeup, fingernail polish, jewelry, or perfume." She told Christina that she must have short hair. At the time, Christina's hair was long. She wore it loosely tied back in a ponytail that reached a third of the way down her back. "Yes, ma'am," she said. "But I can keep it tied back and pull it back tighter to make it smaller." Christina tried politely to reason with her employer. Mrs. Wong firmly pronounced that Christina's hair *must* be short because she would be working with small children.

Before reaching the flat, Mrs. Wong parked the car in front of a barber-shop. As Christina described it, "It was the sort of place where old men go to get their hair cut." Mrs. Wong said something in Chinese to the barber and left. Christina was upset; still, she felt she had little choice but to obey her employer if she wanted to keep her job. So she tried to communicate to the barber, in English and with gestures, the kind of short, shoulder-length cut she would like. He understood and complied. But when Mrs. Wong returned she was furious and insisted that he give Christina a "man's cut." She watched and waited while the barber cropped off Christina's hair. As one of Christina's friends commented: "*Bruha* [witch] obviously didn't know you'd look even more beautiful with short hair!"

For the next two days Christina worked hard washing clothes and dishes, cleaning windows, and scrubbing the walls and floors as her employer care-fully scrutinized her work. Shortly before midnight on the third day, Mrs. Wong began to shout at Christina loudly, saying that she could not have ever worked as a maid before. Mrs. Wong then ordered Christina to leave the house. One of the last things Christina remembered Mrs. Wong shouting was that she was still entitled to three free replacements from the employment agency. Christina had worked for her employer for less than three days. She was now doing "aerobics" (illegal part-time work) when she could, and patiently awaiting her hearing at the Labour Tribunal.

Even more common than hair-length restrictions, and at least as annoying, are rules relating to bathing. At least fifteen different Filipinas told me that their employers dictated that they follow the Chinese custom of bathing in the evening, before bed. Most were required to bathe after ironing, or some other work, in the evening. Some workers were assigned a specific time to bathe.

Several women explained that in the Philippines they would bathe in the morning, and sometimes in both the morning and the evening. Bathing in the evening, when one is still hot from work, they believe, can make one more susceptible to colds, bronchitis, pneumonia, or *pasma* (chills). They believe it can make the veins in the hands or legs "bulge," and that it can cause permanent varicose veins. Jane showed me the bulging veins on her hands and explained that this only happened after she came to Hong Kong. Maria said, "I had to iron many, many [clothes], and then I had to hand-wash [more clothes] again. So we have, you see"—she pointed to her hands—"veins. I didn't have hands like this in the Philippines! Because if we iron in the afternoon we never even take a bath or wash our hands, our parents get angry at us. . . . Because we will get colds, rheumatism, arthritis."

In the Philippines, I was told, parents and elders advise young girls to rest for at least an hour after ironing, or preferably to wait until the next morning to bathe so as not to become ill. Back home, one worker explained, she was not allowed to wash the dishes if she had just ironed. Her employer, however, always made her wash dishes, iron, and then bathe. She interpreted her employer's order as dangerous to her health. Another worker said that forcing her to bathe in the evening was just another way in which her employer tried to destroy her health and beauty. Acosta advised friends who had to shower in the evening to threaten their employers with the medical bills that might ensue should they become sick.

Cathy was particularly upset about her bathing situation. Mrs. Leung criticized the length of her showers. Cathy quoted her: " 'Why when you take a bath do you take such a long time? It takes you one hour—a half hour or something?' She said 'Why? Why?' She said to me, 'In the Philippines, you do that?' 'Yes' I said. 'Well, you're in Hong Kong already. You can follow what I want!' 'Okay,' I said." Ms. Leung would not allow Cathy to bathe before going out on her day off. She told Cathy to wash once a day, in the evening, and would not allow her to wash her hair every day. I asked Cathy to describe her usual bathing pattern in the Philippines. "My hair and my body every day! In the morning, I wash it all—hair and body and everything. . . . Every day [in the Philippines] I clean my body at least twice a day, but at my employer's it's only once. One time, and in the evening! So it's terrible! So she said on my day off I cannot take a bath normally. So every week I would bring some clothes and I go to my friend's house just to take a bath."

Acosta's first employer would not let her wash her hair every day, as was her custom in the Philippines, and if she came out of the bathroom with wet hair, the family members laughed at her or scolded her. Cora, another worker, explained that Filipinos prefer bathing daily, usually in the morning, and that they will wear their clothes only once. "To the Chinese," she reflected, "we are being spoiled and not behaving like maids."

The most common complaints I heard from domestic workers related to food. Many Filipinas commented on their difficulties using chopsticks, and their disgust at the customary communal dish, which everyone dips into, using his or her own chopsticks. Some women continued to use spoons, as they had in the Philippines, despite criticism or teasing. Others found it difficult to get used to Chinese food. Elsa described how her stomach turned the first time she saw "the way the blood is left in the steamed chicken." Employers, conversely, complained about the smell of Filipino food.

The main food-related problem, which I heard repeatedly, concerned quantity. Employers of foreign workers often thought that domestic workers ate too much, sometimes pointing out that Filipinas are, by Hong Kong standards, overweight. Filipinas, conversely, often think that the Chinese are "too thin," and that their employers eat very little.

In most parts of the Philippines, I was told, rice constitutes an important part of every meal. Especially for those who are expected to work hard, three solid meals that include rice are considered essential. In Hong Kong, domestic workers are often expected to eat a slice of bread or toast for breakfast, or perhaps a bowl of "watery rice" cereal (*juk* or congee). Employers, Filipinas note, are often in a great rush to get to work in the morning. To their amazement, employers sometimes skip breakfast, or are satisfied with just a cup of tea or coffee. For lunch, especially if the employer is not at home, a worker may be expected to eat just a bowl of noodles. One woman I met was only given three dry packets of instant noodles a day, one for each meal.

When domestic workers complain to their employers that they need more food, they are sometimes told that they should eat less and lose a bit of weight. By Hong Kong standards Filipinas may be overweight, but in the Philippines, I was told, it is desirable for a woman to be "chubby." Chubbiness (as opposed to obesity) is considered attractive and a sign of good health. Maria and Elsa both noted that when they came to Hong Kong, their complexions suffered and they lost about fifteen pounds. Very few women were pleased when they lost weight, and most were very happy to put it on. Putting on weight was reassuring to their families back home, where it was seen as evidence that they were getting along well in Hong Kong. One employer described her worker, Rina, as "much slimmer and more attractive when she first started to work for us." Rina, by contrast, was pleased only when she started regaining the weight she'd lost when she'd lived with her first employer. She had been miserable and anxious and was not allowed to eat what she wanted. Like many others, she associated her weight loss with stress, hard work, lack of food, and an uncaring employer. She felt that her recent weight gain reflected well on her new employer, Mrs. Chin.

Cathy complained that Mrs. Leung did not give her enough food, and that what she did give her included overripe fruit and leftovers that no one else wanted. She recalled:

> We ate together, using chopsticks and no serving spoons. Sometimes the bone of the chicken was all that was left for me. I ate the same food as them but there wasn't enough. When we went to a restaurant there were only small bowls, so they ate just a little. . . . Not like in the Philippines. There we eat twice the rice, and for breakfast, lunch, and dinner. But here they eat just bread. Only one piece of bread and it's okay [for them]. For me it's okay, but at least at lunch and in the evening I need some vitamins and some nutritious food so that I can work. Sometimes . . . we eat just one kilo of cabbage and HK$5 of pork for a family of four! Fried only, because

they like fried food. And sometimes just fried eggs for dinner. Not much. It was very strange for me at first, because in the Philippines I never ate like this. Because I ate well in my family.

The official employment contract specifies that domestic workers should be provided with "food free of charge" or, "if no food is provided, a food allowance of not less than HK$300 a month." The contract does not stipulate how much food an employer must provide. Some employers apparently think that if they provide any food at all, they need not provide an allowance. Most workers I spoke to did not receive a food allowance, but those who did received no more than HK$300 a month. For some, the food allowance was meant to cover meat and vegetables, whereas rice, sugar, tea, soy sauce, and other common ingredients were provided by the employer. For others, HK$300 was meant to cover everything for the entire month, and most found that it was not enough. As if in recognition of this insufficiency, the Hong Kong Institute advises women that "if FOOD ALLOWANCE is given, use your money to buy your food supplies. Do not complain about [buying] food with salary received. A small part of your salary can buy more than enough food than one wishes to eat."[17]

Food and eating arrangements vary greatly. Some women eat with their employers. More often they eat separately in the kitchen. Some are permitted to cook their own food, but others, like Acosta, were not allowed to cook Filipino food because members of the employers' family did not like the smell of it. When cooking Chinese food, workers are usually required to follow specific instructions. As Elsa explained, buying the wrong cut of beef or slicing the meat or the vegetables the wrong size, shape, or direction for a particular dish sent one of her employers into a rage. For a broccoli-and-beef dish, the broccoli and the beef are cut in a particular way; for a tomato-and-beef dish, the meat is sliced in a different way. Some domestic workers assist in preparing the food—they wash, chop, slice, pare, and peel—but leave the actual cooking to the employer. Employers can determine not only what a domestic worker cooks for the family meal but also what, where, when, and how much a domestic worker eats.

Besides hygiene and food, workers often comment on territorial restrictions in the house. Although employers and workers occupy the same household, certain privileged spaces may be off-limits to the worker, or may be entered only for work. Jane's prospective employer's list indicated that although she would be required to clean the living room and dining room, she would not be permitted to relax or eat there. In extreme cases, workers cannot sit or lean on furniture except their own bed and chair. One worker was told to clean the vinyl-covered dining room chairs with rubbing alcohol after she sat on them. Others were chastised for walking in front of the air conditioner or fan, because it would blow the domestic worker's "air" onto the employer.

Some domestic workers have their own "quarters," often a small window-less bedroom and bathroom, separated from the rest of the flat by the kitchen or a hallway. The "servant's bathroom" typically has less modern fixtures than the family bathroom: a squat toilet rather than one with a seat, and a shower that drains into a hole in the floor rather than a separate bath or shower stall. If the domestic worker does not have a separate bathroom, the employer often designates certain times for her to use theirs. Many workers are not allowed to keep their things—soap, shampoo, towels—in the family bathroom. In one case, an employer insisted on providing the worker with generic brands of soap and shampoo that could easily be distinguished from the more expensive brands used by the rest of the family.

Many domestic workers do not have private rooms. Some, like Cathy, sleep in the family storeroom. Commonly the "servant's quarters" or "amah room" in a Hong Kong flat resembles a large closet. It is frequently without electrical fixtures, and even if the rest of the flat is air-conditioned, often this room is not. In many apartments, there is a separate back door, back stairs, or back elevator that is most accessible from the kitchen and the "servant's area."

Despite the lack of privacy, some workers consider themselves fortunate to share a bedroom with their employer's children because they are less isolated from the rest of the family and because the rooms are usually nicer. The bedroom may be small, but it is often more comfortable and has better lighting than servant's quarters. Elsa once shared a room with her employer's two young daughters while the Chinese cook slept in the servant's quarters near the kitchen. Elsa was pleased with this arrangement because she was not "kept at a distance" from her employer's family. As she explained, "My room was much better [than that of the Chinese cook] because I am staying in my employer's vicinity. And you know what? If my employer is watching television, and it's English television, they sometimes ask me to watch downstairs [with them]! And we talk, and we make up stories about what we are watching. Or if it is a beauty contest we rate the contestants—like that!" Indeed, Elsa's situation is infinitely better than that of workers who sleep in a hallway or on the kitchen or bathroom floor.

Wherever a domestic worker sleeps, her relationship to her employers' space is also distinguished by the fact that, unlike other members of the household, she is not free to come and go as she pleases. In the most extreme, but not uncommon, cases, domestic workers may be locked inside the flat or in a room of the house. I met several workers who were locked inside without a key on weekdays when their employers went out. At the mission, I read the files of several workers who were treated similarly. Although many employers say they lock domestic workers in to keep them safe, this is obviously false. Otherwise, workers could lock the door themselves or be given a key. Clearly this practice has more to do with keeping the worker in the house and curtailing her freedom.

Not all domestic workers resent their employers' assertion of control. Linda, a thirty-year-old who wore blue jeans and a neatly ironed T-shirt when I met her at Chater Garden one Sunday, worked for four years in Abu Dhabi before coming to Hong Kong in early 1992. She had no complaints about the jobs and employers she had had, and the pay was good in both places. She was happier in Hong Kong because her sister was there. Her Hong Kong employer enforced many strict rules regarding work and dress. Some were written, but most were explained to her verbally. One rule was that she must go to bed at 9:30 and wake up at 6:30. Even if her employers were still awake, she had to be in bed, or in her room with the light out, at 9:30. On her day off she had to be home by 8:30.

I asked her how she felt about all these rules, and she said, "I tell her, 'Thank you ma'am.'" Asked if she minded the restrictions at all, she replied, "No. Why would I?" I answered that some workers in similar situations felt they were treated like children. "No, ma'am. I don't mind," she explained, "because my employer is looking out for me like she does her daughter."

Linda eats with her employer's family. As she describes it, they all serve themselves from the main dishes at the center of the table, but her food is placed ahead of time in a small side dish next to her bowl. Linda said this "special treatment" is probably because her employers noted her shock and disgust the first time she ate with them from the communal dish. A more critical observer, however, might wonder if this is another attempt to establish the worker's place as a subordinate member of the household, rather than an expression of concern for her welfare. As James Watson has illustrated, eating from the same pot serves as a symbol of shared identity among members of the same Chinese lineage.[18] Conversely, being served separately may function as a symbol of exclusion.

In Hong Kong, as elsewhere, domestic workers often express a desire to be treated "like one of the family." But, as Mary Romero points out, the family analogy has a coercive side, as it serves to "distort working conditions" and disguise the exploitative side of the relationship.[19] Many Filipinas expressed their awareness of the coercive side of the familial analogy with a popular joke. This joke, I was told, is often heard in Statue Square, but I learned it as I chatted with a group of domestic workers at the mission. Two women were comparing work situations. One woman complained of overwork, and the other grumbled about her early curfew. A third woman suddenly cut in and said, in a serious tone, "So you're a member of the family too, eh?" The crowd burst out laughing.

What I had heard was the punch line of a longer joke so widely known that the punch line was all that was necessary to evoke laughter. The original joke, as it was told to me, goes like this: A Filipina domestic helper arrives in Hong Kong at the home of her new employer. The employer says to her, "We want to treat you as a member of the family." The domestic helper is very happy to hear this. On Sunday, the helper's day off, her employer says to her, "You must work before you leave the house on Sundays because you are a member of the family." And the employer adds, "And you must come home in time to cook dinner for the family." "But sir, ma'am, I would like to eat with my friends today, because it is my day off," says the helper. "But you are a member of the family," says her employer, "and because you are a member of the family, you must eat with us."

Domestic workers who say they would like to be treated "like a member of the family" refer to the positive way they are treated by their own families in the Philippines—not, as the joke implies, when the rhetoric of "family" is purely coercive. Mrs. Leung told Cathy she would treat her like a younger sister, and said, "You can treat me as your elder sister and my husband is your elder brother, and my daughter—you can treat her as your younger sister." As Cathy reflected, it sounded nice. "But later I thought they treated me lower than an animal sometimes. It was May—summer—and we had a small dog at that time. . . . My room is very hot and I have no electric fan. But our dogs have a fan! They bought it for the dog. . . . They all have air-conditioning. But in my room, I don't even have an electric fan."

Domestic workers may share close relationships with certain family members, but some fairly typical conflicts can develop with others. The employer's mother or mother-in-law often does not get along well with the domestic worker. Mrs. Chin was considered an ideal employer because she was out all day and had no mother or mother-in-law in the house. A *pohpoh* at home all day "is constantly watching to see that her son is getting his money's worth." The tension in this relationship is reminiscent of the tension that once existed between a Chinese mother-in-law and daughter-in-law. The daughter-in-law, however, now goes to work, and the criticism she once endured—over her household duties, her cooking, and her way of raising the children—is transferred to the domestic worker. But the situation is different, because a domestic worker, unlike a daughter-in-law, lacks the support of the husband, which can help to counterbalance the conflicts his wife might have with his mother.

Domestic workers may also bear the brunt of generational conflicts between elderly members of the household and their adult children, who—often because they speak English—are the ones who give instructions to the domestic worker. If an employer goes against his or her parents' wishes and instructs the worker to put less oil, salt, or soy sauce in the cooking, to disallow the children from going outside before they finish their homework, or to do the shopping three times a week rather than every day, the *pohpoh* may direct her dissatisfaction toward the domestic worker. Criticism of the domestic worker, however, does not automatically free the female employer from her mother-in-law's criticism. She may still be held responsible for not having trained, instructed, or disciplined the domestic worker properly.

According to many domestic workers, children are also a source of conflict between employers and workers. As one Filipina explained, workers are in a double bind. If a worker loves the children and the children become fond of her, the mother may become jealous and try to undermine the relationship.[20] To put the domestic worker in her place, some mothers, I was told, tell their children that the domestic worker is "just your maid." Some parents will not punish their children for hitting, kicking, or verbally abusing the domestic worker. One worker reported, "Children are very impolite because they are the same as their parents. Their parents show them how to treat the Filipinas like their *gungyahn* [literally "workers," figuratively "servants"]. So if the parents growl, then the children will growl too."

Jealousy on the part of the female employer, I was told by both domestic workers and some Chinese informants, is a common problem. As a Chinese social worker from the Catholic Centre explained, employers are often mothers working outside their homes for the first time. They may be insecure leaving the housework and child care to someone else. When they realize that their children are getting attached to the domestic worker, they sometimes feel that their position in the family is being undermined. Especially if the domestic worker is young and attractive, and if the wife is also worried about her husband, the female employer may become jealous or hostile toward the domestic helper.

Mrs. Chin says she knows "some women who feel jealous or threatened" by their domestic workers. She speculates that "some uneducated people may feel threatened" because they think Filipinas are "desperate enough to do anything to come to Hong Kong. They fear their maids want to ensnare whatever ugly husband they might have." As Mrs. Chin points out, there is a popular fear in Hong Kong that, for the economic benefits, foreign domestic workers will go to any length to find a man to marry.

In the past, male members of the household entered into sexual relations with *muijai* and other Chinese domestic workers,[21] and at least among the wealthy and elite, extramarital liaisons were expected. But such relationships were extremely unlikely to result in divorce, and only in rare circumstances would such a liaison disempower the first or primary wife. Chinese wives in Hong Kong today, influenced in part by Western romantic ideals, are far less likely to view their husband's affairs with nonchalance.

Elsa's Chinese employer did not see her as a threat, but she confided in Elsa about her fear that her husband would take a "mistress," as his brothers, father, and uncle all had. Like the domestic workers described by Romero, Elsa was expected to listen and to express sympathy, to do "emotional labor" for her employer.[22] As Judith Rollins points out, when an employer confides in a domestic worker, it is not necessarily a sign of equality between them. As a member of a different class and social group, a domestic worker may be a "safe confidante." Confiding in her, Rollins has written, "may, in fact, be evidence of the distance in even the closest of these relationships. Employers can feel free to tell domestics secrets they would not share with their family or friends precisely because the domestic is so far from being socially and psychologically significant to the employer."[23] Elsa described listening, nodding, and trying to empathize with her employer, but she never really considered her a friend.

> When she went to America to arrange her things because the eldest son was going there to study in America, my employer he was not sleeping in the house. And he was playing a trick on us—both maids. Because one time when we came in the house I observed that my employer, the male employer, he put out his shoes, pretending that he came back that night. And so me and my cousin were laughing because he mistakenly put two different kinds of shoes! We were laughing because we didn't care if he is staying out. We will not tell our employer. It's not our business. But we kept laughing and laughing.

Despite the emotional labor she did for her employer, Elsa managed to maintain some "professional distance."[24] Her first commitment was to keeping her job, so she refused to get caught taking sides between her two employers.

Belying the egalitarian implications of being "like a member of the family," domestic workers are often required to address women employers as "ma'am" or "Mrs. So-and-so." Female employers may refer to themselves or be referred to as "mistress." Male employers are most often referred to as "sir," "master," or "Mr. So-and-so." Often domestic workers view their male employers as their silent allies, henpecked by their domineering wives. Although most domestic workers receive instructions from and interact exclusively with female employers, male employers usually sign their contracts. Most share a sense that their male employers are often neutral in domestic affairs and allow their wives to make decisions regarding domestic work; but many nonetheless sense that the man is more on their side. So as to not incur the wrath or jealousy of the female employer, many workers are careful to avoid, as much as possible, any interaction with the men in the household.

———

Like gender, class can be a source of conflict in Hong Kong homes that employ domestic workers. Employers today may be upwardly mobile, or aspiring to be, but most are not among Hong Kong's wealthiest elite. Their middle-class status is often quite recent and may appear precarious to them. In short, the employer's class position may seem uncomfortably close to that of the Filipina domestic workers themselves: women employers often work as schoolteachers, bank tellers, shop clerks, or office staff—occupations that some Filipinas held before coming to Hong Kong.

One Filipina domestic worker with a degree in education felt that her employer, a schoolteacher, acted very cool and condescending. In the Philippines, she said, her female employer could have been her friend, or a teacher at the same school, but in Hong Kong "she is my employer and I am just her maid." Other domestic workers, like some of their employers, were until recently "housewives" who worked in their own homes.

Certain conflicts between employers and workers are directly related to the assumed economic inferiority of domestic workers. From the employer's point of view, the problem is that the worker will not accept her inferior status or behave deferentially. In the course of describing more serious complaints, domestic workers who came to the mission for advice often interjected their hurt feelings about employers who shouted, scolded, shook fingers at them, or called them "only a maid," "just a poor maid," or worse. As one employer bluntly stated, "Of course Filipinas are poor. Why else would they become maids?"

Domestic workers often resent such attitudes. After all, if they receive the wages, food, and lodging stipulated in their contracts, and if they can pay off their recruitment debts and remit a reasonable portion of their salaries home, their families may be quite well off, particularly by Philippine standards. A domestic worker's salary in Hong Kong may be more than that of a doctor, lawyer, or a politician in the Philippines.

I talked to Dally and Rosa, two workers who were staying at the mission-sponsored shelter in Kowloon, about the discomfort they felt when their employers labeled them "poor." Dally told me that she did not deny it when her employer spoke of how poor she must be in the Philippines, even though the characterization was false. "I don't like arguments and shouting," she explained. "But I *want* to say, 'In the Philippines I have a lot of land—but you, you don't have even one cup of land!'" Rosa fumed that her employer generalized about Filipinos on the basis of knowing only Rosa, and even then, for only one month. "I say, 'I've only been here one month and you only know me! Why do you generalize? Why you say that *all* Filipinos?' I say, 'You know, we are not beggars in the Philippines! We are rich in the Philippines, you know?' I said to her, 'Before I came here, do you know what my job was in the Philippines? I was a promotions manager in a business in Manila.'"

Some employers are genuinely shocked to discover that their domestic workers come from comfortable families in the Philippines. Such was the case for Rina and Mrs. Chin. Rina's family is in the jewelry business. Before coming to Hong Kong, she worked as an office manager in Manila. Her aunt had just arrived to work as a domestic helper in Hong Kong, as well, Rina explained, "not because she needs the money" but "because she wants to see Hong Kong." When Rina returned from a holiday in the Philippines, she brought a videotape of her brother's wedding to show to Mrs. Chin's family. Mrs. Chin was surprised at the extravagance of the affair. She described it to me:

> When Rina's brother was married there was a tremendous feast in the Philippines. I think they may be quite well off in the Philippines! They own a farm with lots of ducks. She showed me photographs and all that. When her brother was married she went home and brought all these gifts, and when she came back she brought one of those home movies of the whole wedding. And she very unselfconsciously, you know, put it in our television and showed it to us. I'm very polite. I sat through the whole thing. And then, you know, my husband was struggling to be very polite and making comments. But my children disappeared—to my embarrassment—in the middle of the performance. But she was obviously very proud. She wanted to share this experience and all this. I think she's quite well off. I don't see that there's any cause for resentment. She was an office worker in metro Manila—accounting or something—and made about five hundred dollars a month, which was not too bad.

Fortunately for Rina, her relationship with Mrs. Chin was a secure one. Mrs. Chin and her husband both came from an elite background. Rina's display did not evoke any sense of class insecurity. If anything, they were amused by what they considered a rather conspicuous display, an attempt to impress them that was more befitting the middle class than of the truly wealthy. Other employers might not have taken it so well.

More often domestic workers are like Dally and Rosa. They want to tell their employers a thing or two—that they own land, that they have a house (not just a tiny flat), and that they have maids of their own in the Philippines— but they refrain from doing so because their financial security depends on maintaining the pretense that they are "just poor maids."

After all, timetables, dress codes, restrictions on the use of space, and special eating arrangements, among other household rules and regulations, do not simply control a domestic worker's labor. They also convey the employer's sense of the domestic worker's inferior position, and they clarify social boundaries between employers and domestic workers. Informal rules of this nature are first imposed within the private domain of the household; but they may also extend to the still *more* private domain of a domestic worker's body, personality, voice—even her emotions. Through stories like those of Cathy, Jane, and Christina, however, we can begin to see that domestic workers do not just passively acquiesce to their employers' demands. As often as not, they carefully weigh their options, devising ways to improve their situations and to leave abusive, controlling employers for better ones.

America's Dirty Work:
Migrant Maids and Modern-Day Slavery

Joy M. Zarembka

Imagine you are locked away in a strange home. You do not speak your captor's language. On the rare occasions when you are escorted off the premises, you are forbidden to speak to anyone. You are often fed the leftover food of the children you are required to watch while completing your around-the-clock household duties. You have never been paid for your labors, and the woman of the house physically abuses you.

While this scenario seems to hark back to an earlier time in U.S. history, it describes Noreena Nesa's* recent working conditions in the Washington, D.C., area. Tucked behind the manicured lawns and closed doors of our wealthiest residents live some of the most vulnerable people in the United States: abused migrant domestic workers, who are sometimes the victims of slavery and human trafficking.

Marie Jose Perez, for example, left Bolivia in 1997, excited because she had always dreamed of flying on an airplane and hopeful that she would soon be able to support her family in Bolivia with her wages as a live-in maid. But once her plane landed in Washington, D.C., her employer, a

---

* Some names have been changed.

human rights lawyer for the Organization of American States, confiscated her passport and forced her to work days more than twelve hours long, for less than one dollar per hour. She was not allowed to leave the house without her employer. When a friend of her employer's raped her, the human rights lawyer refused to take her to the hospital, claiming that medical care would be too expensive.

Ruth Gnizako, a fifty-two-year-old West African woman, says she was approached by a wealthy relative who worked for the World Bank. The relative promised her a house and a car if she would come serve as a housekeeper and nanny to his five children in suburban Maryland. When she arrived, she was required to sleep with a pair of one-year-old twins in her arms every night, essentially providing twenty-four-hour care with no days off. When the family went out, Ruth was forced to wait outside, in the hallway of the apartment building, until they returned. Both husband and wife repeatedly beat Ruth, and they ignored her request to return to West Africa.

When neighbors heard Ruth screaming during the beatings, they called the Prince George's County Police Department. But the police were unable to understand her broken French, so they relied on her abusive employers for translation. Ruth attempted to reenact the beatings by gesturing physical blows to herself. Her employers, seeing an opportunity, told the police, "See, she's showing you how she beats herself. She's crazy." Ruth was taken to a local mental institution where she was forcibly sedated, her arms and legs tied to the bedposts. By the time the doctors contacted a French interpreter by phone, Ruth was feeling the effects of the psychoactive drugs, and, in her limited French, she could not manage to recount the traumatic events. Frustrated, the hospital staff called Ruth's employers and asked them to retrieve her.

When Ruth returned to the couple's home, they told her that if she upset them, they would call the police again and send her to the hospital permanently. They went on to claim that the security guard who patrolled the area was specifically sent to monitor her behavior and to make sure she did not harm their children. Intimidated by the barriers of language and culture, and still shaken from her terrifying experience at the mental institution, Ruth believed these threats. She suffered many more solitary months of beatings and servitude before the couple's neighbors finally managed to help her escape and contact the local authorities. In the end, Ruth found herself emotionally unable to participate in the U.S. Justice Department's criminal investigation of her former employers and returned home without collecting a dime.

Global Mothers

Noreena, Marie Jose, and Ruth are among a growing number of migrant women known to suffer under conditions that look very much like slavery after they legally enter the United States as domestic workers. The global economic changes that push women from developing nations to migrate for domestic work have also contributed to the recent rise of domestic worker abuse. Developed countries and international lending organizations such as the International Monetary Fund (IMF) and World Bank often prescribe preconditions for loans to developing countries that include cutting basic social services, devaluing local currencies, and imposing wage freezes. These structural adjustment programs create hardships that are borne most severely by those at the bottom of the economic ladder, a significant proportion of whom are women. The world's poor are often faced with few better options than to leave their home countries in search of work overseas, even if they do so with no assurances and at grave personal risk. Once they arrive in the United States, migrant women are sometimes forced into employment situations to which they did not agree and from which they have no escape.

Modern-day slavery, trafficking, and migrant domestic worker abuse result from the illegal manipulation and deception of hopeful migrants, most of whom believe they are going to the United States in order to better their situations. The new global economy permits transnational corporations and other actors in developed countries to transport capital, labor, goods, and services across state lines with relative ease. In the case of slavery and human trafficking, these goods, services, and labor become one: an unpaid or poorly paid person becomes a commodity that can be used again and again for accumulating profit. Traffickers tell migrants that they will earn many times more money abroad than they could at home. If they were employed by law-abiding people, these workers could indeed increase their earnings. Dora Mortey, an articulate Ghanaian schoolteacher, was one of those who believed the odds were on her side. Little did she know she would be worked around the clock as a nanny and housekeeper, and paid only around forty cents an hour.

Dora had signed an employment agreement with a World Bank official in Ghana. Nonetheless, when she got to the Washington area, she was handed a daily schedule that began at 5:45 A.M. and ended at 9:30 P.M., far exceeding the agreed-upon forty-hour workweek. After four months of working for only $100 a month, Dora asked that her contract be honored. The family decided to terminate her services and put her on the next plane to Ghana. She managed to escape from the moving car as her employer drove her to the airport; but the employer scratched an 'X' across her visa and promptly delivered her passport to the Immigration and Naturalization Service (INS), requesting her immediate arrest and deportation. Uncertain what to do, Dora took a cab from Washington to New Jersey to seek refuge with the one person she knew in the United States. Back at the airport, an astute INS official suspected foul play. Eventually, Dora was granted a stay of deportation while she pursued legal action against her former employers.

Each year, thousands of domestic workers like Dora enter the United States on special visas issued by the U.S. State Department. Foreign nationals, diplomats, officials of international agencies, and, in some cases, U.S. citizens with permanent residency abroad, are permitted to "import" domestic help on A-3, G-5, and B-1 visas. Nearly four thousand A-3 and G-5 visas are issued annually—A-3 visas for household employees of diplomats and G-5 visas for employees of international agencies such as the World Bank, IMF, and United Nations. The B-1 visa is a catch-all business category that, in part, allows other foreign nationals and American citizens with permanent residency abroad the option of bringing household employees with them when they visit the United States. Every year, 200,000 B-1 visas are issued, but the State Department does not keep records of B-1 domestic workers. As a result, their locations and working conditions remain particularly obscure. And the B-1 domestic workers may be at special risk for exploitation. All three visa types list the name of the worker's legal employer, but unlike the A-3 and G-5 visa holders, B-1 domestic workers have no option of legally transferring to another employer. They are left with few alternatives if they are enslaved or abused.

Even for A-3 and G-5 domestic workers, who are allowed to transfer to other diplomats or international officials, it is often difficult to find a suitable employer while suffering in an exploitative arrangement. Although the State Department, embassies, and international institutions involved (including the IMF, World Bank, and UN) keep records of the whereabouts of A-3 and G-5 domestic workers, this information is classified as confidential, for the privacy of the employer. Domestic violence and anti-incest advocates have challenged the privacy justification on the grounds that a lot of abuse occurs behind closed doors; other advocates have argued that in addition to being domiciles, these homes are also workplaces, subject to employment standards. Nonetheless, social service agencies remain uninformed of the whereabouts of domestic workers, which leaves them unable to prevent abuse or act on it before it is too late.

Patterns

Abuse and exploitation follow such uncannily predictable patterns that many in the social service world almost wonder if there is an "Abusers Manual" being circulated like samizdat. Typically, when the woman arrives in the United States, her employer illegally confiscates her passport and other travel documents. If the worker signed an official contract in a U.S. embassy abroad, that contract is often replaced with a new contract that stipulates longer hours and lower pay. Even the false contract is often subsequently ignored. Although U.S. labor law dictates that all workers be paid at least minimum wage, it is not uncommon to hear reports of women being paid fifty cents or a dollar an hour—in some cases, nothing at all. With yearly salaries at the World Bank and IMF averaging over $120,000 tax-free, the income disparity is striking, especially in situations where domestic workers are told that all or part of their meager wage is being withheld to offset their room and board.

Many women find themselves working nearly around the clock, seven days a week. The exploitative employer usually tells the worker that she may not leave the house unaccompanied, use the telephone, make friends, or even converse with others. The worker is often denied health insurance and social security, even if these benefits have been deducted from her pay. Some domestic workers are subjected to physical battery and sexual assault; others who have serious health conditions are denied medical treatment, which can result in long-term illness. Some domestic workers are given as gifts to the mistresses of diplomats, or traded and loaned out to American families who further exploit them. One Ghanaian woman reported that her employer's American wife referred to her not by name but rather as "the Creature." Yet another woman reported being called "the Slave." Others have been required to sleep on the floor, sometimes in the kitchen, laundry room, or unfurnished basement. An Ivy League professor, who paid her domestic worker $40 a month, slapped her for smoking outside. One domestic worker reported that she was made to kiss her employer's feet. A Malawian man recalls being forced to bathe in a bucket in the backyard rather than in the home of his American employer. A Filipina was forced to wear a dog collar and, at times, sleep outside with the family's dogs.

Typically, if an abused domestic worker complains, the employer threatens to send her home or turn her over to the police. The employer may also threaten to retaliate against her family if she speaks out; on several occasions, family members have been contacted and harassed after a domestic worker has escaped from an abusive situation. Legal issues in the United States also militate against leaving exploitative jobs: women who flee abusive employers are immediately considered "out of status," ineligible for other employment, and liable to be deported by the Immigration and Naturalization Service. As one neighbor who helped a Haitian domestic worker escape says, "When she ran away, she was out of a job, out of money, out of a home, out of status, and, quite frankly, out of her mind."

While some abusive employers use violence and the threat of violence to keep their domestic workers captive, others rely on psychological coercion. In one recent case, Hilda Rosa Dos Santos, a dark-skinned housekeeper from Brazil, was trapped for twenty years, with no pay and insufficient food, in the home of a Brazilian couple who convinced her that Americans disliked black people so intensely that she would likely be raped or killed if she went outside. Similarly, an Indonesian maid was informed by her Saudi Arabian bosses that Americans disliked Muslims so much that it was unsafe for her to leave the house. Abusive employers often point to violence on television to bolster claims about the dangers of American life. Unfamiliar with the English language or with American culture and laws, these women live as prisoners in the homes they clean.

Many women suffer in silence because they do not know their rights, nor do they have any idea where to go to seek help. Some may leave an abusive situation only to find themselves in even worse circumstances. Consider Tigris Bekele, who quickly found herself in jail on two felony counts of child abuse and grand larceny, all because she fled her job as a live-in maid after being exploited, sexually harassed, and threatened. Unfortunately, the day she decided to escape from her abusive employer, there was a bomb scare at the employer's children's school. The children were sent home at 10:00 A.M., a time when Tigris was not required to work as a nanny. But finding themselves alone, the children called the Virginia police. Tigris was arrested for leaving the children unattended.

The police record does not mention that Tigris was paid only $100 a week for around-the-clock chores because her Middle Eastern employer claimed that "that was enough money for a black person." Nowhere does it mention that the man of the house attempted to fondle and kiss her on various occasions. Nor does it mention that the woman of the house forced her to cut her hair and stop wearing makeup, threatening to kill Tigris if she had sex with her husband. Instead, the police record indicates that she is being held on $20,000 bail. It states that she allegedly stole a piece of jewelry, a claim that is often wielded against runaway domestic workers. Her employers had confiscated her passport and visa; when Tigris scoured the house to "steal" her belongings back, her employers accused her of stealing their personal effects.

Even though she came legally to the United States on a domestic worker visa program, if Tigris is convicted, she will be deported to her home country in East Africa, where she is fleeing political persecution. Tigris had been sending remittances to her father, and she has recently learned from relatives that she will be arrested if she returns because the government claims that the money is being used to launch political opposition. A felony conviction in the United States will automatically render it impossible for her to seek asylum here. While some domestic workers end up in court seeking judgments against their abusers, Tigris finds herself on the wrong side of the courtroom.

A Comparison

Some migrant workers who come to the United States to perform child care and light housework do so as participants in another, markedly different visa program. The congressionally sponsored au pair program—au pair means "an equal" in French—largely recruits young, middle-class women from Europe for "educational and cultural exchange" on J-1 visas. Ava Sudek, from the Czech Republic, experienced life in the United States both as a J-1 and as an A-3 visa holder. She thoroughly enjoyed her time as a J-1 au pair and thoroughly despised her time as an A-3 domestic worker. Ava's experience with the two visa programs highlights their striking dissimilarity.

When Ava arrived as an au pair, she was flown to a New York hotel for a week-long orientation session. There she was introduced to other nannies who would be living in the same region, so that they could form a network of friendships. Once she joined the employer's family, she attended another orientation program, where she received information on community resources and educational opportunities, as well as the contact numbers of other nannies in her local support network. Every month, she and her employers were required to check in with a counselor, who would help them resolve any disputes that arose or report any problems.

After completing a successful year with her au pair family, Ava decided to stay on an A-3 visa and work as a domestic worker for a French diplomat's family. There were no orientations, no information booklets, no contact numbers, no counselors, and no educational programs. In practice, for A-3 domestic workers, there is often no freedom. Ava felt like she was being held captive. She was not allowed to leave the house even during her off hours without a day's advance notice. Work hours and nonwork hours blurred together. When she asked for days off, her employers often refused to grant her request, telling her, "Perhaps another time." They did not pay her overtime. Within a month of obtaining her A-3 visa, Ava fled for the Czech Republic, where she dreamed of opening an au pair agency in her hometown. She did not bother to try to collect the overtime wages she was owed: her employer, as a high-level diplomat, was protected by diplomatic immunity.

Ava had the opportunity to hold both a J-1 and an A-3 visa, but few women of color from developing countries are so lucky. Most of them migrate on A-3, B-1, or G-5 visas, which do not come remotely close to offering the protections or the comforts J-1 visas provide European women. The different policies governing the temporary workers on these two visa programs are thick with racist and classist implications. Simply put, women of color in the domestic worker program deserve the same safety net and rigorous oversight granted to white women in the nanny program.

Solutions

Theoretically, the domestic worker visa program provides a window of opportunity for people from developing countries to enter the United States and earn a decent wage. What the program fails to do, however, is to ensure adequate protection for its visa holders. One simple improvement would be to establish independent monitoring and counseling like that which is provided to au pairs. Access to independent social workers, lawyers, and monitors would furnish live-in domestic workers with a system of safeguards to protect their legal rights and ensure employer compliance with contract conditions and labor laws.

By and large, migrant domestic workers belong to a hidden work force tucked away in private homes. Severe cases of domestic worker abuse differ from other cases of slavery and trafficking, such as those uncovered in brothels, farms, and sweatshops, because workers under the latter conditions have contact with one another. Each domestic worker, by contrast, is employed by an individual boss. Not only are the workers without peer support, but their cases involve no smuggling or trafficking rings for law enforcement to target for investigation. The result is that less attention is paid to these seemingly isolated incidents.

Far from their home countries, abused domestic workers are cut off from their families and their cultures, not to mention the protection that social networks and familiar institutions would provide. Many abusive employers incur the expense of hiring overseas precisely for this reason: they believe that they can increasingly control non-English speaking help. Such workers are less likely to run away in the United States. Lack of familiarity with the American legal system also works to the disadvantage of abused domestic workers.

So where do these workers turn for help? A loose network of churches, lawyers, social service agencies, and good Samaritans have formed a modern-day underground railroad for women attempting to escape abusive employers. Because some domestic workers are only allowed out of the house on Sundays, churches are frequently a first stop on the path to freedom. One Catholic sister has files on several hundred G-5 and A-3 workers she has assisted over the years, beginning in the 1970s. Other good Samaritans have just happened to take initiatives when they've encountered domestic workers in need. Street vendors, taxicab drivers, neighbors, and complete strangers have been known to assist domestic workers in distress. Social service organizations and pro bono lawyers then help domestic workers with housing, medical care, mental health needs, and legal assistance.

Policy on matters affecting domestic workers has improved, but there are still troubling gaps in the protections these workers receive. Congress passed trafficking legislation in 2000 that allows federal law enforcement to convict not only traffickers who control their victims by force but also those who coerce workers by means of threats, psychological abuse, fraud, or deception. Domestic workers who bring criminal claims (such as sexual and physical abuse, or psychological coercion) against their former employers are granted work authorization, while domestic workers with civil claims (back pay, overtime, and the like) remain out of status and are considered illegal. Although the INS often turns a blind eye to out-of-status G-5, A-3, and B-1 domestic workers with civil claims, the threat of deportation and the lack of work authorization makes it unappealing for these workers to seek legal redress. It is time-consuming and difficult to find a pro bono lawyer, and migrants who come to the United States as temporary workers often have families to feed in their home countries; they are not really at liberty to sit around waiting for lengthy and uncertain court proceedings. Moreover, domestic workers with civil cases are so vulnerable and have so little bargaining power that they are sometimes re-enslaved as they wait out the long court process without job or housing options. It is certainly disheartening to think that a migrant domestic worker in a potentially violent situation is legally better off staying and getting beaten because she will later be able to receive a work permit, social services, and legal status. If she leaves before violence erupts, she receives nothing.

No shelters currently exist in the United States for trafficked women, and this remains one of the biggest obstacles facing nongovernmental organizations (NGOs) that attempt to assist domestic workers. NGOs sometimes have to ask women who are not in grave physical danger to stay in their exploitative situations while advocates scramble to find culturally appropriate housing. The Justice Department faces a small housing crisis every time a new criminal case involving trafficking is filed. On one occasion, police dropped a domestic worker on the private doorstep of an NGO worker in the middle of the night, for lack of housing alternatives.

Because few housing options are available to abused domestic workers, NGOs often turn to ethnic communities for assistance with housing, clothing, medical care, and mental health needs. Most of these communities are small and tight-knit. This presents a safety risk for some domestic workers, who find temporary housing in their ethnic communities only to be easily located by their abusers, who sometimes hail from the same background and know those communities well. Most domestic violence shelters will not accommodate domestic workers because they were not beaten by romantic partners; most homeless shelters refuse to assist due to language barriers and lack of beds. Domestic workers often end up relying on compassionate strangers— everyday people who open their homes and hearts to individuals in need.

Fortunately, advocates and domestic workers have been organizing to find solutions to these problems at both the policy and the grassroots levels. Groups such as CASA de Maryland's Mujeres Unidas de Maryland (United Women of Maryland) are forming workplace cooperatives to advocate for improved conditions for all workers. Former and current domestic workers take to the streets, parks, buses, and churches looking for potentially abused domestic workers and educating them about their rights, using Spanish-language legal literature. When a volunteer encounters an exploited employee, she directs her to bilingual legal assistance. The increase in outreach has resulted in an increase in the number of reported cases of domestic worker abuse. Mujeres Unidas has developed self-esteem classes, in which formerly abused or exploited domestic workers extend their support to others suffering under similar circumstances. The group has now formed a twenty-four-member, democratically controlled cleaning cooperative whose goal is to provide dignified day jobs and equitable working conditions. Most impressive, 10 percent of all the cleaning service's proceeds are funneled to social justice organizations.

While most members of Mujeres Unidas are Latina, other ethnically based organizations in the Washington, D.C., area are also engaged in efforts to curb domestic worker abuse; among them are a Filipina organization, Shared Communities, and the Ethiopian Community Development Council. More than twenty-five Washington-based organizations have joined forces to create the Campaign for Migrant Domestic Workers Rights (now Break the Chain Campaign), a coalition whose aim is to change public policy and to strengthen the safety net available to G-5, A-3, and B-1 domestic workers. These efforts involve lawyers, feminists, labor activists, human rights activists, community-based organizations, and social service agencies.

Related campaigns have sprung up elsewhere in the country. In New York, groups such as Andolan, Worker's Awaaz, and the Committee Against Anti-Asian Violence's Women Workers Project are working together; and in California, the Coalition Against Slavery and Trafficking, and the Korean Immigrant Workers Advocates, address similar issues. Workers rights' clinics in Washington, Los Angeles, and New York often provide relief to individuals escaping slavelike conditions. A nationwide Freedom Network (USA) to Empower Enslaved and Trafficked Persons recently formed in response to incidents of trafficking and slavery uncovered among laborers and sex workers.

Noreena, Marie Jose, Ruth, Dora, Hilda, Tigris, and Ava were all able to seek assistance from concerned neighbors, lawyers, and advocates. But it remains unclear how many other women currently toil in isolation, unpaid and abused. In the 1970s, the battered women's movement established a network of advocacy groups and shelters for women who were abused by their spouses; the movement even managed, through arduous grassroots efforts, to change public policy and public consciousness about domestic violence. Its work is not done. But the groups that have committed their time and resources to assisting trafficked and enslaved domestic workers have only now embarked on a similar movement: they are building a new underground railroad, one stretch of track at a time.

Selling Sex for Visas:
Sex Tourism as a Stepping-stone to
International Migration

Denise Brennan

On the eve of her departure for Germany to marry her German client-turned-boyfriend, Andrea, a Dominican sex worker, spent the night with her Dominican boyfriend.[1] When I dropped by the next morning to wish her well, her Dominican boyfriend was still asleep. She stepped outside, onto her porch. She could not lie about her feelings for her soon-to-be husband. "No," she said, "it's not love." But images of an easier life for herself and her two daughters compelled her to migrate off the island and out of poverty. She put love aside—at least temporarily.[2]

Andrea, like many Dominican sex workers in Sosúa, a small town on the north coast of the Dominican Republic, makes a distinction between marriage *por amor* (for love) and marriage *por residencia* (for visas). After all, why waste a marriage certificate on romantic love when it can be transformed into a visa to a new land and economic security?

Since the early 1990s, Sosúa has been a popular vacation spot for male European sex tourists, especially Germans. Poor women migrate from throughout the Dominican Republic to work in Sosúa's sex trade; there, they hope to meet and marry foreign men who will sponsor their migration to Europe. By migrating to Sosúa, these women are engaged in an economic strategy that is both familiar and altogether new: they are attempting to capitalize on the very global linkages that exploit them. These poor single mothers are not simply using sex work in a tourist town with European clients as a survival strategy; they are using it as an *advancement* strategy.

The key aims of this strategy are marriage and migration off the island. But even short of these goals, Sosúa holds out special promise to its sex workers, who can establish ongoing transnational relationships with the aid of technologies such as fax machines at the phone company in town (the foreign clients and the women communicate about the men's return visits in this manner) and international money wires from clients overseas. Sosúa's sex trade also stands apart from that of many other sex-tourist destinations in the developing world in that it does not operate through pimps, nor is it tied to the drug trade; young women are not trafficked to Sosúa, and as a result they maintain a good deal of control over their working conditions.

Certainly, these women still risk rape, beatings, and arrest; the sex trade is dangerous, and Sosúa's is no exception. Nonetheless, Dominican women are not coerced into Sosúa's trade but rather end up there through networks of female family members and friends who have worked there. Without pimps, sex workers keep all their earnings; they are essentially working freelance. They can choose the bars and nightclubs in which to hang out, the number of hours they work, the clients with whom they will work, and the amount of money to charge.

There has been considerable debate over whether sex work can be anything but exploitative. The stories of Dominican women in Sosúa help demonstrate that there is a wide range of experiences within the sex trade, some of them beneficial, others tragic.[3] As Anne McClintock writes, "Depicting all sex workers as slaves only travesties the myriad, different experiences of sex workers around the world. At the same time, it theoretically confuses social *agency* and identity with social *context*."[4] I have been particularly alarmed at the media's monolithic portrayal of sex workers in sex-tourist destinations, such as Cuba, as passive victims easily lured by the glitter of consumer goods. These overly simplistic and implicitly moralizing stories deny that poor women are capable of making their own labor choices.[5] The women I encountered in Sosúa had something else to say.

Sex Workers and Sex Tourists

Sex workers in Sosúa are at once independent and dependent, resourceful and exploited. They are local agents caught in a web of global economic relations. To the extent that they can, they try to take advantage of the men who are in Sosúa to take advantage of them. The European men who frequent Sosúa's bars might see Dominican sex workers as exotic and erotic because of their dark skin color; they might pick one woman over another in the crowd, viewing them all as commodities for their pleasure and control. But Dominican sex workers often see the men, too, as readily exploitable—potential dupes, walking visas, means by which the women might leave the island, and poverty, behind.

Even though only a handful of women have actually married European men and migrated off the island, the possibility of doing so inspires women to move to Sosúa from throughout the island and to take up sex work. Once there, however, Dominican sex workers are beholden to their European clients to deliver visa sponsorships, marriage proposals, and airplane tickets. Because of the differential between sex workers and their clients in terms of mobility, citizenship, and socioeconomic status, these Dominican sex workers might seem to occupy situations parallel to those that prevail among sex workers throughout the developing world. Indeed, I will recount stories here of disappointment, lies, and unfulfilled dreams. Yet some women make modest financial gains through Sosúa's sex trade—gains that exceed what they could achieve working in export-processing zones or domestic service, two common occupations among poor Dominican women. These jobs, on average, yield fewer than 1,000 pesos ($100) a month, whereas sex workers in Sosúa charge approximately 500 pesos for each encounter with a foreign client.

Sex tourism, it is commonly noted, is fueled by the fantasies of white, First-World men who exoticize dark-skinned "native" bodies in the developing world, where they can buy sex for cut-rate prices. These two components—racial stereotypes and the economic disparity between the developed and the developing worlds—characterize sex-tourist destinations everywhere. But male sex tourists are not the only ones who travel to places like Sosúa to fulfill their fantasies. Many Dominican sex workers look to their clients as sources not only of money, marriage, and visas, but also of greater gender equity than they can hope for in the households they keep with Dominican men. Some might hope for romance and love, but most tend to fantasize about greater resources and easier lives.

Yet even for the women with the most pragmatic expectations, there are few happy endings. During the time I spent with sex workers in Sosúa, I, too, became invested in the fantasies that sustained them through their struggles. Although I learned to anticipate their return from Europe, disillusioned and divorced, I continued to hope that they would find financial security and loving relationships. Similarly, Sosúa's sex workers built their fantasies around the stories of their few peers who managed to migrate as the girl-friends or wives of European tourists—even though nearly all of these women returned, facing downward mobility when they did so. Though only a handful of women regularly receive money wires from clients in Europe, the stories of those who do circulate among sex workers like Dominicanized versions of Hollywood's *Pretty Woman*.

The women who pursue these fantasies in Sosúa tend to be pushed by poverty and single motherhood. Of the fifty women I interviewed and the scores of others I met, only two were not mothers. The practice of consensual unions (of not marrying but living together), common among the poor in the Dominican Republic, often leads to single motherhood, which then puts women under significant financial pressure. Typically, these women receive no financial assistance from their children's fathers. I met very few sex workers who had sold sex before migrating to Sosúa, and I believe that the most decisive factor propelling these women into the sex trade is their status as single mothers. Many women migrated to Sosúa within days of their partners' departure from the household and their abandonment of their financial obligations to their children.

Most women migrated from rural settings with meager job oppor-tunities, among them sporadic agricultural work, low-wage hairstyling out of one's home, and waitressing. The women from Santo Domingo, the nation's capital, had also held low-paying jobs, working in domestic service or in *zonas francas* (export-processing zones). Women who sell sex in Sosúa earn more money, more quickly than they can in any other legal job available to poor women with limited educations (most have not finished school past their early teens) and skill bases. These women come from *los pobres*, the poorest class in the Dominican Republic, and they simply do not have the social networks that would enable them to land work, such as office jobs, that offer security or mobility. Rather, their female-based social networks can help them find factory jobs, domestic work, restaurant jobs, or sex work.

Sex work offers women the possibility of making enough money to start a savings account while covering their own expenses in Sosúa and their children's expenses back home. These women tend to leave their children in the care of female family members, but they try to visit and to bring money at least once a month. If their home communities are far away and expensive to get to, they return less frequently. Those who manage to save money use it to buy or build homes back in their home communities. Alternatively, they might try to start small businesses, such as *colmados* (small grocery stores), out of their homes.

While saving money is not possible in factory or domestic work, sex workers, in theory at least, make enough money to build up modest savings. In practice, however, it is costly to live in Sosúa. Rooms in boardinghouses rent for 30 to 50 pesos a day, while apartments range from 1,500 to 3,000 pesos a month, and also incur start-up costs that most women cannot afford (such as money for a bed and cooking facilities). Since none of the boardinghouses have kitchens, women must spend more for take-out or restaurant meals. On top of these costs, they must budget for bribes to police officers (for release from jail), since sex workers usually are arrested two to five times a month. To make matters worse, the competition for clients is so fierce, particularly during the low-volume tourist seasons, that days can go by before a woman finds a client. Many sex workers earn just enough to cover their daily expenses in Sosúa while sending home modest remittances for their children. Realizing this, and missing their children, most women return to their home communities in less than a year, just as poor as when they first arrived.

In order to grasp why Dominican women would use the sex trade in Sosúa as a way to migrate overseas, it helps to consider how the past three decades of Dominican migration to New York have led many Dominicans to look *outside* (*fuera*) for solutions to economic problems *inside* Dominican borders. So adept are Dominicans at migrating off the island that Ninna Sørensen even calls them "natives" to transnational space.[6] The quest for a visa to Canada, the United States, and now to Europe is virtually a national pastime. The Dominican musician Juan Luis Guerra captures this preoccupation with *fuera* and the visas to get there in his hit song *Visa para un sueño* (Visa for a Dream). One of Eugenia Georges's[7] interviewees summed up how class and opportunity are tied to migration networks to New York: "In the Dominican Republic there are three kinds of people: the rich, the poor, and those who travel to New York." Some would-be migrants are so desperate to get off the island that they take dangerous *yolas* (small boats or rafts) to Puerto Rico. Feigning love appears, at the very least, to be less risky.

The sex workers I interviewed, who generally have no immediate family members abroad, have never had reliable transnational resources available to them. Not only do they not receive remittances but they cannot migrate legally through family sponsorship. Sex workers' transnational romantic ties act as surrogate family-migration networks. Consequently, migration to Sosúa from other parts of the Dominican Republic can be seen as both internal and international, since Sosúa is a stepping-stone to migration to other countries. For some poor young women, hanging out in the tourist bars of Sosúa is a better use of their time than waiting in line at the United States embassy in Santo Domingo. Carla, a first-time sex worker, explained why Sosúa draws women from throughout the country: "We come here because we dream of a ticket," she said, referring to an airline ticket. But without a visa—which they can obtain through marriage—that airline ticket is of little use.

If sex workers build their fantasies around their communities' experiences of migration, the fantasies sex tourists hope to enact in Sosúa are often first suggested through informal networks of other sex tourists. Sosúa first became known among European tourists by word of mouth. Most of the sex tourists I met in Sosúa had been to other sex-tourist destinations as well. These seasoned sex tourists, many of whom told me that they were "bored" with other destinations, decided to try Sosúa and Dominican women based on the recommendations of friends. This was the case for a group of German sex tourists who were drinking at a bar on the beach. They nodded when the German bar owner explained, "Dominican girls like to fuck." One customer chimed in, "With German women it's over quickly. But Dominican women have fiery blood. . . . When the sun is shining it gives you more hormones."

The Internet is likely to increase the traffic of both veteran and first-time sex tourists to previously little-known destinations like Sosúa. On-line travel services provide names of "tour guides" and local bars in sex-tourism hot spots. On the World Sex Guide, a Web site on which sex tourists share information about their trips, one sex tourist wrote that he was impressed by the availability of "dirt cheap colored girls" in Sosúa, while another gloated, "When you enter the discos, you feel like you're in heaven! A tremendous number of cute girls and something for everyone's taste (if you like colored girls like me)!"

As discussions and pictures of Dominican women proliferate on the Internet sites—for "travel services" for sex tourists, pen-pal services, and even cyber classified advertisements in which foreign men "advertise" for Dominican girlfriends or brides—Dominican women are increasingly often associated with sexual availability. A number of articles in European magazines and newspapers portray Dominican women as sexually voracious. The German newspaper *Express* even published a seven-day series on the sex trade in Sosúa, called "Sex, Boozing, and Sunburn," which included this passage: "Just going from the street to the disco—there isn't any way men can take one step alone. Prostitutes bend over, stroke your back and stomach, and blow you kisses in your ear. If you are not quick enough, you get a hand right into the fly of your pants. Every customer is fought for, by using every trick in the book."[8] A photo accompanying one of the articles in this series shows Dieter, a sex tourist who has returned to Sosúa nine times, sitting at a German-owned bar wearing a T-shirt he bought in Thailand; the shirt is emblazoned with the words SEX TOURIST.

With all the attention in the European press and on the Internet associating Dominican women with the sex industry, fear of a stigma has prompted many Dominican women who never have been sex workers to worry that the families and friends of their European boyfriends or spouses might wonder if they once were. And since Dominican women's participation in the overseas sex trade has received so much press coverage in the Dominican Republic,[9] women who have lived or worked in Europe have become suspect at home. "I know when I tell people I was really with a folk-dance group in Europe, they don't believe me," a former dancer admitted. When Sosúans who were not sex workers spoke casually among themselves of a woman working overseas as a domestic, waitress, or dancer, they inevitably would raise the possibility of sex work, if only to rule it out explicitly. One Dominican café owner cynically explained why everyone assumes that Dominican women working overseas must be sex workers: "Dominican women have become known throughout the world as prostitutes. They are one of our biggest exports."

"Love" in a Global World:
Transnational Courtship

Sex workers the world over pretend that they desire their clients and enjoy the sex; it is one of the defining charades of the industry.[10] In Sosúa, sex workers also pretend to be in love. They have staked much on this performance. Maintaining transnational ties becomes a daily task for some sex workers. Many correspond by fax with four or five foreign clients at the same time (it costs under a dollar to send or receive a fax at Codetel, the national phone company). Dropping by the Codetel office to see if they have received any faxes is a daily ritual for these women. The lucky ones receive faxes instructing them to pick up money at the Western Union office in downtown Sosúa. Others receive word that their European sweethearts are planning a return visit. The most envied women receive "letters of invitation," the first step to obtaining a tourist visa.

In the faxes the women send, they typically express how much they miss the men, and they urge them to return to Sosúa on their next vacation. They might also mention that they need money for their children and remind the men that there is a Western Union in town. Some sex workers have become so adept at capitalizing on the resources available to them that novices come to them for advice. At the top of this hierarchy are sex workers who can read and write and who have a proven track record of receiving money wires or faxes from clients. One such sex worker, Elena, has given a lot of advice and even helped compose letters and faxes for sex workers who were uncertain what to do with the addresses, fax numbers, and telephone numbers clients gave them. She helped Carmen, for example, write a letter to a Belgian client who had sent her a money wire and then abruptly stopped corresponding with her. Carmen came to Elena because, at the time, Elena was living with Jürgen, a German man and former client. She was experienced, indeed successful, at transnational courting. Elena's advice was simple: "You have to write that you *love* him and that you miss him. Write that you cannot wait to see him again. Tell him you think about him every day." Following Elena's guidelines, Carmen composed the following letter, which I helped her translate into English, since her client's English was better than his Spanish:

Dear——

I have been thinking of you every day and have been waiting for a fax to hear how you are. I got your money wire, thanks. But I still want to see you. Please send me a fax at the following number . . . and, if possible, a fax number where I can reach you.

I miss you very much and think of you all the time. I love you very much.

I wait to hear from you. I hope you come to visit again very soon.

Many kisses,
Carmen

Carmen never heard from this client again.

Since women can enlist the help of friends who are more literate than they are, being able to read and write is not a critical skill in transnational courting. Sensing which men are unmarried, likely to continue corresponding, and likely to return for future vacations proves a more valuable—and elusive—skill. While sorting through all the pictures and letters of her European clients, Nanci, for example, commented on which ones seemed the most serious about keeping in touch. She pronounced several too young, and thus unlikely to follow through on the relationship. Of course, even those sex workers who are veterans of transnational dating cannot easily predict their European clients' actions (or inactions). Yet some seem better at assessing their prospects than others. Nora, who had never received an international fax or letter, kept a German client's business card among her valuables. He had not responded to the numerous faxes she'd sent him, but she clung to his card as if it were a winning lottery ticket. Many of her coworkers, by contrast, quickly begin cultivating new relationships when faced with a client's silence.

Of course, not all sex workers in Sosúa are solely motivated by the prospect of migrating off the island. Some women go to great lengths to establish relationships with European men because they seek an alternative to Dominican machismo. They hope that foreign husbands will be more reliable financial providers and more sexually faithful. As we will see in Elena's story below, Dominican sex workers often dismiss foreign men's imperfections, describing these men in idealized terms. It was only toward the end of Elena's relationship with Jürgen, when his drinking was obviously out of control, that her friends finally admitted that, like the Dominican men they constantly criticized, Jürgen was trouble.

Sex Workers' Stories

Elena, twenty-two when I met her, had initially migrated from the country-side to Sosúa's sex trade after the father of her baby girl left her. She followed her older sister, who was also working in the sex trade at the time. Elena became the main breadwinner for her extended family. She brought remittances back home to pay her parents' monthly *colmado* bill, and she eventually became the surrogate mother for two younger sisters, a stepsister, and a younger sex worker who came to rely on her. All these girls, plus Elena and her daughter, lived in a one-room shack, where they rotated between sharing the bed and sleeping on the floor.

In addition to being generous, Elena was a leader to whom other women in the community turned for advice. It was little surprise to her friends that she, literate and savvy, turned a fax relationship with a middle-aged German man into what many of them called a "marriage." After returning several times to spend time with Elena, Jürgen decided to move to Sosúa. He would return to Germany only a few months out of the year to supervise his construction company, which would support him for the rest of the year in his new Caribbean lifestyle.

To Elena and her friends, she appeared to be living out a fantasy: she had quit sex work and set up house with a German man. Elena's friends and her older sisters envied the two-bedroom apartment with running water, electricity, and a full kitchen that she, Jürgen, and all of her dependents (her daughter and three younger sisters) now inhabited. But her actual relationship with Jürgen was far from ideal. Soon after Jürgen moved to town, Elena found out that she was pregnant. At first, he was helpful around the house and doted on Elena. But the novelty eventually wore off, and he returned to his routine of spending most days drinking in the German-owned bar beneath their apartment. He also went out drinking every night with German friends.

Most of the time he was drunk, and Elena saw him less and less frequently. What's more, he did not treat her any better than the previous Dominican men in her life had. The couple constantly fought over money, which Jürgen controlled tightly. Since they were living together and Jürgen was paying the bills (including private-school tuition for her daughter), Elena considered them to be married. As her "husband" (in a consensual union), Jürgen was financially responsible for the household, in Elena's view; but she felt that he was not fulfilling this role. "Why isn't he giving me any money? He is my *esposo* (husband) and is supposed to give me money," she complained to me. "I need to know if he is with me or someone else. He pays for this house and paid for everything here. I need to know what is going on."

They fought so regularly that Elena started sleeping on the couch. One day, without warning, Jürgen packed his bags and left for Germany on business. Elena had no cash flow into the household. In Jürgen's absence, Elena took her daughter out of private school, since the tuition was overdue. She started working at a small Dominican-owned restaurant. When Jürgen returned a couple of months later, they split up for good. Elena and her family returned to living in a shack without running water or electricity. She had not accumulated any savings or items she could pawn during her time with Jürgen. When they vacated their apartment, he took most of the furniture, and the television, with him.

In many ways, Elena had been better off, financially and emotionally, before she'd met Jürgen. Even though she appeared to have all the coveted trappings that come with "marrying" a foreign tourist, she ended up returning to the same conditions of poverty as before. What's more, her relationship with a foreign man replicated many of the failings sex workers so often criticize in their relationships with Dominican men. Jürgen turned out to be a volatile alcoholic who slept with other women, thus putting Elena, and possibly her baby, at risk for acquiring AIDS. Moreover, soon after he returned to Sosúa, Jürgen set up house with another sex worker. He now lives, Elena hears, somewhere in Asia.

Elena's experience with Jürgen raises an important question: to what degree are the sex workers' fantasies about foreign men shaped by the experience of migrating to Sosúa? Studies reveal that the experience of migration, combined with wage labor, often increases women's social and economic independence and status.[11] Dominican women who migrate internally for the sex trade, however, find their gender roles both reaffirmed and reconfigured. Although the sex trade allows women to outearn male Dominican migrants in Sosúa, they lack any similar source of authority or independence in their relationships with foreign men. In fact, they become completely dependent on these men, not only for money but often for much else.

The case of Nanci, a sex worker who moved to Germany, illustrates this phenomenon. Unlike most sex workers, who explain their transnational relationships in terms of economic strategy, Nanci recounted a love story. "This is completely for love," she gushed. Frank was a German man close to her age (she was twenty-three, and he, twenty-eight); he spoke Spanish and got along well with her three-year-old son; he bought her a plane ticket and helped her get a tourist visa so she could visit him in Germany for a month. When she returned, she showed me pictures of her visit, including pictures of Frank's parents and their middle-class home.

Frank and Nanci agreed never to tell his family or friends that she had been a sex worker. But since they decided to marry and made plans for Nanci to move to Germany with her son, she feared that they would find out. A former coworker of Nanci's, Rosa, lived thirty miles away from Frank's family with a German man she had also met in Sosúa's sex trade. "Rosa's mother-in-law knows what Rosa did in Sosúa," Nanci worried. "And she knows I'm a friend of Rosa's. What if she ever said anything to Frank's parents?" Nanci's ties to Sosúa put a new twist on the importance of social networks in the migration process: the nascent networks linking Sosúan sex workers to towns in Germany can be sources of both support and concern for sex workers–turned–migrants. In many instances, women prefer struggling in isolation in their new European settings to being found out.

After marrying and living in Germany for a year, Frank and Nanci moved to Sosúa, where they had a little girl together. But soon afterward, Frank ran off with another Dominican sex worker and stopped all financial support to Nanci and her children. Nanci went to a lawyer and got Frank to pay child support, which lasted for one month; there is little that Nanci can do now, since Frank and this other woman have moved to Germany. Like Elena,

Nanci has experienced a reversal of fortune. She and her two children now live in a two-room shack in Sosúa, under much worse conditions than when I first met her, before she married Frank. I was quite shaken to see that the one relationship I knew of that seemed to grow out of love, respect, and romance had crumbled.

Despite this turn of events, Nanci returned to sex work and continued to depend exclusively on foreign men for her income. Another sex worker, Carmen, adopted a different strategy, diversifying her risk in the sex trade by working with both foreign and Dominican men. She supplemented unpredictable income from foreign tourists by establishing long-term relationships with Dominican *amigos* (friends), or *clientes fijos* (regular clients), who supplied her with a small but steady income. Ani, another sex worker, explains the function of *amigos*: "You don't always have a client. You need *amigos* and *clientes fijos*. If you have a problem, like something breaks in your house, or your child is sick and you need money for the doctor or medicine, they can help."

After four years of sex work, Carmen has saved enough money to build a small house for her mother and children in Santo Domingo. I asked her why she thinks she was able to save money while so many of her friends in Sosúa did not have an extra *centavo*. She replied, "Because they give it to their men. Their husbands wait at home and drink while their women work. Not me. If I'm in the street with all the risks of disease and the police, I'm keeping the money or giving it to my kids. I'm not giving it to a man, no way."

She was careful not to let the men in her life know how much money she had saved or where it came from. While she was involved with the Belgian client who later declined to answer her letter, she says, "I did not tell him I am building the house. I don't have money and it would seem like I do." She also kept the possibility of her moving to Belgium (and the information-gathering trip she and the client took to the Belgian embassy in Santo Domingo) from Jorge, her young Dominican *amigo*. The nephew of the owner of the boardinghouse where Carmen lived, Jorge visited her periodically from Santiago, about two hours from Sosúa. "He is very young," she told me, scrunching up her nose disapprovingly. "He lives with his mother in Santiago and works in a *zona franca*. He gives me money, even though he does not make a lot."

Jorge was her economic safety net, especially in times of crises. At times, the money Jorge gave Carmen was the only money she had. Though these sums were smaller than the transnational money wires other sex workers received, it was money she could count on regularly.

Living with Foreign Men: Fantasies Versus Realities

Because migrating to Europe is a relatively new phenomenon, not many former sex workers—Nanci is an exception—have returned to Sosúa to dispel the myths and gossip of an easy and fantasy-filled life *allá* (over there). Instead, the women imagine that foreign men will provide them with material comfort and possibly better treatment. They dream of European men "rescuing" them from a lifetime of poverty and foreclosed opportunities. They expect to trade love and romance for financial security and mobility. After all, these relationships are for *residencia,* not for *amor.*

Even after relationships end and women return to Sosúa broke, sex workers in the Sosúa community often still idealize their failed migration stories. Jürgen's alcoholism, for example, and his fighting with Elena were never mentioned in the gossip mill. Elena's friends focused on the money he gave her to feed the household, not on the fact that she did all the food shopping and preparation, on top of all the other household chores. Similarly, Nanci's friends never mentioned the social and economic isolation she suffered when they spoke of her time in Germany. And while Carmen's careful hedging strategy earned her snickers from sex workers who disdained lower-paying Dominican clients, she became the talk of the sex-work community when she later married an Austrian man and moved to Austria.

Because actually going to Europe is a rare prize, sex workers often talk about what they would do to make the most of it if they won the opportunity to migrate. Sex workers fancy that they would do what Andrea did: after marrying her German boyfriend and moving with her two girls to Germany, Andrea left him for another German man. This second German man, her cousin in Sosúa explained to me, "had more money." It was common knowledge that Andrea did not love her first husband. "He is very fat," various sex workers made a point of repeating. Nor did her friends pretend that she loved her current boyfriend. But Andrea was lucky enough to get off the island. Now she is expected—and willingly acquiesces—to help the other single mothers in her family, her parents, and her good friends, such as

Elena, with remittances. She has even sent new sneakers, jeans, and belts to a circle of her closest friends (all sex workers).

With so many financial expectations and demands on Andrea, there is pressure on her to keep her relationship afloat, no matter what. Women such as Andrea become symbols of all that is possible in Europe, while Nanci's friends blame her for the breakup of her marriage. After her own experience with Jürgen, Elena says "Nanci never should have moved to Sosúa with her husband with all these sex workers here. No man would stick around."[12] Considering the benefits for family, and even friends, it is easy to see why sex workers, sporting new fashions from Europe, perpetuate the fiction that marriage in Europe is without significant conflict. Language barriers, cultural differences, and racism are all waved aside. Life *allá* (over there) in Europe is, for now at least, better than *aquí* (here).

Marginalized women in a marginalized economy can and do fashion creative strategies to control their economic lives. Globalization and the accompanying transnational phenomena, including sex tourism, do not simply shape everything in their paths. Individuals react and resist. Dominican sex workers use sex, romance, and marriage as means of turning Sosúa's sex trade into a site of opportunity and possibility, not just exploitation and domination. But exits from poverty are rarely as permanent as the sex workers hope; relationships sour, and subsequently, an extended family's only lifeline from poverty disintegrates. For every promise of marriage a tourist keeps, there are many more stories of disappointment. Dominican women's attempts to take advantage of these "walking visas" call attention, however, to the savviness and resourcefulness of the so-called powerless.

Among Women: Migrant Domestics and Their Taiwanese Employers Across Generations

PEI-CHIA LAN

The relationship between mother-in-law and daughter-in-law has long been a fertile subject for soap operas. It is also a real-life family drama in most societies—not least in Taiwan, where increasing numbers of women hire Southeast Asian migrant workers to fulfill their duties to their mothers-in-law.[1] In her now-classic book *Between Women*, Judith Rollins exposed the contentious dyad between maid and madam.[2] Triangular links bind maid, madam, and mother-in-law in Taiwanese domestic employment arrangements that span generations.

In Taiwan, the relationship between mother-in-law and daughter-in-law is structured by Chinese traditions of filial piety and patriarchal authority. Child rearing is viewed as a process of social investment with an expectation of delayed repayment, or, in Chinese, *bau-da* (payback). Parents undergo economic and emotional costs in bearing and raising children, this tradition stipulates, so children, especially sons, are obligated to return the debts through the provision of care for their aging parents. *San-dai-tone-tang* (three-generation cohabitation) is viewed as the ideal arrangement for elders and the realization of filial piety.[3]

According to the Han Chinese tradition, family membership, inheritance of property, and distribution of authority are defined through the axis of father and son. A daughter is considered "spilled water," given away after marriage to another family headed by her husband's father. In contrast, giving birth to sons assures parents more security for their future welfare.[4] As a Chinese proverb says: "To protect yourself in old age, raise a son." The eldest married son is obligated to reside with and care for his aging parents; placing parents in a nursing home is stigmatized as immoral and irresponsible. But the actual work of serving a man's aging parents is performed mostly by his wife. The son, the major breadwinner, mainly provides economic support for his parents while his wife serves as his filial surrogate, offering care and service on a daily basis.

Intergenerational power dynamics have transformed over the last few decades of Taiwan's economic development. Taiwanese women served as a cheap work force for the labor-intensive, export-oriented manufacturing industries of the 1960s and 1970s.[5] The service sector, whose employment has surpassed that of manufacturing since the mid-1980s, offers further job opportunities for Taiwanese women. In 2002, almost half of Taiwanese women over the age of fifteen were employed. The rate of labor participation is particularly high among young, highly educated urban women. Dual-earner households have become a social norm as well as an economic necessity as housing prices and living expenses rise in urban areas.

As women's employment has grown, the conjugal, or nuclear, household has become the predominant residential structure in contemporary Taiwan. Current generations of young married couples, especially if they are well educated and have arranged their own marriages, expect to live separately from their parents. Adult children who resist three-generation cohabitation may still be blamed for violating filial norms, but they face less severe financial punishment than before. Since a couple's wages now constitute the major source of household income, the cost of losing family property on account of disobeying one's parents has lessened.[6]

The decline of parental authority varies across class backgrounds. As Rita Gallin has observed, mothers-in-law in wealthy families still enjoy the power to distribute properties; hence they maintain traditional family authority. By contrast, poorer mothers-in-law have to "strive to make themselves dependable sources in order to ensure a measure of security."[7] The poverty of these elders is exacerbated by the Taiwanese government's failure to introduce a comprehensive social security system until very recently. Means-tested elder benefits are available to only a small segment of the elderly population, and nearly half of Taiwanese elders are financially dependent on their adult children.[8] The government also actively promotes the privatization of elder care by favoring three-generation households with tax cuts, public housing subsidies, and moral education that emphasizes the family as the unit of filial care.[9]

Although the proportion of parents living alone has been increasing, the social ideology continues to pressure sons to take care of their elderly parents. Almost 60 percent of contemporary Taiwanese households are nuclear units; three-generation cohabitation, mostly on a patrilocal principle, still describes about one-third of the households.[10] More than half of Taiwanese elders live with their sons, and only 3 percent are placed in care facilities.[11] Young generations balance the social norm of filial piety against their desire for autonomy and privacy by making other arrangements, including living in different apartments in the same building, living apart yet having meals together or making frequent visits, and hiring nonfamily care workers. The recently available migrant labor force, which costs less than half the wage of a local caregiver and offers live-in stand-by service, has become a popular arrangement for elder care in Taiwan.[12]

The Maid Trade in the Global South

Significant numbers of undocumented migrants have worked in Taiwanese households since the early 1980s, but the government officially opened the gate to migrant domestic workers in 1992. Taiwan first granted work permits to "domestic caretakers," employed to take care of the severely ill or disabled; later, the government released a limited number of quotas for the employment of "domestic helpers" in households with children under the age of 12 or elders over the age of 70.[13] This policy is viewed as a solution to the growing demand for paid care work among both nuclear households and the aging population. Despite quota control and regulated employer qualification, the number of Taiwanese households hiring migrant domestic workers has rapidly increased in the last decade. Currently, more than 120,000 foreigners are legally employed as domestic workers in Taiwan. Women from the Philippines and Indonesia constitute 93 percent of these migrant domestic; the rest are from Thailand and Vietnam.[14]

Taiwan's case is indicative of a regional pattern. The increasing prosperity of East Asia and the Gulf countries since the mid-1970s has stimulated substantial international migratory flow within this region. Most migrant women in Asia are concentrated in particular occupations, such as the entertainment industry, health services, and especially domestic service. It is estimated that more than one million women from countries like Bangladesh, India, Pakistan, Sri Lanka, Indonesia, and the Philippines are employed as domestic workers, with or without legal documents, in Hong Kong, Singapore, Taiwan, Malaysia, and the Middle East. Scholars have named this regional migration flow the "trade in maids" in Asia.[15]

Globalization has simplified the gendered household burdens for more privileged women even as it complicates the racial and class stratification of domestic work. The supply of Third World women for paid domestic work in the West is historically and structurally linked to the uneven development of the global economy, the legacy of colonialism, and the increasing indebtedness of Third World countries.[16] In the emerging "new domestic world order," migrant women work not only in the households of postindustrial societies like the United States, Canada, and Western Europe, but also in those of the oil-rich nations of the Middle East and the "newly industrialized countries" of Asia.[17]

According to the official data, the majority of Taiwanese employers are dual-income, middle-class households formed by couples between the ages of 25 and 44. More than 30 percent of them reside in metropolitan Taipei.[18] Most employers of domestic workers in Taiwan grew up without maids or baby-sitters in their homes. They are the so-called new middle class, made up of professionals and owners of small- to medium-sized businesses.[19] Employing foreign domestic workers allows them to upgrade their lifestyles and confirm their newly achieved social status.

Many female employers are also the first generation of career women in their families. Their mothers and mothers-in-law quit their jobs after marriage or childbirth, but the daughters and daughters-in-law yearn for career advancement and "couple egalitarianism" in the performance of household labor.[20] Caught between traditional ideals and modern values, these young

Taiwanese women seek to transfer their gendered domestic duties and kin work to the market. Low-cost migrant workers thus become vital to their ability to negotiate intergenerational relations as they pursue gender equality and career achievement.

Subcontracting Filial Duty[21]

Mrs. Chang[22] is a fifty-eight-year-old retired high school teacher. She and her husband, also a teacher, own a modest three-bedroom apartment in Taipei. When Mr. Chang's father died, his mother moved from the countryside to reside with him, her eldest son. Mr. and Mrs. Chang rented the apartment across the hall from their own to accommodate her, so that they could maintain the ideal of three-generation cohabitation without sacrificing their own and their two adult daughters' privacy. Two years ago, Mrs. Chang convinced her husband to hire a Filipina worker to take care of his increasingly frail mother, who now needed daily assistance and personal care. Mrs. Chang then transferred most of her previous duties, including preparing meals, bathing, and changing diapers, to the Filipina worker. More than once during our interview, Mrs. Chang felt compelled to legitimize her decision to hire someone to take care of her mother-in-law:

> I may sound like I have no sense of filial piety to you, but I have been serving her for twenty years! If you want to be a good daughter-in-law, you can no longer be yourself. Fortunately, it doesn't cost that much to hire a Filipina maid these days.... After I retired from school, I'm still doing some part-time work. I don't want to stay home, not a single day. And I can make some money. But all the money goes to the Filipina maid [*smiles*].

Mrs. Chang's remarks highlight the conflict she senses between performing her traditional gender role (being a "good daughter-in-law," "serving" one's mother-in-law) and seeking individual autonomy and self-achievement (being oneself). Zhong-Dong Liu has argued that the traditional ideal of caregiving in Chinese societies is associated with the hierarchical concept of "serving" rather than with the more egalitarian notion of "caring."[23] The typical image of a caregiver in Chinese families is a female relative in a subordinate position, such as a wife serving her husband, or a daughter-in-law serving her parents-in-law. The act of caregiving is strongly tied to the ideal of womanhood, and the failure to fulfill these gendered responsibilities incurs social stigma. Mrs. Chang continues working even after retirement in order to avoid the full-time duty of "serving" her mother-in-law. She volunteers to contribute the wage she earns at her part-time job to hire another woman as her filial agent, but both her mother-in-law and her husband oppose this plan:

> *What did* Amah *say when you first wanted to hire a Filipina maid?*[24]
> She always says bad things about the Filipina maid because she wishes we could stop the employment so she could live with us.
> *How about your husband? He objected, too?*
> Of course. First, it costs money. Second, in this way, it doesn't seem that we are a family, and he won't be able to make the ideal of a filial son.

The mother-in-law considers the care worker a barrier between her and her son's family. The son worries that employing a domestic worker may ruin his filial reputation. But it is the daughter-in-law's unpaid labor that sustains the social myth of intergenerational family unity. Mrs. Chang expressed anguish over the unequal division of filial labor between her and her husband:

> I worked as hard as he did, but he said taking care of children was women's business; serving the mother-in-law was women's business. I feel this is really unfair. I am also an educated person; I cannot accept this. If you want to be a dutiful son, then you should be the one who serves your mother, not me! My mother brought me up. I should take care of my mother, not yours. She is the mother of you and your six siblings, not mine. You cannot just leave her to the daughter-in-law.

To change the terms of this "unfair" gendered assignment, Mrs. Chang seeks a surrogate worker to perform her filial duty. In so doing, she enacts a transfer chain of "filial kin work," which I define as care work to maintain patrilineal intergenerational ties.[25] This transfer chain consists of two components: *gender transfer* of the filial duty from the son to the daughter-in-law, and *market transfer* of elder care from the daughter-in-law to a nonfamily care worker, who is usually a woman. The subcontracting of elder care reveals a transformation in cultural practices, but it does not present a radical challenge to the gendered division of filial kin work. As another woman employer explained, "Many husbands say women today are luckier than ever because they have Filipina maids to help. But actually, who's your wife taking care of? She's taking care of your mother!"

Some young women employers continue doing some portion of housework or elder care in order to affirm the ideal of the filial daughter-in-law and to avoid negative judgments imposed by their mothers-in-law. Rowena, a Filipina domestic worker, observed the struggle of her employer, a successful coffee shop owner who nonetheless remained a powerless daughter-in-law in her patriarchal extended family. With great sympathy, Rowena described how her employer managed to do some housework even though she hired Rowena for exactly that purpose:

> My employer works hard during the day, but she still works very hard after she gets home! I don't understand. I wouldn't if I were her! If you've worked hard all day, you should rest when you get home. . . . When I complained to her that I had too much work to do, she told me there was nothing she could do about it. She belongs to another family. She always needed to ask for [the mother-in-law's] permission to do anything.

The daughter-in-law and the domestic worker may develop a sisterly camaraderie when they face the mother-in-law's authority together. Mrs. Chang refreshes her rusty English in order to better communicate with her Filipina worker, Sheila. The time they spend together doing the grocery shopping and cooking allows Sheila to get away from the mother-in-law and to seek emotional support from Mrs. Chang. When I interviewed Sheila in the Changs' living room about the renewal of her contract, the interaction between the two women clearly expressed the bond they had come to share:

Sheila: I don't know if I will work here next year. Maybe the husband does not like.

Mrs. Chang: I like! I like! Never mind my husband!

Sheila: I like my ma'am very much, but Amah is very difficult.

PCL: Why is she difficult?

Sheila [lowers her voice]: I am afraid to talk about his mother
[points at the husband in the dining room].

Mrs. Chang: It's okay. He does not understand English.

Sheila: Her husband never talks to me. I am here for two years.
Only my ma'am talks to me.

Mrs. Chang [explains to me in Mandarin]: He forgot all his English
and he feels embarrassed talking to a woman.

Sheila: The husband was good to me before, but Amah told him
bad words about me. So he is not good to me now. Sometimes I am thinking of going back to the Philippines, but I
think of my ma'am. If I go back, she will be the one to take
care of Amah! She does not like to. I know that. Amah
sometimes says bad words to me, but I am always patient. I
always talk to my ma'am. She understands me.

Mrs. Chang [nodding]: Yes, I understand. I am like you before!

Sheila [smiles at Mrs. Chang]: That's why I can understand you,
too.

After the interview, Mrs. Chang invited me to stay for dinner. Her
mother-in-law declined Mrs. Chang's dinner invitation, saying she felt sick.
(Mrs. Chang said, "Well, she is still mad at me.") While cooking together in
the kitchen, Mrs. Chang and Sheila taught each other the words for cooking
utensils and materials in English and Chinese; they exchanged complaints
about the hardships of serving the mother-in-law; and they chatted about
each other's children and family. During dinner, Mr. Chang asked me about
my research topic and mentioned a news report about a crime committed by
a migrant worker. "They cause a lot of problems for our society, don't they?
And they are not really that cheap. We have to provide lodging and food and
everything," he remarked. Rather than acknowledging the real person who
was helping meet his mother's pressing need for care, Mr. Chang discussed
the presence of migrant workers as an abstract social problem. From across

the table, Mrs. Chang threw me a look that seemed to say, "Well, now you understand what I was talking about."

Safeguarding the Nuclear Family

Some daughters-in-law use domestic workers to protect their nuclear families from the intervention of extended kin. Young mothers-in-law who are in good health may not yet become recipients of "filial kin work," but they often provide "kin labor" for their sons and daughters-in-law in the form of unpaid or underpaid child care, cooking, and housekeeping for dual-earner young couples. In return for this labor, these mothers-in-law expect to secure three-generation cohabitation and close bonds to their sons' families. From the perspective of adult children, however, especially daughters-in-law, this assistance also threatens to allow mothers-in-law to interfere with or dominate the conjugal family.

Child care is often the source of conflicts between women across generations. In addition to the child's mother, the mother-in-law is traditionally defined as a child's primary caregiver. She supervises her daughter-in-law in the care of her son's children and intervenes when the job is not being done in a way she deems proper.[26] It is common for Taiwanese mothers-in-law to care for grandchildren if their daughters-in-law work outside of the home. This happens not only in three-generation households but also in situations where mothers-in-law live nearby. Catherine and her husband, in their early thirties, both received M.B.A.s in the United States and work in Taipei as market consultants. When Catherine returned to work after three months of maternity leave, her mother-in-law took over caring for the couple's newborn baby. The couple sent the baby to her grandparents' house every morning and picked her up after work. Without being asked to, Catherine paid the mother-in-law NT$18,000 (US$530) per month, an amount equivalent to the lower-end wage of a local caregiver. Although she did not have to worry the way she might have had she left the child with a stranger, Catherine felt that this arrangement caused difficulty and tension between her and her mother-in-law:

> We argued almost every day. . . . She was just exhausted, unhappy, and then she gave me a poker face. Every time when we picked up

our daughter, we didn't know if we should leave or stay. If we left, she would say you guys just want to get your child. If we stayed, she would say I had been working so hard, I took care of your child, and I also have to cook your dinner? She was not saying these things to her son, only to her daughter-in-law.

Not only was Catherine's mother-in-law exhausted by the work of caring for a newborn baby, but she also felt deprived. She felt that she had sacrificed the comfort of her old age in order to maintain her son's family, a duty that was supposed to fall to her daughter-in-law. Catherine later hired a migrant live-in worker to care for her daughter. She spent the money in order to spare the emotional cost.

Adult children who seek a way out of binds like Catherine's often generate parenting practices that deviate from tradition. Neophyte Taiwanese parents seek guidance not only from their parents but also through books by experts, many of which are translated from English. Young mothers hire nannies to safeguard their parental autonomy and to avoid confrontations with the older generation. For example, Ann, a thirty-two-year-old bank manager, explained why she preferred a migrant caregiver to her mother-in-law:

> When there are different opinions regarding child care, you somehow have to listen to the elderly. Then you lose your autonomy. I cannot control my mother-in-law, but I can control my Filipina maid, right?

By hiring a foreign maid, women employers not only solve the problem of child care but also avoid arguing with their husbands over who does the laundry and the dishes. Some Taiwanese husbands, mostly from younger generations, are willing to share some housework, but their mothers object. For example, when I asked Hsiu-Yun, a forty-three-year-old real estate agent, if her husband helped out with housework, she answered:

> More or less. He's a neat person. Once he saw some dirt on the floor and couldn't help but mop it. The maid was on vacation or something. Then his mom came to our house and was shocked when she saw this. She must be thinking, "My son never did anything like this

in *my* house! Now he is mopping the floor!" So I rushed to ask my husband to stop. I would do that later.

This scenario demonstrates not only a divide between traditional and modern notions of marriage, but also an implicit competition between the mother-in-law and the daughter-in-law over the son. The extended family and conjugal family are marked as separate territories dominated by the two women across generations ("my house" versus "your floor"). The mother-in-law viewed the son's participation in housework as an indicator of his subordination to his wife, and concomitantly, of the weakening of his ties to his mother and extended family. Some daughters-in-law, such as Emily, a thirty-year-old financial consultant, hire a maid to avoid potential disputes on the division of housework:

> I'm thinking that when my daughter gets married in the future, I'll also hire a Filipina maid for her. That way she can avoid a lot of problems with her mother-in-law. You can't let your mother-in-law do housework, like cleaning and cooking, but you also feel reluctant to do it alone—there's no way she'll let her son do it, right?

Some female employers more assertively use the employment of domestic workers as a strategy to resist three-generation cohabitation. Hsiao-Li, thirty-six years old, has a junior college degree and worked as a nurse before giving birth to her son. Her mother-in-law volunteered to move to Taipei to be the family's live-in caretaker, but Hsiao-Li rejected this proposal, saying that she would seek a migrant caretaker. Hsiao-Li described what happened then:

> My mother-in-law is a very sharp woman. She said to me, "Your father-in-law thinks hiring a Filipina maid is a bad idea." She wouldn't say that it was she who thought it was a bad idea. Whoever she ran into—my friends, relatives—she told them, "You talk to Hsiao-Li, tell her to let me watch the child." Anyway, the main point is that she wants to live with her son. She doesn't really love the grandson. She loves her son!

Hsiao Li's mother-in-law exerted her social pressure by proxy, framing her objection as though it were that of her husband. After all, he was the extended family's patriarchal authority. I went on to ask Hsiao-Li what her husband thought. She replied, "Him? Of course he'd like to live with both his wife and his mother! Then he could be a baby forever. Everything would be taken care of by others."

In another interview, I heard a story about a mother-in-law who, when visiting her son's house, expressed her anger by throwing out the baggage of the migrant worker. She thought that if there were no Filipina maid, the couple would have invited her to live with them and take care of her grandchildren. These mothers-in-law feel anguish not because their grandchildren have been "taken away" by the domestic workers, but because they have been denied the link they would have enjoyed with their sons' families even in lieu of cohabitation.

Unlike Mrs. Chang, Hsiao-Li has a contentious relationship with her Filipina worker, Julia. Julia is college-educated and plans to pursue a master's degree after saving enough money from working overseas. Hsiao-Li bluntly admits that she has been "a mean boss" to Julia, but she explains this as more a product of contextual factors than an innate personality clash. She has not yet found a suitable job after quitting her nursing position prior to giving birth. Being a stay-at-home mother has brought her a sense of loss and isolation. Her insecurity is aggravated by the presence of a well-educated maid and by the pressure from her husband and mother-in-law:

> The reason I don't get along with the maid is because of all the pressure my mother-in-law and my husband put on me. They complained, "Why are you not working? What are you doing at home every day?" Well, every day I watch her [the maid] and I pick on her. She has an advanced degree, so she feels humiliated. If I were working, all this wouldn't have happened. Because you gain nothing at home, so you become picky and cranky all day long.

A Chinese proverb says: "A daughter-in-law must suffer to become a mother-in-law" (*Si-fu-au-cheng-po*). A young bride who experiences hardships in a patriarchal extended family, in other words, eventually accedes to authority by controlling the next generation of daughters-in-law. Women offset patriarchal domination by controlling other, subordinate women— daughters-in-law in the case of mothers-in-law, and foreign maids in the case of young women employers. Daughters-in-law like Hsiao-Li seek domestic help to lessen the gendered obligations placed upon them, but ironically they then become authority figures similar to their mothers-in-law.

Smoothing Tensions and Anxieties at Home

Jessica, thirty-two, has worked in several international banks and has been promoted to a managerial position in her current job. She married a coworker four years ago and moved in with her husband's parents. Although she abides by the tradition of three-generation cohabitation, Jessica is determined to continue her career after giving birth to her daughter. To solve the thorny problems of child care and housework, she wishes to hire a Filipina worker, as many of her coworkers have. However, she recounts, "I went through a revolution to hire my Filipina maid!" She spent half a year convincing her mother-in-law, who threw out various objections, such as, "This is a waste of money," "Hiring a foreigner at home is not safe," and, "Maybe it's better for you to quit and stay home."

Jessica's story is not atypical. Many daughters-in-law have to fight to convince their mothers-in-law that they are not irresponsible mothers or lazy wives. After all, most older Taiwanese women were full-time homemakers and mothers when they were the age of their daughters-in-law. Shin-Yi, a homemaker in a nuclear household, recalls:

> My mother-in-law always said that it was kind of "weird" that I don't work but still hire a maid. "Weird" is the word she used. Of course, I know what she meant by that. . . . She thinks I am just lazy and I shouldn't have hired a maid.

Similar pressures came to bear on Wan-Ru, an employed woman in an extended household, when she brought her new Filipina maid to see her mother-in-law. When I asked Wan-Ru why she brought the maid to meet her mother-in-law directly on her arrival, she replied:

Well, you have to let the mother-in-law know about this. You have to let her understand that you hire a maid to help, not because you want to be a *shau-nai-nai* [young mistress in the house]. My mother-in-law had a misunderstanding like this in the beginning. She would say, wow, someone else has done everything for you; you have no work to do; you have such a great fortune.

Many of these mothers-in-law fear not only that their links to their sons will be weakened but that they will be replaced by the domestic workers. Pei-Chi and her husband, both in their forties, own and manage a small company that produces and exports computer chips. The husband's mother moved from the province to live with them in Taipei and to help raise her three grandchildren. Five years ago Pei-Chi and her husband decided to hire a Filipina maid to take over the household chores so that the mother-in-law could focus on child care. Pei-Chi's mother-in-law, however, expresses not relief but anxiety, as Pei-Chi recounts:

The first time the Filipina maid moved in, my mother-in-law was really, really upset. She felt that we had deprived her of her rights of working. . . . Raising children and doing housework are not only her responsibilities, but also her only achievement. She values herself solely based on that. So in the beginning, she was wondering if we didn't want her anymore, if we wanted to kick her out, if she still had any "surplus value." We had to communicate with her again and again, and finally we decided to save one job for her—cooking! [*laughs*]

Because Pei-Chi's mother-in-law has been a full-time homemaker all her life, domestic labor is her domain of mastery and the foundation of her identity. She interpreted Pei-Chi's hiring of a Filipina maid as an expression of doubt about her professional skills and a diminishment of her contribution to the family. She was also worried that Pei-Chi and her husband "didn't want her anymore," that they would "kick her out" once her work was transferred to the migrant worker. The social norm of three-generation cohabitation has attenuated, and the moral ideal of filial piety can no longer guarantee paybacks from children. Parents thus struggle to present their "surplus value" to their sons' families because they worry that they will lose economic and emotional support at frail ages.

Frequently, the mother-in-law feels threatened by the arrival of a "professional" domestic worker on her territory. Because older Taiwanese speak little English, the language barrier further exacerbates the tension between mothers-in-law and Filipina domestic workers. Says Jessica of her mother-in-law:

> She feels lost in her life. Her life has no more goals. All her jobs have been taken away by the Filipina maid, and the maid does even a better job than she did. . . . To her, everything is out of her control now. And she cannot even control the Filipina maid because she doesn't speak English!

A daughter-in-law who hires a migrant worker may have lightened her physical workload, but she has often taken on the additional emotional labor of soothing her mother-in-law's tensions and anxieties. One common strategy among female employers is to confirm the mother-in-law's authority. For example, they intentionally have their mothers-in-law release wages to the migrant workers even though the money is actually from the young couple. Women employers also manipulate translations to minimize tensions between mothers-in-law and migrant domestic workers. Jessica's mother-in-law felt so anxious about the worker's presence that she tried to outperform the worker around the house, especially in cooking, a domestic duty with considerable cultural and affective significance. One day, the mother-in-law made an unusual and complicated dish for the family. The message behind this dish, Jessica says, was clear: "I have been married into this family for years, and I never saw her cook that dish! She did this on purpose. It's a performance." But for whom was Jessica's mother-in-law performing? "For the Filipina maid! She was trying to tell the maid, 'See, it's not that easy to take over my job. This is my territory. I can do a lot of things you cannot. So don't think that you can replace me.'"

Jessica took the opportunity to translate the worker's comments on that dish in a way that she knew would mitigate her mother-in-law's anxieties. By exaggerating the worker's compliments of the mother-in-law's cooking skills, she validated a hierarchical distinction between the mother-in-law and the maid:

I tried to sugarcoat the words of the Filipina maid when I translated them. I said, "Mama, the maid said it's delicious. Chinese food becomes like magic at your hands. You can compete with those chefs in five-star restaurants!" Then my mother-in-law was happy, and she put more food on the maid's plate!

The loss of status these mothers-in-law fear is no small thing. Indeed, the subordination of daughters-in-law and the authority accorded to mothers-in-law have affected the quality of life for generations of Taiwanese women. Margery Wolf reported that in 1905, young adult women in Taiwan had a high rate of suicide compared with senior women, who had a relatively low suicide rate, coinciding with their empowered status.[27] Yet, Yow-Hwey Hu later found that, in 1984, the suicide rate for young women significantly dropped, even as older women became more likely to take their own lives.[28] This suicidal tendency among older women is partly explained by their decline in family status and economic security. Such women have been adversely affected by the transformation of gender and intergenerational relations in Taiwan. As young adults, this generation of women sacrificed career achievement for the welfare of family. All the while, they looked forward to enjoying a secure and easy old age. But after surviving their own difficulties as daughters-in-law, they are not accorded the authority their mothers-in-law received in the past. Facing modern daughters-in-law who seek self-realization and autonomy as wage earners, mothers-in-law struggle to enhance their status in the family, even by contributing their kin labor in exchange for economic security and social support.

Fictive Kin Across Ethnic Boundaries

Migrant domestic workers constitute a potential threat for some mothers-in-law, but these foreign workers may also become primary caregivers and fictive kin for Taiwanese elders whose adult children subcontract their filial duty. I conducted some interviews in a small town in mid-Taiwan, where most residents make their living on farms or in factories. The town's population is aging, because many younger villagers have left their parents and gone to cities in search of advanced education and white-collar jobs. This small town is, however, not untouched by globalization. Advertisements for agencies recruiting foreign caretakers are posted all over mailboxes and telephone poles. In the early morning, Filipina or Indonesian women are seen wheeling Taiwanese elders for walks along the field; in the afternoon, they gather in front of the temple, with Taiwanese elders sitting in one circle and migrant women chatting to each other in another.

Amah Lin was born to a poor farming family in 1913. She never attended formal school, and she married a farmer's son when she was sixteen. Discovering that she was infertile, she adopted a daughter and a son. The daughter committed suicide in her early thirties; the son got married and moved to Taipei. After her husband died, Amah Lin lived on her own until she had a bad fall and became half paralyzed three years ago. She disliked Taipei and did not get along well with her daughter-in-law. After the accident, she lived in a nursing home for a year until her son hired a Filipina caretaker, which allowed her to move back to her old house. When I met her, she was eighty-six years old and frail, but with a clear mind. Talking about her own children through tears, Amah Lin pointed at her neighbor who has five sons, and said with envy: "She had a good fortune. She has a lot of children."

Rural grandmothers, who have accumulated only limited economic resources and rely mostly on their children's financial support, occupy the bottom of the elder social ladder. Amah Chen, the neighbor Amah Lin described as "having a good fortune," is actually attended by a Filipina caregiver, too. Amah Chen has no major illness except diabetes and arthritis; the latter commonly afflicts Taiwanese seniors who used to do heavy farm work. Her two sons live in concrete apartments only a few blocks away from Amah Chen's old brick house. When I asked her why she was not living with her sons, she could barely finish her answer for weeping:

> The house is theirs, not mine. Children today don't like to live with elders anyway. I am dying but not dead yet. This is most painful [*rubbing her knees in tears*]. . . . Every day I cry and cry. . . . I don't want to hire someone, but my son said no, nobody is watching you during the day. I'm a useless person, but only cost them a lot of money [*sigh*]. It's better for me to die soon.

Poor senior women commonly express feelings of being useless and a burden on their children. Among Taiwan's elderly, widowed women have the least access to social security, the heaviest reliance on children's support, and the strongest preference for three-generation cohabitation. The suicide rate among rural women over sixty-five is the second highest in the national population, next to that of old, rural men.[29] When I asked Amah Lin what she would do when her Filipina caregiver, Sylvia, finished her contract, she answered me in a flat tone: "Me? I don't know. Maybe it's better for me to just die." Sylvia then patted Amah's shoulder, speaking in broken Taiwanese with a heavy Filipino accent: "No say that!"

Sylvia is a forty-year-old high school graduate and a mother of three. She and her husband used to run a small chicken farm and sell eggs in the village. Driven by financial depression at home and drawn by the success stories of migrant villagers, her husband worked in the Middle East until the decline of construction and manufacturing jobs after the Gulf war. Sylvia then took her turn to work abroad, first in Malaysia and then in Taiwan, as a domestic worker and caregiver. Pleasant and patient, Sylvia has earned a reputation in town for being a great caregiver, tolerant with difficult Amah Lin. As we talked in the living room, Sylvia frequently went to the kitchen to check on the pork stew, Amah Lin's favorite dish. She explained that the meat had to be cooked for more than three hours, until it was tender, because Amah Lin has lost most of her teeth. In addition to Chinese cooking, Sylvia has also picked up a good deal of Taiwanese vocabulary in a short time. When street vendors pass by the house hawking their food or wares, she diligently asks Amah Lin what they are saying, and she repeats the words a few times to memorize their pronunciation.

Compared to Amah Lin's son, who visits her only once or twice a month, Sylvia knows a lot about the personal needs and idiosyncrasies of her client. Out of concern for Amah Lin, Sylvia complains to me about the irresponsibility of her children in the provision of medical care:

> Nobody brings Amah to see the doctor. She doesn't have medicine! During the night, she cried and shouted. She had pain, so I gave her my Filipino medicine. I complained to my employer. They bring her medicine only once a month.

To Amah Lin, Sylvia is not merely an employee but something like "fictive kin," a term that describes "those who provide care like family and do what family does [and] are given the labor of kin with its attendant affection, rights, and obligations."[30] In general, the kinship analogy works best when elderly clients and their care workers are of similar ethnic backgrounds and share cultural knowledge.[31] In this case, Sylvia transcends ethnic and cultural boundaries by learning Chinese cooking, studying the local language, and even sharing the medicine she brought from the Philippines.

On the one hand, a fictive kin relationship improves the quality of care and retrieves personal meanings for both the provider and the recipient. On the other hand, when employers place kin expectations on care workers they may blur the distinction between employees and family members, assigning workers extra labor beyond what was contractually agreed. For example, Ms. Lai, a forty-one-year-old widowed employer, hired a Filipina worker to take care of her ill mother-in-law. After one year, the worker ran away and filed an official complaint on account of extra work and long hours. Ms. Lai, however, considered the workload reasonable because she measured it based on the social expectations placed on daughters-in-law:

> She complained I gave her too much work. Come on, what work? Housework and cooking? What's the big deal? Didn't I have to do all these things before? Which working woman is not like this? Which daughter-in-law doesn't do all these?

Migrant workers who are adopted into the families of their care recipients risk subordinating their own families to the needs of their employers. Sylvia forfeited the annual one-week vacation her contract specified out of loyalty to Amah Lin. During her two years in Taiwan, she had had no chance to visit her three children, who were attended by her mother in the Philippines. Sylvia said with a deep sigh: "My son always says, 'Mom, when are you coming back to the Philippines?' I keep saying, 'maybe next year, maybe.' It will be two years this June, but they don't want me to take a vacation. Nobody can take care of her if I am not here."

When migrant mothers sell their reproductive labor to maintain their employers' families, they depend on other people's paid or unpaid reproductive labor to fill the void they leave in their own families. Some husbands quit jobs and become full-time homemakers, while other households hire local domestic workers. The majority of migrant workers rely on female kin—grandmothers, aunts, sisters, or other relatives—to take care of their children.[32] These relatives provide care in exchange for a secure flow of monthly remittances from the migrant mothers.[33] Unlike Taiwanese daughters-in-law, who use domestic workers as a means of securing distance from their mothers-in-law, migrant women strengthen their extended kin networks in order to maintain their transnational families while they serve as others' fictive kin overseas.

Conclusion

Globalization has participated in the transformation of intergenerational relations among Taiwanese women. As local cultural practices meet global labor forces, three types of labor reproduce kin ties. The first is "filial kin work," or care work conducted in order to maintain intergenerational, patrilineal ties. The filial duty of serving aging parents is transferred first from the son to the daughter-in-law (a gender transfer); later, it is outsourced to migrant care workers (a market transfer). The second is "kin labor," which is provided by extended kin in order to sustain ties to other family members; the unpaid domestic labor parents offer their adult children is one example of kin labor. Modern daughters-in-law often prefer to hire migrant workers rather than accept the kin labor offered by their mothers-in-law, because they fear excessive intervention in their families' domestic lives. The third kind of labor is that of "fictive kin," or nonfamily migrant workers who provide familylike care for elderly clients in lieu of the filial kin work of adult children.

As migrant domestic workers have entered Taiwanese households, intergenerational domestic dynamics have become triangulated, with the three women forming alliances or antagonisms. In some cases, when daughters-in-law hire migrant workers to subcontract the filial duty, the wives and workers become comrades under the mother-in-law's authority. Other daughters-in-law hire domestic workers in order to resist three-generation cohabitation or to minimize the intervention of their mothers-in-law in domestic affairs. These daughters-in-law may become authority figures similar to their mothers-in-law, reproducing the oppressive relationship they seek to escape. Still other daughters-in-law apply themselves to smoothing the tensions that arise in the daily interactions between mothers-in-law and migrant workers. Finally, mothers-in-law who live apart from their children may develop strong personal ties with their migrant caregivers, who become fictive kin across ethnic and cultural boundaries.

The dominant East Asian model of three-generation cohabitation has been praised by policy makers and academics as a time-honored solution to elder care.[34] This romanticized image of family unity obscures intergenerational power struggles. A family-based model of elder care also exacerbates class inequalities among the elderly: the poorer the elderly are, the more dependent they are on their children. Migrant care workers only present a solution to relatively privileged households, which outsource elder care to low-wage migrant women, who then leave their own families to care for others.

If senior citizens are to age with independence and dignity, the government should assume elder care as a collective responsibility, providing public pensions and subsidized care. Universal social security and health insurance would go a long way toward removing the stigma attached to "living on welfare," and toward lessening class disparities among the elderly. The market transfer of elder care is unavoidable. Therefore, we should recognize the value of paid care work by better regulating the working conditions of migrant laborers.[35] If we do so, care providers and recipients may be better able to form emotional ties without reproducing the most oppressive aspects of family relationships—the very dynamics that employers are themselves seeking to avoid.

Breadwinner No More

MICHELE GAMBURD

"He's good-hearted guy, but what a fool!" Priyanthi exclaimed, laughing, as we sat in her living room three days after her return to Sri Lanka from two years' work as a domestic servant in the Middle East. Any money her alcoholic husband had, she told me, he spent right away: "Today he's like a white man, tomorrow like a beggar." Every time she came home from abroad, she found only the four walls of their house remaining; during her last trip, he even sold the kitchen knives. Nonetheless, Priyanthi radiated an affectionate, good-humored conviction that she could reform her husband and build a better life for her four sons with the money she had earned abroad.

When Sri Lankan village women like Priyanthi leave their families to work abroad, their men remain at home, often unemployed and subsisting on the money their wives remit. The migration of these married women has expanded common notions of motherhood in Sri Lanka to include long absences from home. At the same time, female migration has reconfigured male gender roles in an often uncomfortable fashion. Many men feel a loss of self-respect and dignity when their wives become breadwinners. Such men only reluctantly take over the "women's work" of child care and cooking; if possible, they arrange to have female relatives assume these duties instead, in accordance with strongly felt local gender roles. Scenarios that circulate in television shows, newspaper articles, and local gossip suggest that uneducated, slothful husbands waste the money their wives earn abroad and turn to alcohol to drown their sorrows. Representations of delinquent, emasculated men appear in these stories in tandem with images of promiscuous, selfish, pleasure-seeking women who neglect their husbands and children.

The prevalence of migration, itself a response to high unemployment in Sri Lanka, has introduced new social and economic realities in villages like Naeaegama, where Priyanthi lives. In so doing, migration also forces villagers to violate old gender norms and to generate new ideals. This sort of change affects the gut-level, commonsense conceptions of how the world is organized that Raymond Williams calls "structures of feeling."[1]

In Sri Lanka, many people believe that women should stay at home and tend their families while men earn a living for the household. Local poverty and scarce job opportunities for men, however, drive many women to migrate for work. In the Naeaegama area in 1997, 90 percent of all migrants were women. Of the migrant women, 30 percent were single, and 70 percent were married, separated, or divorced. Most of the women in this latter group had at least one child, and approximately half had husbands who contributed regularly to their household income; the other half had husbands who were under- or unemployed. Despite the relatively high proportion of employed husbands, many villagers lump together all the husbands of migrant women as lazy spendthrifts.

Common local stereotypes devalue these husbands' competence as breadwinners and as lovers. A number of housemaids in Naeaegama told me that "Arab people say that Sri Lankan men must be 'donkeys' because they send their wives abroad." The phrase carries two sets of implications. First, it emphasizes Sri Lankan men's inability to provide for their families. Second, the phrase implies that Sri Lankan women are not sexually satisfied with their husbands; if they were, they would not travel to the Middle East (and, presumably, sleep with Arab men). These images of Sri Lankan men rest on certain popular assumptions about migrant women: "If they can't eat grapes and apples, they go abroad. If they can't eat cheese and butter, they go abroad," runs one common adage. Grapes and apples, luxury fruits imported from abroad, signify a life of leisure and affluence. Cheese and butter, also luxury products, signify a rich and satisfying sexual life. This remark suggests that migrant women, dissatisfied with their lives and husbands in Sri Lanka, travel abroad in search of more gratifying economic and sexual situations.

When my research associates, Siri and Sita, and I repeated the story about Arab men calling Sri Lankan men "donkeys" to people I interviewed, it often sparked a lively conversation. Many people, after a moment's contemplation, replied by detailing their financial situations. Some slightly shamefacedly, some matter-of-factly, cited poverty as the reason women went abroad. A family, they explained, could not make ends meet on a man's wages as a casual laborer. Migrant women did not seek anything as fancy as "grapes and apples"; they merely hoped to support their families above the poverty line. Fewer respondents addressed the implicit suggestion of sexual impotence. Pradeep, an articulate young man, bounced his two-year-old son on his knee and replied that he knew and trusted his wife. Despite his hard work, his family could not afford to buy land, build a house, and start a business on his salary alone. If he could save the money his wife sent from abroad and build a house, and if she came home without being unchaste, that would prove he was not a donkey.

Despite the widespread awareness of such pragmatic concerns as local poverty and economic opportunities abroad, negative stereotypes continue to circulate, stigmatizing local men whose wives migrate for their inability to live up to older gender ideals. Both the stereotype of the Sri Lankan man as a "donkey" and the pragmatic discussions of poverty reflect the slow, difficult, and often painful negotiation of changing gender roles and family structures.

Alcohol: Group Bonding and Masculinity

In Naeaegama, alcohol is a business, a medicine, a pleasure, a necessity, and a mark of masculinity. Drinking, an exclusively male activity and a sign of wealth (however fleeting), preoccupies many of the under- and unemployed village men. When families do not prosper from female migration to the Middle East, villagers often blame husbands who quit work and take up drinking in their wives' absence. At once scornful and tolerant of such husbands, villagers commonly tut, "He sits idly, drinks, and wastes." Asked why these men indulge in such behavior, several villagers suggested that the men sought to emulate the rich landowners of the previous generation. One village notable explained to me: "It is good to be rich and look idle; in the absence of riches, looking idle will suffice." Hard work, particularly physical labor, carries significant stigma in the village; light skin, clean white clothing, and a sweatless brow indicate leisure, high status, or at the very least a respectable office job out of the burning sun.

Alcohol is the despair of many a wife, and the basis of community among drinking buddies. When a migrant woman comes home, her husband often demands money to buy drinks for himself and to improve his status by buying rounds for poorer male friends and relatives. Some Naeaegama women anticipate these requests by bringing home prestigious foreign liquor they purchase at duty-free shops. Although they enable their husbands' drinking, these women nevertheless seek to limit it. Blame for bad male behavior—such as gambling, smoking, drinking, and womanizing—often falls on the absent wife, without whose control a husband, considered constitutionally incapable of controlling his baser urges, drifts helplessly into bad habits and bad company. Frequently, however, patterns of drinking, wasteful spending, and failure to prosper predate, and even prompt, female migration. While women are considered responsible for disciplining their families and regulating household finances, they often have little authority to enforce their will, especially while they are abroad.

Drinking norms in Sri Lankan villages do not resemble Western norms of social drinking or before-dinner cocktails. At weddings, funerals, and other mixed-sex get-togethers, the host often "runs a bottle" of hard liquor out of a back room that most of the male guests visit surreptitiously, becoming progressively drunker as the event proceeds. While drinking, men do not eat, because food reduces the "current," or high. This style of drinking spans social classes. I once attended a university dinner party where I learned (a little too late) that respectable unmarried women rarely lingered at such functions past seven or eight in the evening. While their wives (and two uncomfortable female Western academics) huddled together in one room, married and unmarried men drank bottle after bottle in another until, around ten or eleven in the evening, the host decided to serve dinner.

Immediately after eating, the visitors departed, most in cars driven by drunken men. Men strove to get as drunk as possible as quickly as possible; drinking to excess was the norm, not the exception.

The production, distribution, and consumption of alcohol form a significant component of the village economy. A bottle of the legal hard liquor, arrack, costs roughly what a manual laborer might earn in a day; in 1994 a bottle of the officially distilled arrack cost Rs 118 (US$2.36), while a laborer's daily wage was between Rs 100 and Rs 125 (US$2–$2.50). In 1994, one village outfit that offered wages of 150 Sri Lankan Rupees (Rs)—US$3—a night, with free food and drink, went into production twice a week, running three stills all night, each requiring six people's constant attention. Including production crews, complicit landowners and law enforcement officers, and distribution networks, this distillery, one of several in the area, directly involved more than fifty people. Women, who rarely if ever touch liquor, constantly pressure their husbands to spend money on items for family consumption rather than on alcohol. To save money, most local men drink *kasippu*, the local moonshine. A bottle of *kasippu*, a fruit, yeast, and sugar-based fractionally distilled liquor, cost about Rs 60 (US$1.20) in 1994. Despite their families' debts and hunger, many men spend a great deal on alcohol, and some work for local *kasippu* manufacturers who operate stills at night in remote, wooded places.

Alcohol provides a strong basis for social allegiance and identity. Drinking groups often form around a particular *kasippu* producer. Heavy drinkers adopt the values and norms of their groups, which tolerate, even encourage, such activities as gambling, stealing, rape, and assault. Anthropologist Jonathan Spencer glosses *lajja* as shame, shyness, and social restraint—all essential ingredients of good public behavior. He glosses *lajja-baya* as "shame-fear," particularly the fear of ridicule and public humiliation. Those who drink are thought not to know *lajja* or *baya*. Spencer notes, "It is assumed that people who drink alcohol will no longer be in control of their actions and [will be] easily aroused to anger, which would be likely to spill out in physical violence, given the opportunity."[2] Shifting groups of local men, usually of similar age and status, gather regularly to drink, surreptitiously visiting a distribution center or purchasing a bottle to take to a private location. Often those with money spot drinks for those without, who return the favor at a later date.

Although they are rarely acknowledged by respectable village leaders, drinking groups form influential axes of political power. Outsiders occasionally employ such groups to assault opponents and to burn enemies' houses and property.[3] Villagers fear the men in drinking groups, especially those with histories of thuggery and intimidation. And yet, drinking men remain integrated into village kinship and friendship networks. Alcohol producers provide generous support and protection to individuals and to village institutions, including schools and temples. *Kasippu* production groups maintain guardedly friendly ties with some law enforcement officers, and they often lend financial support to local politicians. For reasons ranging from loyalty to fear, villagers rarely challenge drinking groups or report their misdeeds to higher authorities—some of whom are complicit in the network anyway.

For men whose incomes are eclipsed by those of their wives, or who fail to make the most of their wives' salaries, alcohol provides relief from personal responsibility. An extenuating condition that can be entered whenever needed, drunkenness provides the perfect alibi for poor judgment or socially unacceptable behavior.[4] Responsibility falls on the alcohol for any foolish actions and on the absent wife for the drinking itself. With prosperity in the village resting primarily on female migration to the Middle East, involvement with *kasippu* production and distribution provides poor men with alcohol, money, community, political clout, and a means to reassert the male power and respect lost in the face of women's new economic role. Drinkers thus emulate the idle rich of prior generations and reject the work ethic of the contemporary wealthy.

Meaning in the Making: Rukmini and Ramesh

Although many families hope to save a female migrant's earnings for large purchases, such as buying land and building a house, in many cases supporting the family on the husband's wages while putting the wife's earnings aside proves difficult. Men can pursue sporadic, grueling physical labor for very low wages—or they can dip into their wives' remittances. Many men in the Naeaegama area choose to rely on the money their wives earn abroad to finance their daily needs. The following case presents a fairly typical example of voluntary male underemployment and the concomitant use of a migrant woman's wages for family consumption. In a series of interviews, family members struggled to explain to me and to themselves their lack of improvement despite seven years of work abroad. In the process, they wrestled with the meaning of their continued poverty, and with its effect on individual and family identity.

Siri and I interviewed Hema, an elderly woman of a lower caste, and her son Ramesh. Ramesh's wife, Rukmini, was then working abroad as a housemaid. Rukmini, about thirty years old, had spent most of the previous seven years abroad. During the four years Rukmini worked in Jordan, she sent her money to her mother, who was supposed to look after her daughter. But Rukmini's mother had no stable home. She visited all of Rukmini's siblings, staying roughly six weeks with each, and spending lavishly with the checks Rukmini sent. The next time Rukmini went abroad, she left her daughter with Hema, her mother-in-law, instead. While Siri, Hema, Ramesh, and I sat in the shade of Hema's unfinished cement house, Siri half-jokingly explained to me in Sinhala that Rukmini did not send money to her husband Ramesh, an infamous drinker and gambler. Once the ice was broken, Hema took over the story, explaining that she had told Rukmini not to send the money but to keep it herself. Ramesh's gambling and drinking left nothing even to support himself and his daughter, Hema recounted. Ramesh had taken credit with many local stores, and he now owed interest-bearing debts to several moneylenders.

Hema suggested that if Ramesh could earn money for himself and his daughter, his wife could save all of her salary, and the family could then buy land and build a house, as they had originally planned. Sober and embarrassed, Ramesh said nothing to contradict his mother. I asked him about his work. He said he made about Rs 125 (US$2.50, considered a good salary locally) a day doing physical labor, and more than that when he drummed for ceremonies. Silently contradicting the impression that all of his wife's earnings had evaporated, Ramesh took me into the two-room clay house where he, his mother, father, daughter, and several brothers all lived, and he showed us a crowded collection of furniture he had bought with Rukmini's remittances.

When she returned to the village in mid-April 1994, I asked Rukmini to come meet with me at Siri's house for an interview. Usually I spoke with people in their homes, but at that time Rukmini and Ramesh were living in a six-by-twelve-foot lean-to built against the new cement wall of Hema's unfinished house. Unexpectedly, Ramesh accompanied his wife to the interview. Moreover, he was drunk. Siri tried to take Ramesh aside while Sita and I talked to Rukmini. Occasionally, however, Ramesh approached or interjected. When he did so, palpable tension pervaded the interview. Rukmini seemed barely able to finish a sentence. When I asked her about the gifts she had brought back from the Middle East, Ramesh declared that Rukmini had given him a shirt but that he had gotten his sarong for himself. She replied that she had given him a shirt, shoes, and cigarettes.

The full story explained Rukmini's barbed remark. Rukmini had given Ramesh a new pair of sandals, a pack of prestigious foreign cigarettes, and a new shirt. But when the police raided the illegal coconut beer brewery where Ramesh had gone to drink, he ran through a drainage canal toward the ocean. The canal muck claimed his new sandals, and the salt water ruined the pack of cigarettes in his shirt pocket. Rukmini mentioned that she had also brought her husband twelve beers and two whiskey bottles, all of which he had already consumed. But even if he drank, Ramesh retorted to Rukmini, at least he saved her clothing. Siri, Sita, and I assume that he was comparing himself favorably with the husband of another village migrant, who had sold his wife's dresses during her absence.

When Siri had persuaded Ramesh to walk in the garden, I asked Rukmini if she planned to go back to the Middle East. She intended to go back "no matter what," Rukmini replied. She said she was fed up with her husband's habits. There was no use earning money when he was drinking, she lamented, speaking very quickly. Some of the money Rukmini had just brought home had gone to settle Ramesh's debts and to finance drinking and gambling binges. Although she liked to come home to see her daughter, problems with her husband "unsettled her mind." Ramesh never listened to her, Rukmini complained, instead "he breaks things and wastes and drinks." Her variation on the common trope—"He sits idly, drinks, and wastes"— emphasized her dismay at Ramesh's destructive behavior, which she judged worse even than indolence and dissipation.

Ramesh returned to the porch. Reaching for a neutral topic, but inadvertently stumbling into a minefield, I asked Rukmini what had been the worst time in her life. It started after she got married, she replied. Ramesh exclaimed, "Really?" They talked heatedly about a fight several years earlier that had ended with both of them filing separate complaints at the police station at the junction—a common conclusion to serious village disputes. Ramesh accused his wife of abandoning their daughter and neglecting her wifely duties. Silenced, Rukmini picked up an umbrella from the table, examining it with great care. Center stage and unchecked, Ramesh delivered a monologue about himself and how hard he had been working for the family's sake. Siri and Sita made no effort to translate his tirade, and I stopped taking notes. Rukmini slouched low in her cane armchair, turning slightly away from her husband. I caught her eye and winked. Suddenly she sat up straight and relaxed physically, telling Ramesh to go home so that she could answer my questions.

I am not versed in the cross-cultural connotations of winking, and this was my only use of the wink as an interviewing tool, so I can only guess how Rukmini might have interpreted my gesture. I think she might have worried that I would accept at face value everything I heard about how she had neglected her family and about how hard Ramesh had worked to make up her shortfall; maybe my wink positioned me with many local women, who listened to men talk without interrupting or contradicting them, but also without believing all they heard. Aware that Ramesh was drunk, but also recognizing his male prerogative to dominate the conversation, no one on the porch that afternoon directly challenged his assertions beyond Rukmini's initial protest that her married life had been hard. Perhaps Rukmini, caught between the desire to defend herself and the embarrassment of arguing with her drunken husband in front of a foreigner and two higher-caste villagers, chose silence as her best defense until my unvoiced support assured her that none of us took Ramesh's drunken ramblings seriously. That leverage allowed her not to confront his representations directly but to ask him to leave. (In other situations where men or more powerful people dominated conversations, I often found that others approached me later with contradictory information they had not wanted to voice in public.) Although for the most part they accept men's right to dominate the public transcript, women make ample use of other opportunities to communicate their opinions.[5]

That afternoon on the porch, Rukmini and Ramesh each attempted to control the narrative, influence judgments, and shape appraisals. Theirs was a struggle over meaning in the making, as each attempted to define his or her own agency, identity, and self-worth with respect to the story of their family's failure to prosper. By including himself in my invitation to talk, and by excluding Rukmini from the conversation when he could, Ramesh sought to prevent his wife (and me) from portraying Rukmini as the household's decision-maker and breadwinner. Ramesh wanted to be thought of as part of a team, even as a leader, instead of as deadweight, or as someone who "sits at home idle, eating while his wife works." In his monologue, he sought to retell the story of what happened to all the money Rukmini had sent home, simultaneously reworking his own image in my eyes and in his own.

Three years later, Sita and I crowded into a trishaw (a covered, three-wheeled motorcycle) with Hema and her nephew so that Hema could show us the way to Rukmini's new house in a village ten miles from Naeaegama. Some months after the interview related above, Rukmini had gone to work abroad again, this time in Jordan, where she stayed for about a year. When she returned, she and Ramesh bought land and built half of a house. Deciding that they would rather live elsewhere, they sold that property and bought a different one. Their second house, much smaller than the one they had first started, had two rooms and a tin roof. Rukimini had spent Rs 5,000 to add a toilet to their tiny land plot. Bouncing her one-year-old daughter on her lap, Rukmini said that she would like to go abroad again, but neither her mother nor her mother-in-law would look after the girls, because their father would "come fighting" to the house, causing trouble, as he currently did for his wife.

Rukmini had asked a doctor for medicine to stop Ramesh's drinking, but the doctor would only write a prescription to Ramesh himself. Hema suggested asking the alcohol distributors not to sell Ramesh liquor. Although Rukmini still had some money in the bank (and she and her baby both wore gold necklaces), she said that the family had trouble making ends meet on Ramesh's earnings. She did not want to dip into her savings for daily expenses because she wanted to have a large coming-of-age ceremony for her oldest daughter. Fanning herself and her baby under the hot tin roof, Rukmini said that sometimes she thought she would have been better off not going abroad at all; if her husband "had a brain," she could have "brought the family up," but Rukmini wondered if her small plot of land and modest house were worth eight years of hard work abroad.

Back in 1994, I had asked Rukmini how she envisioned her life in another ten years. She said that she would like her whole family to live in a nice house of their own. My research associate greeted this aspiration with skepticism. In 1997, however, villagers voiced different opinions. Despite adversity and a wasteful husband, Rukmini did indeed live in her own home. Although small, the land and house counted as improvement in the eyes of the Naeaegama villagers, and they demonstrated that despite his heavy drinking, Ramesh had not wasted all of the money his wife earned abroad.

Women's Work

Migration has forced men and women in Sri Lankan villages to renegotiate gender roles regarding not only whether a woman can respectably work abroad but also who will take care of a migrant woman's duties and responsibilities in the home she leaves behind. Despite the large number of under- and unemployed husbands in the village, only four or five families of around ninety I interviewed admitted that men had taken over more than the bare minimum of housework. In all but one of these cases, the men in question held other jobs as well, and they shared the domestic duties with female relatives.

In Sri Lankan villages, the gendered division of labor clearly marks child care and cooking as female activities. Most men would feel their sense of masculinity threatened if they took on household chores or cared for young children. Carla Risseeuw writes of a rural Sri Lankan village near Naeaegama:

> Men cannot "stoop down" in the widest sense, without experiencing severe emotional stress. . . . The principle that he is "higher" than a woman, and more specifically his wife, permeates the actions, thoughts and emotions of both men and women. . . . Handling dirt, feces, cleaning toilets, being impure, doing repetitive, relatively less prestigious work, which often lacks the status of work as such or "prestige" of the proximity of danger, is the female expression of the principle of gender hierarchy.[6]

Most of the men and women in Naeaegama accept this division as just, and they judge themselves and others according to it.

Migrants generally told me that they left their children in the care of their mothers or mothers-in-law, but in my daily interactions in the village, I noted more male participation in child care than people reported. Priyanthi, the Naeaegama migrant introduced earlier, left her four sons in the care of her husband and his father while she was abroad. Such men and their families often glossed over men's housework in order to preserve a masculine image. Since Priyanthi's husband, Ariyapala, held a well-paying job at the hospital, he was somewhat sheltered from village ridicule when he took on his wife's work. But in an interview, Ariyapala somewhat defensively explained his assumption of domestic duties as a pragmatic solution to Priyanthi's absence. Ariyapala's heavy drinking also reaffirmed his masculine identity. The few men who did take over their migrant wives' domestic chores both challenged and reaffirmed older gender roles.

Joker, Simpleton, Freethinker: Lal

Indrani and her husband, Chandradasa, belonged to a new elite in the Naeaegama area. They were considered one of the most successful village families involved with the migration of labor to the Middle East. Indrani worked for the same family in Doha, Qatar, for twelve years, earning a very generous salary. Chandradasa worked as a security officer at a hotel near Colombo, returning home for two weekends a month. The couple saved and spent both spouses' salaries wisely. In Indrani's and Chandradasa's absence, Chandradasa's mother and brother took care of their five children and supervised the construction of their new house. Although Indrani named her mother-in-law the primary guardian for her children, the older woman's arthritis severely restricted her movements. The children's uncle Lal, a colorful village character, did the lion's share of the cooking and housekeeping.

Lal lived across the road from Siri's house, where I stayed, and he drew drinking water from the well in our garden. Members of our household replied to the greetings Lal called out every time he entered the compound with teasing comments and questions. About the state of the meal Lal was preparing, Siri invariably asked, "Is the [cooking] course over?" For a man to study cooking in school would be only slightly more astounding than to find him cooking at all. In a world of simple structural reversals, when the house-worker leaves to earn a living, one might expect the former breadwinner to do the housework. In Naeaegama, however, in most cases other women, not men, took over "feminine" chores, with grandmothers and aunts looking after the children. Lal, a man who for the past twelve years had cooked, kept house, fetched water, done laundry and shopping, and taken care of children, was the source of some astonishment and amusement in the village.

Many villagers associate full male adulthood with having a wife and a stable job. Lal had neither. At his mother's insistence, Lal had reluctantly married some years before I met him. His beautiful wife asked him to move to her relatives' home in the capital; when he refused, she found work in the Middle East and never returned to the village. Although he was fairly sure that she had come home safely, Lal had no desire to visit her relatives in the city or to see her again.

Lal had worked as a laborer and as an office clerk, but he had not held a job since he was hit by a van while walking on the side of the road a number of years previous. He had no wish to return to work and no ambition to start a business. His mother, who had persuaded him to marry in the first place, thought that he should do so again. Quoting a proverb, Lal said, "The man who is hit with the firebrand from the fire is afraid even of the firefly" (the local equivalent of "Once bitten, twice shy"). When his mother died and all of his family duties were fulfilled, Lal figured, he would become a priest. In the meantime, when his sister-in-law Indrani left for Qatar, Lal and his mother moved in with Chandradasa to look after the couple's children. The fact that Lal was single, lacked a salaried job, and devoted attention to chores often thought of as women's work caused a number of chuckles in the village.

Curious about Lal's sexuality, two village notables arranged to question him informally. One afternoon Lal, who was nearly illiterate, asked Siri's father, the local Justice of the Peace, to help him write a letter to the Graama Seevaka, the local government administrator, asking to be put on a list to receive aid from a local nongovernmental organization. In jest, the Justice of the Peace wrote a completely unsuitable letter, telling the Graama Seevaka the stark truth—that Lal lived in a good cement house with electricity and a television set. (Lal's official residence, a collapsing clay hut, formed the basis of a subsequent, successful application.) Unable to read the letter, Lal took it to the Graama Seevaka, who laughed and said, "This won't do at all," and suggested that he and Lal both go talk to the Justice of the Peace.

Siri overheard the conversation. The Justice of the Peace and the Graama Seevaka teasingly but somewhat cruelly peppered Lal with questions about his long-absent wife, asking if he had sent her cards and sweets in the Middle East. They also asked about Lal's sex life. In a village where everyone knew everyone else's business, there was not even the hint of a rumor suggesting that Lal might be actively homosexual; several other men were known to be so. The Justice of the Peace and the Graama Seevaka merely determined that Lal did not know "which end was up." Having satisfied their curiosity, the Justice of the Peace wrote a suitable letter for the Graama Seevaka and gave it to Lal, who went home to start the evening meal.

Lal's calm, slow, joking manner made him a hard target for teasing. He was the only male recipient of government aid who waited in line with the women to collect food at the local cooperative store. When villagers mocked his feminine behavior, Lal regaled them with humorous stories about his finicky taste in groceries; those who attempted to laugh at him found themselves instead laughing with him about the dead gecko in the rice bag and the dried fish so smelly it must have been fertilizer. He met comments on his domesticity with exaggerated stories about the latest crises in the kitchen, the rough quality of a new soap, and the price of beans. His complaints were uniformly within his domestic role, not about it. He created an ambiguous self-image, as something between a simpleton with no understanding of his failure to fulfill a man's proper role and a freethinker, impervious to criticism, who held a singularly different set of values. That opacity, along with his nonstop wit, allowed Lal to carve out a unique space for himself as a man whose sole job was women's work. The good-humored probing of the Graama Seevaka and the Justice of the Peace indexed at once the community's awareness of Lal's unusual behavior, and its baffled but amused acceptance.

When I spoke with Lal in 1997, he expressed some ambivalence about his domestic role. At one point he said that he needed to be "bailed out of jail" and set free from the kitchen; a little later, he noted with pride that his family preferred his cooking to Indrani's. When Indrani cooked, Lal recounted,

Chandradasa and the children could tell. "*Bappa* [uncle] didn't cook this," the children would say, with gestures that indicated that they did not like the food. Lal said that his sister-in-law made coconut milk by machine; he scraped coconuts the old-fashioned way, generating a richer milk. Her curries had a foreign taste; his had a better flavor. Neighbors had asked Lal why he still cooked when Indrani was home for a visit. He said that he would like to find a job, but Indrani and his mother had asked him not to leave. If he no longer took care of the family, Indrani would have to give up her job and look after her mother-in-law, a prospect neither of the strong-willed women viewed with pleasure. I asked Lal if he were ashamed or shy (*lajja*) about the work he did. Suddenly completely serious, he held his head up very straight and said that one should never be ashamed of the work one does to eat or drink. He took care of his mother, the house, and the children, and he did not try to hide what he did. He said he was ready to do any job that came his way, either men's work or women's work. He was not ashamed.

While Indrani's migration had changed household gender roles for both Lal and Chandradasa, only Lal's behavior drew extensive village comments. Although Chandradasa took over some of the household chores during his infrequent visits, for the most part his job as a security guard kept him out of the domestic sphere, at the same time reaffirming his breadwinner role. In contrast, Lal's daily routine included many activities commonly thought of as women's work; he lacked any other form of regular employment to reaffirm his masculinity; he had no wife or family of his own; and he did not drink alcohol. When a local committee arranged to resurface the paved road that led into the village, Lal, who had worked in road construction in the past, eagerly volunteered for the overtly masculine job. I believe he sought both the modest paycheck and the highly visible change of gender role.

Lal's ambiguous gender position complemented the new status and prestige Indrani's accumulated wealth gave her in the village. Indrani and Chandradasa contributed yearly to a large ceremony at a popular local shrine, spending over Rs 5,000 (US$100) on food and decorations. Contributing lavishly to community projects elevated the prestige and social standing of villagers; for Indrani and Chandradasa, this entitled them to positions of authority in community politics and temple decision-making formerly monopolized by wealthy, high-caste, elite families. Several days after her return from the Middle East in 1993, Indrani received an invitation from three village youths to "open" a community food distribution event. Indrani accepted the offer and also made a generous contribution. Indrani's financial capital metamorphosed into prestige, symbolic capital, respect, and renown. Watching each other cynically for signs of returning poverty, villagers often recognized that wealth was difficult to maintain. Patrons who sustained their positions for a significant length of time, as Indrani and Chandradasa have, were recognized in the village as people who had truly prospered.

How Lal and Indrani would negotiate the transformation of their roles when Indrani returned permanently to the village remained to be seen. In 1997, returning home for a vacation for the first time in four years, Indrani displayed no desire to relieve Lal of the household chores. Having spent lavishly for her daughter's coming-of-age ceremony, Indrani insisted (against her husband's will) on returning overseas to continue earning money for the family. Many villagers felt that she should have stayed home to look after her daughter instead. Indrani countered that she had spent all of her money on improving her house and holding a grand ceremony for her daughter. Now that they were older, her children needed money for their schooling. She added that she had promised to fund the construction of a new cement house where Lal and his mother would move when Indrani returned from abroad for good. The family also needed money for further improvements on their own house and to start a business, perhaps a small shop.

Indrani's prolonged absence changed not only Lal's social position but also her own. Like many migrant women, she no longer fit into village society the same way she had before she left. Though her primary motivation for migrating was economic, issues of identity, independence, and torn loyalties also impinged on her decision. Like Lal, Indrani seemed ambivalent about assuming the housewife's role in her Sri Lanka home.

Conclusion

When women migrate to the Middle East, gender roles and power relations change in the villages they leave behind. The preceding cases illustrate both the world that could once be taken for granted and the challenges that now face older patterns of behavior. Ramesh, Lal, and Chandradasa, three village men associated with female migrants, all asserted their masculinity differently: Ramesh through idleness and alcohol, Chandradasa through work and wealth, and Lal through a playful self-parody of his feminizing housekeeping role.

Ramesh's drinking, his braggadocio, and his deliberate cultivation of the idle life challenged Rukmini to prosper despite her husband, not with his help. Membership in the drinking group affirmed Ramesh's masculinity, assuaged his shame or guilt (*lajja*) for not improving his family's social status, and provided the economic and social community he may have missed in his wife's absence. Chandradasa, by comparison, found his identity in hard work away from home. The cooperative and trusting relationship he shared with his wife gave him control not only of his own salary but also of the money she earned abroad. Willingly remitted for the construction of their house, her pay enhanced both spouses' standards of living and prestige in the village.

Lal, who took on all of the domestic chores in Indrani's absence, encountered daily teasing about his cooking and household work, but he met these remarks with unfailing good humor. Because he lacked other employment, Lal brought villagers face to face with the possibility of men taking over not just individual chores but entire social roles vacated by migrant women. Lal's behavior projected a crisis in gender categories. He generated a powerful mixture of laughter and unease by assuming a traditionally domestic role as his sister-in-law moved out into the international labor market.

Because She Looks like a Child

KEVIN BALES

When Siri wakes it is about noon.[1] In the instant of waking she knows exactly who and what she has become. As she explained to me, the soreness in her genitals reminds her of the fifteen men she had sex with the night before. Siri is fifteen years old. Sold by her parents a year ago, she finds that her resistance and her desire to escape the brothel are breaking down and acceptance and resignation are taking their place.

In the provincial city of Ubon Ratchathani, in northeastern Thailand, Siri works and lives in a brothel. About ten brothels and bars, dilapidated and dusty buildings, line the side street just around the corner from a new Western-style shopping mall. Food and noodle vendors are scattered between the brothels. The woman behind the noodle stall outside the brothel where Siri works is also a spy, warder, watchdog, procurer, and dinner lady to Siri and the other twenty-four girls and women in the brothel.

The brothel is surrounded by a wall, with iron gates that meet the street. Within the wall is a dusty yard, a concrete picnic table, and the ubiquitous spirit house, a small shrine that stands outside all Thai buildings. A low door leads into a windowless concrete room that is thick with the smell of cigarettes, stale beer, vomit, and sweat. This is the "selection" room (*hong du*). On one side of the room are stained and collapsing tables and booths; on the other side is a narrow elevated platform with a bench that runs the length of the room. Spotlights pick out this bench, and at night the girls and women sit here under the glare while the men at the tables drink and choose the one they want.

Passing through another door, at the far end of the bench, the man follows the girl past a window, where a bookkeeper takes his money and records which girl he has selected. From there he is led to the girl's room. Behind its concrete front room, the brothel degenerates even further, into a haphazard shanty warren of tiny cubicles where the girls live and work. A makeshift ladder leads up to what may have once been a barn. The upper level is now lined with doors about five feet apart, which open into rooms of about five by seven feet that hold a bed and little else.

Scraps of wood and cardboard separate one room from the next, and Siri has plastered her walls with pictures of teenage pop stars cut from magazines. Over her bed, as in most rooms, there also hangs a framed portrait of the king of Thailand; a single bare lightbulb dangles from the ceiling. Next to the bed a large tin can holds water; there is a hook nearby for rags and towels. At the foot of the bed, next to the door, some clothes are folded on a ledge. The walls are very thin, and everything can be heard from the surrounding rooms; a shout from the bookkeeper echoes through all of them, whether their doors are open or closed.

After rising at midday, Siri washes herself in cold water from the single concrete trough that serves the brothel's twenty-five women. Then, dressed in a T-shirt and skirt, she goes to the noodle stand for the hot soup that is a Thai breakfast. Through the afternoon, if she does not have any clients, she chats with the other girls and women as they drink beer and play cards or make decorative handicrafts together. If the pimp is away the girls will joke around, but if not they must be constantly deferential and aware of his presence, for he can harm them or use them as he pleases. Few men visit in the afternoon, but those who do tend to have more money and can buy a girl for several hours if they like. Some will even make appointments a few days in advance.

At about five, Siri and the other girls are told to dress, put on their makeup, and prepare for the night's work. By seven the men will be coming in, purchasing drinks, and choosing girls; Siri will be chosen by the first of the ten to eighteen men who will buy her that night. Many men choose Siri because she looks much younger than her fifteen years. Slight and round faced, dressed to accentuate her youth, she could pass for eleven or twelve. Because she looks like a child, she can be sold as a "new" girl at a higher price, about $15, which is more than twice that charged for the other girls.

Siri is very frightened that she will get AIDS. Long before she understood prostitution she knew about HIV, as many girls from her village returned home to die from AIDS after being sold into the brothels. Every day she prays to Buddha, trying to earn the merit that will preserve her from the disease. She also tries to insist that her clients use condoms, and in most cases she is successful, because the pimp backs her up. But when policemen use her, or the pimp himself, they will do as they please; if she tries to insist, she will be beaten and raped. She also fears pregnancy, but like the other girls she receives injections of the contraceptive drug Depo-Provera. Once a month she has an HIV test. So far it has been negative. She knows that if she tests positive she will be thrown out to starve.

Though she is only fifteen, Siri is now resigned to being a prostitute. The work is not what she had thought it would be. Her first client hurt her, and at the first opportunity she ran away. She was quickly caught, dragged back, beaten, and raped. That night she was forced to take on a chain of clients until the early morning. The beatings and the work continued night after night, until her will was broken. Now she is sure that she is a very bad person to have deserved what has happened to her. When I comment on how pretty she looks in a photograph, how like a pop star, she replies, "I'm no star; I'm just a whore, that's all." She copes as best she can. She takes a dark pride in her higher price and the large number of men who choose her. It is the adjustment of the concentration camp, an effort to make sense of horror.

In Thailand prostitution is illegal, yet girls like Siri are sold into sex slavery by the thousands. The brothels that hold these girls are but a small part of a much wider sex industry. How can this wholesale trade in girls continue? What keeps it working? The answer is more complicated than we might think. Thailand's economic boom and its social acceptance of prostitution contribute to the pressures that enslave girls like Siri.

Rice in the Field. Fish in the River.
Daughters in the Brothel.

Thailand is blessed with natural resources and sufficient food. The climate is mild to hot, there is dependable rain, and most of the country is a great plain, well watered and fertile. The reliable production of rice has for centuries made Thailand a large exporter of grains, as it is today. Starvation is exceedingly rare in its history, and social stability very much the norm. An old and often-repeated saying in Thai is "There is always rice in the fields and fish in the river." And anyone who has tried the imaginative Thai cuisine knows the remarkable things that can be done with those two ingredients and the local chili peppers.

One part of Thailand that is not so rich in necessities of life is the mountainous north. In fact, that area is not Thailand proper; originally the kingdom of Lanna, it was integrated into Thailand only in the late nineteenth century. The influence of Burma here is very strong—as are the cultures of the seven main hill tribes, which are distinctly foreign to the dominant Thai society. Only about a tenth of the land of the north can be used for agriculture, though what can be used is the most fertile in the country. The result is that those who control good land are well-off; those who live in the higher elevations, in the forest, are not. In another part of the world this last group might be called hillbillies, and they share the hardscrabble life of mountain dwellers everywhere.

The harshness of this life stands in sharp contrast to that on the great plain of rice and fish. Customs and culture differ markedly as well, and one of those differences is a key to the sexual slavery practiced throughout Thailand today. For hundreds of years many people in the north, struggling for life, have been forced to view their own children as commodities. A failed harvest, the death of a key breadwinner, or any serious debt incurred by a family might lead to the sale of a daughter (never a son) as a slave or servant. In the culture of the north it was a life choice not preferred but acceptable, and one that was used regularly. In the past these sales fed a small, steady flow of servants, workers, and prostitutes south into Thai society.

One Girl Equals One Television

The small number of children sold into slavery in the past has become a flood today. This increase reflects the enormous changes in Thailand over the past fifty years as the country has gone through the great transformation of industrialization—the same process that tore Europe apart over a century ago. If we are to understand slavery in Thailand, we must understand these changes as well, for like so many other parts of the world, Thailand has always had slavery, but never before on this scale.

The economic boom of 1977 to 1997 had a dramatic impact on the northern villages. While the center of the country, around Bangkok, rapidly industrialized, the north was left behind. Prices of food, land, and tools all increased as the economy grew, but the returns for rice and other agriculture were stagnant, held down by government policies guaranteeing cheap food for factory workers in Bangkok. Yet visible everywhere in the north is a flood of consumer goods—refrigerators, televisions, cars and trucks, rice cookers, air conditioners—all of which are extremely tempting. Demand for these goods is high as families try to join the ranks of the prosperous. As it happens, the cost of participating in this consumer boom can be met from an old source that has become much more profitable: the sale of children.

In the past, daughters were sold in response to serious family financial crises. Under threat of losing its mortgaged rice fields and facing destitution, a family might sell a daughter to redeem its debt, but for the most part daughters were worth about as much at home as workers as they would realize when sold. Modernization and economic growth have changed all that. Now parents feel a great pressure to buy consumer goods that were unknown even twenty years ago; the sale of a daughter might easily finance a new television set. A recent survey in the northern provinces found that of the families who sold their daughters, two-thirds could afford not to do so but "instead preferred to buy color televisions and video equipment."[2] And from the perspective of parents who are willing to sell their children, there has never been a better market.

The brothels' demand for prostitutes is rapidly increasing. The same economic boom that feeds consumer demand in the northern villages lines the pockets of laborers and workers in the central plain. Poor economic migrants from the rice fields now work on building sites or in new factories, earning many times what they did on the land. Possibly for the first time in their lives, these laborers can do what more well-off Thai men have always done: go to a brothel. The purchasing power of this increasing number of brothel users strengthens the call for northern girls and supports a growing business in their procurement and trafficking.

Siri's story was typical. A broker, a woman herself from a northern village, approached the families in Siri's village with assurances of well-paid work for their daughters. Siri's parents probably understood that the work would be as a prostitute, since they knew that other girls from their village had gone south to brothels. After some negotiation they were paid 50,000 baht (US$2,000) for Siri, a very significant sum for this family of rice farmers.[3] This exchange began the process of debt bondage that is used to enslave the girls. The contractual arrangement between the broker and the parents requires that this money be paid by the daughter's labor before she is free to leave or is allowed to send money home. Sometimes the money is treated as a loan to the parents, the girls being both the collateral and the means of repayment. In such cases the exorbitant interest charged on the loan means there is little chance that a girl's sexual slavery will ever repay the debt.

Siri's debt of 50,000 baht rapidly escalated. Taken south by the broker, Siri was sold for 100,000 baht to the brothel where she now works. After her rape and beating Siri was informed that the debt she must repay to the brothel equaled 200,000 baht. In addition, Siri learned of the other payments she would be required to make, including rent for her room, at 30,000 baht per month, as well as charges for food and drink, fees for medicine, and fines if she did not work hard enough or displeased a customer.

The total debt is virtually impossible to repay, even at Siri's higher rate of 400 baht. About 100 baht from each client is supposed to be credited to Siri to reduce her debt and pay her rent and other expenses; 200 goes to the pimp and the remaining 100 to the brothel. By this reckoning, Siri must have sex with three hundred men a month just to pay her rent, and what is left over after other expenses barely reduces her original debt. For girls who can charge only 100 to 200 baht per client, the debt grows even faster. This debt bondage keeps the girls under complete control as long as the brothel owner and the pimp believe they are worth having. Violence reinforces the control, and any resistance earns a beating as well as an increase in the debt. Over time, if the girl becomes a good and cooperative prostitute, the pimp may tell her she has paid off the debt and allow her to send small sums home. This "paying off" of the debt usually has nothing to do with an actual accounting of earnings but is declared at the discretion of the pimp, as a means to extend the brothel's profits by making the girl more pliable. Together with rare visits home, money sent back to the family operates to keep her at her job.

Most girls are purchased from their parents, as Siri was, but for others the enslavement is much more direct. Throughout Thailand agents travel to villages, offering work in factories or as domestics. Sometimes they bribe local officials to vouch for them, or they befriend the monks at the local temple to gain introductions. Lured by the promise of good jobs and the money that the daughters will send back to the village, the deceived families dispatch their girls with the agent, often paying for the privilege. Once they arrive in a city, the girls are sold to a brothel, where they are raped, beaten, and locked in. Still other girls are simply kidnapped. This is especially true of women and children who have come to visit relatives in Thailand from Burma or Laos. At bus and train stations, gangs watch for women and children who can be snatched or drugged for shipment to brothels.

Direct enslavement by trickery or kidnapping is not really in the economic interest of the brothel owners. The steadily growing market for prostitutes, the loss of girls to HIV infection, and the especially strong demand for younger and younger girls make it necessary for brokers and brothel owners to cultivate village families so that they can buy more daughters as they come of age. In Siri's case this means letting her maintain ties with her family and ensuring that after a year or so she send a monthly postal order for 10,000 baht to her parents. The monthly payment is a good investment, since it encourages Siri's parents to place their other daughters in the brothel as well. Moreover, the young girls themselves become willing to go when their older sisters and relatives returning for holidays bring stories of the rich life to be lived in the cities of the central plain. Village girls lead a sheltered life, and the appearance of women only a little older than themselves with money and nice clothes is tremendously appealing. They admire the results of this thing called prostitution with only the vaguest notion of what it is. Recent research found that young girls knew that their sisters and neighbors had become prostitutes, but when asked what it means to be a prostitute their most common answer was "wearing Western clothes in a restaurant."[4]

Drawn by this glamorous life, they put up little opposition to being sent away with the brokers to swell an already booming sex industry.

By my own conservative estimate there are perhaps thirty-five thousand girls like Siri enslaved in Thailand. Remarkably, this is only a small proportion of the country's prostitutes. In the mid-1990s the government stated that there were 81,384 prostitutes in Thailand—but that official number is calculated from the number of registered (though still illegal) brothels, massage parlors, and sex establishments. One Thai researcher estimated the total number of prostitutes in 1997 to be around 200,000.[5] Every brothel, bar, and massage parlor we visited in Thailand was unregistered, and no one working with prostitutes believes the government figures. At the other end of the spectrum are the estimates put forward by activist organizations such as the Center for the Protection of Children's Rights. These groups assert that there are more than 2 million prostitutes. I suspect that this number is too high in a national population of 60 million. My own reckoning, based on information gathered by AIDS workers in different cities, is that there are between half a million and 1 million prostitutes.

Of this number, only about one in twenty is enslaved. Most become prostitutes voluntarily, through some start out in debt bondage. Sex is sold everywhere in Thailand: barbershops, massage parlors, coffee shops and cafés, bars and restaurants, nightclubs and karaoke bars, brothels, hotels, and even temples traffic in sex. Prostitutes range from the high-earning "professional" women who work with some autonomy, through the women working by choice as call girls or in massage parlors, to the enslaved rural girls like Siri. Many women work semi-independently in bars, restaurants, and nightclubs—paying a fee to the owner, working when they choose, and having the power to decide whom to take as a customer. Most bars and clubs cannot use an enslaved prostitute like Siri, as the women are often sent out on call and their clients expect a certain amount of cooperation and friendliness. Enslaved girls serve the lowest end of the market: the laborers, students, and workers who can afford only the 100 baht per half hour. It is low-cost sex in volume, and the demand is always there. For a Thai man, buying a woman is much like buying a round of drinks. But the reasons why such large numbers of Thai men use prostitutes are much more complicated and grow out of their culture, their history, and a rapidly changing economy.

"I Don't Want to Waste It, So I Take Her"

Until it was officially disbanded in 1910, the king of Thailand maintained a harem of hundreds of concubines, a few of whom might be elevated to the rank of "royal mother" or "minor wife." This form of polygamy was closely imitated by status-hungry nobles and emerging rich merchants of the nineteenth century. Virtually all men of any substance kept at least a mistress or a minor wife. For those with fewer resources, prostitution was a perfectly acceptable option, as renting took the place of out-and-out ownership.

Even today everyone in Thailand knows his or her place within a very elaborate and precise status system. Mistresses and minor wives continue to enhance any man's social standing, but the consumption of commercial sex has increased dramatically.[6] If an economic boom is a tide that raises all boats, then vast numbers of Thai men have now been raised to a financial position from which they can regularly buy sex. Nothing like the economic growth in Thailand was ever experienced in the West, but a few facts show its scale: in a country the size of Britain, one-tenth of the workforce moved from the land to industry in just the three years from 1993 to 1995; the number of factory workers doubled from less than 2 million to more than 4 million in the eight years from 1988 to 1995; and urban wages doubled from 1986 to 1996. Thailand is now the world's largest importer of motorcycles and the second-largest importer of pickup tricks, after the United States. Until the economic downturn of late 1997, money flooded Thailand, transforming poor rice farmers into wage laborers and fueling consumer demand.

With this newfound wealth, Thai men go to brothels in increasing numbers. Several recent studies show that between 80 and 87 percent of Thai men have had sex with a prostitute. Most report that their first sexual experience was with a prostitute. Somewhere between 10 and 40 percent of married men have paid for commercial sex within the past twelve months, as have up to 50 percent of single men. Though it is difficult to measure, these reports suggest something like 3 to 5 million regular customers for commercial sex. But it would be wrong to imagine millions of Thai men sneaking furtively on their own along dark streets lined with brothels; commercial sex is a social event, part of a good night out with friends.

Ninety-five percent of men going to a brothel do so with their friends, usu-ally at the end of a night spent drinking. Groups go out for recreation and entertainment, and especially to get drunk together. That is a strictly male pursuit, as Thai women usually abstain from alcohol. All-male groups out for a night on the town are considered normal in any Thai city, and whole neighborhoods are devoted to serving them. One man interviewed in a recent study explained, "When we arrive at the brothel, my friends take one and pay for me to take another. It costs them money; I don't want to waste it, so I take her."[7] Having one's prostitute paid for also brings an informal obliga-tion to repay in kind at a later date. Most Thais, men and women, feel that commercial sex is an acceptable part of an ordinary outing for single men, and about two-thirds of men and one-third of women feel the same about married men.[8]

For most married women, having their husbands go to prostitutes is preferable to other forms of extramarital sex. Most wives accept that men naturally want multiple partners, and prostitutes are seen as less threatening to the stability of the family.[9] Prostitutes require no long-term commitment or emotional involvement. When a husband uses a prostitute he is thought to be fulfilling a male role, but when he takes a minor wife or mistress, his wife is thought to have failed. Minor wives are usually bigamous second wives, often married by law in a district different than that of the men's first marriage (easily done, since no national records are kept). As wives, they require upkeep, housing, and regular support, and their offspring have a claim on inheritance; so they present a significant danger to the well-being of the major wife and her children. The potential disaster for the first wife is a minor wife who convinces the man to leave his first family, and this happens often enough to keep first wives worried and watchful.

For many Thai men, commercial sex is a legitimate form of entertain-ment and sexual release. It is not just acceptable: it is a clear statement of sta-tus and economic power. Such attitudes reinforce the treatment of women as mere markers in a male game of status and prestige. Combined with the new economy's relentless drive for profits, the result for women can be horrific. Thousands more must be found to feed men's status needs, thousands more must be locked into sexual slavery to feed the profits of investors. And what are the police, government, and local authorities doing about slavery? Every case of sex slavery involves many crimes—fraud, kidnap, assault, rape, sometimes murder. These crimes are not rare or random; they are systematic and repeated in brothels thousands of times each month. Yet those with the power to stop this terror instead help it continue to grow and to line the pockets of the slaveholders.

Millionaire Tiger and Billionaire Geese

Who are these modern slaveholders? The answer is anyone and everyone—anyone, that is, with a little capital to invest. The people who *appear* to own the enslaved prostitutes—the pimps, madams, and brothel keepers—are usually just employees. As hired muscle, pimps and their helpers provide the brutality that controls women and makes possible their commercial exploitation. Although they are just employees, the pimps do rather well for themselves. Often living in the brothel, they receive a salary and add to that income by a number of scams; for example, food and drinks are sold to customers at inflated prices, and the pimps pocket the difference. Much more lucrative is their control of the price of sex. While each woman has a basic price, the pimps size up each customer and pitch the fee accordingly. In this way a client may pay two or three times more than the normal rate, and all of the surplus goes to the pimp. In league with the bookkeeper, the pimp systematically cheats the prostitutes of the little that is supposed to be credited against their debt. If they manage the sex slaves well and play all of the angles, pimps can easily make ten times their basic wage—a great income for an ex-peasant whose main skills are violence and intimidation, but nothing compared to the riches to be made by the brokers and the real slaveholders.

The brokers and agents who buy girls in the villages and sell them to brothels are only short-term slaveholders. Their business is part recruiting agency, part shipping company, part public relations, and part kidnapping gang. They aim to buy low and sell high while maintaining a good flow of girls from the villages. Brokers are equally likely to be men or women, and they usually come from the regions in which they recruit. Some are local people dealing in girls in addition to their jobs as police officers, government bureaucrats, or even schoolteachers. Positions of public trust are excellent starting points for buying young girls. In spite of the character of their work, they are well respected. Seen as job providers and sources of large cash payments to parents, they are well known in their communities. Many of the women brokers were once sold themselves; some spent years as prostitutes and now, in their middle age, make their living by supplying girls to the brothels. These women are walking advertisements for sexual slavery. Their lifestyle and income, their Western clothes and glamorous, sophisticated ways promise a rosy economic future for the girls they buy. That they have physically survived their years in the brothel may be the exception—many more young women come back to the village to die of AIDS—but the parents tend to be optimistic.

Whether these dealers are local people or traveling agents, they combine the business of procuring with other economic pursuits. A returned prostitute may live with her family, look after her parents, own a rice field or two, and buy and sell girls on the side. Like the pimps, they are in a good business, doubling their money on each girl within two or three weeks; but also like the pimps, their profits are small compared to those of the long-term slaveholders.

The real slaveholders tend to be middle-aged businessmen. They fit seamlessly into the community, and they suffer no social discrimination for what they do. If anything, they are admired as successful, diversified capitalists. Brothel ownership is normally only one of many business interests for the slaveholder. To be sure, a brothel owner may have some ties to organized crime, but in Thailand organized crime includes the police and much of the government. Indeed, the work of the modern slaveholder is best seen not as aberrant criminality but as a perfect example of disinterested capitalism. Owning the brothel that holds young girls in bondage is simply a business matter. The investors would say that they are creating jobs and wealth. There is no hypocrisy in their actions, for they obey an important social norm: earning a lot of money is good enough reason for anything.

The slaveholder may in fact be a partnership, company, or corporation. In the 1980s, Japanese investment poured into Thailand, in an enormous migration of capital that was called "Flying Geese."[10] The strong yen led to buying and building across the country, and while electronics firms built television factories, other investors found that there was much, much more to be made in the sex industry. Following the Japanese came investment from the so-called Four Tigers (South Korea, Hong Kong, Taiwan, and Singapore), which also found marvelous opportunities in commercial sex. (All five of these countries further proved to be strong import markets for enslaved Thai girls, as discussed below.) The Geese and the Tigers had the resources to buy the local criminals, police, administrators, and property needed to set up commercial sex businesses. Indigenous Thais also invested in brothels as the sex industry boomed; with less capital, they were more likely to open poorer, working-class outlets.

Whether they are individual Thais, partnerships, or foreign investors, the slaveholders share many characteristics. There is little or no racial or ethnic difference between them and the slaves they own (with the exception of the Japanese investors). They feel no need to rationalize their slaveholding on racial grounds. Nor are they linked in any sort of hereditary ownership of slaves or of the children of their slaves. They are not really interested in their slaves at all, just in the bottom line on their investment.

To understand the business of slavery today we have to know something about the economy in which it operates. Thailand's economic boom included a sharp increase in sex tourism tacitly backed by the government. International tourist arrivals jumped from 2 million in 1981 to 4 million in 1988 to over 7 million in 1996.[11] Two-thirds of tourists were unaccompanied men; in other words, nearly 5 million unaccompanied men visited Thailand in 1996. A significant proportion of these were sex tourists.

The recent downturn in both tourism and the economy may have slowed, but not dramatically altered, sex tourism. In 1997 the annual illegal income generated by sex workers in Thailand was roughly $10 billion, which is more than drug trafficking is estimated to generate.[12] According to ECPAT, an organization working against child prostitution, the economic crisis in Southeast Asia may have increased the exploitation of young people in sex tourism:

> According to Professor Lae Dilokvidhayarat from Chulalongkorn University, there has been a 10 percent decrease in the school enrollment at primary school level in Thailand since 1996. Due to increased unemployment, children cannot find work in the formal sector, but instead are forced to "disappear" into the informal sector. This makes them especially vulnerable to sexual exploitation. Also, a great number of children are known to travel to tourist areas and to big cities hoping to find work.

We cannot overlook the impact of the economic crisis on sex tourism, either. Even though travelling costs to Asian countries are approximately the same as before mid 1997, when the crisis began, the rates for sexual services in many places are lower due to increased competition in the business. Furthermore, since there are more children trying to earn money, there may also be more so called situational child sex tourists, i.e. those who do not necessarily prefer children as sexual partners, but who may well choose a child if the situation occurs and the price is low."[13]

In spite of the economic boom, the average Thai's income is very low by Western standards. Within an industrializing country, millions still live in rural poverty. If a rural family owns its house and has a rice field, it might survive on as little as 500 baht ($20) per month. Such absolute poverty means a diet of rice supplemented with insects (crickets, grubs, and maggots are widely eaten), wild plants, and what fish the family can catch. If a family's standard of living drops below this level, which can be sustained only in the countryside, it faces hunger and the loss of its house or land. For most Thais, an income of 2,500 to 4,000 baht per month ($100 to $180) is normal. Government figures from December 1996 put two-thirds of the population at this level. There is no system of welfare or health care, and pinched budgets allow no space for saving. In these families, the 20,000 to 50,000 baht ($800 to $2,000) brought by selling a daughter provides a year's income. Such a vast sum is a powerful inducement that often blinds parents to the realities of sexual slavery.

Disposable Bodies

Girls are so cheap that there is little reason to take care of them over the long term. Expenditure on medical care or prevention is rare in the brothels, since the working life of girls in debt bondage is fairly short—two to five years. After that, most of the profit has been drained from the girl and it is more cost-effective to discard her and replace her with someone fresh. No brothel wants to take on the responsibility of a sick or dying girl.

Enslaved prostitutes in brothels face two major threats to their physical health and to their lives: violence and disease. Violence—their enslavement enforced through rape, beatings, or threats—is always present. It is a girl's typical introduction to her new status as a sex slave. Virtually every girl interviewed repeated the same story: after she was taken to the brothel or to her first client as a virgin, any resistance or refusal was met with beatings and rape. A few girls reported being drugged and then attacked; others reported being forced to submit at gunpoint. The immediate and forceful application of terror is the first step in successful enslavement. Within hours of being brought to the brothel, the girls are in pain and shock. Like other victims of torture they often go numb, paralyzed in their minds if not in their bodies. For the youngest girls, who understand little of what is happening to them, the trauma is overwhelming. Shattered and betrayed, they often have few clear memories of what occurred.

After the first attack, the girl has little resistance left, but the violence never ends. In the brothel, violence and terror are the final arbiters of all questions. There is no argument; there is no appeal. An unhappy customer brings a beating, a sadistic client brings more pain; in order to intimidate and cheat them more easily, the pimp rains down terror randomly on the prostitutes. The girls must do anything the pimp wants if they are to avoid being beaten. Escape is impossible. One girl reported that when she was caught trying to escape, the pimp beat her and then took her into the viewing room; with two helpers he then beat her again in front of all the girls in the brothel. Afterward she was locked into a room for three days and nights with no food or water. When she was released she was immediately put to work. Two other girls who attempted escape told of being stripped naked and whipped with steel coat hangers by pimps. The police serve as slave catchers whenever a girl escapes; once captured, girls are often beaten or abused at the police station before being sent back to the brothel. For most girls it soon becomes clear that they can never escape, that their only hope for release is to please the pimp and to somehow pay off their debt.

In time, confusion and disbelief fade, leaving dread, resignation, and a break in the conscious link between mind and body. Now the girl does whatever it takes to reduce the pain, to adjust mentally to a life that means being used by fifteen men a day. The reaction to this abuse takes many forms: lethargy, aggression, self-loathing, suicide attempts, confusion, self-abuse, depression, full-blown psychoses, and hallucinations. Girls who have been freed and taken into shelters exhibit all of these disorders. Rehabilitation workers report that the girls suffer emotional instability; they are unable to trust or to form relationships, to readjust to the world outside the brothel, or to learn and develop normally. Unfortunately, psychological counseling is virtually unknown in Thailand, as there is a strong cultural pressure to keep mental problems hidden. As a result, little therapeutic work is done with girls freed from brothels. The long-term impact of their experience is unknown.

The prostitute faces physical dangers as well as emotional ones. There are many sexually transmitted diseases, and prostitutes contract most of them. Multiple infections weaken the immune system and make it easier for other infections to take hold. If the illness affects a girl's ability to have sex, it may be dealt with, but serious chronic illnesses are often left untreated. Contraception often harms the girls as well. Some slaveholders administer contraceptive pills themselves, continuing them without any break and withholding the monthly placebo pills so that the girls can work more nights of the month. These girls stop menstruating altogether.

Not surprisingly, HIV/AIDS is epidemic in enslaved prostitutes. Thailand now has one of the highest rates of HIV infection in the world. Officially, the government admits to 800,000 cases, but health workers insist there are at least twice that many. Mechai Veravaidya, a birth-control campaigner and expert who has been so successful that *mechai* is now the Thai word for condom, predicts there will be 4.3 million people infected with HIV by 2001.[14] In some rural villages from which girls are regularly trafficked, the infection rate is over 60 percent. Recent research suggests that the younger the girl, the more susceptible she is to HIV, because her protective vaginal mucous membrane has not fully developed. Although the government distributes condoms, some brothels do not require their use.

Burmese Prostitutes

The same economic boom that has increased the demand for prostitutes may, in time, bring an end to Thai sex slavery. Industrial growth has also led to an increase in jobs for women. Education and training are expanding rapidly across Thailand, and women and girls are very much taking part. The ignorance and deprivation on which the enslavement of girls depends are on the wane, and better-educated girls are much less likely to fall for the promises made by brokers. The traditional duties to family, including the debt of obligation to parents, are also becoming less compelling. As the front line of industrialization sweeps over northern Thailand, it is bringing fundamental changes. Programs on the television bought with the money from selling one daughter may carry warning messages to her younger sisters. As they learn more about new jobs, about HIV/AIDS, and about the fate of those sent to the brothels, northern Thai girls refuse to follow their sisters south. Slavery functions best when alternatives are few, and education and the media are opening the eyes of Thai girls to a world of choice.

For the slaveholders this presents a serious problem. They are faced with an increase in demand for prostitutes and a diminishing supply. Already the price of young Thai girls is spiraling upward. The slaveholders' only recourse is to look elsewhere, to areas where poverty and ignorance still hold sway. Nothing, in fact, could be easier: there remain large, oppressed, and isolated populations desperate enough to believe the promises of the brokers. From Burma to the west and Laos to the east come thousands of economic and political refugees searching for work; they are defenseless in a country where they are illegal aliens. The techniques that worked so well in bringing Thai girls to brothels are again deployed, but now across borders. Investigators from Human Rights Watch, which made a special study of this trafficking in 1993, explain:

> The trafficking of Burmese women and girls into Thailand is appalling in its efficiency and ruthlessness. Driven by the desire to maximize profit and the fear of HIV/AIDS, agents acting on behalf of brothel owners infiltrate ever more remote areas of Burma seeking unsuspecting recruits. Virgin girls are particularly sought after because they bring a higher price and pose less threat of exposure to sexually transmitted disease. The agents promise the women and girls jobs as waitresses or dishwashers, with good pay and new clothes. Family members or friends typically accompany the women and girls to the Thai border, where they receive a payment ranging from 10,000 to 20,000 baht from someone associated with the brothel. This payment becomes the debt, usually doubled with interest, that the women and girls must work to pay off, not by waitressing or dishwashing, but through sexual servitude.[15]

Once in the brothels they are in an even worse situation than the enslaved Thai girls: because they do not speak Thai their isolation is increased, and as illegal aliens they are open to even more abuse. The pimps tell them repeatedly that if they set foot outside the brothel, they will be arrested. And when they are arrested, Burmese and Lao girls and women are afforded no legal rights. They are often held for long periods at the mercy of the police, without charge or trial. A strong traditional antipathy between Thais and Burmese increases the chances that Burmese sex slaves will face discrimination and arbitrary treatment. Explaining why so many Burmese women were kept in brothels in Ranong, in southern Thailand, the regional police commander told a reporter for the *Nation:* "In my opinion it is disgraceful to let Burmese men [working in the local fishing industry] frequent Thai prostitutes. Therefore I have been flexible in allowing Burmese prostitutes to work here."[16]

A special horror awaits Burmese and Lao women once they reach the revolving door at the border. If they escape or are dumped by the brothel owners, they come quickly to the attention of the police, since they have no money for transport and cannot speak Thai. Once they are picked up, they are placed in detention, where they meet women who have been arrested in the periodic raids on brothels and taken into custody with only the clothes they are wearing. In local jails, the foreign women might be held without charge for as long as eight months while they suffer sexual and other abuse by the police. In time, they might be sent to the Immigrant Detention Center in Bangkok or to prison. In both places, abuse and extortion by the staff continue, and some girls are sold back to the brothels from there. No trial is necessary for deportation, but many women are tried and convicted of prostitution or illegal entry. The trials take place in Thai without interpreters, and fines are charged against those convicted. If they have no money to pay the fines, and most do not, they are sent to a factory-prison to earn it. There they make lightbulbs or plastic flowers for up to twelve hours a day; the prison officials decide when they have earned enough to pay their fine. After the factory-prison the women are sent back to police cells or the Immigrant Detention Center. Most are held until they can cover the cost of transportation (illegal aliens are required by law to pay for their own deportation); others are summarily deported.

The border between Thailand and Burma is especially chaotic and dangerous. Only part of it is controlled by the Burmese military dictatorship; other areas are in the hands of tribal militias or warlords. After arriving at the border, the deportees are held in cells by immigration police for another three to seven days. Over this time, the police extort money and physically and sexually abuse the inmates. The police also use this time to make arrangements with brothel owners and brokers, notifying them of the dates and places of deportation. On the day of deportation, the prisoners are driven in cattle trucks into the countryside along the border, far from any village, and then pushed out. Abandoned in the jungle, miles from any major road, they are given no food or water and have no idea where they are or how to proceed into Burma. As the immigration police drive away, the deportees are approached by agents and brokers who followed the trucks from town by arrangement with the police. The brokers offer work and transportation back into Thailand. Abandoned in the jungle, many women see the offer as their only choice. Some who don't are attacked and abducted. In either case, the cycle of debt bondage and prostitution begins again.

If they do make it into Burma, the women face imprisonment or worse. If apprehended by Burmese border patrols they are charged with "illegal departure" from Burma. If they cannot pay the fine, and most cannot, they serve six months' hard labor. Imprisonment applies to all those convicted— men, women, and children. If a girl or woman is suspected of having been a prostitute, she can face additional charges and long sentences. Women found to be HIV-positive have been imprisoned and executed. According to Human Rights Watch, there are consistent reports of "deportees being routinely arrested, detained, subjected to abuse and forced to porter for the military. Torture, rape and execution have been well documented by the United Nations bodies, international human rights organizations and governments."[17]

The situation on Thailand's eastern border with Laos is much more difficult to assess. The border is more open, and there is a great deal of movement back and forth. Lao police, government officials, and community leaders are involved in the trafficking, working as agents and making payments to local parents. They act with impunity, as it is very difficult for Lao girls to escape back to their villages; those who do find it dangerous to speak against police or officials. One informant told me that if a returning girl did talk, no one would believe her *and* she would be branded as a prostitute and shunned. There would be no way to expose the broker and no retribution; she would just have to resign herself to her fate. It is difficult to know how many Lao women and girls are brought into Thailand. In the northeast many Thais speak Lao, which makes it difficult to tell whether a prostitute is a local Thai or has actually come from Laos. Since they are illegal aliens, Lao girls will always claim to be local Thais and will often have false identity cards to prove it. In the brothels their lives are indistinguishable from those of Thai women.

To Japan, Switzerland, Germany, the United States

Women and girls flow in both directions over Thailand's borders.[18] The export of enslaved prostitutes is a robust business, supplying brothels in Japan, Europe, and America. Thailand's Ministry of Foreign Affairs estimated in 1994 that as many as 50,000 Thai women were living illegally in Japan and working in prostitution. Their situation in these countries parallels that of Burmese women held in Thailand. The enticement of Thai women follows a familiar pattern. Promised work as cleaners, domestics, dishwashers, or cooks, Thai girls and women pay large fees to employment agents to secure jobs in rich, developed countries. When they arrive, they are brutalized and enslaved. Their debt bonds are significantly larger than those of enslaved prostitutes in Thailand, since they include airfares, bribes to immigration officials, the costs of false passports, and sometimes the fees paid to foreign men to marry them and ease their entry.

Variations on sex slavery occur in different countries. In Switzerland girls are brought in on "artist" visas as exotic dancers. There, in addition to being prostitutes, they must work as striptease dancers in order to meet the carefully checked terms of their employment. The brochures of the European companies that have leaped into the sex-tourism business leave the customer no doubt about what is being sold:

> Slim, sunburnt, and sweet, they love the white man in an erotic and devoted way. They are masters of the art of making love by nature, an art that we Europeans do not know. (Life Travel, Switzerland)

[M]any girls from the sex world come from the poor north-eastern region of the country and from the slums of Bangkok. It has become a custom that one of the nice looking daughters goes into the business in order to earn money for the poor family . . . [Y]ou can get the feeling that taking a girl here is as easy as buying a package of cigarettes . . . little slaves who give real Thai warmth. (Kanita Kamha Travel, the Netherlands)[19]

In Germany they are usually bar girls, and they are sold to men by the bartender or bouncer. Some are simply placed in brothels or apartments controlled by pimps. After Japanese sex tours to Thailand began in the 1980s, Japan rapidly became the largest importer of Thai women. The fear of HIV in Japan has also increased the demand for virgins. Because of their large disposable incomes, Japanese men are able to pay considerable sums for young rural girls from Thailand. Japanese organized crime is involved throughout the importation process, sometimes shipping women via Malaysia or the Philippines. In the cities, the Japanese mob maintains bars and brothels that trade in Thai women. Bought and sold between brothels, these women are controlled with extreme violence. Resistance can bring murder. Because the girls are illegal aliens and often enter the country under false passports, Japanese gangs rarely hesitate to kill them if they have ceased to be profitable or if they have angered their slaveholders. Thai women deported from Japan also report that the gangs will addict girls to drugs in order to manage them more easily.

Criminal gangs, usually Chinese or Vietnamese, also control brothels in the United States that enslave Thai women. Police raids in New York, Seattle, San Diego, and Los Angeles have freed more than a hundred girls and women.[20] In New York, thirty Thai women were locked into the upper floors of a building used as a brothel. Iron bars sealed the windows and a series of buzzer-operated armored gates blocked exit to the street. During police raids, the women were herded into a secret basement room. At her trial, the brothel owner testified that she'd bought the women outright, paying between $6,000 and $15,000 for each. The women were charged $300 per week for room and board; they worked from 11:00 A.M until 4:00 A.M. and were sold by the hour to clients. Chinese and Vietnamese gangsters were also involved in the brothel, collecting protection money and hunting down escaped prostitutes. The gangs owned chains of brothels and massage parlors, through which they rotated the Thai women in order to defeat law enforcement efforts. After being freed from the New York brothel, some of the women disappeared—only to turn up weeks later in similar circumstances three thousand miles away, in Seattle. One of the rescued Thai women, who had been promised restaurant work and then enslaved, testified that the brothel owners "bought something and wanted to use it to the full extent, and they didn't think those people were human beings."[21]

Official Indifference and a Growth Economy

In many ways, Thailand closely resembles another country, one that was going through rapid industrialization and economic boom one hundred years ago. Rapidly shifting its labor force off the farm, experiencing unprecedented economic growth, flooded with economic migrants, and run by corrupt politicians and a greedy and criminal police force, the United States then faced many of the problems confronting Thailand today. In the 1890s, political machines that brought together organized crime with politicians and police ran the prostitution and protection rackets, drug sales, and extortion in American cities. Opposing them were a weak and disorganized reform movement and a muckraking press. I make this comparison because it is important to explore why Thailand's government is so ineffective when faced with the enslavement of its own citizens, and also to remember that conditions *can* change over time. Discussions with Thais about the horrific nature of sex slavery often end with their assertion that "nothing will ever change this . . . the problem is just too big . . . and those with power will never allow change." Yet the social and economic underpinnings of slavery in Thailand are always changing, sometimes for the worse and sometimes for the better. No society can remain static, particularly one undergoing such upheavals as Thailand.

As the country takes on a new Western-style materialist morality, the ubiquitous sale of sex sends a clear message: women can be enslaved and exploited for profit. Sex tourism helped set the stage for the expansion of sexual slavery.

Sex tourism also generates some of the income that Thai men use to fund their own visits to brothels. No one knows how much money it pours into the Thai economy, but if we assume that just one-quarter of sex workers serve sex tourists and that their customers pay about the same as they would pay to use Siri, then 656 billion baht ($26.2 billion) a year would be about right. This is thirteen times more than the amount Thailand earns by building and exporting computers, one of the country's major industries, and it is money that floods into the country without any concomitant need to build factories or improve infrastructure. It is part of the boom raising the standard of living generally and allowing an even greater number of working-class men to purchase commercial sex.

Joining the world economy has done wonders for Thailand's income and terrible things to its society. According to Pasuk Phongpaichit and Chris Baker, economists who have analyzed Thailand's economic boom,

> Government has let the businessmen ransack the nation's human and natural resources to achieve growth. It has not forced them to put much back. In many respects, the last generation of economic growth has been a disaster. The forests have been obliterated. The urban environment has deteriorated. Little has been done to combat the growth in industrial pollution and hazardous wastes. For many people whose labour has created the boom, the conditions of work, health, and safety are grim.
>
> Neither law nor conscience has been very effective in limiting the social costs of growth. Business has reveled in the atmosphere of free-for-all. The machinery for social protection has proved very pliable. The legal framework is defective. The judiciary is suspect. The police are unreliable. The authorities have consistently tried to block popular organizations to defend popular rights.[22]

The situation in Thailand today is similar to that of the United States in the 1850s; with a significant part of the economy dependent on slavery, religious and cultural leaders are ready to explain why this is all for the best. But there is also an important difference: this is the new slavery, and the impermanence of modern slavery and the dedication of human-rights workers offer some hope.

Clashing Dreams:
Highly Educated Overseas Brides
and Low-Wage U.S. Husbands

Hung Cam Thai

Hours before her husband's plane was due, on a rainy day in July 2000, Thanh Nguyen[1] and about thirty members of her family anxiously waited outside of Tan Son Nhut, Saigon's international airport.[2] Thanh's family was understandably excited. For many families expecting a relative or a close friend from the Vietnamese diaspora, the waiting is an event in itself: they come to the airport long before the plane is due, creating such a commotion outside that it is difficult to follow any one conversation.

I watched and listened, like a waiter at a busy restaurant—intently but discreetly. I could make out only fragments of conversations among people of a culture known for making sure: "Make sure you greet him properly," adults told young children. "Make sure the restaurant knows we are coming," men reminded women. And of course, "Make sure you always show him love and respect," Thanh's parents reminded their thirty-two-year-old daughter.

The Nguyens were prudent people. Although they knew Thanh's husband, Minh, well—he had made the long journey across the Pacific from his home in Quincy, Washington, three times in the last year—they wanted him to feel welcome and important each time he visited. Their instinct was a good one: when I visited him in Quincy, ninety miles from Seattle, the thirty-seven-year-old Minh revealed to me that he often did not feel important or respected in the small suburban town where he lived.

Seattle is one of the most heavily Vietnamese cities outside of Vietnam, and Thanh's husband is one of more than two million *Viet Kieu*, or Vietnamese people living overseas, who make up an aging diaspora that largely began emigrating in the mid-1970s.[3] Thanh will soon join Minh in Quincy as one of more than 200,000 legal marriage migrants who come to the United States each year.[4]

About a quarter of all men and more than 40 percent of all women who currently enter the United States are marriage migrants.[5] Of these marriage migrants, more than 65 percent are women. It is no news that women have dominated U.S.–bound migration since the 1930s[6] and that, historically, more women than men have migrated as spouses.[7] However, despite the fact that marriage remains the number one reason people migrate to the United States,[8] we know very little about the specific contemporary marriage migration streams or about why women overwhelmingly dominate them.[9] More familiar is the often sensationalized phenomenon of mail-order brides;[10] though an important part of the female marriage migration puzzle, such women constitute at most 4 percent of all marriage migrants.[11]

The marriage of Minh and Thanh follows a global trend that has been gathering momentum over the last forty years: immigrant and immigrant-origin men are more and more frequently seeking wives in their countries of origin.[12] An estimated two-thirds of all marriage migrants are of the same ethnicity, and among migrants who come to the United States married to noncitizen permanent residents (presumably immigrants), almost 90 percent are women.[13] Like many international marriages between same-ethnic individuals, especially in Asia, the marriage of Minh and Thanh was arranged. Marriage arrangements come in many forms, and I have addressed these elsewhere.[14] What Minh and Tranh represent is a specific and fairly typical pattern: the marriage of the two "unmarriageables," namely of highly educated women in Vietnam to Vietnamese men who do low-wage work overseas.[15]

The Double Marriage Squeeze

Vietnamese people worldwide are pressed by what demographer Daniel Goodkind calls the "double marriage squeeze."[16] A high male mortality rate during the Vietnam War, combined with the migration of a larger number of men than women during the last quarter of the twentieth century, has produced a low ratio of men to women in Vietnam, as well as an unusually high ratio of men to women in the Vietnamese diaspora, especially in Australia and the United States. Of the fifteen most populous nations in 1989, Vietnam had the lowest ratio of men to women at the peak marrying ages. By 1999, there were approximately 92 men for every 100 women between the ages of 30 and 34 in Vietnam. The reverse situation prevails in the diaspora: in 2000, there were 129 Vietnamese-American men for every 100 women between the ages of 24 and 29. Among Vietnamese-Americans aged 30 to 34, there were about 135 men for every 100 women.[17]

Those who study marriage markets have long documented a nearly universal pattern, called the marriage gradient, whereby women tend to marry men who are older, better educated, and higher earning than they are, while men tend to marry younger women who earn less money and have less education.[18] Men "marry down" economically and socially; women "marry up." Transnational couples like Minh and Thanh, however, seem to reverse the marriage gradient. But depending on the measure one uses, it is often difficult to tell who is really marrying up, and who down.

Thanh belongs to an emerging group of highly educated women in Vietnam who have delayed or avoided marriage with local men. These women have found that too few men in Vietnam are employed and successful relative to them. More important, in the eyes of many men influenced by traditional Asian and Confucian hierarchies of gender, age, and class, a highly educated woman like Thanh is unmarriageable. As with highly educated African-American women in the United States, there is a surfeit of women like Thanh in Vietnam relative to their educated male counterparts. Minh, on the other hand, belongs to a surfeit group of Viet Kieu men, many of whom are unable to find marriage partners partly because they are low-wage workers. Some of these men, though certainly not all, experienced tremendous downward mobility when they migrated overseas after the Vietnam War.

In my study of sixty-nine Vietnamese transpacific marriages, 80 percent of the men were low-wage earners like Minh. These men generally work for hourly wages, though some work in ethnic enterprises where salaries are negotiated under the table. For the most part, they work long hours for low pay. Almost 70 percent of their brides are women like Thanh, who are college-educated; about 40 percent of these women have advanced degrees, which permit them to work as doctors, lawyers, computer programmers, and the like. Of my entire sample about 55 percent were marriages between these two "unmarriageables."[19]

The double marriage squeeze is one force propelling these transpacific marriages of the two unmarriageables, but the cultural belief in the marriage gradient is at least as powerful and probably more so. The marriage gradient is a strict norm in Vietnamese culture. Many Vietnamese, including the unmarriageables themselves, believe that by making these unorthodox matches transnational ones, they somehow get around the discomfort of breaking the marriage gradient norm. It is as though despite their relative incomes and education, if the man is from a First World country, he has the "up," while a woman from Third World Vietnam has the "down." And though it is no surprise that the economic divide between the First and Third Worlds deeply penetrates the private lives of Vietnamese transpacific couples, it is not always clear who has the Third World life in marriages of the two unmarriageables.

While reaching out overseas seems a perfect solution to the double marriage squeeze, it gives rise to an unanticipated collision of gender ideologies in 90 percent of these couples. The reason is that the dreams that led both partners into the arrangement often had as much to do with gender as with economic mobility. Educated women like Thanh hope that a man living overseas in a modern country will respect women more than men at home, who may still be in the sway of ancient Vietnamese traditions. Low-wage working men like Minh, meanwhile, often look to women in Vietnam precisely because they wish to uphold those ancient traditions, which they believe have been eroded in modern American life, but which they expect a woman in Vietnam will maintain.

In their search for spouses, both parties have relied to some extent on tradition, which leads them to agree to a marriage arranged by family members. But it is the modern, globalizing culture of Vietnam that makes the transnational match possible. In 1986, after having had no contact with the outside world for over a decade, the Vietnamese government adopted a new economic policy known as *doi moi*. It did not end state ownership, but it encouraged private enterprise, free markets, and global engagement. In the 1990s, Saigon reemerged as a major international city, first within Asia and then in the world more generally. Vietnam was projected to be one of Asia's next "tigers."[20] Enticed by an emerging labor and consumer market of eighty million people, foreign companies were eager to move their factories there and to make their products known.

Globalization rapidly opened the Vietnamese market for capital, goods, and labor. At the same time, it also opened a more personal exchange of emotions and marriage partners. But while goods and capital tend to flow in two directions, the divide between the First World economy of the West and the Third World economy of Vietnam makes it impossible for women in Vietnam to go abroad to look for grooms but very easy for Viet Kieu men to go to Vietnam for brides. Just as global corporations and factories moved to Vietnam to partake of its large supply of labor, Viet Kieu men go there to choose among its large selection of potential brides. But unlike locals who eagerly take jobs at foreign factories for the pay, Vietnamese transpacific brides have a wide range of reasons for choosing to marry Viet Kieu men.

The Highly Educated Bride

Twenty years ago, Thanh's father was a math teacher at Le Buon Phong, a prestigious high school in Saigon. After the war, Thanh's uncle, her mother's younger brother, and his family were among the several thousand Vietnamese who were airlifted out of Vietnam on April 30, 1975, when Saigon surrendered to the North Vietnamese. They eventually settled in Houston, one of the larger Vietnamese enclaves in the United States, and started a successful restaurant business specializing in *pho*, the popular Vietnamese beef noodle soup. Remittances from Thanh's uncle helped her parents open a small candy factory in the late 1980s; that factory now has more than forty employees. Thanh's parents belong to a small but very visible class of Vietnamese families who enjoy access to overseas resources. They are part of a Viet Kieu economy that has grown from roughly $35 million in 1993 to an estimated $2 billion in 2000.[21]

Thanh was only seven years old when Saigon fell. She is not as old as Minh, whose memory of the war is very strong and formative; nor is she able to put that era completely behind her, like her peers born after the war, who are eager to move forward and to join the global economy. She embraces foreign influences and appreciates the access she has to them. Many of her friends work in foreign companies as translators, or in marketing or sales; some have become local branch supervisors for international corporations such as Citibank and IBM. Nevertheless, Thanh is conscious that her parents have sustained hidden injuries from accepting remittances from her uncle in Houston, and this saddens her. She observes:

> My father is a very strong man; nobody ever tells him what to do with his life, like how to raise his children. But I think it is very hard for him when he has to deal with my uncle. My uncle is a very nice man, and he cares a lot for our family. But even though he's younger than my mother, his older sister, he doesn't respect my father. He thinks my father has to listen to him about everything, like how to run his business. When he comes back to Vietnam, he always tries to change the ways my dad runs things. And my father always defers to him. He feels that because my uncle helped him financially to open up the candy factory, he has to do everything my uncle says. I know he feels very embarrassed and humiliated inside, but would never tell anyone about it.

Thanh's family is not alone in its discomfort with receiving money from abroad. Remittances create social inequality and stress between givers and receivers, and even greater inequalities between receivers and nonreceivers in the same community. Nonetheless, Thanh knows that she owes the lifestyle she enjoys at least partly to her uncle's remittances. After all, the average salary for Saigonese lawyers, according to Thanh, is a little over 2 million Vietnamese *dong* (VND), or US$150 per month, whereas the net profit of her father's candy factory averages close to VND 900 million a year. Thanh earns about VND 2.5 million a month as a part-time lawyer in a small firm that handles legal contracts of all sorts. Although her salary is six times the standard income of the average worker in Saigon, it is still low on a global scale.[22] But the remittances that gave her parents' business a leg up have also allowed Thanh, an only child, to have a greater than average degree of educational and social mobility. She has been able to obtain a good high school education, to study law, and to take lessons at international English schools in Saigon.

Most of Thanh's peers married soon after high school, but Thanh and a small group of her female friends from Le Buon Phong High School decided to continue their schooling instead. Of her seven close female friends from high school, only one did not go to college, choosing instead to marry early. The rest, including Thanh, quietly built professional careers. Most went into fields traditionally reserved for women, including education and nursing. Two pursued advanced degrees. Thanh obtained a law degree, while her friend became a prestigious physician at Vinh Bien, a private hospital catering to Saigon's middle class. Four of the seven, now in their early thirties, remain single. At the time of this writing, there is no available data on the extent of delayed marriages across class and educational levels in Vietnam. But if the paths of Thanh and her four friends who chose singlehood are any indication, a quiet gender revolution is taking place among highly educated Vietnamese women. These women have opted for singlehood in a culture where marriage is not only presumed but often coerced. Women and men who have not yet married at the appropriate age are often dismissively referred to as *"e,"* or unmarketable. By contrast, women (often young and beautiful) and men (often educated and financially secure) who fare well on the marriage market are considered *dat*, or scarce goods. As Thanh explained to me,

> I am already *e* in Vietnam. You know, at thirty-two here, it's hard to find a decent husband. I knew that when I decided to get a good education here that many men would be intimidated by me. But it was important to me to get an education, and I know that for women, marriage is more important. In Asian cultures, but maybe in Vietnam especially, the men do not want their wives to be better than them. I think for me it's harder, too, because my parents are successful here, so to the outsider we seem very successful.

In truth, Thanh is not completely *e:* several men, sometimes with their families, have come to propose marriage to her. Arranged marriages remain common in Vietnam, although they are more common in villages than in urban areas. Young couples who marry by arrangement are susceptible to significant difficulties if class differences divide their families.[23] Individual and family success can make a Vietnamese woman, particularly if she has passed the socially accepted marriageability age, unmarriageable. Thanh had several proposals for marriage arrangements when she was in her mid-twenties, before she got her law degree, from men who wanted to marry down. Now she is thirty-two and educated; she believes that marrying up is no longer an option, since there are few available men in that category. Although she has many suitors of lesser means and education than herself, Thanh explains that she does not find marrying down to be an appealing prospect:

> When I look up, there are few men "up there" who I could see as suit-able husbands. But those men, the few men I know who have more education and who are more successful than I am, usually want to marry young, beautiful women. To them, I am now too old. The backward thing about life is that the men below are very unappeal-ing. And of course there are many of them! There are many, many nonquality men I could choose from, but that's what they are—nonquality.

Thanh's marriage procrastination was partly anchored in her confused class and gender status. Her upward mobility put her at the top locally, but globally, she is at the bottom, since Vietnam has low status among nations. In a traditional marriage, her husband must be the household's provider; but given that she is marrying a low-wage worker, she may end up being the one to seek economic security through her own means. Yet marrying a low-wage worker overseas looks attractive to Thanh because she knows that in Viet-nam, her high educational status will not help her escape the gender subor-dination of marital life. She can think of few men she knows in Vietnam who show respect to their wives.

On our third and final interview, Thanh and I walked along the Saigon River. It was early evening, and the city skyline loomed in the near distance, separated from us by a cacophony of motorcycles, bicycles, and taxis. Disconsolately, Thanh explained:

> In Vietnam, it is hard being single, female, and old. People will criticize and laugh at you. People always ask me, "Where are your husband and children?" And when I think about that, I realize that I have two choices. I can marry a man in Vietnam who is much less educated and less successful than I whom I will have to support and who will likely abuse me emotionally or physically or dominate me in every possible way. Or I can marry a Viet Kieu man. At least Viet Kieu men live in modern countries where they respect women.

Ultimately, what Thanh wants in a marriage partner is someone who will respect her, and who will not seek to control her the way she sees so many Vietnamese men control their wives. As she told me:

> When I find a nice man "below" me I could marry, he wouldn't want to marry me because he's afraid that I'll take control of the house or that if anything goes wrong in the marriage, I could turn to my family for help. Most men in Vietnam want to control their wives, they want their wives to be subordinate even when she is more successful and educated. That leaves me with very few choices in Vietnam, you see, because I for sure don't want a man to take control of me.

The Low-Wage Working Groom

If Thanh's desire for respect stems from her upward mobility, her husband's parallel desire has everything to do with his downward mobility. Minh, whose hands, facial expressions, and graying hair make him seem older than his thirty-seven years, was the only member of his family to leave Vietnam during "Wave II" of the boat exodus that took place after the war.[24] As the eldest son, he was vested with a special status and with a good deal of responsibility for his six siblings. Both of his parents were teachers of philosophy at Le Buon Phong, where they have known Thanh's parents for many years. Today, three of Minh's sisters are teachers and his two brothers are successful merchants in Saigon.

In 1985, at the age of twenty-one, Minh was a man of intellectual ambition and curiosity. He had just completed his third year of engineering school when his parents asked him if he wanted to go to America. They didn't know anyone overseas at the time, but they knew of several people, among the many hundreds of thousands of refugees, who had safely reached a Western country. More than 90 percent of these refugees settled in France, Australia, Canada, or the United States.[25] Minh's parents also knew that as many as half of the refugees on any given boat did not reach their destinations. They died along the way due to starvation, pirate attacks, and often, in the case of women and children, in the combination of rape and murder en route to a refugee camp. Many were also caught by the Vietnamese government and severely punished with long prison sentences.

Nevertheless, Minh's parents were confident that he would survive and find a better life abroad. They spent their entire lives' savings to put him on one of the safest and most reputable boats to leave the Mekong Delta for Western lands of opportunity. These boats and their routes via refugee camps in Southeast Asia were a carefully guarded secret in Vietnam, and they were accessible only to wealthy or well-connected families. Being caught by government officials could lead to severe punishment. Many who were not wealthy, like Minh's family, managed to pool their resources so that one person, usually a son, could go. They saw this as an investment, which they made with the hope it would yield high returns.

Today, Minh considers himself one of the lucky ones who left. After surviving two years in a refugee camp in Malaysia, he was selected in 1987 for entry to the United States. Many people he met at the camp ended up in less desirable places, like Finland, Belgium, or Hungary. Back then, as now, the United States was the top-choice destination, followed by Canada, France, and Australia. Minh arrived in rural Wyoming under the sponsorship of a local Catholic church. Like many of the American churches that sponsored Indochinese refugees from the late 1970s to the mid-1990s, Minh's church sponsored only one person.[26] He spent the first five years of his new life as the only person of color in a rural town in Wyoming, the name of which he doesn't even want to remember.

Like many Vietnamese refugees in the past three decades, Minh decided to migrate a second time. He wanted to go to Little Saigon, the most highly concentrated Vietnamese enclave outside of Vietnam, located in a seemingly quiet Los Angeles suburb that is today plagued by urban problems.[27] But he had little money and no connections in or around Los Angeles. Then one day, in one of the Vietnamese-produced newspapers that flourished in the United States following the influx of refugees, Minh read about a Chinese restaurant called the Panda Garden that needed dishwashers. Unfortunately, it was not in Los Angeles but in a small town called Quincy, ninety miles from Seattle. Minh heard that Seattle also had many Vietnamese people, and he hoped that moving there would bring him closer to other refugees.

Eleven years later, Minh still lives in Quincy and works at the Panda Garden. He is now a deep fryer and an assistant cook, which is several steps up from the dishwashing position he was first given. Although to him, an assistant cook carries less stigma than a dishwasher, it is far from the engineering career he envisaged in his pre-migration years. His responsibilities include helping the main cook with various kitchen tasks and making sure that the restaurant has a constant supply of egg rolls and wontons. Though known as one of the best and most authentic ethnic restaurants in town, the Panda serves a mainly white American clientele that, according to the restaurant's owners, probably wouldn't know the difference between authentic Chinese food and a Sara Lee frozen dinner.

Quincy is similar to many suburban towns in Middle America: it is not quite rural, but far from urban. People who live here drive to Seattle to shop and eat if they have money, but they stay in town if they want to see a movie. The town has two Chinese restaurants, a dozen other ethnic restaurants, and numerous chain-store franchises. Minh knows five other Vietnamese people in Quincy. They are all men, and three of them work with him at the restaurant. He shares a modest three-bedroom apartment with the barest of furnishings with these coworkers.

Like many Viet Kieu people, Minh sends remittances to Vietnam. But though remittances allow their receivers to enjoy First World consumption, givers often only partake of these fruits when they return to their Third World homes. In the First World settings where they live and work, some givers, like Minh, are able to sustain only a Third World consumption pattern. Minh earns approximately $1,400 a month in Quincy and sends $500 of that back to his family. That amount is much higher than the average of $160 the grooms in my study remit to their wives or families on a monthly basis. At $900, his remaining budget would be considered way below the poverty level anywhere in the United States. But the stream of cash he sends his family permits them to stay connected in the small, though conspicuous, circles of families who have overseas kin networks.

In the meantime, however, Minh finds himself lacking not only in material comforts but in the kind of respect he had come to expect before he migrated. Minh remembers vividly that in his early twenties, his peers considered him a good catch. He came from a well-respected family, and he was headed for a career in engineering. Young men he knew had not one but several girlfriends at a time, and this was accepted and celebrated during those difficult postwar years. Minh was relatively fortunate: his parents were respected teachers with small but steady incomes. They could afford to spend small amounts of money on leisure activities, and on materials that bought them some status in their pre-remittance circles. When we talked over beer and cigarettes in the hot kitchen where he worked, Minh told me:

> Life here now is not like life in Vietnam back then. My younger brothers and sisters used to respect me a lot because I was going to college and I was about to get my degree. Many young women I met at the time liked me, too, because I came from a good family and I had status [*dia di*]. But now, because I don't have a good job here, people don't pay attention to me. That's the way my life has been since I came to the United States. And I don't know if I'm lucky or unlucky, but I think it's hard for a [Vietnamese] man to find a wife here if he doesn't make good money. If you have money, everyone will pay attention [to you], but if you don't, you have to live by yourself.

For the most part, that's what Minh has done in the sixteen years since he arrived in the United States. Minh believes that money can, and often does, buy love, and that if you don't have much of it, you live by yourself. Although his yearly income puts him just above the poverty level for a single man, I discovered in a budget analysis of his expenditures that after remittances he falls well below the poverty level. The long hours that often accompany low-wage work have made it particularly difficult for him to meet and court marriage partners. If Minh worked long hours for a law firm or a corporation, he would not only get financial rewards but also the status and prestige that men often use as a trade-off in marriage markets. If he were a blue-collar white man in Quincy, he could go to church functions, bowling alleys, or bars to meet and court local women. For Minh, a single, immigrant man who does low-wage work in a low-status job with long hours in Middle America, the prospect of marriage has been, and remains, low. Even under slightly more favorable circumstances, Viet Kieu men complain of a lack of marriage partners. Men I interviewed in ethnic enclaves such as Little Saigon faced difficulties because, as one man told me, "Viet Kieu women know that there are many of us and few of them!"

Low-wage workers like Minh find it especially difficult to compete in intimate markets. Unlike women like Thanh, men like Minh are at the bottom locally, while globally they are at the top, since the United States enjoys high status among nations. That is one reason they turn to Vietnam. After all, men like Minh are in the market for more than just intimacy. They are in it for respect and for a kind of marital life that they believe they cannot obtain locally. For men in general, but especially for working-class men, as sociologist Lillian Rubin has argued in a compelling study, a worthy sense of self is deeply connected to the ability to provide economically for one's family.[28] As Minh movingly explained to me,

> I don't know if other men told you this, but I think the main reason why a lot of Viet Kieu men go back to Vietnam for a wife is because the women here [Viet Kieu] do not respect their husbands if the husbands cannot make a lot of money. I think that's why there are a lot of Viet Kieu women who marry white men, because the white men have better jobs than us.[29] Many Viet Kieu women, even though they are not attractive and would not be worth much if there were a lot of them, would not even look at men like me because we can't buy them the fancy house or the nice cars. I need my wife to respect me as her husband. If your wife doesn't respect you, who will?

How They Meet

Although Minh was upwardly mobile in 1985 and would have become an engineer had he remained in Vietnam, he is now an assistant cook who has spent the bulk of his adult working life confined to a small Chinese restaurant in Middle America. He hasn't read a book in recent memory. In fact, he says little about what he does, except work, or what he owns, except a used Toyota Tercel he recently bought. Meanwhile, Thanh is a relatively successful lawyer in urban Saigon, where Chanel perfume and Ann Taylor shirts are essential components of her daily life. Thanh speaks very good English, the language we used when she and I met in Vietnam; Minh and I spoke Vietnamese when I interviewed him in Quincy. Thanh is currently working toward an English proficiency degree at an international adult English school, and her reading list includes F. Scott Fitzgerald's *The Great Gatsby*. She often prides herself that she is not as thin as the average woman in Vietnam, nor does she have the stereotypically Vietnamese long, straight black hair. Instead, Thanh has a perm with red highlights, and she spends a large part of her leisure time taking aerobics classes at the Saigonese Women's Union. She likes to joke, "Some people in Vietnam think that I'm a Viet Kieu woman."

Today Minh and Thanh live in seemingly separate worlds. The network of kin and acquaintanceship that unites them was riven by the war, but it still shares the history, memories, and connections of the prewar years. In 1997, when he was nearing his mid-thirties, Minh's family pressed him to find a suitable wife. In Vietnam, there is a strong cultural belief that one should marry in early adulthood, and most certainly before one turns thirty. In 1997, Minh, at thirty-four, was getting old in the eyes of married Vietnamese people. At twenty-eight, Thanh was considered even older as a woman, and both were very old according to Vietnamese notions of fertility. Most people are expected to have a first child, preferably a son, early to ensure patrilineal lineage. Although the average age of marriage has increased in Vietnam in the past few years, as it has worldwide, Vietnamese women are often stigmatized and considered unmarriageable at as young as twenty-five.[30] In the villages, some women are considered unmarriageable at twenty.

Transpacific marriage arrangements are not always the idea of the grooms or brides involved. More than 55 percent of the grooms I interviewed said the idea of a transpacific marriage did not occur to them until a close friend or family member suggested it. The same was true of only 27 percent of the brides. In other words, more brides than grooms expressed an initial desire for an overseas spouse, while grooms were somewhat hesitant until encouraged. The arrangement for Minh and Thanh started when Minh's siblings expressed concern that their eldest brother appeared lonely and needed a wife (though they never asked him if this was the case). After all, he was the eldest sibling but the only one who remained unmarried and childless. The average age of marriage for his three younger sisters was twenty-one and for his two brothers, twenty-four. While these ages seem lower than the current Vietnamese average of twenty-four years for women and twenty-five years for men, they were not unusual at the time, since all five siblings married in the late 1980s and early 1990.[31] Minh's next brother's eldest child is now in her first year at Le Buon Phong High School. Minh feels old when he thinks of this. He is often embarrassed when his family asks him, "Why didn't you bring your lady friend back to visit us, too?" Minh's long work hours, along with the scarcity of Vietnamese women (relative to men) in the United States in general and Quincy in particular, were among the real reasons why the lady friend was generally "too busy to come home *this time.*"

Both Minh and Thanh faced structural and demographic limitations in their local marriage markets, but in different and reversed ways. Minh knew very few Vietnamese-American women, and those he knew usually earned the same amount or more than he did, which made him a less attractive marriage candidate in the United States. Among Asian-Americans, especially in California, women tend to get low-wage jobs more easily, to work longer hours, and to earn more money than men.[32] By contrast, Thanh knew many single men in Saigon, but they were far below her in educational status and made much less money than she did. Her economic and educational status made her a less attractive marriage candidate in Vietnam, but the same qualities served her well on the transpacific marriage market. As Thanh explained to me:

> Any Viet Kieu man can come here to find a wife. And he can surely find a beautiful woman if he wants because there are many beautiful young women willing to marry anyone to go overseas. I think there is something different when you talk about Viet Kieu men coming back here to marry. The women here who marry for money, many of them will marry other foreign men, like Taiwanese and Korean

men, but they have sacrificed their lives for their families because they think they can go off to another country and later send money back home. Those [non–Viet Kieu] men seldom check the family backgrounds of the women they marry, because they don't care. They, the women and the men, know it's something like prostitution, like selling oneself, even though they have weddings and everything. But it's not really a marriage. If the brides are lucky, their foreign husbands will love them and take care of them. But when it has to do with Vietnamese men, they are more selective. They look for a real marriage. And a marriage that will last forever. So it's important to them to check everything about the woman they will marry and her background. These [Viet Kieu] men want a woman who is educated and who comes from an educated family, because that means she comes from a good family. And if her family has money, he knows she just doesn't want to marry him to go overseas because she already has a comfortable life in Vietnam.

News of a split marriage market, one for foreign non–Viet Kieu men and the other for Viet Kieu men who usually have family connections, has circulated extensively throughout the Vietnamese diaspora. Men who want "real" marriages are careful not to meet women on their own, because they fear they will be used as passes for migration. When I visited Saigon nightclubs, cafés, and bars where overseas Vietnamese men and local women converge, I found that both men and women approached public courtship with a lack of trust. Like women in Taiwan, Thailand, Singapore, Malaysia, Hong Kong, and other Asian countries I've visited or studied, Vietnamese women who seek transpacific spouses are so afraid of being seen as prostitutes that they rarely allow themselves to be courted by foreign men in public. Some Viet Kieu men come back and visit local bars and dance clubs in search of "one-night stands" either with prostitutes or non-prostitutes, but they rarely marry women they meet in these public spaces. My sample of marriages yielded only one couple who met by any means other than kinship introduction or arrangement. That couple had met through an international Vietnamese newspaper based in Sydney. Ninety percent of the couples had their marriages arranged, and of the remaining 9 percent, the men had returned to Vietnam to court old school friends or neighbors.

If women are afraid that they will be sexually exploited, Viet Kieu men are wary of being used as a "bridge" to cross the Pacific.[33] These concerns, combined with the availability of transnational networks, have propelled women in Vietnam and Vietnamese men who live overseas to rely on marriage arrangements rather than engaging in individual courtship. As in the case of arranged marriages among other ethnic groups, marriage candidates in the Vietnamese diaspora believe that family members make the best judgments in their interests when looking for a spouse.[34] Thanh explained the logic of marriage arrangement, which may seem illogical to a foreigner:

It's very easy to trick people now. Both men and women can trick each other. Women will pretend to love so they can go abroad and men will pretend to love so they can get a one-night relationship. So that is why people will choose a family member who could investigate both sides for them. Most of the cases I know are similar to mine. Usually a Viet Kieu man says he wants a wife, and then he will call a family member here who will search for him. His family member will try to contact friends, neighbors, whoever he can in search of a suitable wife who happens to also be waiting for an overseas man to court her. There's always a lot of women willing to marry a Viet Kieu man, even though she may never have thought about it until someone asks them. If you have a family member to choose for you, as my uncle helped me get to know my husband, you will end up with a real marriage. Otherwise, it can be risky for both people if they meet each other on their own.

Minh's parents have known Thanh's family for more than two decades. Even though Thanh's father taught at Le Buon Phong two decades ago, and was a friend and colleague of Minh's parents, the current consumption gap between the two families has created a social distance over the years. When Minh's siblings convinced him to search for a wife in Vietnam, he was hesitant at first, but later followed their advice when his parents promised that they would invest time and care in finding the most suitable spouse.

According to Minh, however, they were surprised to discover that arranging a marriage for a Viet Kieu was more complicated than they had anticipated:

> I thought that it would be easy for them to find someone. I thought all they had to do was mention a few things to their friends, and within days they could describe a few possible people to me. But my parents told me that they were afraid that women just wanted to use our family to go abroad. We had many people get involved, many people wanted to be matchmakers for the family, and they added so much anxiety and fear about people's intentions. But the first goal for them was to find a woman from a wealthy family so that they were sure she wasn't just interested in money, because if she has money she would already be comfortable in Vietnam. And it would have been best if she had family in the United States already, because we would then know that they already have overseas people who help them out and they would not expect to become dependent on us. In Vietnamese, you know, there is this saying, "When you choose a spouse, you are choosing his or her whole family."

Minh's parents finally contacted Thanh's parents, after the traditional fashion in which the groom's parents represent him to propose, often with rituals and a centuries-old ceremonial language. Like most brides in my study, Thanh relied on an overseas relative—in this case her uncle, Tuan—for advice on Minh's situation in the United States. The family discovered that Minh was a low-wage worker, but a full-time worker nonetheless. During a walk Thanh and I took through the busy Ben Thanh market in the center of Saigon, she revealed that she and her family were already prepared to support a reversed remittance situation:

> My father and mother didn't care about how much money Minh has. They figured that they could help us out if Minh doesn't do so well; it sounds strange and hard to believe, but my parents said that they could help us open up a business in the United States later on if Minh wants us to do that. They liked the idea that he is a hardworking man and that he comes from a good family. . . . They know he

comes from a good family because he sends money back to his parents. He knows how to take care of them.

Virtually all of the locals I met in Vietnam viewed overseas men as a two-tiered group: the "successful," who were educated or who succeeded in owning ethnic enterprises, and the "indolent," who lacked full-time jobs and were perceived as being welfare-dependent or as participating in underground economies, such as gambling. Some felt that the latter group had taken up valuable spots that others from Vietnam could have filled. "If I had gotten a chance to go, I would be so rich by now," I heard many local men say. Most people, however, could not explain a man like Minh, who is neither lazy nor extremely successful. Thanh's uncle Tuan seemed to know more men in Houston who were not only unemployed but alcoholics and gamblers. Her parents were worried that their daughter was unmarriageable, because there was certainly no shortage of younger women in Vietnam for local men her age to marry. Thanh, too, was already convinced that she was "*e*." Both her parents and her uncle worried that Thanh was facing a life of permanent singlehood. Finally, they all believed that marrying Thanh to Minh, a Viet Kieu man, would be more desirable than arranging her marriage to a local man in Vietnam. Thanh's parents were confident that Minh's status as a full-time worker who sent remittances back home to his family spoke well for him as a suitable husband. Most Viet Kieu single men her uncle knew belonged to an underclass of which Minh was not a part. For Thanh, Minh's geographical advantage translated into something socially priceless: a man living in a modern country, she was sure, would respect women.

A Clash of Dreams

Highly educated women like Thanh resist patriarchal arrangements by avoiding marriages with local men. They do not want to "marry down" economically and socially—though this seems to be their only choice—because they believe that marrying local men will only constrain them to domestic roles in a male-dominated culture. As Thanh told me, some women will endure the often painful stigma of singlehood and childlessness over the oppression they could face from dominating husbands. For some of these women, the transpacific marriage market holds out hope for a different kind of marriage—one in which Vietnamese women imagine that their husbands will believe in, and practice, gender equity. Many such women will instead find themselves back in the pre-modern family life they hoped to avoid. As Minh told me, "A woman's place is in the home to take care of her husband and his family."

All but three of the twenty-eight grooms I interviewed shared Minh's view. But this conflict in gender ideology between the two unmarriageables never seemed to come to the fore until it was too late. During the migration period, each expensive phone call and visit is an occasion for love, not for discussing the details of what life will be like when the woman joins the man abroad. Most couples shared only words of joy about being together in the future.

And yet, as I interviewed the couples in their separate countries during this period, I found that the two parties usually held conflicting views of the life they would soon lead together. I did not interview all of the grooms, but I did ask all of the brides about their husbands' ideas about gender relations, and about how they envisioned the organization of their households after they joined their husbands abroad. Among other things, I asked about household division of labor, about whether the couple would live with or without kin, and about whether or not the women expected to work outside the home. Although these concerns address only a fraction of a marriage's potential promise or pitfalls, they can certainly help us understand the interplay between a husband's gender ideology and his wife's.[35]

Nearly 95 percent of the brides in Vietnam wanted to work for a wage when they joined their husbands abroad. Though wanting to work outside the home is not the ultimate measure of a modernized woman in Vietnam, it does indicate these women's unwillingness to be confined to domestic work. Some women who wanted paid jobs were not averse to the idea of doing second shift work as well.[36] However, most of the women, and virtually all of the educated ones—the unmarriageables—wanted and expected to have egalitarian relationships with their husbands. In general, they objected to traditionally female tasks, although they did not fully embrace what we might call a peer marriage.[37] For the men and women I interviewed, as for mainstream dual-career American couples, marital life consists of much more than just household tasks. But these tasks are important symbols in the economy of gratitude among married people, "for how a person wants to identify himself or herself influences what, in the back and forth of a marriage, will seem like a gift and what will not."[38] As Thanh explained when I asked her about the implications of a purely egalitarian marriage:

> I don't want everything split fifty-fifty. For example, I like to cook. But it's important for me as an educated woman not to be controlled by my husband. I don't mind cooking for my husband, but I don't want it to be forced on me. That's what the men in Vietnam feel like; they feel that their wives are like their domestic workers. Men in Vietnam never do anything in the house. I think they have to know how to respect educated women.

Women like Thanh want a respectful marriage based on principles of gender equality. According to these principles, women expect to work for a wage, to share in making social and economic decisions for their future households, and to have their husbands share in the household division of labor. Above all, they do *not* want to live in multigenerational households, serving as the dutiful daughter-in-law and housewife, the two often inseparable roles historically delegated to women in Vietnam. Many express that reluctance, because they know numerous Viet Kieu men who live with their parents or who plan to do so when their parents are old. In Vietnam, and more generally in Asia, elderly parents often live with their eldest sons. The daily caring work then falls to their sons' wives. Forty percent of the U.S.–based grooms and a third of all Vietnamese grooms live with their parents, most of whom are elderly and require care. Of all low-wage working men married to highly educated women, about 35 percent currently reside with their parents. Virtually all of the men in my study who resided with their parents wanted to continue to do so when their wives joined them abroad.

For Minh, the possibility that a wife will insist on an equal marriage is one of the anxieties of modern life:

> Vietnamese women, they care for their husbands and they are more traditional. I think non-Vietnamese women and Viet Kieu women are too modern. They just want to be equal with their husbands, and

I don't think that is the way husband and wife should be. . . . I mean that husband and wife should not be equal. The wife should listen to husband most of the time. That is how they will have a happy life together. If the woman tries to be equal they will have problems. . . . I know many Vietnamese men here who abandon their parents because their wives refuse to live with their parents. If my parents were in America, I would definitely plan for them to live with me when they are old. But because they are in Vietnam, they are living with one of my brothers.

Instead of seeking peasant village women or uneducated ones, after the fashion of white men who pursue mail-order brides because they believe such women consent to subordination in marriage, men like Minh seek marriage arrangements with educated women. As Minh explains:

For me, I want to marry an educated woman, because she comes from a good, educated family. It's very hard to find a poor woman or an uneducated woman who comes from an uneducated family to teach their daughters about morals and values, because if they are uneducated they don't know how. I know many men, Viet Kieu and foreign men, who go to Vietnam to marry beautiful young women, but they don't ask why do those women marry them? Those women only want to use their beauty to go overseas, and they will leave their husbands when they get the chance. They can use their beauty to find other men. I would never marry a beautiful girl from a poor, uneducated family. You see, the educated women, they know it's important to marry and stay married forever. As they say in Vietnam, "*Tram nam han phuc* [a hundred years of happiness]." Educated women must protect their family's reputation in Vietnam by having a happy marriage, not have it end in divorce.

The Inflated Market of Respect

At first glance, Minh and Thanh seem to come from two vastly different social worlds, assembled only by the complexity of Vietnamese history. But at a closer look, we learn that these two lonely faces of globalization are very much alike. Both of their parents were educated and middle class. Both lack the emotional fulfillment and intimate partnership that adults of their social worlds enjoy. Both long for a kind of marital respect they perceive as scarce in their local marriage markets. Minh has experienced immense, swift downward mobility as a result of migration, and he is eager to regain the respect he has lost. Thanh has practically priced herself out of the local marriage market by acquiring an advanced degree, which she could not have obtained without her uncle's remittances. She wants a husband who respects her as an equal and who accepts that she is a modern woman. He wants to regain something he thinks men like him have lost; she wants to challenge the local marriage norm, including the very preindustrial Vietnamese family life Minh yearns for. Many men in Vietnam do live that life. As Minh told me:

> My younger brothers have control over their homes. Their wives help them with their shops selling fabrics in Saigon, but their wives don't make any decisions. I think that if they live in America, and their wives were working, they would not let my brother make all the decisions in the house. . . . And I think that Vietnamese women, when they come to the United States, they are influenced by a lot of different things. That is why there are a lot of divorces in America.

Minh believes that when he migrated to the United States, he left the respect he now craves behind him in Vietnam. Thanh imagines that the marital respect *she* craves is unobtainable in Vietnam, but awaits her in the United States. Each has inflated the true extent of the respect the other is willing to give. For though there is a quiet feminist revolution of sorts going on among highly educated women in Vietnam, that revolution has not entered the experience or expectations of the less educated, low-wage husbands living overseas. And while many of these Viet Kieu men seek reprieve from modern Western life, the women they marry have washed away those traditions during the long years that the men have been gone.

The Future of Transpacific Marriages

Surely, this clash of dreams and expectations will result in marital conflict when the couple is united overseas. Such conflicts have several potential outcomes. The happiest would have Minh joining the feminist revolution and abandoning his desire for the preindustrial, traditional family life he never had. Some men will go this route, but only a few. In other cases, such marriages may end in divorce—or worse, domestic battery. I believe the latter scenario is an unlikely one for the couples I studied. Many women like Thanh have considered the possibility and are careful to maintain contact with transnational networks that will look out for them. Seventy-five percent of the women in my study have at least one overseas relative. Virtually all the middle-class and college-educated women do.

Most likely, these marriages will resolve themselves with the men getting the respect they want and the women consenting to subordination in the name of family and kinship. Thanh will be going from the patriarchal frying pan to the patriarchal fire, but with one big difference. In the United States, her desire for gender equity will find more support, in a culture where women dare to leave their husbands if they aren't treated equally. But Thanh will still bear the burden of Vietnamese tradition, which will prevent her from leaving her husband. In Vietnam, divorce is stigmatized, and saving face is especially important to educated, middle-class families. If Thanh daringly divorces her husband, she will damage her family's reputation in Vietnam and overseas. She told me she would not be likely to take this risk. If she stays in the marriage, she will probably wind up serving as the traditional wife Minh desires.

Although globalization appears to offer some Vietnamese women an escape from local patriarchal marriages, it may in fact play more to the interests of certain Vietnamese men, offering them the opportunity to create the traditional life they've always wanted within the modern setting where they now live. Strong traditions back in Vietnam protect them against instability in their marriages. But the women they have married don't share their husbands' traditional vision of marital life. The only thing educated women like Thanh have to look forward to is more waiting—waiting for men like their husbands, who live in a modern country, simply to respect women.

Global Cities and Survival Circuits

Saskia Sassen

When today's media, policy, and economic analysts define globalization, they emphasize hypermobility, international communication, and the neutralization of distance and place. This account of globalization is by far the dominant one. Central to it are the global information economy, instant communication, and electronic markets—all realms within which place no longer makes a difference, and where the only type of worker who matters is the highly educated professional. Globalization thus conceived privileges global transmission over the material infrastructure that makes it possible; information over the workers who produce it, whether these be specialists or secretaries; and the new transnational corporate culture over the other jobs upon which it rests, including many of those held by immigrants. In brief, the dominant narrative of globalization concerns itself with the upper circuits of global capital, not the lower ones, and with the hypermobility of capital rather than with capital that is bound to place.

The migration of maids, nannies, nurses, sex workers, and contract brides has little to do with globalization by these lights. Migrant women are just individuals making a go of it, after all, and the migration of workers from poor countries to wealthier ones long predates the current phase of economic globalization. And yet it seems reasonable to assume that there are significant links between globalization and women's migration, whether voluntary or forced, for jobs that used to be part of the First World woman's domestic role. Might the dynamics of globalization alter the course or even reinscribe the history of the migration and exploitation of Third World laborers? There are two distinct issues here. One is whether globalization has enabled formerly national or regional processes to go global. The other is whether globalization has produced a new kind of migration, with new conditions and dynamics of its own.

Global Cities and Survival Circuits

When today's women migrate from south to north for work as nannies, domestics, or sex workers, they participate in two sets of dynamic configurations. One of these is the global city. The other consists of survival circuits that have emerged in response to the deepening misery of the global south.[1]

Global cities concentrate some of the global economy's key functions and resources. There, activities implicated in the management and coordination of the global economy have expanded, producing a sharp growth in the demand for highly paid professionals. Both this sector's firms and the lifestyles of its professional workers in turn generate a demand for low-paid service workers. In this way, global cities have become places where large numbers of low-paid women and immigrants get incorporated into strategic economic sectors. Some are incorporated directly as low-wage clerical and service workers, such as janitors and repairmen. For others, the process is less direct, operating instead through the consumption practices of high-income professionals, who employ maids and nannies and who patronize expensive restaurants and shops staffed by low-wage workers. Traditionally, employment in growth sectors has been a source of workers' empowerment; this new pattern undermines that linkage, producing a class of workers who are isolated, dispersed, and effectively invisible.

Meanwhile, as Third World economies on the periphery of the global system struggle against debt and poverty, they increasingly build survival circuits on the backs of women—whether these be trafficked low-wage workers and prostitutes or migrant workers sending remittances back home. Through their work and remittances, these women contribute to the revenue of deeply indebted countries. "Entrepreneurs" who have seen other opportunities vanish as global firms entered their countries see profit-making potential in the trafficking of women; so, too, do longtime criminals who have seized the opportunity to operate their illegal trade globally. These survival circuits are often complex; multiple locations and sets of actors constitute increasingly far-reaching chains of traders and "workers."

Through their work in both global cities and survival circuits, women, so often discounted as valueless economic actors, are crucial to building new economies and expanding existing ones. Globalization serves a double purpose here, helping to forge links between sending and receiving countries, and enabling local and regional practices to assume a global scale. On the one hand, the dynamics that converge in the global city produce a strong demand for low-wage workers, while the dynamics that mobilize women into survival circuits produce an expanding supply of migrants who can be pushed—or sold—into such jobs. On the other hand, the very technological infrastructure and transnationalism that characterize global industries also enable other types of actors to expand onto the global stage, whether these be money launderers or people traffickers.[2] It seems, then, that in order to understand the extraction from the Third World of services that used to define women's domestic role in the First, we must depart from the mainstream view of globalization.

Toward an Alternative Narrative About Globalization

The spatial dispersal of economic activities and the neutralization of place constitute half of the globalization story. The other half involves the territorial centralization of top-level management, control operations, and the most advanced specialized services. Markets, whether national or global, and companies, many of which have gone global, require central locations where their most complex tasks are accomplished. Furthermore, the information industry rests on a vast physical infrastructure, which includes strategic nodes where facilities are densely concentrated. Even the most advanced sectors of the information industry employ many different types of workplaces and workers.

If we expand our analysis of globalization to include this production process, we can see that secretaries belong to the global economy, as do the people who clean professionals' offices and homes. An economic configuration very different from the one suggested by the concept of an "information economy" emerges—and it is one that includes material conditions, production sites, and activities bounded by place.

The mainstream account of globalization tends to take for granted the existence of a global economic system, viewing it as a function of the power of transnational corporations and communications. But if the new information technologies and transnational corporations can be operated, coordinated, and controlled globally, it's because that capacity has been produced. By focusing on its production, we shift our emphasis to the *practices* that constitute economic globalization: the work of producing and reproducing the organization and management of a global production system and a global marketplace for finance.

This focus on practices draws the categories of place and work process into the analysis of economic globalization. In so broadening our analysis, we do not deny the importance of hypermobility and power. Rather, we acknowledge that many of the resources necessary for global economic activities are not hypermobile and are, on the contrary, deeply embedded in place, including such sites as global cities and export processing zones. Global processes are structured by local constraints, including the work culture, political culture, and composition of the workforce within a particular nation state.[3]

If we recapture the geography behind globalization, we might also recapture its workers, communities, and work cultures (not just the corporate ones). By focusing on the global city, for instance, we can study how global processes become localized in specific arrangements, from the high-income gentrified urban neighborhoods of the transnational professional class to the work lives of the foreign nannies and maids in those same neighborhoods.

Women in the Global City

Globalization has greatly increased the demand in global cities for low-wage workers to fill jobs that offer few advancement possibilities. The same cities have seen an explosion of wealth and power, as high-income jobs and high-priced urban space have noticeably expanded. How, then, can workers be hired at low wages and with few benefits even when there is high demand and the jobs belong to high-growth sectors? The answer, it seems, has involved tapping into a growing new labor supply—women and immigrants—and in so doing, breaking the historical nexus that would have empowered workers under these conditions. The fact that these workers tend to be women and immigrants also lends cultural legitimacy to their non-empowerment. In global cities, then, a majority of today's resident workers are women, and many of these are women of color, both native and immigrant.

At the same time, global cities have seen a gathering trend toward the informalization of an expanding range of activities, as low-profit employers attempt to escape the costs and constraints of the formal economy's regulatory apparatus. They do so by locating commercial or manufacturing operations in areas zoned exclusively for residential use, for example, or in buildings that violate fire and health standards; they also do so by assigning individual workers industrial homework. This allows them to remain in these cities. At its best, informalization reintroduces the community and the household as important economic spaces in global cities. It is in many ways a low-cost (and often feminized) equivalent to deregulation at the top of the system. As with deregulation (for example, financial deregulation), informalization introduces flexibility, reduces the "burdens" of regulation, and lowers costs, in this case of labor. In the cities of the global north—including New York, London, Paris, and Berlin—informalization serves to downgrade a variety of activities for which there is often a growing local demand. Immigrant women, in the end, bear some of the costs.

As the demand for high-level professional workers has skyrocketed, more and more women have found work in corporate professional jobs.[4] These jobs place heavy demands on women's time, requiring long work hours and intense engagement. Single professionals and two-career households therefore tend to prefer urban to suburban residence. The result is an expansion of high-income residential areas in global cities and a return of family life to urban centers. Urban professionals want it all, including dogs and children, whether or not they have the time to care for them. The usual modes of handling household tasks often prove inadequate. We can call this type of house-hold a "professional household without a 'wife,'" regardless of whether its adult couple consists of a man and a woman, two men, or two women. A growing share of its domestic tasks are relocated to the market: they are bought directly as goods and services or indirectly through hired labor. As a consequence, we see the return of the so-called serving classes in all of the world's global cities, and these classes are largely made up of immigrant and migrant women.

This dynamic produces a sort of double movement: a shift to the labor market of functions that used to be part of household work, but also a shift of what used to be labor market functions in standardized workplaces to the household and, in the case of informalization, to the immigrant commu-nity.[5] This reconfiguration of economic spaces has had different impacts on women and men, on male-typed and female-typed work cultures, and on male- and female-centered forms of power and empowerment.

For women, such transformations contain the potential, however limited, for autonomy and empowerment. Might informalization, for example, reconfigure certain economic relationships between men and women? With informalization, the neighborhood and the household reemerge as sites for economic activity, creating "opportunities" for low-income women and thereby reordering some of the hierarchies in which women find themselves. This becomes particularly clear in the case of immigrant women, who often come from countries with traditionally male-centered cultures.

A substantial number of studies now show that regular wage work and improved access to other public realms has an impact on gender relations in the lives of immigrant women. Women gain greater personal autonomy and independence, while men lose ground. More control over budgeting and other domestic decisions devolves to women, and they have greater leverage in requesting help from men in domestic chores. Access to public services and other public resources also allows women to incorporate themselves into the mainstream society; in fact, women often mediate this process for their households. Some women likely benefit more than others from these circumstances, and with more research we could establish the impact of class, education, and income. But even aside from relative empowerment in the household, paid work holds out another significant possibility for women: their greater participation in the public sphere and their emergence as public actors.

Immigrant women tend to be active in two arenas: institutions for public and private assistance, and the immigrant or ethnic community. The more women are involved with the migration process, the more likely it is that migrants will settle in their new residences and participate in their communities. And when immigrant women assume active public and social roles, they further reinforce their status in the household and the settlement process.[6] Positioned differently from men in relation to the economy and state, women tend to be more involved in community building and community activism. They are the ones who will likely handle their families' legal vulnerabilities as they seek public and social services. These trends suggest that women may emerge as more forceful and visible actors in the labor market as well.

And so two distinct dynamics converge in the lives of immigrant women in global cities. On the one hand, these women make up an invisible and disempowered class of workers in the service of the global economy's strategic sectors. Their invisibility keeps immigrant women from emerging as the strong proletariat that followed earlier forms of economic organization, when workers' positions in leading sectors had the effect of empowering them. On the other hand, the access to wages and salaries, however low; the growing feminization of the job supply; and the growing feminization of business opportunities thanks to informalization, all alter the gender hierarchies in which these women find themselves.

New Employment Regimes in Cities

Most analysts of postindustrial society and advanced economies report a massive growth in the need for highly educated workers but little demand for the type of labor that a majority of immigrants, perhaps especially immigrant women, have tended to supply over the last two or three decades. But detailed empirical studies of major cities in highly developed countries contradict this conventional view of the postindustrial economy. Instead, they show an ongoing demand for immigrant workers and a significant supply of old and new low-wage jobs that require little education.[7]

Three processes of change in economic and spatial organization help

explain the ongoing, indeed growing, demand for immigrant workers, especially immigrant women. One is the consolidation of advanced services and
corporate headquarters in the urban economic core, especially in global
cities. While the corporate headquarters-and-services complex may not
account for the majority of jobs in these cities, it establishes a new regime of
economic activity, which in turn produces the spatial and social transformations evident in major cities. Another relevant process is the downgrading of
the manufacturing sector, as some manufacturing industries become incorporated into the postindustrial economy. Downgrading is a response to
competition from cheap imports, and to the modest profit potential of manufacturing compared to telecommunications, finance, and other corporate
services.[8] The third process is informalization, a notable example of which is
the rise of the sweatshop. Firms often take recourse to informalized arrangements when they have an effective local demand for their goods and services
but they cannot compete with cheap imports, or cannot compete for space
and other business needs with the new high-profit firms of the advanced
corporate service economy.

In brief, that major cities have seen changes in their job supplies can be
chalked up both to the emergence of new sectors and to the reorganization
of work in sectors new and old. The shift from a manufacturing to a service-
dominated economy, particularly evident in cities, destabilizes older relationships between jobs and economic sectors. Today, much more than
twenty years ago, we see an expansion of low-wage jobs associated with
growing sectors rather than with declining ones. At the same time, a vast
array of activities that once took place under standardized work arrangements have become increasingly informalized, as some manufacturing relo-
cates from unionized factories to sweatshops and private homes. If we
distinguish the characteristics of jobs from those of the sectors in which they
are located, we can see that highly dynamic, technologically advanced
growth sectors may well contain low-wage, dead-end jobs. Similarly, backward sectors like downgraded manufacturing can reflect the major growth
trends in a highly developed economy.

It seems, then, that we need to rethink two assumptions: that the postindustrial economy primarily requires highly educated workers, and that
informalization and downgrading are just Third World imports or
anachronistic holdovers. Service-dominated urban economies do indeed

create low-wage jobs with minimal education requirements, few advancement opportunities, and low pay for demanding work. For workers raised in an ideological context that emphasizes success, wealth, and career, these are not attractive positions; hence the growing demand for immigrant workers. But given the provenance of the jobs these immigrant workers take, we must resist assuming that they are located in the backward sectors of the economy.

The Other Workers in the Advanced Corporate Economy

Low-wage workers accomplish a sizable portion of the day-to-day work in global cities' leading sectors. After all, advanced professionals require clerical, cleaning, and repair workers for their state-of-the-art offices, and they require truckers to bring them their software and their toilet paper. In my research on New York and other cities, I have found that between 30 and 50 percent of workers in the leading sectors are actually low-wage workers.[9]

The similarly state-of-the-art lifestyles of professionals in these sectors have created a whole new demand for household workers, particularly maids and nannies, as well as for service workers to cater to those professionals' high-income consumption habits.[10] Expensive restaurants, luxury housing, luxury hotels, gourmet shops, boutiques, French hand laundries, and special cleaning services, for example, are more labor-intensive than their lower-priced equivalents. To an extent not seen in a very long time, we are witnessing the reemergence of a "serving class" in contemporary high-income households and neighborhoods. The image of the immigrant woman serving the white middle-class professional woman has replaced that of the black female servant working for the white master in centuries past. The result is a sharp tendency toward social polarization in today's global cities.

We are beginning to see how the global labor markets at the top and at the bottom of the economic system are formed. The bottom is mostly staffed through the efforts of individual workers, though an expanding network of organizations has begun to get involved. (So have illegal traffickers, as we'll see later.) Kelly Services, a Fortune 500 global staffing company that operates in twenty-five countries, recently added a home-care division that is geared toward people who need assistance with daily living but that also offers services that in the past would have been taken care of by the mother or wife figure in a household. A growing range of smaller global staffing organizations offer day care, including dropping off and picking up school-children, as well as completion of in-house tasks from child care to cleaning and cooking.[11] One international agency for nannies and au pairs (EF Au Pair Corporate Program) advertises directly to corporations, urging them to include the service in their offers to potential hires.

Meanwhile, at the top of the system, several global Fortune 500 staffing companies help firms fill high-level professional and technical jobs. In 2001, the largest of these was the Swiss multinational Adecco, with offices in fifty-eight countries; in 2000 it provided firms worldwide with 3 million workers. Manpower, with offices in fifty-nine different countries, provided 2 million workers. Kelly Services provided 750,000 employees in 2000.

The top and the bottom of the occupational distribution are becoming internationalized and so are their labor suppliers. Although midlevel occupations are increasingly staffed through temporary employment agencies, these companies have not internationalized their efforts. Occupations at the top and at the bottom are, in very different but parallel ways, sensitive. Firms need reliable and hopefully talented professionals, and they need them specialized but standardized so that they can use them globally. Professionals seek the same qualities in the workers they employ in their homes. The fact that staffing organizations have moved into providing domestic services signals both that a global labor market has emerged in this area and that there is an effort afoot to standardize the services maids, nannies, and home-care nurses deliver.

Producing a Global Supply of the New Caretakers: The Feminization of Survival

The immigrant women described in the first half of this chapter enter the migration process in many different ways. Some migrate in order to reunite their families; others migrate alone. Many of their initial movements have little to do with globalization. Here I am concerned with a different kind of migration experience, and it is one that is deeply linked to economic global-ization: migrations organized by third parties, typically governments or illegal traffickers. Women who enter the migration stream this way often (though not always) end up in different sorts of jobs than those described above. What they share with the women described earlier in this chapter is that they, too, take over tasks previously associated with housewives.

The last decade has seen a growing presence of women in a variety of cross-border circuits. These circuits are enormously diverse, but they share one feature: they produce revenue on the backs of the truly disadvantaged. One such circuit consists in the illegal trafficking in people for the sex industry and for various types of labor. Another circuit has developed around cross-border migrations, both documented and not, which have become an important source of hard currency for the migrants' home governments. Broader structural conditions are largely responsible for forming and strengthening circuits like these. Three major actors emerge from those conditions, however: women in search of work, illegal traffickers, and the governments of the home countries.

These circuits make up, as it were, countergeographies of globalization. They are deeply imbricated with some of globalization's major constitutive dynamics: the formation of global markets, the intensifying of transnational and translocal networks, and the development of communication technologies that easily escape conventional surveillance. The global economic system's institutional support for cross-border markets and money flows has contributed greatly to the formation and strengthening of these circuits.[12] The countergeographies are dynamic and mobile; to some extent, they belong to the shadow economy, but they also make use of the regular economy's institutional infrastructure.[13]

Such alternative circuits for survival, profit, and hard currency have grown at least partly in response to the effects of economic globalization on developing countries. Unemployment is on the rise in much of the developing world; small and medium-sized enterprises oriented to the national, rather than the export, market have closed; and government debt, already large, is in many cases rising. The economies frequently grouped under the label "developing" are often struggling, stagnant, or even shrinking. These conditions have pressed additional responsibilities onto women, as men have lost job opportunities and governments have cut back on social services.[14] In other words, it has become increasingly important to find alternative ways of making a living, producing profits, and generating government revenues, as developing countries have faced the following concurrent trends: diminishing job prospects for men, a falloff in traditional business opportunities as foreign firms and export industries displace previous economic mainstays, and a concomitant decrease in government revenues, due both to the new conditions of globalization and to the burden of servicing debts.[15]

The major dynamics linked to economic globalization have significantly affected developing economies, including the so-called middle-income countries of the global south. These countries have had not only to accommodate new conditions but to implement a bundle of new policies, including structural adjustment programs, which require that countries open up to foreign firms and eliminate state subsidies. Almost inevitably, these economies fall into crisis; they then implement the International Monetary Fund's programmatic solutions. It is now clear that in most of the countries involved, including Mexico, South Korea, Ghana, and Thailand, these solutions have cost certain sectors of the economy and population enormously, and they have not fundamentally reduced government debt.

Certainly, these economic problems have affected the lives of women from developing countries. Prostitution and migrant labor are increasingly popular ways to make a living; illegal trafficking in women and children for the sex industry, and in all kinds of people as laborers, is an increasingly popular way to make a profit; and remittances, as well as the organized export of workers, have become increasingly popular ways for governments to bring in revenue. Women are by far the majority group in prostitution and in trafficking for the sex industry, and they are becoming a majority group in migration for labor.

Such circuits, realized more and more frequently on the backs of women, can be considered a (partial) feminization of survival. Not only are households, indeed whole communities, increasingly dependent on women for their survival, but so too are governments, along with enterprises that function on the margins of the legal economy. As the term *circuits* indicates, there is a degree of institutionalization in these dynamics; that is to say, they are not simply aggregates of individual actions.

Government Debt: Shifting Resources
from Women to Foreign Banks

Debt and debt-servicing problems have been endemic in the developing world since the 1980s. They are also, I believe, crucial to producing the new countergeographies of globalization. But debt's impact on women, and on the feminization of survival, has more to do with particular features of debt than with debt *tout court*.

A considerable amount of research indicates that debt has a detrimental effect on government programs for women and children, notably education and health care. Further, austerity and adjustment programs, which are usually implemented in order to redress government debt, produce unemployment, which also adversely affects women[16] by adding to the pressure on them to ensure household survival. In order to do so, many women have turned to subsistence food production, informal work, emigration, and prostitution.[17]

Most of the countries that fell into debt in the 1980s have found themselves unable to climb out of it. In the 1990s, a whole new set of countries joined the first group in this morass. The IMF and the World Bank responded with their structural adjustment program and structural adjustment loans, respectively. The latter tied loans to economic policy reform rather than to particular projects. The idea was to make these states more "competitive," which typically meant inducing sharp cuts in various social programs.

Rather than becoming "competitive," the countries subjected to structural adjustment have remained deeply indebted, with about fifty of them now categorized as "highly indebted poor countries." Moreover, a growing number of middle-income countries are also caught in this debt trap. Argentina became the most dramatic example when it defaulted on $140 billion in debt in December 2001—the largest ever sovereign default. Given the structure and servicing of these debts, as well as their weight in debtor countries' economies, it is not likely that many of these countries will ever be able to pay off their debts in full. Structural adjustment programs seem to have made this even less likely; the economic reforms these programs demanded have added to unemployment and the bankruptcy of many small, nationally oriented firms.

It has been widely recognized that the south has already paid its debt several times over. According to some estimates, from 1982 to 1998, indebted countries paid four times their original debts, and at the same time their debt increased four times.[18] Nonetheless, these countries continue to pay a significant share of their total revenue to service their debt. Thirty-three of the officially named forty-one highly indebted poor countries paid $3 in debt service to the north for every $1 they received in development assistance. Many of these countries pay more than 50 percent of their government revenues toward debt service, or 20 to 25 percent of their export earnings.

The ratios of debt to GNP in many of the highly indebted poor countries exceed sustainable limits; many are far more extreme than the levels considered unmanageable during the Latin American debt crisis of the 1980s. Such ratios are especially high in Africa, where they stand at 123 percent, compared with 42 percent in Latin America and 28 percent in Asia.[19] Such figures suggest that most of these countries will not get out of their indebtedness through structural adjustment programs. Indeed, it would seem that in many cases the latter have had the effect of intensifying debt dependence. Furthermore, together with various other factors, structural adjustment programs have contributed to an increase in unemployment and in poverty.

Alternative Survival Circuits

It is in this context—marked by unemployment, poverty, bankruptcies of large numbers of firms, and shrinking state resources to meet social needs—that alternative circuits of survival emerge, and it is to these conditions that such circuits are articulated. Here I want to focus on the growing salience of the trafficking of women as a profit-making option and on the growing importance of the emigrants' remittances to the bottom lines of the sending states.

Trafficking, or the forced recruitment and transportation of people for work, is a violation of human, civil, and political rights. Much legislative effort has gone into addressing trafficking: international treaties and charters, U.N. resolutions, and various bodies and commissions have all attempted to put a stop to this practice.[20] Nongovernmental organizations have also formed around this issue.[21]

Trafficking in women for the sex industry is highly profitable for those running the trade. The United Nations estimates that 4 million people were trafficked in 1998, producing a profit of $7 billion for criminal groups.[22] These funds include remittances from prostitutes' earnings as well as payments to organizers and facilitators. In Poland, police estimate that for each woman delivered, the trafficker receives about $700. Ukrainian and Russian women, highly prized in the sex market, earn traffickers $500 to $1,000 per woman delivered. These women can be expected to service fifteen clients a day on average, and each can be expected to make about $215,000 per month for the criminal gang that trafficked her.[23]

It is estimated that in recent years, several million women and girls have been trafficked from and within Asia and the former Soviet Union, both of which are major trafficking areas. The growing frequency of trafficking in these two regions can be linked to increases in poverty, which may lead some parents to sell their daughters to brokers. In the former Soviet republics and Eastern Europe, unemployment has helped promote the growth of criminal gangs, some of which traffic women. Unemployment rates hit 70 percent among women in Armenia, Russia, Bulgaria, and Croatia after the implementation of market policies; in Ukraine, the rate was 80 percent. Some research indicates that need is the major motivation for entry into prostitution.[24]

The sex industry is not the only trafficking circuit: migrant workers of both sexes can also be profitably trafficked across borders. According to a U.N. report, criminal organizations in the 1990s generated an estimated $3.5 billion per year in profits from trafficking migrants. Organized crime has only recently entered this business; in the past, trafficking was mostly the province of petty criminals. Some recent reports indicate that organized-crime groups are creating strategic intercontinental alliances through networks of coethnics in various countries; this facilitates transport, local distribution, provision of false documents, and the like. These international networks also allow traffickers to circulate women and other migrants among third countries; they may move women from Burma, Laos, Vietnam, and China to Thailand, while moving Thai women to Japan and the United States.[25] The Global Survival Network reported on these practices after it conducted a two-year investigation, establishing a dummy company itself in order to enter the illegal trade.[26]

Once trafficked women reach their destination countries, some features of immigration policy and its enforcement may well make them even more vulnerable. Such women usually have little recourse to the law. If they are undocumented, which they are likely to be, they will not be treated as victims of abuse but as violators of entry, residence, and work laws. As countries of the global north attempt to address undocumented immigration and trafficking by clamping down on entry at their borders, more women are likely to turn to traffickers to help them get across. These traffickers may turn out to belong to criminal organizations linked to the sex industry.

Moreover, many countries forbid foreign women to work as prostitutes, and this provides criminal gangs with even more power over the women they traffic. It also eliminates one survival option for foreign women who may have limited access to jobs. Some countries, notably the Netherlands and Switzerland, are far more tolerant of foreign women working as prostitutes than as regular laborers. According to International Organization for Migration data, in the European Union, a majority of prostitutes are migrant women: 75 percent in Germany and 80 percent in the Italian city of Milan.

Some women know that they are being trafficked for prostitution, but for many the conditions of their recruitment and the extent of the abuse and bondage they will suffer only become evident after they arrive in the receiving country.[27] Their confinement is often extreme—akin to slavery—and so is their abuse, including rape, other forms of sexual violence, and physical punishment. Their meager wages are often withheld. They are frequently forbidden to protect themselves against AIDS, and they are routinely denied medical care. If they seek help from the police, they may be taken into detention for violating immigration laws; if they have been provided with false documents, there will be criminal charges.

With the sharp growth of tourism over the last decade, the entertainment sector has also grown, becoming increasingly important in countries that have adopted tourism as a strategy for development.[28] In many places, the sex trade is part of the entertainment industry, and the two have grown in tandem. Indeed, the sex trade itself has become a development strategy in some areas where unemployment and poverty are widespread, and where governments are desperate for revenue and hard currency. When local manufacturing and agriculture no longer provide jobs, profits, or government revenue, a once marginal economic wellspring becomes a far more important one. The IMF and the World Bank sometimes recommend tourism as a solution to the troubles of poor countries, but when they provide loans for its development or expansion, they may well inadvertently contribute to the expansion of the entertainment industry and, indirectly, of the sex trade. Because it is linked to development strategies in this way, the trafficking of women may continue to expand in these countries.

Indeed, the global sex industry is likely to expand in any case, given the involvement of organized crime in the sex trade, the formation of cross-border ethnic networks, and the growing transnationalization of tourism. These factors may well lead to a sex trade that reaches out to more and more "markets." It's a worrisome possibility, especially as growing numbers of women face few if any employment options. Prostitution becomes—in certain kinds of economies—crucial to expanding the entertainment industry, and thereby to tourism as a development strategy that will in turn lead to increased government revenue. These links are structural; the significance of the sex industry to any given economy rises in the absence of other sources of jobs, profits, and revenues.

Women, and migrants generally, are crucial to another development strategy as well: the remittances migrant workers send home are a major source of hard-currency reserves for the migrant's home country. While remittances may seem minor compared to the financial markets' massive daily flow of capital, they are often very significant for struggling economies. In 1998, the latest year for which we have data, the remittances migrants sent home topped $70 billion globally. To understand the significance of this figure, compare it to the GDP and foreign currency reserves in the affected countries, rather than to the global flow of capital. For instance, in the Philippines, a major sender of migrants generally and of women for the entertainment industry in particular, remittances were the third largest source of foreign currency over the last several years. In Bangladesh, which sends significant numbers of workers to the Middle East, Japan, and several European countries, remittances totaled about a third of foreign-currency transactions.

Exporting workers is one means by which governments cope with unemployment and foreign debt. The benefits of this strategy come through two channels, one of which is highly formalized and the other a simple by-product of the migration process. South Korea and the Philippines both furnish good examples of formal labor-export programs. In the 1970s, South Korea developed extensive programs to promote the export of workers, initially to the Middle Eastern OPEC countries and then worldwide, as an integral part of its growing overseas construction industry. When South Korea's economy boomed, exporting workers became a less necessary and less attractive strategy. The Philippine government, by contrast, expanded and diversified its labor exports in order to deal with unemployment and to secure needed foreign-currency reserves through remittances.

The Philippines Overseas Employment Administration (POEA) has played an important role in the emigration of Filipina women to the United States, the Middle East, and Japan. Established by the Filipino government in 1982, POEA organized and supervised the export of nurses and maids to high-demand areas. Foreign debt and unemployment combined to make the export of labor an attractive option. Filipino workers overseas send home an average of almost $1 billion a year. For their parts, labor-importing countries had their own reasons to welcome the Filipino government's policy. The OPEC countries of the Middle East saw in the Filipina migrants an answer to their growing demand for domestic workers following the 1973 oil boom. Confronted with an acute shortage of nurses, a profession that demanded years of training yet garnered low wages and little prestige, the United States passed the Immigration Nursing Relief Act of 1989, which allowed for the importation of nurses.[29] And in booming 1980s Japan, which witnessed rising expendable incomes but marked labor shortages, the government passed legislation permitting the entry of "entertainment workers."[30]

The largest number of migrant Filipinas work overseas as maids, particularly in other Asian countries.[31] The second largest group, and the fastest growing, consists of entertainers, who migrate mostly to Japan. The rapid increase in the number of women migrating as entertainers can be traced to the more than five hundred "entertainment brokers" that now operate in the Philippines outside the state umbrella. These brokers provide women for the Japanese sex industry, which is basically controlled by organized gangs rather than through the government-sponsored program for the entry of entertainers. Recruited for singing and entertaining, these women are frequently forced into prostitution as well.[32]

The Filipino government, meanwhile, has also passed regulations that permit mail-order-bride agencies to recruit young Filipinas to marry foreign men. This trade rapidly picked up pace thanks to the government's organized support. The United States and Japan are two of the most common destinations for mail-order brides. Demand was especially high in Japan's agricultural communities in the 1980s, given that country's severe shortage of people in general and of young women in particular, as the demand for labor boomed in the large metropolitan areas. Municipal governments in Japanese towns made it a policy to accept Filipina brides.

A growing body of evidence indicates that mail-order brides frequently suffer physical abuse. In the United States, the Immigration and Naturalization Service has recently reported acute domestic violence against mail-order wives. Again, the law discourages these women from seeking recourse, as they are liable to be detained if they do so before they have been married for two years. In Japan, foreign mail-order wives are not granted full legal status, and considerable evidence indicates that many are subject to abuse not only by their husbands but by their husbands' extended families as well. The Philippine government approved most mail-order-bride brokers before 1989, but during Corazon Aquino's presidency, the stories of abuse by foreign husbands led the Philippine government to ban the mail-order-bride business. Nonetheless, such organizations are almost impossible to eliminate, and they continue to operate in violation of the law.

The Philippines may have the most developed programs for the export of its women, but it is not the only country to have explored similar strategies. After its 1997–1998 financial crisis, Thailand started a campaign to promote migration for work and to encourage overseas firms to recruit Thai workers. Sri Lanka's government has tried to export another 200,000 workers in addition to the 1 million it already has overseas; Sri Lankan women remitted $880 million in 1998, mostly from their earnings as maids in the Middle East and Far East. Bangladesh organized extensive labor-export programs to the OPEC countries of the Middle East in the 1970s. These programs have continued, becoming a significant source of foreign currency along with individual migrations to these and other countries, notably the United States and Great Britain. Bangladesh's workers remitted $1.4 billion in each of the last few years.[33]

Conclusion

Globalization is not only about the hypermobility of capital and the ascendance of information economies. It is also about specific types of places and work processes. In order to understand how economic globalization relates to the extraction of services from the Third World to fulfill what was once the First World woman's domestic role, we must look at globalization in a way that emphasizes some of these concrete conditions.

The growing immiserization of governments and economies in the global south is one such condition, insofar as it enables and even promotes the migration and trafficking of women as a strategy for survival. The same infrastructure designed to facilitate cross-border flows of capital, information, and trade also makes possible a range of unintended cross-border flows, as growing numbers of traffickers, smugglers, and even governments now make money off the backs of women. Through their work and remittances, women infuse cash into the economies of deeply indebted countries, and into the pockets of "entrepreneurs" who have seen other opportunities vanish. These survival circuits are often complex, involving multiple locations and sets of actors, which altogether constitute increasingly global chains of traders and "workers."

But globalization has also produced new labor demand dynamics that center on the global cities of the north. From these places, global economic processes are managed and coordinated by increasing numbers of highly paid professionals. Both the firms and the lifestyles of these professionals are maintained by low-paid service workers, who are in growing demand. Large numbers of low-wage women and immigrants thus find themselves incorporated into strategic economic sectors in global cities. This incorporation happens directly, as in the case of low-wage clerical and blue collar workers, such as janitors and repair workers. And it happens indirectly, through the consumption practices of high-income professionals, which generate a demand for maids and nannies as well as low-wage workers in expensive restaurants and shops. Low-wage workers are then incorporated into the leading sectors, but under conditions that render them invisible.

Both in global cities and in survival circuits, women emerge as crucial economic actors. It is partly through them that key components of new economies have been built. Globalization allows links to be forged between countries that send migrants and countries that receive them; it also enables local and regional practices to go global. The dynamics that come together in the global city produce a strong demand for migrant workers, while the dynamics that mobilize women into survival circuits produce an expanding supply of workers who can be pushed or sold into those types of jobs. The technical infrastructure and transnationalism that underlie the key global-ized industries also allow other types of activities, including money-laundering and trafficking, to assume a global scale.

Migration Trends:
Maps and Chart

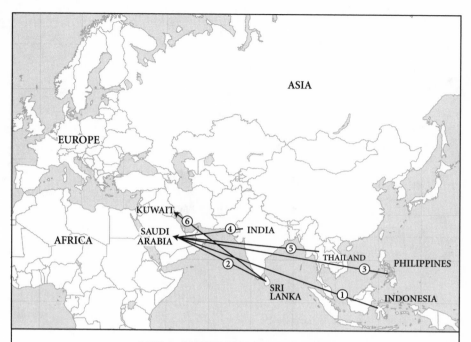

MAP 1. SOUTH ASIA TO THE GULF

1 = Indonesia to Saudi Arabia
As of 1992, 100,000 overseas domestic workers were in Saudi Arabia, many working illegally. It is estimated that at least 230,000 women left Indonesia between 1983 and 1990 to work in Saudi Arabia. The Rural Foundation report (1992) as cited in Heyzer, Lycklama à Nijehold, and Weerakoon, 1994.

In 1986, 36,244 or 61.4 percent of Indonesian workers in Saudi Arabia were women domestic workers. Women's Study Centre (1992) as cited in Heyzer, Lycklama à Nijehold, and Weerakoon, 1994.

2 = Sri Lanka to Saudi Arabia
In 1994, 640,000 Sri Lankan women immigrated to the Middle East for jobs in the domestic service industry. Momsen, 1999.

3 = Philippines to Saudi Arabia
As cited in Momsen, 1999.

4 = India to Saudi Arabia
As cited in Momsen, 1999.

5 = Thailand to Saudi Arabia
As cited in Momsen, 1999.

6 = Sri Lanka to Kuwait
It is estimated that the number of domestic workers in 1989 was in the range of 45,000 to 52,000. Shah et al., as cited in Heyzer, Lycklama à Nijehold, and Weerakoon, 1994.

In 1994, 640,000 Sri Lankan women immigrated to the Middle East for jobs in the domestic service industry. Momsen, 1999.

Key:
——— = domestic worker*

* Please note that the title "domestic worker" includes domestic workers, nannies, and maids. This title was chosen because in many cases a distinction could not be made.

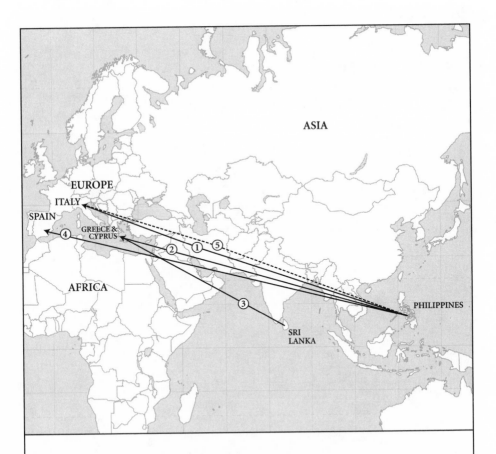

MAP 2. SOUTH ASIA TO EUROPE

1 = Philippines to Italy
Campani (1993) in Momsen, 1999, reported that in 1984 non–European Union foreign female domestic workers made up only 6 percent of the total number of registered domestic workers and that by 1987 they constituted 52.5 percent.

2 = Philippines to Greece and Cyprus
Approximately 12,000 domestic workers/maids as of 1997. Anthias and Lazaridis, 2000.

3 = Sri Lanka to Greece and Cyprus
As cited in Anthias and Lazaridis, 2000.

4 = Philippines to Spain
As cited in Anthias and Lazaridis, 2000.

5 = Philippines to Italy
Presentation by Anny Misa Hefti entitled "Globalization and Migration" at the European Solidarity Conference on the Philippines, September 19–21, 1997, Boldern House, Mannedorf, Zurich, Switzerland.

Key:
——— = domestic worker
- - - - = sex worker

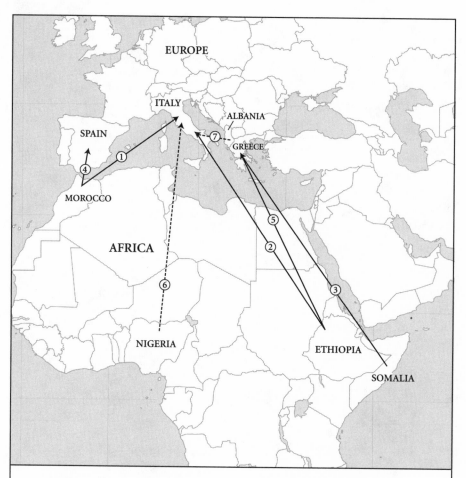

MAP 3. EASTERN EUROPE AND AFRICA TO WESTERN EUROPE

1 = **Morocco to Italy**
   As cited in Anthias and Lazaridis, 2000.

2 = **Ethiopia to Italy**
   As cited in Anthias and Lazaridis, 2000.

3 = **Somalia to Greece**
   As cited in Anthias and Lazaridis, 2000.

4 = **Morocco to Spain**
   Approximately 11,414 Moroccan female domestic workers as of 1997. Anthias and Lazaridis, 2000.

5 = **Ethiopia to Greece**
   As cited in Anthias and Lazaridis, 2000.

6 = **Nigeria to Italy**
   As cited in Anthias and Lazaridis, 2000. In addition, Hopper (1998) as cited in Momsen, 1999, reported that there were 25,000 foreign prostitutes in Italy including Nigerians, Albanians, and Poles.

7 = **Albania to Italy**
   As cited in Anthias and Lazaridis, 2000.

Key:
    = domestic worker
    = sex worker

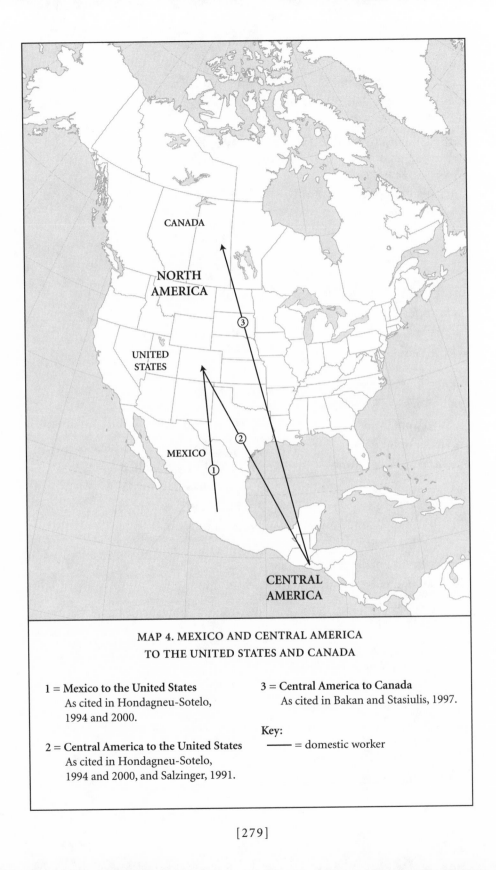

MAP 4. MEXICO AND CENTRAL AMERICA
TO THE UNITED STATES AND CANADA

1 = Mexico to the United States
As cited in Hondagneu-Sotelo,
1994 and 2000.

2 = Central America to the United States
As cited in Hondagneu-Sotelo,
1994 and 2000, and Salzinger, 1991.

3 = Central America to Canada
As cited in Bakan and Stasiulis, 1997.

Key:
——— = domestic worker

Other important migration trends for women not
documented in the four regional maps:

Latin America to Europe

Domestic Workers:
Dominican Republic to Spain
Peru to Spain

Sex Workers:
Guatemala to Spain
Columbia & Brazil to Western
    Europe

Within Asia

Domestic Workers:
Philippines to Hong Kong,
    Singapore, Malaysia
Sri Lanka to Singapore
Thailand to Hong Kong

Sex Workers:
Philippines to Japan, Taiwan, Hong
    Kong, Malaysia
Cambodia to Thailand & Malaysia
Vietnam to Thailand & Cambodia
Laos to Thailand
China to Thailand
Burma to Thailand
Bangladesh to Pakistan & India
Nepal to India
India to Pakistan & Sri Lanka
Sri Lanka to Pakistan

Within Europe

Domestic Workers:
Poland to Greece
Albania to Greece
Bulgaria to Greece

Sex Workers:
Albania to Greece
Romania to Turkey
Russia & Ukraine to Western
    Europe

Other

Domestic Workers:
Philippines to United States
Caribbean to United States
Sri Lanka to Canada
Philippines to Canada
Peru to Spain

Appendix: Activist Organizations

Women migrant workers around the world face many potential difficulties, including low wages, poor working conditions, trafficking, domestic violence, problematic immigration status, and various human rights violations. A number of organizations now provide information and services; coordinate the activities of grassroots advocacy groups; and serve as clearinghouses for services available to migrant women workers. Below is a small sampling of the many organizations devoted to these important issues.

International Organization for Migration (IOM)
http://www.iom.int
Established in 1951 to resettle displaced persons in Europe, IOM now has offices on every continent and maintains close working relations with the United Nations and a wide range of NGOs. It is a good source of information. IOM's Working Group on Gender Issues prepares a helpful quarterly, *Gender Bulletin*.

International Labor Organization (ILO)
http://www.ilo.org
Established in 1944, the ILO gathers information and prepares reports on various issues vital to migrant women workers. The ILO has also coordinated efforts with the United Nations and other international organizations to address the problems of migrant women workers. A joint project between the ILO and the United Nations Children's Fund (UNICEF) has addressed the trafficking of children in Africa. A joint project with the World Health Organization (WHO) has tackled debt bondage

in Asia. In 1998 the ILO issued a Declaration of Fundamental Principles and Rights at Work, which called for the eradication of forced labor.

The Global Alliance Against Traffic in Women (GAATW)
http://www.inet.co.th/org/gaatw/
GAATW was formed in 1994 in Thailand. It promotes grassroots activism on behalf of trafficked women and has published a handbook for NGOs and activists concerned with trafficking.

> The International Coordination Office
> P.O. Box 36, Bangkok Noi Office
> Bangkok 10700, Thailand
> Phone: (662) 864-1427-8
> Fax: (662) 864-1637
> E-mail: gaatw@mozart.inet.co.th

The Coalition Against Trafficking in Women (CATW)
http://www.catwinternational.org.
CATW is a clearinghouse for a variety of anti-trafficking organizations that fight sexual exploitation around the world (e.g., in Bangladesh, France, the United States, and the Philippines). Having spearheaded the drive to establish a new United Nations Convention Against Sexual Exploitation, CATW now seeks to establish this convention as an article of international law.

International Movement Against All Forms of Discrimination and Racism (IMADR)
http://www.imadr.org
IMADR is an international nonprofit human rights organization that publishes resources for anti-racism NGOs and activists.

American Federation of Labor and Congress of Industrial Organizations (AFL-CIO)
http://www.aflcio.org
Among other things, the AFL-CIO addresses the concerns of immigrant workers in the United States. It has an excellent set of resources, including written materials on the legal rights of immigrants and union activities on behalf of migrants. (Also see http://www.aflcio.org/immigrantworkers/index.htm.) The AFL-CIO also has branches outside the United States. The Sri Lankan branch of the AFL-CIO, called the American Center for International Labor Solidarity, works on the migration of labor from Sri Lanka to the Middle East. ACILS's address is:

> 9, Kinross Avenue
> Colombo 4, Sri Lanka
> Phone: +94-1-580080
> Fax: +91-1-593123

Kalayaan! Justice for Migrant Domestic Workers
Kalayaan! works with documented and undocumented migrant domestic workers in the United Kingdom. It maintains strong links with sister organizations in the European Union.

St. Francis Centre
13 Hippodrome Place
London W11 4SF, England
Phone: 020-7243-2942
Fax: 020-7792-3060
E-mail: kalayaanuk@aol.com

Center for Filipino Migrant Workers (CFMW)
CFMW publishes two newsletters on migrant issues, called *Kababayan* and *Migration Monitor*. It also coordinates services and activism on behalf of Filipino migrant workers in the European Union.

CFMW International
Paulus Potterstraat 20
1071 Amsterdam, The Netherlands
Phone: 20-664-6927
Fax: 20-664-7093
E-mail: cfmw@open.net

Stop-Traffic
http://www.stop-traffic.org
Stop-Traffic is an open, international, electronic mailing list funded by the Women's Reproductive Health Initiative of the Program for Appropriate Technology in Health. It addresses human rights abuses associated with forced labor trafficking around the world.

National Interfaith Committee for Worker Justice
http://www.nationalinterfaith.org
The National Interfaith Committee for Worker Justice is a network of religious activists that works to improve the wages, benefits, and working conditions of migrant workers. Based in the United States, it has a partnership with the Department of Labor. The organization hopes to help enforce workers' rights to engage in collective bargaining.

1020 Bryn Mawr Avenue, 4th Floor
Chicago, IL 60660
Phone: 773-728-8400

Migrants.Net
http://www.migrants.net
Migrants.Net provides online resources for migrant workers.

The Mission for Filipino Migrant Workers (MFMW)
Established in 1981 by various churches, MFMW provides information and out-reach to Filipino migrant workers in Hong Kong. The Mission focuses on crisis intervention and prevention, and offers legal and social services.
St. John's Cathedral
Garden Road, Central
Hong Kong, SAR
Phone: 25228264
E-mail: migrant@pacific.net.hk

Coalition for Humane Immigrant Rights in Los Angeles (CHIRLA)
Formed in 1986, CHIRLA serves as a clearinghouse and library for agencies and individuals with an interest in immigrants' rights. It also provides training and technical assistance to 125 grassroots organizations in Southern California.
1521 Wilshire Boulevard
Los Angeles, CA 90017
Phone: 213-353-1333
Fax: 213-353-1344
E-mail: chirla@earthlink.net

Notes

Introduction

1. See Ellen Galinsky and Dana Friedman, *Women: The New Providers,* Whirlpool Foundation Study, Part 1 (New York: Families and Work Institute, 1995), p. 37.

2. Special thanks to Roberta Espinoza, who gathered and designed the flow maps shown in Appendix I. In addition to material directly cited, this introduction draws from the following works: Kathleen M. Adams and Sara Dickey, eds., *Home and Hegemony: Domestic Service and Identity Politics in South and Southeast Asia* (Ann Arbor: University of Michigan Press, 2000); Floya Anthias and Gabriella Lazaridis, eds., *Gender and Migration in Southern Europe: Women on the Move* (Oxford and New York: Berg, 2000); Stephen Castles and Mark J. Miller, *The Age of Migration: International Population Movements in the Modern World* (New York and London: The Guilford Press, 1998); Noeleen Heyzer, Geertje Lycklama à Nijehold, and Nedra Weerakoon, eds., *The Trade in Domestic Workers: Causes, Mechanisms, and Consequences of International Migration* (London: Zed Books, 1994); Eleanore Kofman, Annie Phizacklea, Parvati Raghuram, and Rosemary Sales, *Gender and International Migration in Europe: Employment, Welfare, and Politics* (New York and London: Routledge, 2000); Douglas S. Massey, Joaquin Arango, Graeme Hugo, Ali Kouaouci, Adela Pellegrino, and J. Edward Taylor, *Worlds in Motion: Understanding International Migration at the End of the Millennium* (Oxford: Clarendon Press, 1999); Janet Henshall Momsen, ed., *Gender, Migration, and*

Domestic Service (London: Routledge, 1999); Katie Willis and Brenda Yeoh, eds., *Gender and Immigration* (London: Edward Elgar Publishers, 2000).

3. Illegal migrants are said to make up anywhere from 60 percent (as in Sri Lanka) to 87 percent (as in Indonesia) of all migrants . In Singapore in 1994, 95 percent of Filipino overseas contract workers lacked work permits from the Philippine government. The official figures based on legal migration therefore severely underestimate the number of migrants. See Momsen, 1999, p. 7.

4. Momsen, 1999, p. 9.

5. Sri Lanka Bureau of Foreign Employment, 1994, as cited in G. Gunatilleke, *The Economic, Demographic, Sociocultural and Political Setting for Emigration from Sri Lanka International Migration,* vol. 23 (3/4), 1995, pp. 667–98.

6. Anthias and Lazaridis, 2000; Heyzer, Nijehold, and Weerakoon, 1994, pp. 4–27; Momsen, 1999, p. 21; "Wistat: Women's Indicators and Statistics Database," version 3, CD-ROM (United Nations, Department for Economic and Social Information and Policy Analysis, Statistical Division, 1994).

7. Geovanna Campani, "Labor Markets and Family Networks: Filipino Women in Italy," in Hedwig Rudolph and Mirjana Morokvasic, eds., *Bridging States and Markets: International Migration in the Early 1990s* (Berlin: Edition Sigma, 1993), p. 206.

8. This "new" source of the Western demand for nannies, maids, child-care, and elder-care workers does not, of course, account for the more status-oriented demand in the Persian Gulf states, where most affluent women don't work outside the home.

9. For information on male work at home during the 1990s, see Arlie Russell Hochschild and Anne Machung, *The Second Shift: Working Parents and the Revolution at Home* (New York: Avon, 1997), p. 277.

10. Kevin Bales, *Disposable People: New Slavery in the Global Economy* (Berkeley: University of California Press, 1999), p. 43.

11. Andrea Tyree and Katharine M. Donato, "A Demographic Overview of the International Migration of Women," in *International Migration: The Female Experience,* ed. Rita Simon and Caroline Bretell (Totowa, N.J: Rowman & Allanheld, 1986), p. 29. Indeed, many immigrant maids and nannies are more educated than the people they work for. See Pei-Chia Lan's paper in this volume.

12. Momsen, 1999, pp. 10, 73.

13. Grete Brochmann, *Middle East Avenue: Female Migration from Sri Lanka to the Gulf* (Boulder, Colo.: Westview Press, 1993), pp. 179, 215.

14. On this point, thanks to Raka Ray, Sociology Department at the University of California, Berkeley.

Love and Gold

1. Information about Rowena Bautista is drawn from Robert Frank, "High-Paying Nanny Positions Puncture Fabric of Family Life in Developing Nations," *Wall*

Street Journal, December 18, 2001. All interviews not otherwise attributed were conducted by the author. Also see Arlie Hochschild, "The Nanny Chain," *American Prospect,* January 3, 2000, pp. 32–36. Rhacel Parreñas's discussion of the "globalization of mother" in her dissertation first got me thinking about this subject; see her *Servants of Globalization: Women, Migration, and Domestic Work* (Palo Alto: Stanford University Press, 2001). Also see the film *When Mother Comes Home for Christmas,* directed by Nilita Vachani. On the whole, until very recently there has been little focus on a "care drain," even among academics who focus on gender issues. Much writing on globalization focuses on money, markets, and, presumably, male labor. Much research on women and development, on the other hand, has focused on the impact of "structural adjustments" (World Bank loan requirements that call for austerity measures) and deprivation. Meanwhile, most research on working women in the United States and Europe focuses on the picture of a detached, two-person balancing act or the lone "supermom," omitting child-care workers from the picture. Fortunately, in recent years, scholars such as Evelyn Nakano Glenn, Janet Henshall Momsen, Mary Romero, Grace Chang, and the authors included and referenced in this volume have produced the important research on which this book builds.

2. *New York Times,* September 1, 2001, A8.

3. William Greider, *One World, Ready or Not: The Manic Logic of Global Capitalism* (New York: Simon and Schuster, 1997), p. 21.

4. Castles and Miller, 1998, p. 8. See also Hania Zlotnik, "Trends of International Migration Since 1965: What Existing Data Reveal," *International Migration,* vol. 37, no. 1 (1999), pp. 22–61.

5. Castles and Miller, 1998, p. 5.

6. Castles and Miller, 1998, p. 9. Also see the Technical Symposium on International Migration and Development, the United Nations General Assembly, Special Session on the International Conference on Population and Development, The Hague, The Netherlands, June 29–July 2, 1998, Executive Summary, p. 2. See also *Migrant News,* no. 2 (November 1998), p. 2.

7. Castles and Miller, 1998, p. xi.

8. Arlie Russell Hochschild, *The Time Bind: When Work Becomes Home and Home Becomes Work* (New York: Avon, 1997) pp. xxi, 268.

9. Nancy Folbre, *The Invisible Heart: Economics and Family Values* (New York: The New Press, 2001), p. 55.

10. Rhacel Parreñas, "The Global Servants: (Im)Migrant Filipina Domestic Workers in Rome and Los Angeles," Ph.D. dissertation, Department of Ethnic Studies, University of California, Berkeley, 1999, p. 60.

11. Parreñas, 1999, pp. 123, 154.

12. Parreñas, 1999, p. 154.

13. Parreñas, 1999, p. 123.

14. Frank, 2001.
15. Sau-Ling Wong, "Diverted Mothering: Representations of Caregivers of Color in the Age of 'Multiculturalism,' " in *Mothering: Ideology, Experience and Agency,* ed. Evelyn Nakano Glenn, Grace Chang, and Linda Rennie Forcey (London: Routledge, 1994), pp. 67–91.
16. Philippe Ariès, *Centuries of Childhood: A Social History of Family Life* (New York: Vintage, 1962); Sharon Hays, *The Cultural Contradictions of Motherhood* (New Haven: Yale University Press, 1996).

The Care Crisis in the Philippines: Children and Transnational Families in the New Global Economy

1. The data collection for this project benefited from the research assistance of Jason David, Luisa Gonzaga, Maria Eva Cecilia Lesondra, Ella Liu, and Sauro Solis. The project received research support from the University of California President's Postdoctoral Fellowship Program, the Ford Foundation Postdoctoral Fellowship Program, and the Graduate School of the University of Wisconsin, Madison.
2. Arlie Hochschild, "The Culture of Politics: Traditional, Post-modern, Cold Modern, Warm Modern Ideals of Care," *Social Politics,* vol. 2, no. 3 (1995): pp. 331–46.
3. While women made up only 12 percent of the total worker outflow in 1975, this figure grew to 47 percent twelve years later in 1987 and surpassed the number of men by 1995. IBON Facts and Figures, "Filipinos as Global Slaves," 22, nos. 5–6 (March 15–31, 1999), p. 6.
4. Notably, Filipino women have responded to the care crisis in more developed nations in other ways. They also alleviate the care crisis plaguing hospitals and hospices in more developed nations by providing services as professional nurses. At the expense of the quality of professional care in the Philippines, nurses have sought the better wages available outside the country. Between 1992 and 1999, the government deployed more than thirty-five thousand nurses. See Maruja Asis, *Female Labour Migration in South-East Asia: Change and Continuity* (Bangkok, Thailand: Asian Research Centre for Migration, Institution of Asian Studies, Chulalongkorn University, 2001).
5. Using a 1997 national labor force survey, Hector Morada, the director of the Bureau of Labor and Employment Statistics in the Philippines, found that female-headed transnational households have an average of 2.74 children, with .56 aged less than seven years.
6. Gina Mission, "The Breadwinners: Female Migrant Workers," *WIN: Women's International Net Issue* (November 1998): p. 15A.
7. Hochschild and Machung, 1989. By "stalled revolution," Hochschild refers to the fact that the economic contributions of women to the family have not been met with a corresponding increase in male responsibility for household work.

8. Agence France-Presse, "Ramos: Overseas Employment a Threat to Filipino Families," *Philippine Inquirer* (May 26, 1995), p. 11.

9. I base this claim on a survey of articles that appeared in Philippine dailies from 1995 to 1998. I obtained the newspaper articles from the library of the Philippine Overseas Employment Agency, which catalogs media reports on migrant Filipino workers.

10. Perfecto G. Caparas, "OCWs Children: Bearing the Burden of Separation," *Manila Times* (September 30, n.d.), pp. 1–2.

11. Susan Fernandez, "Pamilya ng OFWs maraming hirap" (Many hardships in the families of OFWs), *Abante* (January 27, 1997), p. 5.

12 Lorie Toledo, "Child Sexual Abuse Awareness," *People's Journal* (February 19, 1996), p. 4. Although incest is a social problem in the Philippines, its direct correlation to the emigration of mothers is an unproven speculation. For instance, studies have yet to show that there are higher rates of incest among children of migrant mothers than in other families.

13. Lorie Toledo, "Overseas job vs. family stability," *People's Journal* (December 15, 1993), p. 4.

14. Bureau of Employment and Labor Statistics, "Remittances from Overseas Filipino Workers by Country of Origin Philippines: 1997–Fourth Quarter 1999," *Pinoy Migrants, Shared Government Information System for Migration,* http://emisd.web.dfa.gov.ph/~pinoymigrants/.

15. Rosemarie Samaniego is a pseudonym. This excerpt is drawn from Rhacel Salazar Parreñas, *Servants of Globalization: Women, Migration, and Domestic Work* (Stanford, Calif.: Stanford University Press, 2001).

16. Ellen Seneriches and the names of the other children whom I quote in this article are all pseudonyms.

17. Pierrette Hondagneu-Sotelo and Ernestine Avila, " 'I'm Here, but I'm There': The Meanings of Latina Transnational Motherhood," *Gender and Society,* vol. 11, no. 5 (1997), pp. 548–71.

18. A two-part special report by Caparas, "OCWs Children," which appeared on the front page of the *Manila Times,* summarized the media's incredibly negative view on the plight of children in transnational families. It reported that children suffer from a "psychological toll," "extreme loneliness," "unbearable loss," "strained relations," "incest," and consequently delinquency, as indicated, for instance, by rampant "premature pregnancies." See also Caparas's "OCWs and the Changing Lives of Filipino Families," *Manila Times* (August, 29, n.d.), pp. 1, 5.

19. Similarly, I found that children use the corollary image of the struggling "breadwinner" father to negotiate the emotional strains of their transnational household arrangement.

20. Scalabrini Migration Center (SMC), *Impact of Labor Migration on the Children Left Behind* (Quezon City, Philippines: Scalabrini Migration Center, 2000).

21. SMC, 2000, p. 65.
22. SMC, 2000, p. 57.
23. SMC, 2000, p. 65.
24. Arjun Appadurai, "Globalization and the Research Imagination," *International Social Science Journal,* vol. 160 (June 1999), p. 231.
25. National Commission for the Role of Filipino Women, *Philippine Plan for Gender-Responsive Development, 1995–2025* (Manila, Philippines: National Commission for the Role of Filipino Women, 1995).
26. Marije Meerman, "The Care Chain," episode 42 of *The New World* (Netherlands: VPRO-TV); www.dnv.vpro.nl/carechain.
27. Policies in various receiving countries restrict the migration of workers' families. Such restrictions can be found both in countries, such as Singapore and Taiwan, that have illiberal policies and in those, like Canada, with liberal policies. See Abigail Bakan and Daiva Stasiulis, eds., *Not One of the Family: Foreign Domestic Workers in Canada* (Toronto: University of Toronto Press, 1997).

Blowups and Other Unhappy Endings

1. Note that each case is reconstructed from one person's story.
2. Alejandro Portes, "When More Can Be Less: Labor Standards, Development, and the Informal Economy," in *Contrapunto: The Informal Sector Debate in Latin America,* ed. Cathy A. Rokowski (Albany: State University of New York Press, 1994), pp. 113–29.
3. James Bates, "Disney Settles Up with Its Former Studio Boss," *Los Angeles Times,* July 8, 1999, pp. A1, A10.
4. Julia Wrigley, *Other People's Children: An Intimate Account of the Dilemmas Facing Middle-Class Parents and the Women They Hire to Raise Their Children* (New York: Basic Books, 1995), p. 26.
5. Deborah Stone, "Valuing 'Caring Work': Rethinking the Nature of Work in Human Services," typescript, Radcliffe Public Policy Institute, April 1998.
6. Albert O. Hirschman, *Exit, Voice and Loyalty: Responses to Decline in Firms, Organizations and States* (Cambridge, Mass.: Harvard University Press, 1970).

Invisible Labors: Caring for the Independent Person

1. Thanks to all who agreed to tell me their stories. This research was supported by fellowships from the Ford Foundation as well as the graduate division of the University of California, Berkeley.
2. Studies of the nationwide personal attendant workforce have not considered the issue of immigration status; see, e.g., William Crown, Margaret MacAdam et al.,

"Home Care Workers: A National Profile," *Caring Magazine,* vol. 11, no. 4 (1992), pp. 34–38. However, the Service Employees International Union reports: "In larger cities, these workers tend to be minority and immigrant women." See Service Employee International Union, "Home Care Workers: A Briefing Paper," submitted to the U.S. Department of Labor and the U.S. Department of Health and Human Services (Washington, D.C., May 1999). Grace Chang (*Disposable Domestics: Immigrant Women Workers in the Global Economy* [Cambridge, Mass.: South End Press, 2000]) reports that in California, 40 percent of the personal attendants paid for by IHSS (In-Home Supportive Services) are immigrants. Candace Howes and Richard Zawadski ("The Effect of Changes in the Wage/Benefit Package on the Supply of Home Care Workers in San Francisco," paper presented at the Institute of Industrial Relations Seminar, [Berkeley, February 2001]) report that the majority of IHSS workers in the California counties of Alameda, Contra Costa, and San Francisco are immigrant women.

3. The racial and ethnic composition of the home-care workforce varies substantially by location. In Los Angeles County the composition of the personal attendants funded by IHSS is the following: 30 percent Latina, 25 percent African-American, and 14 percent of Armenian and Russian descent (M. Cousineau, "Providing Health Insurance to IHSS Providers [Home Care Workers] in Los Angeles County," report to the California Health Care Foundation [June 2000]). In contrast, the IHSS personal attendant workforce in San Francisco County is approximately 28 percent Chinese, 29 percent Russian, 8 percent Latina, 22 percent white non-Russian, and 8 percent African-American (Howes and Zawadski, 2001).

4. Cousineau reports that of the personal attendants working for IHSS, most were poor or nearly poor: "80 percent live in a household with income below 200 percent of Federal Poverty Level." Crown et al. report that the median income of personal attendants in 1988 was $7,999.

5. Noticeably absent from my study are the average users of personal-attendant services in the United States, specifically disabled elderly women. However, the consumers in my study are typical of individuals identified as constituents of the Independent Living Movement. See Gerben DeJong, "Defining and Implementing the Independent Living Concept," in *Independent Living for Physically Disabled People: Developing, Implementing, and Evaluating Self-Help Rehabilitation Programs,* ed. Nancy M. Crewe and Irving K. Zola (San Francisco: Jossey-Bass, 1983).

6. DeJong, 1983.

7. S. L. Dawson et al., *Direct-Care Health Workers: The Unnecessary Crisis in Long-term Care* (Washington, D.C., The Domestic Strategy Group of the Aspen Institute, 2001), p. 44.

8. Generally minimum wage, however there are exceptions, the most striking of which is the county of San Francisco where, because of a living-wage law that was strongly supported by the Service Employees International Union (SEIU), personal attendants paid by In-Home Supportive Services receive an hourly wage of $9.70 an hour, which is more than $3 above the minimum wage of $6.25.

9. Personal attendant is the fastest-growing job category in the United States (see D. Murphy, "Health Opportunities," *San Francisco Examiner* [May 23, 1999] pp. J1–J2; and M. Farr, L. LaVerne, et al., *Best Jobs of the 21st Century* [Indianapolis, JIST Works Inc., 1999]).

10. Andrew I. Batavia, Gerben DeJong, et al., "Toward a National Personal Assistance Program: The Independent Living Model of Long-term Care for Persons with Disabilities," *Journal of Health Politics, Policy and Law*, vol. 16, no. 3 (1991), pp. 523–545.

11. Remarkably, despite the structure of their jobs, SEIU has, in recent years, managed to organize many of these workers. See S. Greenhouse, "In Biggest Drive Since 1937, Union Gains a Victory," *New York Times* (February 26, 1999), pp. A1, A15.

12. In the Independent Living paradigm, caregivers have no professional authority and personal attendants must not be professionals; formal training and skills are not required and are in fact discouraged. See G. DeJong and T. Wenker, "Attendant Care," in *Independent Living for Physically Disabled People: Developing, Implementing, and Evaluating Self-Help Rehabilitation Programs*, ed. Nancy M. Crewe and Irving K. Zola (San Francisco: Jossey-Bass, 1983).

13. Rare exceptions include the California counties of San Francisco, Alameda, and Contra Costa, which introduced health-care benefits in 1999, 2001, and 2001 respectively. In all three cases health benefits were the result of contract negotiations between the counties and the SEIU.

14. Robert Bellah, R. Madsen, et al., *Habits of the Heart: Individualism and Commitment in American Life* (Berkeley: University of California Press, 1985).

15. Bellah et al., 1985, argue that "it is individualism . . . that has marched inexorably through our history" (p. vii). I use the word *man* because the history of the independent individual is gendered. Michael Kimmel points out that independence has become part of common definitions of masculinity. See Michael Kimmel, *Manhood in America: A Cultural History* (New York: Free Press, 1986).

16. That individuals are not independent but rather interdependent is not a new idea, and feminist critics of liberalism (e.g., Dorothy Smith, *The Everyday World as Problematic: A Feminist Sociology* [Boston: Northeastern University Press, 1987]) have pointed out that making women's reproductive labor invisible helps sustain the myth of the independent man.

17. Joan Tronto, *Moral Boundaries: A Political Argument for an Ethic of Care* (New York: Routledge, 1993), p. 20.

18. The "doing" of identity in Candace West and Donald Zimmerman ("Doing Gender," in *The Social Construction of Gender*, ed. Judith Lorber and Susan Farrell [Newbury Park: Sage Publications, 1991]) as well as Candace West and Sarah Fenstermaker ("Doing Difference," *Gender and Society*, vol. 9, no. 1 [1995], pp. 8–37) is conceived of as something that people accomplish through interaction. One does not do identity alone; the real or imagined presence of another is necessary. However, while their conception involves interaction, it does not involve collaboration.

19. Evelyn Nakano Glenn, "From Servitude to Service Work: Historical Continuities in the Racial Division of Paid Reproductive Labor," *Signs: Journal of Women in Culture and Society,* vol. 18, no. 1 (1991).

20. Arlie Russell Hochschild (*The Managed Heart: Commercialization of Human Feeling* [Berkeley: University of California Press, 1983]) found that it was the flight attendant's job to "naturally" love the job of caring, which erased the emotional labor involved.

21. Lise Isaksen, "Toward a Sociology of Gendered Disgust: Perceptions of the Organic Body and the Organization of Care," *Working Papers Series* (Berkeley, University of California, Center for Working Families, 2000).

22. Isaksen, 2000; Thomas Scheff and Suzanne Retzinger, "Shame as the Master Emotion of Everyday Life," *Journal of Mundane Behavior,* vol. 1, no. 3 (2000).

23. Naturalizing and essentializing a particular activity does not have the same effect on a high-status group as it has on a low-status group. For example, when men act in accord with gender stereotypes, their contribution is usually visible, but when women act within their gender roles their contributions are often invisible. See Barbara Stanek Kilborne, P. England, et al., "Returns to Skill, Compensating Differentials, and Gender Bias: Effects of Occupational Characteristics on the Wages of White Women and Men," *American Journal of Sociology*, vol. 100, no. 3 (1994), pp. 689–719. Ironically, when lower-status groups act outside of their social roles, while their contributions are more likely to be visible, they are also more likely to be stigmatized.

24. Hochschild, 1983.

25. In *Manufacturing Consent* (Chicago: University of Chicago Press, 1979), Michael Burawoy describes the process by which the workers in a machine shop actively participate in the appropriation of their labor by the company.

26. Deborah Stone in her 1991 article, "Caring Work in a Liberal Polity," observes that one of her students (Kim Smith, draft dissertation, Heller School, Brandeis University, Waltham, Mass., 1991) also found this tendency of disabled individuals to use active verbs in the first person to describe activities that they could not have done themselves. However, it's important to note that disabled individuals are not the only ones who do this. Stone uses the example of a disabled person

offering a cup of coffee but we can just as easily imagine an able-bodied executive offering, "Can I get you a cup of coffee?" when in fact it is his secretary that will be doing the getting.

27. Personal attendants were present in three of the eight interviews with consumers.

28. In *Moral Boundaries*, Joan Tronto distinguishes between caring for and caring about. "Caring about" refers to emotional attachment.

29. George also told me that *consumers* (of personal-attendant services) is the politically correct term to use, as opposed to the term *disabled*. Individuals I interviewed used both terms.

30. Dejong, 1983. See also A. D. Ratzka, "Independent Living and Attendant Care in Sweden: A Consumer Perspective" (New York: World Rehabilitation Fund, 1986).

31. For example, Irving K. Zola, "Developing Self-Images and Interdependence," in *Independent Living for Physically Disabled People: Developing, Implementing, and Evaluating Self-Help Rehabilitation Programs*, ed. Nancy M. Crewe and Irving K. Zola.

32. Other studies (e.g., N. N. Eustis and L. R. Fischer, "Relationships Between Home Care Clients and Their Workers: Implications for Quality of Care," *The Geronotologist*, vol. 31, no. 4 [1991], pp. 447–456) show that higher levels of consumer satisfaction are correlated to longer-term relationships with attendants, in which consumers regarded attendants as friends. However, Crown et al., 1992, assert that high rates of turnover are widespread; they specifically report that, according to 1988 Current Population Survey data: "42 percent of home care workers left the field in a one-year period."

33. Eustis and Fischer found that "clients with formal relationships reported more problems with workers than those with other types of relationships" (1991, p. 455).

34. Stone, 1991, pp. 547–552.

35. The consumers who did think that their personal attendants did things that went "beyond the call of duty" cited times when their attendants brought them gifts or visited them in the hospital on off-hours. With one exception, none of the consumers mentioned an activity performed during work hours as something above and beyond the call of duty. Eustis and Fischer, by contrast, reported that during work hours "most workers did extra jobs—that is, beyond what they were assigned or paid to do according to perceptions of both clients and workers" (1991, p. 455). It's important to remember, however, that their study was of a completely different population of both clients and workers. The mean age of the consumers in their sample was 62.4; the relationships they investigated were between a consumer and one particular personal attendant, generally someone who had worked for that client for some time. Also, unlike the attendants in this study, more than half of the personal attendants in their sample worked for home health-care agencies.

36. Independent Living adherents, by describing themselves as consumers, made claims about their right to choose and to control their own care. In particular they demanded the right to hire and fire their personal attendants (DeJong 1983; DeJong and Wenker 1983).

37. Jessica Benjamin, *The Bonds of Love: Psychoanalysis, Feminism, and the Problem of Domination* (New York: Pantheon Books, 1980).

Maid to Order

1. Cheryl Mendelson, *Home Comforts: The Art and Science of Keeping House* (New York: Scribner, 1999), p. 501.

2. Quotes are from Phyllis Palmer, "Outside the Law: Agricultural and Domestic Workers Under the Fair Labor Standards Act," *Journal of Policy History*, vol. 7, no. 4 (1995), pp. 416–440.

3. Suzanne Bianchi et al., "Is Anyone Doing the Housework? Trends and Gender Differentials in America's Least Favorite Activity," University of Maryland, July 1999.

4. "With More Equity, More Sweat," *Washington Post*, March 22, 1998.

5. Mary Romero, *Maid in the U.S.A.* (New York: Routledge, 1992), p. 92.

6. Quoted in Romero, 1992, p. 72.

7. See Palmer, 1995, pp. 12–13.

8. Judith Rollins, *Between Women: Domestics and Their Employers* (Philadelphia: Temple University Press, 1985).

9. "Détente in the Housework Wars," *Toronto Star*, November 20, 1999.

10. "Molding Loyal Pamperers for the Newly Rich," *New York Times*, October 24, 1999.

Just Another Job? The Commodification of Domestic Labor

1. Nicky Gregson and Michelle Lowe, *Servicing the Middle Classes: Class, Gender and Waged Domestic Labour in Contemporary Britain* (London: Routledge, 1994).

2. Margaret Healy, "Exploring the Slavery of Domestic Work in Private House-holds," unpublished M.A. thesis, University of Westminster, 1994.

3. Judith Rollins, *Between Women: Domestic Workers and Their Employers* (Philadelphia: Temple University Press, 1985).

4. Miranda Miles, "Working in the City: The Case of Migrant Women in Swazi-land's Domestic Service Sector," in *Gender, Migration and Domestic Service*, ed. Janet Momsen (London: Routledge, 1999).

Filipina Workers in Hong Kong Homes: Household Rules and Relations

1. Catholic Institute for International Relations (CIIR), *The Labour Trade: Filipino Migrant Workers Around the World* (London: Catholic Institute for International Relations, 1987), p. 104.

2. Hong Kong Immigration Department, "Employment Contract for Domestic Workers Recruited from Outside of Hong Kong" (Hong Kong: Immigration Department, 1993). For further discussion of the employment contract, see also Nicole Constable, *Maid to Order in Hong Kong: Stories of Filipina Workers* (Ithaca, N.Y.: Cornell University Press, 1997), pp. 131–51.

3. Hong Kong Institute of Household Management (HKIHM) (Manila, Philippines, n.d.), p. 3 (Hong Kong University Foreign Domestic Worker Project Files).

4. HKIHM, p. 2.

5. HKIHM, p. 2.

6. HKIHM, p. 3.

7. Edward P. Thompson, "Time, Work-Discipline, and Industrial Capitalism," *Past and Present*, vol. 38 (1967), pp. 56–97.

8. As Michel Foucault has written, timetables are "based on the principle of non-idleness" and were designed to "eliminate the danger of wasting it—a moral offense and economic dishonesty." Michel Foucault, *Discipline and Punish: The Birth of the Prison* (New York: Vintage Books, 1979), p. 154.

9. For a discussion of "maternalism" in employer-worker relationships, see Rollins, 1985, pp. 173–203.

10. Jennifer Gaff, *The Maid's Manual* (Hong Kong: Redcoat Investments, 1983). This book is advertised as a "guide to all household matters," as "the perfect answer for use by employer and maids in achieving on the job training," and as the "perfect gift for maids to take home to their younger sisters" (back cover). It provides "A to Z" entries intended to help train domestic workers to meet their employer's expectations.

11. Carolyn French, "Filipina Domestic Workers in Hong Kong" (Ph.D. dissertation, University of Surrey, 1986), p. 186.

12. Asian Migrant Centre (AMC), *Foreign Domestic Workers in Hong Kong: A Baseline Study* (Hong Kong: Asian Migrant Centre, 1991), pp. 38–39.

13. A. Lam, "Most Overseas Workers Inefficient," *South China Morning Post* (August 23, 1993).

14. See, for example, Shellee Cohen, " 'With Respect and Feelings': Voices of West Indian Child Care and Domestic Workers in New York City," in *All American Women: Lives That Divide, Ties That Bind*, ed. Johnetta Cole (New York: Free Press, 1986), p. 57; and Soroya Moore Coley, "And Still I Rise: An Exploratory Study of Contemporary Private Black Household Workers" (Ph.D. dissertation, Bryn Mawr College, 1981), p. 238.

15. Rollins, 1985, p. 129; and Mary Romero, *Maid in the U.S.A.* (New York: Routledge, 1992), p. 112.
16. Evelyn Nakano Glenn, *Issei, Nisei, War Bride: Three Generations of Japanese American Women in Domestic Service* (Philadelphia: Temple University Press, 1986), p. 158.
17. HKIHM, p. 3.
18. James L. Watson, "From the Common Pot: Feasting with Equals in Chinese Society," *Anthropos,* vol. 82 (1987), pp. 389–401.
19. Romero, 1992, p. 123. See also Alice Childress, *Like One of the Family: Conversations from a Domestic's Life* (Boston: Beacon Press, 1986).
20. For a discussion of jealousy, see Rollins, 1985, pp. 99–100; and Nicole Constable, "Jealousy, Chastity and Abuse: Chinese Maids and Foreign Helpers in Hong Kong," *Modern China,* vol. 22, no. 4 (1996), pp. 448–79.
21. See Maria Jaschok, *Concubines and Bondservants: The Social History of a Chinese Custom* (Hong Kong: Oxford University Press, 1988).
22. Romero, 1992, pp. 105–111.
23. Rollins, 1985, pp. 166–67.
24. For further discussion of the importance of "professional distance," see Romero, 1992, pp. 126–27.

Selling Sex for Visas: Sex Tourism as a Stepping-stone to International Migration

1. I have changed the names of all the sex workers I interviewed, as well as those of their clients.
2. I am deeply grateful to two research assistants, former sex workers whose names I agreed not to use, who generously introduced me to their community. Without their insights and patience, I would have had a difficult time conducting this field research. I am also greatly indebted to Dr. Bayardo Gómez and the staff of COVI-COSIDA, a Dominican nongovernmental agency that conducts AIDS education with sex workers. I would like to thank Marybeth McMahon for her helpful comments on this chapter, as well as Ann Jordan and Melanie Orhant, with whom I have shared many fruitful discussions on the global sex trade.
3. The debate on how to conceive of women's sexual labor centers on issues of agency and victimization, as well as economic empowerment and powerlessness. Some scholars, activists, and sex workers assert that women who are forced to choose sex work because of their race, class, nationality, colonial status, and gender are not in fact exercising "choice." To them, all forms of sex work are exploitative and oppressive, which is why they usually use the terms *prostitute* and *prostitution* rather than *sex worker* and *sex work.* On the other side of the debate are scholars, activists, and sex workers who do not see sex work solely as exploitative but rather emphasize women's right to choose to exchange sexual services on

their own terms and under their preferred conditions. They embrace the terms *sex worker* and *sex work,* since they define sexual labor for pay as work, which, as such, therefore should be protected and safe.

4. Anne McClintock, "Sex Workers and Sex Work: An Introduction," *Social Text,* vol. 11, no. 4 (1993), pp. 1–10.

5. Here I am referring only to situations in which women are not sold or coerced into the sex trade.

6. Ninna Nyberg Sorensen, "Narrating Identity Across Dominican Worlds," in *Transnationalism from Below,* ed. M. P. Smith and L. E. Guarnizo (New Brunswick, N.J.: Transaction Publishers, 1998), pp. 241–69. It is estimated that at least 10 percent of all Dominicans live outside of the Dominican Republic.

7. Eugenia Georges, *The Making of a Transnational Community: Migration, Development and Cultural Change in the Dominican Republic,* (New York: Columbia University Press, 1990).

8. Jorg Heikaus, "Heisse Nachte in Sosúa: Die Sundigste Meile der Karibe" (Hot Nights in Sosúa: The Most Sinful Mile in the Caribbean), part of a series: *Sex, Suff, und Sonnenbrand* (Sex, Boozing, and Sunburn), Cologne (Germany) *Express,* May 23, 1995.

9. Dominican newspapers have been full of stories, over the past decade, about the participation of Dominican women in Europe's sex trade. An estimated fifty thousand Dominican women have been trafficked to Europe as sex workers in the 1980s and early 1990s, either voluntarily or forcibly (Renaldo Parejo and Santo Rosario, *Sexo, Trabajo, Sida, y Sociedad: el mundo del trabajo sexual, su dinámica, sus reglas, y sus autores* [Santo Domingo: COIN, 1992]). One researcher estimated that during this time, thirty to forty trafficking rings specialized in the international trafficking of Dominican women (Martina Van Den Berg, *Trafica de Mujeres y Prostitucion de Mujeres de la Republica Dominicana en Holanda* [Santa Domingo: CIPAF, 1991]). However, a number of European countries, such as Spain, have made it more difficult to obtain "entertainment" visas, which were used to traffic women in the 1980s. What's more, having read the Dominican newspapers and heard stories passed on by women returning from Europe's sex trade, Dominican women are now generally more savvy (than in 1980) about sex work overseas.

10. See sex workers' accounts in Frederique Delacoste and Priscilla Alexander's edited volume: *Sex Work: Writings by Women in the Sex Industry* (Pittsburgh: Cleis Press, 1987) and in a special edition of *Social Text,* edited by Anne McClintock, vol. 11, no. 4, (1993).

11. For research on women and migration that tackles the issue of reconfiguration or reaffirmation of gender roles through the migration process, see Pierrette Hondagneu-Sotelo, *Gendered Transitions: Mexican Experiences of Immigration* (Berkeley: University of California Press, 1994). Sarah Mahler, "Theoretical and

Empirical Contributions Toward a Research Agenda for Transnationalism," in *Transnationalism from Below*, ed. Michael P. Smith and Luis Guarnizo (New Brunswick, N.J.: Transaction Publishers, 1998), pp. 64–100; Patricia Pessar, "The Role of Gender, Households, and Social Networks in the Migration Process: A Review and Appraisal," in *The Handbook of International Migration: The American Experience*, ed. Charles Hirschman, Philip Kasinitz, and Josh DeWind (New York: Russell Sage Foundation, 1999), pp. 53–70. For research on women's increased authority in the household through wage work—and the experience of migration—see Jennifer Hirsch, "En el Norte la Mujer Manda: Gender, Generation, and Geography in a Mexican Transnational Community," in *American Behavioral Scientist*, vol. 42, no. 9 (1994), pp. 1332–49; Nazli Kibria, *Family Tightrope: The Changing Lives of Vietnamese Americans* (Princeton, N.J.: Princeton University Press, 1993); Patricia Pessar, "The Linkage between the Household and Workplace of Dominican Women," in *U.S. International Migration Review*, vol. 18, no. 4 (1994), pp. 1188–1211; and Terry A. Repack, *Waiting on Washington: Central American Workers in the Nation's Capital* (Philadelphia: Temple University Press, 1995).

12. I write about the gossip within the sex workers' community that reveals the "code of behavior" or "script" sex workers learn within days of arriving in Sosúa in *What's Love Got to Do with It? Transnational Desires and Sex Tourism in Sosúa, the Dominican Republic* (Durham, N.C.: Duke University Press, forthcoming). Newcomers quickly catch on to the major themes their coworkers expect them to stress: motherhood, suffering, sacrifice, frustration with Dominican men's infidelity, and safe sex. Within a matrix of maternal responsibility and morality, sex workers depict themselves as selfless, responsible, and caring mothers. Their gossip reveals hierarchies that pit Dominicans against one another based on perceived differences in class and community of origin—particularly urban versus rural communities—and that aligns Dominican against Haitian sex workers, based on race and ethnicity. Since Dominican sex workers come from similar backgrounds of limited opportunity, they accentuate minor differences based on dress and competence with clients (including whether or not they practice safe sex).

Among Women: Migrant Domestics and Their Taiwanese Employers Across Generations

1. I am grateful to all my informants. My data collection was funded by a Dissertation Year Fellowship at Northwestern University, Chiang Ching-Kwo Foundation, and the Institute of Sociology at Academia Sinica. The writing process was supported by the Alfred Sloan Foundation Center for Working Families at the University of California, Berkeley.

2. Judith Rollins, *Between Women: Domestics and Their Employers* (Philadelphia: Temple University Press, 1985).

3. For a comprehensive literature review on the Chinese family, see Thomas E. Fricke, Jui-Shan Chang, and Li-Shou Yang, "Historical and Ethnographic Perspectives on the Chinese Family," in *Social Change and the Family in Taiwan,* ed. Arland Thorton and Hui-shang Lin (Chicago: Chicago University Press, 1994), pp. 22–48.

4. Kandiyoti has insightfully discussed how the mother-in-law may internalize patriarchy as a rational strategy to maximize her interests in a patrilocally extended household. Because a woman's well-being in old age is guarded only by her sons, she has a vested interest in suppressing romantic love between her sons and daughters-in-law as a means to secure the married sons' loyalty. See Deniz Kandiyoti, "Bargaining with Patriarchy," in *The Social Construction of Gender,* ed. Judith Lorber and Susan Farrell (London: Sage, 1991), pp. 104–18.

5. Ping-Chun Hsiung, *Living Rooms as Factories: Class, Gender, and the Satellite Factory System in Taiwan* (Philadelphia: Temple University Press, 1996).

6. Maxine Weinstein, Te-Hsiung Sun, M. C. Chang, and Ronald Freedman, "Co-Residence and Other Ties Linking Couples and Their Parents," in *Social Change and the Family in Taiwan,* ed. Arland Thornton and Hui-shang Lin (Chicago: Chicago University Press, 1994), pp. 305–34. Tai-Li Hu, *My Mother-in-law's Village: Rural Industrialization and Change in Taiwan* (Taipei: Institute of Ethnology, Academia Sinica, 1994).

7. Rita Gallin, "The Intersection of Class and Age: Mother-in-law/Daughter-in-law Relations in Rural Taiwan," *Journal of Cross-Cultural Gerontology,* vol. 9 (1994), p. 138.

8. Ministry of Interior, *Report on the Living Conditions of the Elderly in Taiwan Area* (Taipei: Executive Yuan, Republic of China, 1996).

9. Yow-Hwey Hu, *Three Generation Families: Myth or Trap?* (in Chinese) (Taipei: Ju-Liu Publisher, 1995).

10. Chronological demographic data show that the increases in nuclear units are associated primarily with the decline of joint households (of those extended both laterally and across generations), but the percentage of stem households (of those with at least one of the husband's parents alive) containing one or two grandparents has decreased only slightly. The decline in both mortality and fertility rates has also increased the propensity for stem co-residence across generations, because older generations have a higher survival rate and the supply of married sons has shrunk. See Weinstein et al., 1994, p. 332.

11. Directorate-General Budget, Accounting and Statistics, ROC, Report on the Housing Status Survey in the Taiwan Area (Taipei: Executive Yuan, Republic of China, 1996).

12. The monthly wage of a migrant domestic worker was NT$15,840 (approxi-

mately US$466) in 2002. A full-time, local domestic worker or caregiver is paid from NT$35,000 to $45,000.

13. Taiwan's government has stopped releasing quotas for the employment of domestic helpers, but it places no quota restriction on the employment of foreign caretakers. Many households thus apply for caretakers with forged medical documents but in fact assign them household chores or child care.

14. Council of Labor Affairs, *Monthly Bulletin of Labor Statistics*, February 2002 (Taipei: Executive Yuan, Republic of China).

15. Noeleen Heyzer, Geertje Lycklama à Nijehold, and Nedra Weerakoon, eds., *The Trade in Domestic Workers: Causes, Mechanisms and Consequences of International Migration* (London: Zed Books, 1994).

16. Kim England, and Bernadette Stiell, " 'They Think You're as Stupid as Your English Is': Constructing Foreign Domestic Workers in Toronto," *Environment and Planning A*, vol. 29 (1997), pp. 195–215.

17. Pierrette Hondagneu-Sotelo, *Domestica: Immigrant Workers Cleaning and Caring in the Shadows of Affluence* (Berkeley: University of California Press, 2001).

18. Council of Labor Affairs, *The 1998 Investigation Report on the Management and Employment of Foreign Workers in R.O.C.* (Taipei: Executive Yuan, Republic of China, 1999).

19. Jou-Ju Chu, "Taiwan: A Fragmented 'Middle' Class in the Making," in *The New Rich in Asia: Mobile Phones, McDonald's, and Middle-class Revolution*, ed. Richard Robison and David Goodman (New York: Routledge, 1996), pp. 207–24.

20. Rozanna Hertz, *More Equal Than Others: Women and Men in Dual-career Marriage* (Berkeley: University of California Press, 1986).

21. The following analysis is based on data collected for a broader project on transnational domestic employment in Taiwan. I conducted open-ended, in-depth interviews with forty-six Taiwanese employers, mostly women of younger generations, and fifty-eight Filipina migrant domestic workers. For more details, see Pei-Chia Lan, "Global Divisions, Local Identities: Filipina Migrant Domestic Workers and Their Taiwanese Employers" (Ph.D. dissertation, Northwestern University, 2000).

22. All names are pseudonyms. I use Chinese first names for younger employers and follow the local practice of calling senior women employers by the last names of their husbands. I apply English pseudonyms to those who are employed by multinational companies and use an English first name at work.

23. Zhong-Dong Liu, *Women's Medical Sociology* (in Chinese) (Taipei: Feminist Bookstore, 1998).

24. *Amah*, literally meaning "grandmother" in Taiwanese, is a general term used to refer to senior women. It is also what most foreign caregivers call their Taiwanese elder clients.

25. The concept of "kin work" is borrowed from di Leonardo, who refers in a

broader sense to "the conception, maintenance, and ritual celebration of kin ties." See Micaela di Leonardo, "The Female World of Cards and Holidays: Women, Families, and the Work of Kinship," in *Families in the U.S.: Kinship and Domestic Politics*, ed. Karen V. Hansen and Anita Garey (Philadelphia: Temple University Press, 1998), pp. 419–30.

26. Margery Wolf, "Child Training and the Chinese Family," in *Family and Kinship in Chinese Society*, ed. M. Freedman (Stanford, Calif.: Stanford University Press, 1970), pp. 37–62.

27. Margery Wolf, "Women and Suicide in China," in *Women in Chinese Society*, ed. M. Wolfe and R. Witke (Stanford, Calif.: Stanford University Press, 1975), pp. 111-14.

28. Yow-Hwey Hu, "Elderly Suicide Risks in the Family Context: A Critique of the Asian Family Care," *Journal of Cross-Cultural Gerontology*, vol. 10 (1995), pp. 199–217.

29. Hu, 1995.

30. Tracy Karner, "Professional Caring: Homecare Workers as Fictive Kin," *Journal of Aging Studies*, vol. 12, no. 1 (1998), p. 70.

31. In another study, I found that ethnic Chinese households in the San Francisco Bay Area preferred care workers of the same ethnic cultural background, who come closer to the ideal of fictive kin. Chinese adult children employ the kinship metaphor to maintain a cultural sense of filial care; home care workers also understand the cultural significance of kinship analogy and accept the job obligation of being the surrogate children of care recipients. See Pei-Chia Lan, "Subcontracting Filial Piety: Elder Care in Ethnic Chinese Immigrant Families in California," *Journal of Family Issues*, forthcoming.

32. According to a survey conducted in the Philippines, 60 percent of married migrant women entrusted their children to the care of their parents, 28 percent reported leaving the children with their husbands, 5 percent leaned on their husbands' parents or family members, and 7 percent hired caretakers outside of the family.

33. Rhacel Salazar Parreñas, *Servants of Globalization: Women, Migration, and Domestic Work* (Stanford, Calif.: Stanford University Press, 2001).

34. Hu, 1995.

35. A growing body of literature examines the social organization and policy implication of care work. See, for example, Emily Abel and Margaret Nelson, eds., *Circles of Care: Work and Identity in Women's Lives* (Albany: State University of New York Press, 1990); Madonna Harrington Meyer, ed., *Care Work: Gender, Labor and the Welfare State* (New York: Routledge, 2000).

Breadwinner No More

1. Raymond Williams, *Marxism and Literature* (Oxford: Oxford University Press, 1977), p. 132.
2. Jonathan Spencer, *A Sinhala Village in a Time of Trouble* (Delhi: Oxford University Press, 1991), pp. 169–72.
3. Nandasena Ratnapala, *Alcohol and People* (Ratmalana, Sri Lanka: Sarvodaya Research, 1985).
4. Hans Olav Fekjaer, *Alcohol and Illict Drugs: Myths and Realities* (Colombo, Sri Lanka: IOGT Alcohol and Drug Information Centre, 1993).
5. James Scott, *Domination and the Arts of Resistance: Hidden Transcripts* (New Haven: Yale University Press, 1990).
6. Carla Risseeuw, *Gender Transformation, Power, and Resistance among Women in Sri Lanka: The Fish Don't Talk about the Water* (New Delhi: Manohar, 1991), p. 271.

Because She Looks like a Child

1. Siri is, of course, a pseudonym; the names of all respondents have been changed for their protection. I spoke with them in December 1996.
2. "Caught in Modern Slavery: Tourism and Child Prostitution in Thailand," Country Report Summary prepared by Sudarat Sereewat-Srisang for the Ecumenical Consultation held in Chiang Mai in May 1990.
3. Foreign exchange rates are in constant flux. Unless otherwise noted, dollar equivalences for all currencies reflect the rate at the time of the research.
4. From interviews done by Human Rights Watch with freed child prostitutes in shelters in Thailand, reported in Jasmine Caye, *Preliminary Survey on Regional Child Trafficking for Prostitution in Thailand* (Bangkok: Center for the Protection of Children's Rights, 1996), p. 25.
5. Kulachada Chaipipat, "New Law Targets Human Trafficking," Bangkok *Nation*, November 30, 1997.
6. Thais told me that it would be very surprising if a well-off man or a politician did not have at least one mistress. When I was last in Thailand there was much public mirth over the clash of wife and mistress outside the hospital room of a high government official who had suffered a heart attack, as each in turn barricaded the door.
7. Quoted in Mark Van Landingham, Chanpen Saengtienchai, John Knodel, and Anthony Pramualratana, *Friends, Wives, and Extramarital Sex in Thailand* (Bangkok: Institute of Population Studies, Chulalongkorn University, 1995), p. 18.
8. Van Landingham et al., 1995, pp. 9–25.

9. Van Landingham et al., 1995, p. 53.

10. Pasuk Phongpaichit and Chris Baker, *Thailand's Boom* (Chiang Mai: Silkworm Books, 1996), pp. 51–54.

11. Center for the Protection of Children's Rights, *Case Study Report on Commercial Sexual Exploitation of Children in Thailand* (Bangkok, October 1996), p. 37.

12. David Kyle and John Dale, "Smuggling the State Back In: Agents of Human Smuggling Reconsidered," in *Global Human Smuggling: Comparative Perspectives,* ed. David Kyle and Rey Koslowski (Baltimore: Johns Hopkins University Press, 2001).

13. "Impact of the Asian Economic Crisis on Child Prostitution," *ECPAT International Newsletter* 27 (May 1, 1999), found at http://www.ecpat.net/eng/Ecpat_inter/IRC/articles.asp?articleID=143&NewsID=21.

14. Mechai Veravaidya, address to the International Conference on HIV/AIDS, Chiang Mai, September 1995. See also Gordon Fairclough, "Gathering Storm," *Far Eastern Review,* September 21, 1995, pp. 26–30.

15. Human Rights Watch, *A Modern Form of Slavery,* p. 3.

16. "Ranong Brothel Raids Net 148 Burmese Girls," *Nation* (July 16 1993), p. 12.

17. Dorothy O. Thomas, ed., *A Modern Form of Slavery: Trafficking of Burmese Women and Girls into Brothels in Thailand* (New York: Human Rights Watch, 1993), p. 112.

18. *International Report on Trafficking in Women (Asia-Pacific Region)* (Bangkok: Global Alliance Against Traffic in Women, 1996); Sudarat Sereewat, *Prostitution: Thai-European Connection* (Geneva: Comission on the Churches' Participation in Development, World Council of Churches, n.d.). Women's rights and antitrafficking organizations in Thailand have also published a number of personal accounts of women enslaved as prostitutes and sold overseas. These pamphlets are disseminated widely in the hope of making young women more aware of the threat of enslavement. Good examples are Siriporn Skrobanek, *The Diary of Prang* (Bangkok: Foundation for Women, 1994); and White Ink (pseud.), *Our Lives, Our Stories* (Bangkok: Foundation for Women, 1995). They follow the lives of women "exported," the first to Germany and the second to Japan.

19. The brochures are quoted in Truong, *Sex, Money, and Morality: Prostitution and Tourism in Southeast Asia* (London: Zed Books, 1990), p. 178.

20. Carey Goldberg, "Sex Slavery, Thailand to New York," *New York Times* (September 11, 1995), p. 81.

21. Quoted in Goldberg.

22. Phongpaichit and Baker, 1996, p. 237.

Clashing Dreams: Highly Educated Overseas Brides and Low-Wage U.S. Husbands

1. All names have been changed to protect the privacy of informants. In most cases, I have also changed the names of peasant villages in Vietnam or small towns in the United States. I have kept the real names of all metropolitan areas.

2. Although Saigon's name changed to Ho Chi Minh City when the South surrendered to Northern Vietnam in 1975, most people I met in contemporary Vietnam still refer to the city as Saigon, or simply Thanh Pho (the City). I use the name Saigon and Saigonese in deference to local usage.

3. More than two million people have emigrated from Vietnam since April 1975, which comes to about 3 percent of the country's current population of eighty million. Approximately 60 percent left as boat refugees; the remaining 40 percent went directly to resettlement countries. Ninety-four percent of those who left Vietnam eventually resettled in Western countries. Between 1975 and 1995, the United States accepted 64 percent of that group; 12 percent went to Australia and 12 percent to Canada. Among European countries, France received the largest number, although this comes to only 3 percent of total resettlements. As the refugee outflux declines, family reunification and family sponsorship may dominate Vietnamese out-migration during this century. See Giovanna M. Merli, "Estimation of International Migration for Vietnam 1979–1989," unpublished paper, Department of Sociology and Center for Studies in Demography and Ecology (University of Washington, Seattle, 1997).

4. I would like to thank Pierrette Hondagneu-Sotelo for pointing out the complexity and danger of lumping all migrants—legal and illegal—into one category.

5. These figures refer to individuals aged twenty and over, since aggregate data from the Immigration and Naturalization Service includes in one bracket the ages fifteen through nineteen, thus making it impossible to calculate the legal marriage age of eighteen into the marriage migration figure. Therefore, we can assume that these percentages are slightly lower than the actual numbers of marriage migrants. See United States Immigration and Naturalization Service, "Statistical Yearbook of the Immigration and Naturalization Service, 1997," *Statistics Branch* (1999); United States Immigration and Naturalization Service, "International Matchmaking Organizations: A Report to Congress By the Immigration and Naturalization Service," *A Report to Congress* (1999); and United States Immigration and Naturalization Service, "Annual Report: Legal Immigration, Fiscal Year 1997," *Statistics Branch* (1999), pp. 1–13.

6. Marion F. Houstoun, Roger G. Kramer, and Joan Mackin Barrett, "Female Predominance in Immigration to the United States since the 1930s: A First Look," *International Migration Review,* vol. 18, no. 4 (1984), pp. 908–63.

7. Guillermina Jasso, *The New Chosen People: Immigrants in the United States* (New York: Russell Sage Foundation, 1990). In recent years, there has been a lively discussion among feminist scholars about family migration, but no one has specifically looked at processes of marriage migration. See, for example, Alan Booth, Ann C. Crouter, and Nancy Landale, *Immigration and the Family: Research and Policy on U.S. Immigrants* (Mahwah, N.J.: Lawrence Erlbaum Associates Press, 1997); Nancy Foner, "The Immigrant Family: Cultural Legacies and Cultural Changes," *International Migration Review*, vol. 31, no. 4 (1997), pp. 961–74; Yen Le Espiritu, *Asian American Women and Men* (Thousand Oaks, Calif.: Sage Publications, 1997); Pierrette Hondagneu-Sotelo, *Gendered Transitions: Mexican Experiences of Immigration* (Berkeley: University of California Press, 1994); Silvia Pedraza, "Women and Migration: The Social Consequences of Gender," *Annual Review of Sociology*, vol. 17 (1991), pp. 303–25; and Patricia R. Pessar, "Engendering Migration Studies: The Case of Immigrants in the United States," *American Behavioral Scientist*, vol. 42, no. 4 (1999), pp. 577–600.

8. Ruben G. Rumbaut, "Ties That Bind: Immigration and Immigrant Families in the United States," in *Immigration and the Family: Research and Policy on U.S. Immigrants*, ed. Alan Booth, Ann C. Crouter, and Nancy Landale (Mahwah, N.J.: Lawrence Erlbaum Associates Press, 1997).

9. Migrants in at least three different streams of marriage migration can obtain, with relative ease, the papers to go abroad. The first is the *commercialized* mail-order bride stream. In their communities of origin, these brides are seen as occupying a continuum that runs from prostitutes (most commonly) to women seeking their dream husbands. Men on the receiving end are usually Caucasians from the United States, Australia, Canada, and Europe who go to "exotic lands" in search of submissive wives. See Mila Glodava and Richard Onizuka, *Mail-Order Brides: Women for Sale* (Colorado: Alaken, 1994). The second stream includes the *non-commercialized* transracial spousal migrant. This has historically included war brides of U.S. servicemen. In contemporary Vietnam and elsewhere, these couples tend to meet by working together in multinational firms, embassies, or universities. The third stream is composed of same-ethnic individuals who live in different countries and have married each other. This third stream is the topic of my research.

10. See, for example, Eve Tahmincioglu, "For Richer or Poorer: Mail-Order Brides Make for Big Business Online," *Ziff Davis Smart Business for the New Economy*, (Jan. 1, 2001), p. 40.

11. Although it is difficult to calculate whether or not marriage migrants are in transracial relationships, or how many are part of systems of commercialized mail-order brides, the best estimate we have is that about one-third of all marriage migrant couples are transracial, and that 2.7 to 4.1 percent are mail-order brides. See *Report to Congress*, 1999; Michael C. Thornton, "The Quiet Immigra-

tion: Foreign Spouses of U.S. Citizens, 1945–1985," in *Racially Mixed People in America*, ed. Maria P. Root (Newbury Park, Calif.: Sage Publications, 1992), pp. 64–76.

12. Guillermina Jasso and Mark R. Rosenzweig, "Sponsors, Sponsorship Rates and the Immigration Multiplier," *International Migration Review*, vol. 23, no. 4 (1989), pp. 856–888; Jasso, 1990.

13. In the United States from 1960 to 1997, the number of marriage migrants multiplied by approximately three times. In the 1960s, only 9 percent of all immigrants were marriage migrants; by 1997, this number jumped to 25 percent. See *Report to Congress*, 1999; Jasso, 1990. Most of those who migrate to marry permanent residents are women. In 1997, for example, a total of 201,802 individuals came to the United States through legal marriage migration. Of these, 84 percent were marrying U.S. citizens and 16 percent were marrying permanent residents. Of those marrying U.S. citizens, 61 percent were women, whereas 87 percent of those marrying permanent residents were women.

14. This paper is based on extensive interviews with ninety-eight people (mainly brides and their families) in Vietnam and thirty-one people (mainly grooms) in the United States. I interviewed the brides in their homes in Saigon and in six villages dotted along a main road in the Mekong Delta. I interviewed the grooms in their homes in San Francisco, Los Angeles, Seattle, and Boston. For further details, see Hung Cam Thai, "Marriage Across the Pacific: Family, Gender and Migration in Vietnam and in the Vietnamese Diaspora" (Ph.D. dissertation, University of California, Berkeley, in progress).

15. Except in a few cases, the men who do low-wage work are also less educated than their wives; most of these grooms have barely a grade school education. Education and income are often, but not always, linked. Plumbers, for example, may earn more money than teachers. In this chapter, I refer to the men as both "low-wage workers" and "undereducated" men. The brides I describe in this chapter are "highly educated" women compared to most women in Vietnam, meaning that they all have at least a college degree and many have advanced degrees. Most of them, though not all, come from solidly middle-class Vietnamese backgrounds.

16. Daniel Goodkind, "The Vietnamese Double Marriage Squeeze," *The Center for Migration Studies of New York*, vol. 31, no. 1 (1997), pp. 108–28.

17. These calculations are based on Goodkind's 1990 data. See Goodkind, 1997. I simply added ten years to each cohort, though mortality for either sex as a whole may have caused a shift in sex ratio since 1990.

18. Tina Katherine Fitzgerald, "Who Marries Whom? Attitudes in Marital Partner Selection" (Ph.D. dissertation, Department of Sociology, University of Colorado, 1999).

19. When low-wage men travel to search for spouses abroad, they are unlikely to

advertise that they work in low-wage jobs. In my study, however, most men did inform their wives, vis-à-vis matchmakers and go-betweens. Thus, I base my 55 percent figure of low-wage men married to highly educated women on information provided by the brides and their families, as well as interviews with some of the grooms. I did not find that any grooms had misrepresented themselves when I matched their stories to those of their brides. Nonetheless, although I estimate that 80 percent of the grooms in my study are low-wage workers, that number may, in fact, be higher if they misinformed their wives.

20. Andrew J. Pierre, "Vietnam's Contradictions," *Foreign Affairs,* vol. 79, no. 6 (2000).

21. Pierre, 2000.

22. Henry Dietz, "The Rich Get Richer: The Rise of Income Inequality in the United States and the World," *Social Science Quarterly* (Sept. 1991), p. 639; *Saigon: 20 Years After Liberation* (Hanoi, Vietnam: The Gioi Publishers, 1995); Vu Thi Hong, Le Van Thanh, and Troung Si Anh, *Migration, Human Resources, Employment and Urbanization in Ho Chi Minh City* (Hanoi: National Political Publishing House, 1996).

23. Daniele Belanger and Khuat Thu Hong, "Marriage and Family in Urban North Vietnam, 1965–1993," *Journal of Population,* vol. 2, no. 1 (1996), pp. 83–112; Charles Hirschman and Vu Manh Loi, "Family and Household Structures in Vietnam: Some Glimpses from a Recent Survey," *Pacific Affairs,* vol. 69 (1996), pp. 229–49; Nazli Kibria, *Family Tightrope: The Changing Lives of Vietnamese Americans* (Princeton, N.J.: Princeton University Press, 1993); Dinh Huou Tran, "Traditional Families in Vietnam and the Influence of Confucianism," in *Sociological Studies on the Vietnamese Family,* ed. Rita Lijestrom and Tuong Lai (Hanoi, Vietnam: Social Sciences Publishing House, 1991), pp. 27–53; and Steven K. Wisensale, "Marriage and Family Law in a Changing Vietnam," *Journal of Family Issues,* vol. 20 (1999), pp. 602–16.

24. Min Zhou and Carl L. Bankston, *Growing Up American: How Vietnamese Children Adapt to Life in the United States* (New York: Russell Sage Foundation, 1998).

25. Giovanna M. Merli, "Estimation of International Migration for Vietnam 1979–1989" (unpublished paper, Department of Sociology and Center for Studies in Demography and Ecology, University of Washington, Seattle, 1997).

26. Zhou and Bankston, 1998.

27. Jack Leonard and Mai Tran, "Probes Take Aim at Organized Crime in Little Saigon; Crackdown: Numerous Agencies Target Gambling, Drug Sales, Counterfeit Labels and Credit Card Scams," *Los Angeles Times,* Oct. 7, 2000, p. B-7; Richard C. Paddock and Lily Dizon, "3 Vietnamese Brothers in Shoot-out Led Troubled Lives," *Los Angeles Times,* April 15, 1991, p. A3; Richard Marosi and Mai Tran,

"Little Saigon Raids Dismantle Crime Ring, Authorities Say," *Los Angeles Times*, Sept. 29, 2000, p. B-3.

28. Lillian Rubin, *Families on the Fault Line: America's Working Class Speaks About the Family, the Economy, Race and Ethnicity* (New York: HarperCollins, 1994).

29. Racial and ethnic disparities, including in interethnic and interracial intimate markets, loom large in some of the marriages I studied. For these low-wage working men, categories of class and gender are more internalized, and more to the fore in their reflections on their lived experiences.

30. Huu Minh Nguyen, "Age at First Marriage in Vietnam: Patterns and Determinants" (unpublished M.A. thesis, Department of Sociology, University of Washington, 1995); *The World's Women, 2000: Trends and Statistics*, 3rd ed., Social Statistics and Indicators, series K, no. 16 (New York: United Nations, 2000).

31. *World's Women*, 2000.

32. Yen Le Espiritu, "Gender and Labor in Asian Immigrant Families," *American Behavioral Scientist* (1999), pp. 628–47.

33. Aihwa Ong, *Flexible Citizenship* (London: Duke University Press, 1999). In one highly publicized case that spread throughout the Vietnamese diaspora, a transpacific groom "arrived to meet his bride at Los Angeles International Airport with a dozen red roses only to watch her blithely wave good-bye before she left with friends for San Jose" (Lily Dizon, "Journey Home for a Bride," *Los Angeles Times*, Sept. 19, 1994, p. A1).

34. Reena Jana, "Arranged Marriages, Minus the Parents; for Some South Asians, Matrimonial Sites Both Honor and Subvert Tradition," *New York Times*, August 17, 2000, p. D1; Molly Moore, "Changing India, Wedded to Tradition; Arranged Marriages Persist with '90's Twists," *Washington Post*, Oct. 8, 1994; Shanthy Nambiar, "Love with the Proper Stranger," *Washington Post*, 1993; Shoba Narayan, "When Life's Partner Comes Pre-Chosen," *New York Times*, 1995; Najma Rizvi, "Do You Take This Man? Pakistani Arranged Marriages," *American Anthropologist* (Sept. 1993), p. 787.

35. According to sociologist Arlie Russell Hochschild, there are differences between what people say they believe about their marital roles and how they seem to feel about those roles. Furthermore, what they believe and how they feel may also differ from what they actually do. She distinguishes between gender ideologies and gender strategies to point out that ideology has to do with how men and women draw on "beliefs about manhood and womanhood, beliefs that are forged in early childhood and thus anchored to deep emotions." Gender strategies refer to people's plans of action and their emotional preparations for pursuing them. See Arlie Russell Hochschild and Anne Machung, *The Second Shift: Working Parents and the Revolution at Home* (New York: Viking, 1989), p. 15.

36. Hochschild with Machung, *The Second Shift; Working Parents and the Revolution at Home* (New York: Avon, 1997).
37. Pepper Schwartz, *Love Between Equals: How Peer Marriage Really Works* (New York: Free Press, 1995).
38. Hochschild and Machung, 1997.

Global Cities and Survival Circuits

1. For more detailed accounts of each of these configurations please see my "Towards a Feminist Analytics of Globalization," in Saskia Sassen, *Globalization and Its Discontents: Essays on the Mobility of People and Money* (New York: The New Press, 1998); and my article, "Women's Burden: Countergeographies of Globalization and the Feminization of Survival," *Journal of International Affairs,* vol. 53, no. 2 (spring 2000) pp. 503–24.

2. In my larger research project, I also focus on a range of liberating activities and practices that globalization enables; for example, some aspects of the human-rights and environmental movements, as well as of the antiglobalization network. In this sense, globalization enables the production of its own countergeographies, some of which are exploitative, others emancipatory.

3. By emphasizing that global processes are at least partly embedded in national territories, such a focus introduces new variables into current conceptions of economic globalization and the shrinking regulatory role of the state. That is to say, new transnational economic processes do not necessarily occur within the global/national spatial duality that many analysts of the global economy presuppose. That duality suggests two mutually exclusive spaces, one beginning where the other ends. National states play a role in the implementation of global economic systems, and this role can assume different forms, depending on the level of development, political culture, and mode of articulation with global processes. By reintroducing the state into our analysis of globalization, we open the way toward examining how this transformed state articulates the gender question. One way in which states have been reconfigured is through the political ascendance of ministries of finance and the decline of departments dealing with social concerns, including housing, health, and welfare.

4. Indeed, women in many of these settings are seen, rightly or wrongly, as better cultural brokers, and these skills matter to global firms. In the financial-services industry, women are considered crucial to interfacing with consumers, because they are believed to inspire more trust and thereby to make it easier for individual investors to put their money in what are often known to be highly speculative endeavors. See Melissa Fisher, "Wall Street Women's 'Herstories' in Late Financial Corporate Capitalism," in *Constructing Corporate America: History, Politics, Cul-*

ture, ed. Kenneth Lipartito and David B. Sicilia (New York: Oxford University Press, 2002).

5. I have developed this at length in *Globalization and Its Discontents.*

6. Pierrette Hondagneu-Sotelo, *Gendered Transitions: Mexican Experiences of Immigration* (Berkeley: University of California Press, 1994); Sarah Mahler, *American Dreaming: Immigrant Life on the Margins* (Princeton, N.J.: Princeton University Press, 1995).

7. Frank Munger, ed., *Laboring Under the Line* (New York: Russell Sage Foundation, 2002); Laurance Roulleau-Berger, ed., *Youth and Work in the Postindustrial City of North America and Europe* (Leiden and New York: Brill, 2002); Hector R. Cordero-Guzman, Robert C. Smith, and Ramon Grosfoguel, eds., *Migration, Transnationalization, and Race in a Changing New York* (Philadelphia: Temple University Press, 2001); see generally for data and sources, Saskia Sassen, *The Global City* (Princeton, N.J.: Princeton University Press, 2001), chapters 8 and 9.

8. At issue here is a type of manufacturing that requires an urban location because it is geared toward urban markets and belongs to a fairly developed network of contractors and subcontractors. We have called this type of manufacturing "urban manufacturing" to distinguish it from sectors that respond to very different constraints and advantages. It generally consists of design-linked manufacturing done on contract: jewelry making, woodwork and metalwork for architecture and real estate firms, the production of fashion, furniture, lamps, and so on. Many components of urban manufacturing are not downgraded, or at least not yet. One major policy implication is that city governments should support this type of manufacturing and cease to subsidize the kind that will leave the city sooner or later anyhow (see Matthew T. Mitchell, "Urban Manufacturing in New York City" [Master's thesis, Department of Urban Planning, Columbia University, 1996]). Women, especially immigrant women, are the key labor force in urban manufacturing.

9. For evidence and multiple sources, see Sassen, 2001, chapters 8 and 9.

10. The consumption needs of the growing low-income population in large cities are also increasingly often met through labor-intensive, rather than standardized and unionized, forms of producing goods and services: manufacturing and retail establishments that are small, rely on family labor, and often fall below minimum safety and health standards. Cheap, locally produced sweatshop garments and bedding, for example, can compete with low-cost Asian imports. A growing range of products and services, from low-cost furniture made in basements to "gypsy cabs" and family day care, are available to meet the demands of the growing low-income population in these cities. Inequality reshapes the consumption structure of cities in innumerable ways, and this in

turn has feedback effects on the organization of work, in both the formal and the informal economy.

11. Very prominent in this market are the International Nanny and Au Pair Agency, headquartered in Britain; Nannies Incorporated, based in London and Paris; and the International Au Pair Association (IAPA) based in Canada.

12. I have argued this for the case of international labor migrations (e.g., Saskia Sassen, *Guests and Aliens* [New York: The New Press, 1999]). See also Max Castro, ed., *Free Markets, Open Societies, Closed Borders?* (Berkeley: University of California Press, 2000); and Frank Bonilla, Edwin Melendez, Rebecca Morales, and Maria de los Angeles Torres, eds., *Borderless Borders* (Philadelphia: Temple University Press, 1998).

13. Once there is an institutional infrastructure for globalization, processes that have previously operated at the national level can scale up to the global level, even when they do not need to. This phenomenon contrasts with processes that are by their very nature global, such as the network of financial centers underlying the formation of a global capital market.

14. An older literature on women and debt links the implementation of a first generation of structural adjustment programs to the growth of government debt in the 1980s; this literature documents the disproportionate burden these programs put on women. It is a large literature in many different languages, and including a vast number of limited-circulation items produced by various activist and support organizations. For overviews, see Kathryn Ward, *Women Workers and Global Restructuring* (Ithaca, N.Y.: School of Industrial and Labor Relations Press, 1990); Kathryn Ward and Jean Pyle, "Gender, Industrialization and Development," in *Women in the Latin American Development Process: From Structural Subordination to Empowerment,* ed. Christine E. Bose and Edna Acosta-Belen (Philadelphia: Temple University Press, 1995), pp. 37–64; Christine E. Bose and Edna Acosta-Belen, eds., *Women in the Latin American Development Process* (Philadelphia: Temple University Press, 1995); Lourdes Beneria and Shelley Feldman, eds., *Unequal Burden: Economic Crises, Persistent Poverty, and Women's Work* (Boulder, Colo.: Westview Press, 1992); York Bradshaw, Rita Noonan, Laura Gash, and Claudia Buchmann, "Borrowing Against the Future: Children and Third World Indebtness," *Social Forces,* vol. 71, no. 3 (1993), pp. 629–656; Irene Tinker, ed., *Persistent Inequalities: Women and World Development* (New York: Oxford University Press, 1990); and Carolyn Moser, "The Impact of Recession and Structural Adjustment Policies at the Micro-Level: Low-Income Women and Their Households in Guayaquil, Ecuador," *Invisible Adjustment,* UNICEF, vol. 2 (1989). Now there is also a new literature on structural adjustment's second generation. These studies are more directly linked to globalization; I will cite them later in this article.

15. In many of these countries, a large number of firms in traditional sectors ori-

ented to the local or national market have closed, and export-oriented cash crops have increasingly often replaced survival agriculture and food production for local or national markets.

16. See Michel Chossudovsky, *The Globalisation of Poverty* (London: Zed/TWN, 1997); Guy Standing, "Global Feminization Through Flexible Labor: A Theme Revisited," *World Development,* vol. 27, no. 3 (1999), pp. 583–602; Aminur Rahman, "Micro-credit Initiatives for Equitable and Sustainable Development: Who Pays?" *World Development,* vol. 27, no. 1 (1999), pp. 67–82; Diane Elson, *Male Bias in Development,* 2nd ed. (Manchester, 1995). For an excellent overview of the literature on the impact of the debt on women, see Kathryn Ward, "Women and the Debt," paper presented at the Colloquium on Globalization and the Debt, Emory University, Atlanta (1999). On file with author at kbward@siu.edu.

17. On these various issues, see Diana Alarcon-Gonzalez and Terry McKinley, "The Adverse Effects of Structural Adjustment on Working Women in Mexico," *Latin American Perspectives,* vol. 26, no. 3 (1999), 103–17; Claudia Buchmann, "The Debt Crisis, Structural Adjustment and Women's Education," *International Journal of Comparative Studies,* vol. 37, nos. 1–2 (1996), pp. 5–30; Helen I. Safa, *The Myth of the Male Breadwinner: Women and Industrialization in the Caribbean* (Boulder, Colo.: Westview Press, 1995); Nilufer Cagatay and Sule Ozler, "Feminization of the Labor Force: The Effects of Long-term Development and Structural Adjustment," *World Development,* vol. 23, no. 11 (1995), pp. 1883–94; Erika Jones, "The Gendered Toll of Global Debt Crisis," *Sojourner,* vol. 25, no. 3, pp. 20–38; and several of the references cited in the preceding footnotes.

18. Eric Toussaint, "Poor Countries Pay More Under Debt Reduction Scheme?" (July 1999), www.twnside.org.sg/souths/twn/title/1921-cn.htm. According to Susan George, the south has paid back the equivalent of six Marshall Plans to the north (Asoka Bandarage, *Women, Population, and Crisis* [London: Zed, 1997]).

19. The IMF asks HIPCs to pay 20 to 25 percent of their export earnings toward debt service. In contrast, in 1953 the Allies canceled 80 percent of Germany's war debt and only insisted on 3 to 5 percent of export-earnings debt service. These general terms were also evident as Central Europe emerged from communism. For one of the best critical examinations of globalization, see Richard C. Longworth, *Global Squeeze: The Coming Crisis for First World Nations* (Chicago: Contemporary Books, 1998).

20. See Janie Chuang, "Redirecting the Debate over Trafficking in Women: Definitions, Paradigms, and Contexts," *Harvard Human Rights Journal,* vol. 10 (winter 1998). Trafficking has become sufficiently recognized as an issue that it was addressed in the G8 meeting in Birmingham in May 1998, a first for the G8 (*Trafficking in Migrants,* International Office of Migration quarterly bulletin, Geneva: IOM, 1998). The heads of the eight major industrialized countries

stressed the importance of cooperating against international organized crime and people trafficking. President Clinton issued a set of directives to his administration in order to strengthen efforts against trafficking in women and girls. This in turn generated a legislative initiative by Senator Paul Wellstone, which led to a Senate bill in 1999. (For a good critical analysis, see Dayan, "Policy Initiatives in the U.S. against the Illegal Trafficking of Women for the Sex Industry," Department of Sociology, University of Chicago, 1999, on file with the author).

21. The Coalition Against Trafficking in Women has centers and representatives in Australia, Bangladesh, Europe, Latin America, North America, Africa, and Asia Pacific. The Women's Rights Advocacy Program has established the Initiative Against Trafficking in Persons to combat the global trade in persons. Other organizations are referred to throughout this article.

22. See, generally, the Foundation Against Trafficking in Women (STV) and the Global Alliance Against Traffic in Women (GAATW). For regularly updated sources of information on trafficking, see http://www.hrlawgroup.org/site/programs/traffic.html. See also Sietske Altink, *Stolen Lives: Trading Women into Sex and Slavery* (New York: Harrington Park Press, 1995); Kamala Kempadoo and Jo Doezema, *Global Sex Workers: Rights, Resistance, and Redefinition* (London: Routledge, 1998); Susan Shannon, "The Global Sex Trade: Humans as the Ultimate Commodity," *Crime and Justice International* (May 1999), pp. 5–25; Lap-Chew Lin and Wijers Marjan, *Trafficking in Women, Forced Labour and Slavery-like Practices in Marriage, Domestic Labour and Prostitution* (Utrecht: Foundation Against Trafficking in Women [STV], and Bangkok: Global Alliance Against Traffic in Women [GAATW], 1997); Lin Lim, *The Sex Sector: The Economic and Social Bases of Prostitution in Southeast Asia* (Geneva: International Labor Office, 1998).

23. For more detailed information, see the STV-GAATW reports; IOM 1996; CIA, "International Trafficking in Women to the United States: A Contemporary Manifestation of Salvery and Organized Crime," prepared by Amy O'Neill Richard (Washington, D.C.: Center for the Study of Intelligence, 2000). www.cia.gov/csi/monograph/women/trafficking.pdf

24. There is also a growing trade in children for the sex industry. This has long been the case in Thailand, but it is now present in several other Asian countries, eastern Europe, and Latin America.

25. There are various reports on trafficking routes. Malay brokers sell Malay women into prostitution in Australia. Women from Albania and Kosovo have been trafficked by gangs into prostitution in London. Teens from Paris and other European cities have been sold to Arab and African customers; see Susan Shannon, "The Global Sex Trade: Humans as the Ultimate Commodity," *Crime and*

Justice International (May 1999), pp. 5–25. In the United States, the police broke up an international Asian ring that imported women from China, Thailand, Korea, Malaysia, and Vietnam; see William Booth, "Thirteen Charged in Gang Importing Prostitutes," *Washington Post*, August 21, 1999. The women were charged between $30,000 and $40,000 in contracts to be paid through their work in the sex trade or the garment industry. The women in the sex trade were shuttled around several states in the United States in order to bring continuing variety to the clients.

26. See Global Survival Network, "Crime and Servitude: An Expose of the Traffic in Women for Prostitution from the Newly Independent States," at www.globalsurvival.net/femaletrade.html, November 1997.

27. A fact sheet by the Coalition to Abolish Slavery and Trafficking reports that one survey of Asian sex workers found that rape often preceded their being sold into prostitution and that about one-third had been falsely led into prostitution.

28. Nancy A. Wonders and Raymond Michalowski, "Bodies, Borders, and Sex Tourism in a Globalized World: A Tale of Two Cities—Amsterdam and Havana," *Social Problems*, vol. 48, no. 4 (2001), pp. 545–71. See also Dennis Judd and Susan Fainstein, *The Tourist City* (New Haven: Yale University Press, 1999).

29. About 80 percent of the nurses imported under the new act were from the Philippines. See generally, Satomi Yamamoto, "The Incorporation of Women Workers into a Global City: A Case Study of Filipina Nurses in the Metropolitan New York Area," (2000). On file with the author at syamamot@uiuc.edu.

30. Japan passed a new immigration law—strictly speaking, an amendment of an older law—that radically redrew the conditions for entry of foreign workers. It allowed professionals linked to the new service economy—specialists in Western-style finance, accounting, law, et cetera—but made the entry of what is termed "simple labor" illegal. The latter provision generated a rapid increase in the entry of undocumented workers for low-wage jobs. But the new law did make special provisions for the entry of "entertainers."

31. Brenda Yeoh, Shirlena Huang, and Joaquin Gonzalez III, "Migrant Female Domestic Workers: Debating the Economic, Social and Political Impacts in Singapore," *International Migration Review*, vol. 33, no. 1 (1999), pp. 114–136; Christine Chin, "Walls of Silence and Late 20th-Century Representations of Foreign Female Domestic Workers: The Case of Filipina and Indonesian Houseservants in Malaysia," *International Migration Review*, vol. 31, no. 1 (1997), pp. 353–85; Noeleen Heyzer, *The Trade in Domestic Workers* (London: Zed Books, 1994).

32. These women are recruited and transported both through formal legal channels and through informal or illegal ones. Either way, they have little power to resist. Even as they are paid below minimum wage, they produce significant profits for

their brokers and employers. There has been an enormous increase in so-called entertainment businesses in Japan.

33. Natacha David, "Migrants Made the Scapegoats of the Crisis," *ICFTU Online* (International Confederation of Free Trade Unions, 1999). www.hartford-hwp. com/archives/50/012.html

Bibliography

Abel, Emily, and Margaret Nelson. "Circles of Care: An Introductory Essay," in *Circles of Care: Work and Identity in Women's Lives*. Ed. Emily Abel and Margaret Nelson, Albany: State University of New York Press, 1990.

Adams, Kathleen M., and Sara Dickey, eds. *Home and Hegemony: Domestic Service and Identity Politics in South and Southeast Asia*. Ann Arbor: University of Michigan Press, 2000.

Afshar, Halef, and Carolyn Dennis, eds. *Women and Adjustment Policies in the Third World*. New York: St. Martin's Press, 1992.

Anderson, Benedict. "Exodus." *Critical Inquiry* 20, no. 2 (1994), pp. 314–27.

Anderson, Bridget. *Doing the Dirty Work? The Global Politics of Domestic Labour*. London and New York: Zed Books, 2000.

Anthias, Floya, and Gabriella Lazaridis, eds. *Gender and Migration in Southern Europe: Women on the Move*. Oxford and New York: Berg, 2000.

Ariès, Philippe. *Centuries of Childhood: A Social History of Family Life*. New York: Vintage Books, 1962.

Asian Migrant Centre. *Asian Migrant Yearbook: Migration Facts, Analysis and Issues in 2000*. Hong Kong: Asian Migrant Centre Ltd., 2001.

Bakan, Abigail, and Daiva Stasiulis. "Making the Match: Domestic Placement Agencies and the Racialization of Women's Household Work." *Signs*, vol. 20, no. 2 (1995), pp. 303–35.

———, eds. *Not One of the Family: Foreign Domestic Workers in Canada*. Toronto: University of Toronto Press, 1997.

Bales, Kevin. *Disposable People: New Slavery in the Global Economy*. Berkeley: University of California Press, 1999.

———. *New Slavery: A Reference Handbook*. Santa Barbara, Calif.: ABC-Clio, Inc., 2000.

———. "The Social Psychology of Modern Slavery." *Scientific American* (April, 2002), pp. 66–74.

Bales, Kevin, and Peter Robbins. " 'No One Shall Be Held in Slavery or Servitude': A Critical Analysis of International Slavery Agreements and Concepts of Slavery." *Human Rights Review,* vol. 2, no. 2: (2001), pp. 18–45.

Beneria, Lourdes, and M. J. Dudley, eds. *Economic Restructuring in the Americas*. Ithaca, N.Y.: Latin American Studies Program, Cornell University, 1996.

Brennan, Denise. "Tourism in Transnational Places: Dominican Sex Workers and German Sex Tourists Imagine One Another." *Identities,* vol. 7, no. 4 (2001), pp. 621–63.

———. *What's Love Got to Do with It? Transnational Desires and Sex Tourism in Sosúa, the Dominican Republic*. Durham, N.C.: Duke University Press, forthcoming.

Brochmann, Grete. *Middle East Avenue: Female Migration from Sri Lanka to the Gulf*. Boulder, Colo.: Westview Press, 1993.

Brown, Karen McCarthy. *Mama Lola: A Vodou Priestess in Brooklyn*. Berkeley: University of California Press, 1991.

Buijs, Gina, ed. *Migrant Women: Crossing Boundaries and Changing Identities*. Oxford: Berg, 1993.

Castles, Stephen, and Mark J. Miller. *The Age of Migration: International Population Movements in the Modern World*. New York and London: The Guilford Press, 1998.

Chan, Sucheng. *Asian Americans: An Interpretive History*. Boston: Twayne Publishers, 1991.

Chaney, Elsa M., and Maria Garcia Castro, eds. *Muchachas No More: Household Workers in Latin American and the Caribbean*. Philadelphia: Temple University Press, 1989.

Chang, Grace. *Disposable Domestics: Immigrant Women Workers in the Global Economy*. Cambridge, Mass.: South End Press, 2000.

Chant, Sylvia. *Women-Headed Households: Diversities and Dynamics in the Developing World*. New York: St. Martin's Press, 1997.

Chant, Sylvia, and Kathy McIlwaine. *Women of a Lesser Cost: Female Labour, Foreign Exchange and Philippine Development*. London and Boulder, Colo.: Pluto Press, 1995.

Chin, Christine B. N. *Service and Servitude: Foreign Domestic Workers and the Malaysian "Modernity" Project*. New York: Columbia University Press, 1998.

Clifford, James. "Diasporas." *Cultural Anthropology,* vol. 9, no. 3 (1994), pp. 302–38.

Cock, Jacklyn. *Maids and Madams: A Study in the Politics of Exploitation*. Johannesburg, So. Africa: Raven Press, 1980.

Constable, Nicole. "Jealousy, Chastity and Abuse: Chinese Maids and Foreign Helpers in Hong Kong." *Modern China,* vol. 22, no. 4 (1996), pp. 448–79.

———. *Maid to Order in Hong Kong: Stories of Filipina Workers.* Ithaca, N.Y.: Cornell University Press, 1997.

———. "Sexuality and Discipline Among Filipina Domestic Workers in Hong Kong." *American Ethnologist,* vol. 24, no. 3 (1997), pp. 539–58.

Cornia, G., R. Jolly, and F. Stewart, eds. *Adjustment with a Human Face.* Oxford: Clarendon Press, 1987.

Delacoste, Frederique, and Priscilla Alexander, eds. *Sex Work: Writings by Women in the Sex Industry.* Pittsburgh: Cleis Press, 1987.

Dill, Bonnie Thornton. *Across the Boundaries of Race and Class: An Exploration of the Relationship Between Work and Family Among Black Female Domestic Servants.* New York: Garland, 1994.

Elson, D. "Micro, Meso and Macro: Gender and Economic Analysis in the Context of Policy Reform," in *The Strategic Silence: Gender and Economic Policy.* Ed. I. Bakker, London and Atlantic Highlands, N.J.: Zed Books with North-South Institute, 1994.

Espiritu, Yen Le. *Asian American Women and Men.* Thousand Oaks, Calif.: Sage Publications, 1997.

Feber, Marianne, and Julie Nelson, eds. *Beyond Economic Man: Feminist Theory and Economics.* Chicago: University of Chicago Press, 1993.

Fernandez Kelly, M. P. *For We Are Sold, I and My People: Women and Industrialization in Mexico's Frontier.* Albany: State University of New York Press, 1983.

Fisher, B., and J. Tronto. "Toward a Feminist Theory of Caring," in *Circle of Care: Work and Identity in Women's Lives.* Ed. E. K. Abel and M. K. Nelson. Albany: State University of New York Press, 1990.

Gamburd, Michele. *The Kitchen Spoon's Handle: Transnationalism and Sri Lanka's Migrant Housemaids.* Ithaca, N.Y.: Cornell University Press, 2000.

Gladwin, Christina. H., ed. *Structural Adjustment and African Women Farmers.* Gainesville, Fla: University Press of Florida, 1991.

Glenn, Evelyn Nakano. *Issei, Nisei, War Bride: Three Generations of Japanese American Women in Domestic Service.* Philadelphia: Temple University Press, 1986.

———. "From Servitude to Service Work: Historical Continuities in the Racial Division of Paid Reproductive Labor." *Signs: Journal of Women in Culture and Society,* vol. 18, no. 1 (1991), pp. 1–43.

Glenn, Evelyn Nakano, Grace Chang, and Linda Forcey, eds. *Mothering: Ideology. Experience, and Agency.* New York: Routledge, 1994.

Glick Schiller, Nina, Linda Basch, and Cristina Blanc-Szanton. *Towards a Transnational Perspective on Migration: Race, Class, Ethnicity, and Nationalism.* New York: Annals of the New York Academy of Sciences, vol. 645, 1992.

Gray, Breda. "Irish Women in London: National or Hybrid Diasporic Identities?" *National Women's Studies Association Journal,* vol. 8, no. 1 (1996), pp. 85–109.

Gregson, Nicky, and Michelle Lowe. *Servicing the Middle Classes: Class, Gender and Waged Domestic Labour in Contemporary Britain.* London: Routledge, 1994.

Grieder, William. *One World, Ready or Not: The Manic Logic of Global Capitalism.* New York: Simon and Schuster, 1997.

Guarnizo, Luis, and Michael P. Smith. *Transnationalism from Below.* New Brunswick, N.J.: Transaction Publishers, 1998.

Gupta, Akhil. "The Song of the Nonaligned World: Transnational Identities and the Reinscription of Space in Late Capitalism." *Cultural Anthropology,* vol. 7, no. 1 (1992), pp. 63–79.

Hansen, Karen T. *Distant Companions: Servants and Employers in Zambia, 1900–1985.* Ithaca, N.Y.: Cornell University Press, 1989.

Harrington Meyer, Madonna, ed. *Care Work: Gender, Labor, and the Welfare State.* New York: Routledge, 2000.

Harrison, Faye V. "The Gendered Politics and Violence of Structural Adjustment," in *Situated Lives: Gender and Culture in Everyday Life.* Ed. Louise Lamphere, Helena Ragone, and Patricia Zavella, New York: Routledge, 1997, pp. 451–68.

Hays, Sharon. *The Cultural Contradictions of Motherhood.* New Haven: Yale University Press, 1996.

Heyzer, Noeleen, Geertje Lycklama à Nijehold, and Nedra Weerakoon, eds. *The Trade in Domestic Workers: Causes, Mechanisms and Consequences of International Migration.* London: Zed Books, 1994.

Hochschild, Arlie Russell. *The Managed Heart: Commercialization of Human Feeling.* Berkeley, Calif.: University of California Press, 1983.

———. *The Time Bind: When Work Becomes Home and Home Becomes Work.* New York: Metropolitan Books, 1997.

———. "Global Care Chains and Emotional Surplus Value," in *On the Edge: Living with Global Capitalism.* Ed. Will Hutton and Anthony Giddens, London: Jonathan Cape, 2000.

Hochschild, Arlie Russell, and Anne Machung. *The Second Shift: Working Parents and the Revolution at Home.* New York: Avon, 1997.

Hondagneu-Sotelo, Pierrette. *Gendered Transitions: Mexican Experiences of Immigration.* Berkeley: University of California Press, 1994.

———. *Doméstica: Immigrant Workers Cleaning and Caring in the Shadow of Affluence.* Berkeley: University of California Press, 2001.

Hondagneu-Sotelo, Pierrette, and Ernestine Avila. " 'I'm Here, But I'm There': The Meanings of Latina Transnational Motherhood," in *Gender and Society,* vol. 11, no. 5 (1997), pp. 548–71.

Jasso, Guillermina. *The New Chosen People: Immigrants in the United States.* New York: Russell Sage Foundation, 1990.

Kaplan, Elaine. " 'I Don't Do No Windows': Competition Between Domestic Worker and Housewife," in *Competition: A Feminist Taboo?* Ed. Valerie Miner and Helen Longino. New York: Feminist Press, 1987.

Karner, Tracy. "Professional Caring: Homecare Workers as Fictive Kin," *Journal of Aging Studies,* vol. 12, no. 1 (1998), pp. 69–82.

Kempadoo, Kamala, and Jo Doezema, eds. *Global Sex Workers: Rights, Resistance and Redefinition.* New York: Routledge, 1998.

Kibria, Nazli. *Family Tightrope: The Changing Lives of Vietnamese Americans.* Princeton, N.J.: Princeton University Press, 1993.

Kofman, Eleonore, Annie Phizacklea, Parvati Raghuram, and Rosemary Sales. *Gender and International Migration in Europe: Employment, Welfare, and Politics.* New York and London: Routledge, 2000.

Kyle, David, and Rey Koslowski, eds. *Global Human Smuggling: Comparative Perspectives.* Baltimore: Johns Hopkins University Press, 2001.

Lamphere, Louise. *From Working Daughters to Working Mothers: Immigrant Women in a New England Industrial Community.* Ithaca, N.Y.: Cornell University Press, 1987.

Levitt, Peggy. "Social Remittances: Migration Driven Local-Level Forms of Cultural Diffusion." *International Migration Review,* vol. 32, no. 4 (1998), pp. 926–48.

Lozano, Beverly. *The Invisible Workforce: Transforming American Business with Outside and Home-based Workers.* New York: The Free Press, 1989.

Mahler, Sarah. *American Dreaming: Immigrant Life on the Margins.* Princeton, N.J.: Princeton University Press, 1996.

Massey, Douglas S. "March of Folly: U.S. Immigration Policy after NAFTA." *The American Prospect,* vol. 9, no. 37 (1998).

McClintock, Anne. "Sex Workers and Sex Work: An Introduction." *Social Text,* vol. 11, no. 4 (1993), pp. 1–10.

Mendez, Jennifer. "Of Mops and Maids: Contradictions and Continuities in Bureaucratized Domestic Work." *Social Problems,* vol. 45, no. 1 (1998), pp. 114–35.

Mies, Maria. *The Lacemakers of Narsapur: Indian Housewives Produce for the World Market.* Westport, Conn.: Zed Press, 1982.

Miyoshi, Masao. "A Borderless World? From Colonialism to Transnationalism and the Decline of the Nation-State." *Critical Inquiry,* vol. 19, no. 4 (1993), pp. 726–51.

Momsen, Janet Henshall. *Gender, Migration and Domestic Service.* London: Routledge, 1999.

Moon, Katherine. *Sex Among Allies: Military Prostitution in U.S.-Korea Relations.* New York: Columbia University Press, 1997.

Morrison, Toni. *The Bluest Eye.* New York: Plume Books, 1994.

Ozyegin, Gul. *Untidy Gender: Domestic Service in Turkey.* Philadelphia: Temple University Press, 2001.

Palmer, Phyllis. *Domesticity and Dirt: Housewives and Domestic Servants in the United States, 1920–1940s.* Philadelphia: Temple University Press, 1989.

Panda, Pradeep Kumar. "Gender and Structural Adjustment: Exploring the Connections." Center for Development Studies, Thiruvananthapuram, Kerala, India (unpublished paper), 1997.

Parreñas, Rhacel Salazar. "The Global Servants: (Im)Migrant Filipina Domestic Workers in Rome and Los Angeles." Ph.D. dissertation, Department of Ethnic Studies, University of California, Berkeley, 1999.

————. *Servants of Globalization: Women, Migration, and Domestic Work.* Stanford, Calif.: Stanford University Press, 2001.

Pessar, P. "On the Homefront and in the Workplace: Integrating Immigrant Women into Feminist Discourse." *Anthropological Quarterly* 68, no. 1 (1995), pp. 37–47.

Pruitt, Deborah, and Suzanne LaFont. "For Love and Money: Romance Tourism in Jamaica." *Annals of Tourism Research,* vol. 22, no. 2 (1995), pp. 422–40.

Richard, Amy O'Neill. *International Trafficking in Women to the United States: A Contemporary Manifestation of Slavery and Organized Crime.* Washington, D.C.: Center for the Study of Intelligence, Central Intelligence Agency, 1999.

Rollins, Judith. *Between Women: Domestics and their Employers.* Philadelphia: Temple University Press, 1985.

Romero, Mary. *Maid in the U.S.A.* New York: Routledge, 1992.

————. "Life as the Maid's Daughter: An Exploration of the Everyday Boundaries of Race, Class, and Gender," in *Challenging Fronteras: Structuring Latina and Latino Lives in the U.S.* Ed. Mary Romero, Pierrette Hondagneu-Sotelo, and Vilma Ortiz. New York, Routledge, 1997.

Rumbaut, Ruben G. "Ties That Bind: Immigration and Immigrant Families in the United States," in *Immigration and the Family: Research and Policy on U.S. Immigrants.* Ed. Alan Booth, Ann C. Crouter, and Nancy Landale. Mahwah, N.J.: Lawrence Erlbaum Associates Press, 1997.

Russell, Sharon Stanton. "Remittances from International Migration: A Review in Perspective." *World Development,* vol. 14, no. 6 (1986), pp. 677–96.

Sachs, Wolfgang. *The Development Dictionary: A Guide to Knowledge as Power.* London and Atlantic Highlands, N.J.: Zed Books, 1992.

Salzinger, Leslie. "A Maid By Any Other Name: The Transformaiton of 'Dirty Work' by Central American Immigrants," in *Ethnography Unbound: Power and Resistance in the Modern Metropolis.* Ed. Michael Burawoy et al. Berkeley: University of California Press, 1991.

Sanjek, Roger, and Shellee Colen, eds. *At Work in Homes: Household Workers in World Perspective.* American Ethnological Society Monograph Series, no. 3. Washington, D.C.: American Anthropological Society, 1990.

Sankar, Andrea. "Female Domestic Service in Hong Kong," in *Female Servants and*

Economic Development. Ed. Louise Tilly et al. Michigan Occasional Papers in Women's Studies. Ann Arbor: University of Michigan, 1978.

Sassen, Saskia. *The Mobility of Labor and Capital: A Study in International Investment and Labor Flows.* New York: Cambridge University Press, 1988.

Seager, J. *The State of Women in the World Atlas.* New York: Penguin Books, 1997.

Simon, Rita James, and Caroline B. Brettell, eds. *International Migration: The Female Experience.* Totowa, N.J.: Rowman & Allanheld, 1986.

Sinke, Suzanne. "Migration for Labor, Migration for Love: Marriage and Family Formation Across Borders." *Magazine of History,* vol. 14, no. 1 (1999), pp. 17–21.

Stone, Deborah. "Care and Trembling." *The American Prospect,* vol. 10, no. 43 (1999).

———. "Caring Work in a Liberal Polity." *Journal of Health Politics, Policy and Law,* vol. 16, no. 3 (1991): 547–52.

Sturdevandt, Saundra Pollock, and Brenda Stoltzfus. *Let the Good Times Roll: Prostitution and the U.S. Military in Asia.* New York: New Press, 1992.

Tolentino, Roland B. "Bodies, Letters, Catalogs: Filipinas in Transnational Space." *Social Text,* vol. 48 (fall, 1996), pp. 49–76.

Truong, Thanh-dam. *Sex, Money, and Morality: Prostitution and Tourism in Southeast Asia.* London: Zed Books, 1990.

———. "Gender, International Migration, and Social Reproduction: Implications for Theory, Policy, Research, and Networking." *Asian and Pacific Migration Journal,* vol. 5, no. 1 (1996), pp. 27–52.

Tucker, Robert C., ed. *The Marx-Engels Reader,* 2nd ed. New York: W. W. Norton & Company, Inc., 1978.

Tung, Charlene. "The Cost of Caring: The Social Reproductive Labor of Filipina Live-In Home Health Caregivers." *Frontiers: A Journal of Women's Studies,* vol. 21, no. 1 (2000), pp. 61–82.

Tyree, Andrea, and Katharine M. Donato. "A Demographic Overview of the International Migration of Women," in *International Migration: The Female Experience.* Ed. Rita James Simon and Caroline B. Brettell. Totowa, N.J.: Rowman & Allanheld, 1986.

United Nations Research Institute for Social Development. *Working Towards a More Gender Equitable Macro-Economic Agenda,* report of conference held in Rajendrapur, Bangladesh, November 26–28, 1996. Geneva, Switzerland: UNRISD, 1997.

Varley, Ann. "Women Heading Households: Some More Equal Than Others?" *World Development,* vol. 24, no. 3 (1996), pp. 505–20.

Ward, Kathryn, ed. *Women Workers and Global Restructuring.* Ithaca, N.Y.: School of Industrial and Labor Relations Press, 1990.

Willis, Katie, and Brenda Yeoh, eds. *Gender and Immigration.* The International Library of Studies on Migration, 10. London: Edward Elgar Publishers, 2000.

Wong, Sau-Ling C. "Diverted Mothering: Representation of Caregivers of Color in the Age of 'Multiculturalism,'" in *Mothering: Ideology, Experience and Agency*. Ed. Evelyn Nakano Glenn, Grace Chang, and Linda Rennie Forcey. New York: Routledge, 1994.

Wrigley, Julia. *Other People's Children: An Intimate Account of the Dilemmas Facing Middle-Class Parents and the Women They Hire to Raise Their Children*. New York: Basic Books, 1995.

Yeoh, Branda S., and Shirlena Huang. "Negotiating Public Space: Strategies and Styles of Migrant Female Domestic Workers in Singapore." *Urban Studies*, vol. 35, no. 3 (1998), pp. 583–602.

Zarembka, Joy. "Modern Slavery: Abuse of Domestic Workers." *Off Our Backs*, vol. 30, no. 6 (2000), p. 12.

———. "Maid to Order." *Colorlines Magazine*, vol. 4, no. 3 (2001), pp. 26–28.

Acknowledgments

Special thanks to Kerri McLean, who added to the duties of her busy Key West classroom the job of helping shepherd this project to completion; many thanks also to Bonnie Kwan for superb help with the bibliography and appendix and for keeping every marble on the table through final galleys. Thanks to Roberta Espinoza, our "map wizard," for careful research on migration patterns, and to those who advised or directed us to articles—Stephen Castles, Judith Kazantsis, Janet McIntosh, and Ann Jordan. Thanks to Shara Kay for very skillful editorial assistance, and to Laura Secor, for her distinguished editing. And many thanks from get-go to finish line to our editor at Metropolitan Books, Sara Bershtel, who combines a brilliant editorial eye with a caring heart.

The Contributors

Bridget Anderson is a research fellow under the Transnational Communities Program, studying the pathways to legitimacy of undocumented workers. She is also the chair of Kalayaan, an organization working with migrant domestic workers in the United Kingdom. She is the author of *Doing the Dirty Work? The Global Politics of Domestic Labour*.

Kevin Bales is a professor of sociology at the University of Surrey, Roehampton, London, and director of Free the Slaves, the American sister organization of Anti-Slavery International (www.freetheslaves.net).

Denise Brennan is an assistant professor of anthropology at Georgetown University, Washington, D.C.

Susan Cheever is the author of ten books, including *Home Before Dark, Treetops: A Family Memoir*, and *As Good As I Could Be: A Memoir of Raising Wonderful Children in an Imperfect World*.

Nicole Constable is a professor of anthropology at the University of Pittsburgh. She is the author of *Christian Souls and Chinese Spirits* and *Maid to Order in Hong Kong*, and is currently writing a book entitled *Romance on a Global Stage*, about correspondence relationships between Filipinas, Chinese women, and U.S. men.

Barbara Ehrenreich is the author of *Nickel and Dimed: On (Not) Getting by in America, Blood Rites: Origins and History of the Passions of War*, and numerous other works.

Arlie Russell Hochschild is the author of *The Second Shift, The Time Bind*, and the forthcoming *Commercialization of Intimate Life and Other Essays*. She teaches sociology at the University of California at Berkeley.

Pierrette Hondagneu-Sotelo is the author of *Gendered Transitions: Mexican Experiences of Immigration* and *Doméstica: Immigrant Workers Cleaning and Caring in the Shadows of Affluence*. She teaches sociology at the University of Southern California and is currently researching clergy mobilization for economic justice.

Michele Gamburd, author of *The Kitchen Spoon's Handle: Transnationalism and Sri Lanka's Migrant Housemaids*, is assistant professor of anthropology at Portland State University in Portland, Oregon.

Pei-Chia Lan is an assistant professor of sociology at National Taiwan University and a 2000 postdoctoral research fellow at the Center for Working Families at the University of California, Berkeley.

Rhacel Salazar Parreñas is an assistant professor in the department of Women's Studies and Asian American Studies at University of Wisconsin, Madison, and author of *Servants of Globalization: Women, Migration, and Domestic Work*.

Lynn May Rivas is a Ph.D. candidate in the Sociology Department at the University of California at Berkeley, where she is working on a dissertation that examines the intersections among the disability rights movement, the movement to organize personal attendants, and the state.

Saskia Sassen is the Ralph Lewis Professor of Sociology at the University of Chicago, and Centennial Visiting Professor at the London School of Economics. She is the author of *Guests and Aliens* and the forthcoming *Denationalization: Economy and Polity in a Global Digital Age*, as well as the editor of *Global Networks/Linked Cities*.

Hung Cam Thai is a Ph.D. candidate in the Sociology Department at the University of California at Berkeley. *The Two Unmarriageables* is drawn from his dissertation, which he is currently writing as a scholar-in-residence at Pomona College in Claremont, California.

Joy M. Zarembka, the daughter of a domestic worker from Kenya, is the director of Break the Chain Campaign, She is also the author of *The Pigment of Your Imagination: Mixed Race Families in Britain, Kenya, Zimbabwe and Jamaica* (www.ThePigment.com), which explores the various configurations of "race" in different countries.